SURPLUS HISTORY & EMANCIPATION
Another Ethiopia is Possible

SURPLUS HISTORY & EMANCIPATION
Another Ethiopia is Possible

Maimire Mennasemay

Surplus History & Emancipation: Another Ethiopia is Possible
Copyright © 2025 by Maimire Mennasemay. All rights reserved.

Apart from any fair dealing for the purpose of private study, research, criticism or review, as permitted under the Copyright Act, no part of this publication may be reproduced in\any form, stored in a retrieval system or transmitted in any form by any means—electronic, mechanical, photocopy, recording or otherwise—without the prior permission of the publisher. Enquiries should be sent to the undermentioned address.

TSEHAI books may be purchased for educational, business, or sales promotional use. For more information, please contact our special sales department.

TSEHAI Publishers
www.tsehaipublishers.com
info@tsehaipublishers.com

ISBN: 978-1-59907-294-4 (Paperback)
ISBN: 978-1-59907-295-1 (Hardcover)
ISBN: 978-1-59907-296-8 (EBook)

First Edition

Publisher: Elias Wondimu
Book Layout: Befikadu Teka
Cover design: Sara Martine

A Catalog Record for this book is available from:
Wemezekir Ethiopian National Library, Addis Ababa, Ethiopia
United States Library of Congress, Washington, DC., USA
British Library, London, UK

10 9 8 7 6 5 4 3 2 1

Printed in the United States of America

For Liya, Milo, Isaiah, and Joshua

Contents

Preface ix
Introduction: Epistemic autonomy in Ethiopian Studies 1
Chapter 1. Critical *Qiné* Hermeneutical Concepts 19

    1.1. *Nägär* (ነገር); 21
    1.2. *Säm ena wärq* (ሰም እና ወርቅ) / wax and gold; 23
    1.3. *Ena* (እና) / "and" or conflictual interinvolvement; 24
    1.4. *Gädl* (ገድል) / struggle; 25
    1.5. *Ewnät* (እውነት) / truth or "the hidden good"; 29
    1.6. *Ewqät* (እውቀት) / knowledge; 30
    1.7. *Enkän* (እንከን) / incompleteness; 31
    1.8. *Qisäla* (ቅጸላ) / propaedeutic to mirmära (research); 34
    1.9. *Mirmära* (ምርመራ) / research; 35
    1.10. *Säwrä bahil* (ሰውረ ባሕል) / non-tradition; 37
    1.11. *Säwrä hiywät* (ሰውረ ሕይወት) / surplus life; 39
    1.12. *Säwrä ras* (ሰውረ ራስ) / surplus self; 42
    1.13. *Säwrä tarik* (ሰውረ ታሪክ) / surplus history; 44
    1.14. *Arnät* (አርነት) human emancipation; 44
    1.15. *Hiss* (ሂስ) / critique; 44
    1.16. *Zäybé* (ዘይቤ) / symptom, signal, way; 46
    1.17. *Hibrä qal* (ሕብረ ቃል) / harmonizer; 48
    1.18. *Andem* (አንድም) / and one; 50
    1.19. *Arat ayn* (አራት ዓይን) / "four-eyed"; 51
    1.20. *Zäräfa* (ዘረፋ) / decentering and diverting; 53
    1.21. *Quanqua* (ቋንቋ) / language as a discourse of domination; 57
    1.22. *Lissan* (ልሳን) / language of emancipation; 58
    1.23. *Tsinsä hassab* (ፅንስ ሐሳብ) / concept; 61
    1.24. *Admas* (አድማስ) / horizon; 63
    1.25. *Wihdät* (ውህደት) / unity; 64
    1.26. *Andemta* (አንድምታ) / "fusion of wärq horizons"; 67
    1.27. *Silt* (ስልት) / method-approach; 70
    1.28. *Mädämamät* (መደማመጥ) / critical dialogical dialogue; 74
    1.29. *Minab* (ምናብ) / utopianism without utopia; 76
    1.30. *Yäwäl* (የወል) / the commons; 76
    1.31. *Dagmawi Tinsa'e* (ዳግማዊ ትንሳኤ) / The Second Resurrection; 77
    1.32. *Bähig amlak* (ባሕግ አምላክ) / the God of Law, ፍትህ (fithe) justice; 78
    1.33. *Tirgum* (ትርጉም) / critical translation; 81

Contents

1. 34. *Antsar nibab* (አንጻር ንባብ) / distanciation reading;   82
1. 35. *Wistä wäyra nibab* (ውስጠ ወይራ ንባብ), symptomatic reading;   84
1. 36. *Säwrä fitch* (ሰውረ ፍች) / surplus meaning.   87

Chapter 2. Surplus History / *Säwrä tarik*: Immanent Critique   89

2.1. *Säwrä tarik* and the entangled streams of Ethiopian history.   90
2.2. *Säwrä tarik* as embodied knowledge.   94
2.3. *Säwrä tarik* and the *people's people* and the *official people*.   99
2.4. *Säwrä tarik*, ideology critique, and *Oromummaa*.   105
2.5. *Säwrä tarik* and politics as the art of the impossible.   121
2.6. *Säwrä tarik* and "standing upright."   128

Chapter 3. *Säwrä tarik*: Overcoming the triple domination   133

3.1 *Säwrä tarik* and *arnät*: beyond Potemkin democracy.   133
3.2 *Säwrä tarik* and *minab*: beyond adaptive preferences.   141
3.3 *Säwrä tarik* and *yäwäl*: from property to use.   154

Chapter 4. *Säwrä tarik*: The emergence of *hizb* and *agär*   161

4.1. The transition from primary to secondary identification.   162
4.2. Becoming a *hizb*, becoming *agär*.   170
4.3. The primacy of *hizb* and *agär* over regimes.   175
4.4. Critique of the concepts of "people" and "nation."   177
4.5. Is a democratic ethnic federalism possible?
     The *Estifanosite* approach.   182
4.6. Critique of *kilil* as a biopolitical space of necropower.   189

Chapter 5. Conclusion: Ethioperspectivism and Becoming Ethiopian   193

5.1. Critique of knowledge welfare.   195
5.2. De-Gibbonizing or de-Westernizing knowledge.   201
5.3. De-Gibbonizing or de-Westernizing Ethiopian poverty.   203
5.4. De-Gibbonizing or de-Westernizing democracy.   211
5.5. Against falling out of world history.   216

Glossary   227
Bibliography   233
Index   239

Preface

The present book focuses on "surplus history" (ሰውረ ታሪh / *säwrä tarik*) as a source of an emancipatory theory immanent to Ethiopian history and society. At the same time, it provides a systematic and detailed presentation of the critical *qiné* hermeneutical concepts necessary for questioning and developing emancipatory ideas through a critical internal journey into Ethiopia's intellectual traditions and a critical external journey into the West's (or other) intellectual traditions. It also deepens and extends the ideas discussed in my previous book, *Qiné Hermeneutics and Ethiopian Critical Theory*, and opens new paths for reflecting on emancipatory democracy and emancipatory development.

The Introduction discusses the crucial issue of epistemic autonomy in Ethiopian studies. The rest of the book is divided in five chapters. In Chapter I, I consider thirty-six critical *qiné* hermeneutical concepts that could contribute to the cultivation of epistemic autonomy in Ethiopian Studies.. These concepts are indispensable for conducting a critical internal journey into Ethiopian intellectual traditions, history and society, and for effecting a critical external journey into the intellectual traditions and practices of the West (or others). The purpose of these two critical journeys is to produce through "a fusion of horizons" or *andemta* (see Chapter1 # 26) and the critical language or *lissan* (see Chapter 1 # 22) necessary for considering the issue of emancipation or *arnät* (see Chapter 3) in ways that speak to the emancipatory needs and interests of Ethiopians. I examine separately four of the thirty-six concepts, namely *säwrä tarik*, *arnät*, *minab*, and *yäwäl*. In Chapter 2, I discuss *säwrä tarik* (surplus history) as immanent critique and in Chapter 3, *arnät* (emancipation), *minab* (utopia), and *yäwäl* (the commons). Chapter 2 is divided in six sections: the sources and meaning of surplus history (*säwrä tarik*), *säwrä tarik* as embodied knowledge, the distinction between the "people's people" and the "official people," *säwrä tarik* and the ideology critique of *Oromummaa*, the distinction between politics as the art of the possible and politics as the art of the impossible, and the 15th century concept of "standing upright" that one finds among the *Estifanosites*, the *Ewostatewosites*, and the *Zamika'elites*. Chapter 3 deals with the issue of overcoming the triple domination—political, economic, and epistemic—that stifles the life of Ethiopians. It is divided in three sections: *säwrä tarik* and *arnät*: beyond Potemkin democracy; *säwrä tarik* and *minab*: beyond adaptive preferences; *säwrä tarik* and *yäwäl*: from property to use. Though repressed historically, these four concepts—*säwrä tarik*, *arnät*, *minab*, and *yäwäl*—are crucial for a critical consideration of Ethiopia's conditions and her possible futures. They are the emancipatory surplus meanings or *säwrä fitch* (see Chapter 1 # 36) of Ethiopian social practices, past and present.

Chapter 4 examines the contentious question of whether Ethiopia is a nation in six sections: the transition from primary to secondary identification, becoming *hizb* and becoming *agär*, the primacy of *hizb* and *agär* over regimes, critique of the concepts of "people" and "nation," the question of whether a democratic ethnic federalism is possible and mines the surplus meanings of the *Estifanosites* ideas and practices to propose an answer to the question, and a critique of *kilil* (ክልል) as a biopolitical space of necropower. Chapter 5 discusses Ethio-perspectivism as the approach that enables us to reflect on and bring about emancipation in Ethiopia, which I discuss as the issue of Becoming Ethiopian. I conduct the discussion in five sections: critique of knowledge welfare, de-Gibbonizing or de-Westernizing knowledge, de-Gibbonizing or de-Westernizing Ethiopian poverty, de-Gibbonizing or de-Westernizing democracy, and against falling out of world history.

I would like to point out that my effort to develop *qiné* hermeneutics in a way that contributes to our epistemic autonomy, political imaginary, and critical thinking is more of a propaedeutic than a finished work. Rather, it is an invitation to others to develop and expand the intellectual heritage of Ethiopia in terms of the modern emancipatory needs of Ethiopians. This heritage, which includes, among others, *qiné* hermeneutics, is vast and complex, and requires the collective effort of Ethiopian intellectuals and scholars to make it flourish in light of the questions and challenges with which the modern world confronts Ethiopians. If this book provokes others to give consideration to this issue, the book would have fulfilled its purpose.

I would like to acknowledge the support I received from Dawson College under its program of Scholar in Residence during the research and writing of this manuscript. Thanks to Gerardo Mosquera and James Ring of the Humanities/Philosophy Department for their constructive comments on parts of the manuscript. Thanks to Aba Ergete Tesfaye, Hibrat Agonafir, and Terefe Reta for helping me procure out-of-print *qiné* books and Amharic literary works, to Betty G. for her permission to use a stanza from her song አዲስ ሰማይ / Addis Semay, and Elias Wondimu of Tsehai Publishers, for facilitating my research on out-of-print *qiné* documents. My thanks to my department colleagues Michael Smith, Leon Jacobs, Mendel Kramer, Stan Nachfolger, Albert Kudsizadeh,

Marvin Hershorn, and to members of S.P.A.C.E—a trans-disciplinary program that conjoins the natural sciences, the arts, and philosophy in which I participated for the last twenty years and which provided me a space for examining cross-cultural epistemological issues. My thanks to Ken Milkman (philosophy and mathematics), Joel Trudeau (physics), Richard Shoemaker (Physics), Lois Valliant (Fine Arts), and Andrew Katz (English). Above all, my gratitude goes to Geneviève, my wife and friend, and to my daughters Elsa and Sara, without whose constant support and counsel this book would still be in its embryonic state.

Introduction:

Epistemic autonomy in Ethiopian Studies

ሩቅ ነው ጉዟችን
ድንቅም ነው ጉዟችን

"Our destination is distant,
But our journey is glorious."
            Debebe Seyfu, የብርሃን ፍቅር [1]

The book is motivated by the question: Why is Ethiopia stuck in an ongoing crisis since 1960? It stands to reason that one cannot change a condition that one misunderstands or does not understand. If we Ethiopians have failed to change Ethiopia for the better after almost a century of "modern thinking," it is because our modern thinking has failed to correctly grasp the aspirations of Ethiopians and the nature and workings of the material and cognitive conditions of their life context, past and present. What we Ethiopians need is an Ethiopian-generated knowledge that gives theoretical clarity to our conditions and needs, and offers a guidance to an alternative Ethiopia in ways that grasp the intelligence, affects and desires of Ethiopians, and engenders enthusiasm for and fidelity to the project of an Ethiopian society in which every Ethiopian flourishes. Modern Ethiopian Studies have failed in this task. The discourse of Ethiopian Studies on politics, economics, society, and culture have turned out to be an elaborate intellectual façade that hides the painful reality of a sophisticated and educated thoughtlessness that has landed Ethiopians in the *cul-de-sac* of ethnic fantasies that masquerade as thinking.[2] A crucial reason for this reign of thoughtlessness

---

1   Debebe Seyfu, የብርሃን ፍቅር (Addis Ababa: Hassab Publishers, 2013), p.115.
2   The distance between the concerns of Ethiopian Studies and the aspirations of Ethiopians are so great that one is tempted to call Ethiopian Studies "Potemkin Knowledge."

is the fact that thinking on Ethiopia by Ethiopians has been radically severed from Ethiopia's intellectual traditions. "A tree without roots does not bear fruits," says a Gurage saying. Modern thinking in contemporary Ethiopia is rootless thinking. We have failed to dig out the forms and contents of our intellectual traditions, question them, confront them with the questions and ideas of Western (or other) civilization, and develop a fusion of horizons or *andemta* (see Chapter 1 # 26)) of historically rooted emancipatory ideas. Unwilling to engage in this demanding task, many Ethiopians have resorted to the facile exercise of "inventing traditions" (see Chapter 2.4 below). Invented traditions add another layer of opacity, thus thickening our ignorance of Ethiopia's conditions and making our policies and actions based on them ever more destructive.

The present book does not pretend to give an exhaustive answer to the question of the failure of "modern thinking" in Ethiopia and its catastrophic consequences. It focuses on the epistemic aspect of the mis-self-understanding of Ethiopians and the misunderstanding of Ethiopia that emerged with the hegemony of the Western social sciences in the study of Ethiopian society, politics and economics. These misunderstandings first manifested themselves in the "modern" political ideas and visions of the Ethiopian Student movement that came to life in the 1960s: a liberal vision and a Marxist vision of development and democracy. These two were the major currents of political thought, with the Marxist vision gaining the upper hand in the 1970s.[3] Despite the radical differences between these two visions, they shared the same approach in the sense that both treated Ethiopia as a *tabula rasa* on which liberalism or Marxism were to be written without any consideration of the ideas of change, transformation, power, and emancipation that were gestating in Ethiopian intellectual traditions and social practices, past and present. Both approaches treated Ethiopians as political patients and not as political agents, hence the "verticalism" that characterized their political activities and organizations.[4] The Ethiopian Student movement created the intellectual and ideological environment that incubated all the major Ethiopian political movements and parties—The Ethiopian People's Revolutionary Party (EPRP), The All-Ethiopia Socialist Movement (MEISON), the 1974 revolution and the DERG, the Tigray

---

3 Bahru Zewde, *The Quest for Socialist Utopia: The Ethiopian Student Movement c.1960-1974* (Suffolk: James Currey, 2014); Elleni Centime Zeleke, *Ethiopia in Theory: Revolution and Knowledge Production, 1964-2016* (Leiden and Boston: Brill 2019).
4 Verticalism is a term that Jeremy Gilbert uses to refer to the political practice of organizing politics in a top-down manner, Jeremy Gilbert, *Common Ground: Democracy and Collectivity in an Age of Individualism* (London: Pluto Press, 2014), pp. 69-70.

People Liberation Front (TPLF), the Eritrean People Liberation Front (EPLF), the Oromo Liberation Front (OLF), and other liberation movements. Its first political offspring was the 1974 "phantom revolution." Seen from the perspective of the present which still bears within itself the traces of the past, the 1974 Revolution was not a progressive one but rather the beginning of a catastrophe that is still unfolding. As if to confirm the historical experiences of other countries that "behind every fascism, there is a failed revolution," the failed 1974 revolution furnished the ground for the emergence of successive authoritarian regimes—the DERG regime, (1974-1991), the EPRDF regime (1991-2018), and the Prosperity Party regime, (2019...).[5]

The leaders of all the political parties and movements that have been active in Ethiopian politics were the progenies of "modern" education whose contents and forms were based on uncritically borrowed Western social sciences. Modern Ethiopian education was, and still is, an extravertive education that generates understandings of Ethiopian society and Ethiopians, of "development," democracy, reform, revolution, education, people, nation, and knowledge production, with minimal roots in the history, social practices, intellectual traditions, and the "subjugated knowledge" and emancipatory aspirations of Ethiopians.[6] Modern education has evicted the intellectual traditions of Ethiopia from the education of Ethiopians. It treats Ethiopians as an intellectual blank slate on which to write Western knowledge.

The cognitive vacuum created by the complete exclusion of Ethiopia's intellectual traditions from the cultural formation of modern educated Ethiopians stranded modern Ethiopians on the shifting sands of spontaneous consciousness feeding on revolutionary fantasies and mercurial convictions. The result is what Messay Kebede has described as "cultural dislocation," procreating processes of political, social, and economic disasters, psychological

---

5   The EPRDF is dominated by the TPLF, and the PP is dominated by the OPP. TPLF stands for *Tigrean People Liberation Front*, EPRDF *for* Ethiopian People's Revolutionary Democratic Front, PP for Prosperity Party, OPP for Oromo Prosperity Party. The statement, "behind every fascism, there is a failed revolution," is generally attributed to Walter Benjamin.
6   On "subjugated knowledge" Michel Foucault writes, "knowledges that have been disqualified as nonconceptual knowledges, as insufficiently elaborated knowledges: naive knowledges, hierarchically inferior knowledges, knowledges that are below the required level of erudition or scientificity." Michel Foucault, *Society must be defended*, trans. David Macey (New York: Picador, 2003), pp. 7-8. Subjugated knowledge inhabits mutual aid associations (*iddir, iqqub*, etc.) labour sharing associations (*däbo*, etc.) and conflict resolution institutions (*enashma*, etc.. Maimire Mennasemay, *Qiné Hermeneutics and Ethiopian Critical Theory* (Los Angeles: Tsehai Publishing, 2021), pp. 376-434.

confusions and cultural alienations.[7] I argue in this book that a crucial reason for this historical catastrophe is the absence of epistemic autonomy among Ethiopians engaged in the study of Ethiopian society, politics, economics, and of her manuscript and non-manuscript cultures. The absence of epistemic autonomy in Ethiopian Studies has deprived Ethiopians of the capacity to create knowledge that grasps them and their conditions cognitively and affectively in ways that enthuse Ethiopians to transform Ethiopia willingly, collectively and rationally into a free, just, prosperous, and knowledge producing society.

Ethiopia's internally generated resistance to and victory over European political designs during the 19th century were possible because Ethiopians practiced epistemic autonomy in the sense that they were the thinkers and conceptualizers of their problems and solutions.[8] Bahru Zewde, the Ethiopian historian, hints at this idea when he writes, "Ethiopia was more Feudal in 1896 than in 1936. Ethiopia was defeated [in 1936] because she was less feudal…."[9] In pre-twentieth century, Ethiopians themselves conceptualized their problems, formulated their questions, and generated their own answers with their epistemic feet firmly grounded in the intellectual traditions of Ethiopians, with their ideas and imagination resolutely turned to a future that they saw as of their own making. Though often articulated in quasi-religious terms, pre-twentieth century Ethiopians conceived political and social problems and solutions and understood their conditions within a cognitive framework that exuded epistemic autonomy, as we could see in the Ethiopian Royal Chronicles and the numerous *gädl* of Medieval Ethiopia.[10] However, the epistemic autonomy that guaranteed the conceptualization and the successful pursuit of Ethiopian political, economic, and cognitive independence in pre-twentieth century is currently absent. The result is, as we could see, the hollowing out of the self-understanding of Ethiopians and of their understanding of Ethiopian society, leading to the erosion of Ethiopia's political independence, a spiraling

---

7   Messay Kebede, *Radicalism and Cultural Dislocation in Ethiopia, 1960-1974* (Rochester: University of Rochester Press, 2008).
8   The highpoint of the 19th century Ethiopian history is the Adwa Victory. ተክለ ጻድቅ መኩርያ: የኢትዮጵያ ታሪክ: ከዓጼ ቴዎድሮስ እስከ ቀዳማዊ ኃይለ ሥላሴ (አዲስ አበባ, ብርሃንና ሰላም: 1961 ዓ.ም); Harold G. Marcus, *The Life and Times of Menelik II: Ethiopia 1844–1913.* (Lawrenceville: Red Sea Press, 1995).
9   Bahru Zewde, *A History of Modern Ethiopia* (London: James Curry, 1991), p. 159.
10 Richard Pankhurst, *The Ethiopian Royal Chronicles* (Los Angeles: Tsehai Publishing, 2010); Maimire Mennasemay, *Qiné Hermeneutics and Ethiopian Critical Theory* (Los Angeles: Tsehai Publishing, 2021), pp. 267-296. On *gädl*, see Chapter 1, # 4, below.

economic decline, and the flight into the anesthetising vision of Ethiopia's systemic problems and their solutions as ethnic problems and solutions.

How did this historical regression happen? One may roughly situate the beginning of this decline with the Ethiopian defeat in 1936 by Fascist Italy, and the use of the British army to liberate Ethiopia (1941). It is as if these two back-to-back events have thrown Ethiopians in a "cultural cringe" and sapped their intellectual will to recover and develop in new directions their intellectual traditions to confront the new political, economic, and epistemic challenges of the post-Second World War period.[11] These events opened the door for the intervention of Great Britain and the United States in Ethiopian affairs, the former in the post-1941 years, and the latter from 1951 onwards.[12] The 1951 Point Four Program agreement between Ethiopia and the USA laid down the cornerstone of Ethiopia's loss of epistemic autonomy, with the introduction of the Western concept of "development" without any critical reflection on what development means.[13] Neither in 1951 nor since have Ethiopians critically reflected on the meaning of "development" in the Ethiopian intellectual and historical context and in terms of their emancipatory needs and interests. Rather, they fled away from this task of reflection with abandon such that an observer of modern Ethiopian students noted "the speed with which they gave up their traditional habits and manners" by comparing them to "their Japanese counterparts," who followed Western education but "continued to adhere to their traditions."[14] The loss of epistemic autonomy took the particular form of Gibbonism. I have discussed Gibbonism elsewhere.[15] However, since the

---

11 A.A. Philips, the Australian writer and critic, in his comment on Australian intellectual life, called "cultural cringe": "an internalized inferiority complex which causes people in a country to dismiss their own culture as inferior to the cultures of other countries." A.A. Phillips, 'The Cultural Cringe', *Meanjin*, vol. 9, no. 4, Summer 1950, pp. 299–302. See also Katie Pickles, "Transnational History and Cultural Cringe: Some Issues for Consideration in New Zealand, Australia and Canada: Transnational History and Cultural Cringe", *History Compass*, (2011), vol. 9, no. 9., pp. 657-673.

12 A. Sbacchi, *Legacy of Bitterness: Ethiopia and Fascist Italy, 1935–1941.* (Lawrenceville, New Jersey: Red Sea Press, 1997). Harold G. Marcus, *Ethiopia, Great Britain, and the United States, 1941-1974: The Politics of Empire* (Los Angeles: University of California Press, 1983).

13 U.S.A. Operations Mission to Ethiopia, *Point Four Agreements between the Imperial Ethiopian Government and the Government of the United States* (Washington: Information, Mission to Ethiopia Subject Files, 1954).

14 Bahru Zewde, *Pioneers of Change in Ethiopia: The Reformist Intellectuals of the early Twentieth Century* (Oxford: James Curry, 2002), p. 80.

15 Maimire Mennasemay, *Qiné Hermeneutics and Ethiopian Critical Theory*, *supra*, pp. 15-35.

understanding of Gibbonism is necessary for following the arguments made in this book, I will give a succinct summary of its main characteristics.

In a section on Ethiopia in *The Decline and Fall of the Roman Empire*, Edward Gibbon wrote, "Æthiopians *slept near a thousand years*, forgetful of the world, by whom they were forgotten" and "were *awakened* by the Portuguese, who... appeared in [Ethiopia], as if they had descended through the air from a distant planet."[16] He adds, "Conscious of their own indigence, the Abyssinians had formed the rational project of importing the arts and ingenuity of Europe," inspired by the "native valor of Europeans."[17] Gibbon represented Ethiopia as all that the West is not, a perception of Ethiopia that still persists and that one finds in Donald Levine characterization of Ethiopia as "exotic."[18] In the post-1951 period, Ethiopians have taken to heart Gibbon's advice, or so it seems. They have in their quest of modernization uncritically borrowed Western social sciences—"the arts and ingenuity of Europe"—to "awaken" themselves, to understand themselves and their conditions, to formulate their problems and questions, and to generate solutions.

Four ideas constitute Gibbonism: the Newtonian idea of change, the epistemology of ignorance, an anamorphic perception of Ethiopia, and the "backward-looking" conception of "progress" as a "fact" that has already taken place in the West.[19] The Newtonian idea of change through an external push informs Gibbon's diagnosis of Ethiopia as a sleeping nation that needs external agents (the West) to "awaken" her. Boris Groys notes that a Newtonian theory of socio-cultural change assumes that "the historically new manifests itself in culture only as a consequence of the action of an extra-cultural other."[20] One finds in Ethiopian Studies assertions such as "In the context of Ethiopia, history is tantamount to preservation rather than to succession of events and changes," or Ethiopia is devoid of the "the rationalistic aspects of modern culture."[21] Thus, the

---

16   Edward Gibbon, *The History of the Decline and Fall of the Roman Empire*, Book IV, Chapter XLVII, Part V. (Kindle edition, 2008), unpaginated. Emphasis added. Gibbon is an 18th century British historian (1737-1794),
17   Ibid.
18   Donald N. Levine's *Wax and Gold* (Chicago: University of Chicago Press, 1972), pp. ix, 10-11.
19   On backward-looking conception of "progress," Amy Allen, *The End of Progress*, (New York: Columbia University Press, 2015). pp. 15-24.
20   Boris Groys, *On the New,* trans. G. M. Goshgarian (London: Verso, 2014), p. 29. Though Groys writes on artistic production, his ideas on the Newtonian mechanics of cultural change are apropos for the topic I am discussing. I operate a *zäräfa* of his discussion of the Newtonian mechanics of cultural change.
21   Messay Kebede, *Survival and Modernization Ethiopia's Enigmatic Present: A Philosophical Discourse* (Lawrenceville: The Red Sea Press, 1999), p. 57; Donald

concepts and practices of "development," assumed to be necessary to transform Ethiopia, are drawn from the history of the West's political-economic transformations and self-reflections, and introduced externally to put Ethiopia in "motion." However, to say, "In the context of Ethiopia, history is tantamount to preservation rather than to succession of events and changes" is to forget that history that does not change is also history in all its senses.[22] It all depends by what we mean by "change." It does not justify abandoning the quest for an immanent theory in a history that is not "a succession of events and changes."

Second, Gibbonism imposes on Ethiopian Studies an "epistemology of ignorance."[23] The "epistemology of ignorance" frames what is knowable and unknowable about Ethiopia in light of the dominant Western epistemology and its methodology. These smuggle in certain assumptions about reality, rationality, history, the individual as a discrete free-standing agent, and society as an aggregation of such individuals. Given that these assumptions circumscribe what is knowable and unknowable, what is normative and deficient, and given that Ethiopian social practices are not constitutively internal to Western social practices from which the currently dominant epistemology and methodology and their assumptions emerge, Ethiopian Studies confine Ethiopia to what the borrowed social sciences consider "knowable" or worthy of "knowing" in Ethiopian reality in light of their epistemology, methodology, and their conception of "change."[24] One cannot presume that what is "unknowable" according to the epistemology and methodology of the borrowed social sciences is also "unknowable" to Ethiopians and their intellectual traditions. A knowledge of Ethiopia built on the assumptions of what is "knowable" and "unknowable" in terms of the epistemology and methodology of Western social sciences

---

N. Levine, *Wax and Gold, supra*, pp. 10-11.

22 As Althusser notes, "a history that fails, makes no headway and repeats itself is… still a history." Louis Althusser, *For Marx* (London: LRB, 1969), pp. 81-2.

23 I will subject to *zäräfa* the literature on the "epistemology of ignorance" and its use of the term "ignorance" to cover both false belief and the absence of true belief. Linda Martín Alcoff, "Epistemologies of Ignorance: Three Types," in Shannon Sullivan and Nancy Tuana, eds. *Race and Epistemologies of Ignorance* (New York: State University of New York Press, 2007), pp. 39-57; Robert N. Proctor and Londa Schiebinger, eds. *Agnotology: The Making and Unmaking of Ignorance* (Stanford: Stanford University Press, 2008), pp. 1-36, 209-229; Bonaventura de Sousa Santos, *Another Knowledge is Possible: Beyond Western Epistemologies* (London: Verso, 2008); Gaston Bachelard, *The Philosophy of No*, trans. G. C. Waterston (New York: Orion Press, 1968).

24 Note for example Donald Levine's assertion that Ethiopia is an "exotic culture" that lacks "the rationalistic aspects of modern culture" Donald N. Levine's *Wax and Gold, supra*, pp. ix, 10-11. One may note that Ethiopians do not see themselves as an "exotic" people.

substitutes what it does not know about Ethiopia with what its social sciences claim to know about Ethiopia. The epistemology of ignorance treats Western concepts as transcendental concepts that swoop in from the Western knowledge firmament to handle Ethiopian issues externally. It produces knowledge that is "a web of positive, tenacious, interdependent errors" that cannot be "destroyed one by one."[25] It thus produces ignorance of things Ethiopian as a positive, non-contingent, systematic knowledge of what Ethiopia is: an aggregate of lacks and absences of what the West counts as "development"—particular ideas, values and practices that the West has generated in the course of its transition from feudalism to capitalism—descriptively and normatively, in light of its epistemology and methodology and their underlying assumptions about "change" and "permanence." Thus, we "know" that Ethiopia lacks "instrumental rationality," "civil society," "democracy," "human capital," "social capital," and so forth. Consequently, development and democratization in Ethiopia are grounded negatively, for what is knowable in Ethiopia is her state of atrophy: a social body without the ideas, norms and practices that characterize a "developed" body, to wit, the West. That is, the epistemology of ignorance produces systematically "knowledge as ignorance" and "ignorance as knowledge" of that which is to be known, i.e., Ethiopia. The epistemology of ignorance makes the self-forgetfulness of Ethiopians a necessary premise for Ethiopians if they want to "know" and "understand" "development," "democracy," themselves, and their society. It is an epistemology that does not allow building a theory immanent to Ethiopian society.

Third, the borrowed social sciences impose an anamorphic perception of Ethiopia. "Anamorphosis" is the distorted projection of the observed (Ethiopia, in our case) that arises from the viewer's use of his "special devices" and specific "vantage points."[26] The social science studies of Ethiopia use "special devices"—theories, concepts, methodologies, teleological models that emerged from the

---

25   Gaston Bachelard, *The Philosophy of No,* trans. G. C. Waterston (New York: Orion Press, 1968), p. 8.
26   I base my arguments on Jurgis Baltrusaitis, *Anamorphic Art,* trans. W. J. Strachan (New York: Harry N. Abrams, 1977) and on Predrag Cicovacki, *Anamorphosis: Kant on Knowledge and Ignorance* (New York: University of America Press, 1997), p. 8. In his study on anamorphosis from a Kantian perspective, Predrag Cicovacki writes that the picture or map of reality we produce "becomes damaging when we are not aware of the limited nature of our approach to reality, when we are not aware of our ignorance. ... In our ignorance, we may presume that our scientific map, which excludes values, freedom, and faith, portrays the only reality that exists." He notes that "anamorphosis" gives us a picture of reality that is "broken and fragmentary" because "there is something wrong with our attitude toward the map."

West's self-interpretation in its quest for self-understanding and self-transformation—and they do it from specific "vantage points," that is, the West's historical experiences and material and intellectual interests. These "special devices" and "vantage points" are assumed to be objective and to have universal validity. They are used to reconstruct Ethiopia as a society that "lacks" its own "special devices" and "vantage points," and the internal resources and impetus that could propel it into self-knowledge and self-transformation. Ethiopia thus appears to be in pre-history—to be precise, pre-Western history—in need of the West's "special devices" and "vantage points" in order to know how to enter history understood as "liberal capitalist democracy,"[27] the sub-text of development and democratization theories.

Fourth, in line with the above considerations, the borrowed social sciences espouse a "backward-looking" conception of "progress"— "development" and "democracy": they consider "progress" as a fact that has already taken place in the West, which Ethiopians must follow.[28] This transcendental approach to Ethiopian issues occludes the possibility that there could be a theory of social transformation immanent to Ethiopian history and society. It deprives Ethiopians of their epistemic independence and intimates the idea that the self-denial of Ethiopians—of their history—and the normalization of cultural cringe is a necessary condition for "progress."

In short, Gibbonism asphyxiates our epistemic autonomy by grounding our knowledge of Ethiopia and of ourselves on Western reality and its cognitive patterns. When we Ethiopians uncritically use the borrowed social sciences to study ourselves, we see ourselves the way the West sees us; we see our actions the way the West sees them; we see our future the way the West sees it; we see the world and others the way the West sees them; and we see the West the way the West sees itself. What emerges is an anamorphically warped understanding of Ethiopia, of the world and our relations to it, of ourselves, of the West, and of Ethiopia's future. Gibbonism occludes the power relations that enable the West to impose on us the knowledge of and the political and economic limits on what development and democracy are. From the perspective of Gibbonism, the condition of Ethiopians appears as "lack" of development—" the arts and

---

27 W. W. Rostow, *The Stages of Economic Growth* (New York: Cambridge University Press, 1962) is the earliest articulation of this idea. A new rendition of this idea is Francis Fukuyama, *The End of History and the Last Man* (Washington: Free Press, 2006). The idea that liberal capitalist democracy, i.e., Western society, is the telos of history is the sometimes overt and sometimes covert backbone of development theories.

28 Amy Allen, *The End of Progress*, (New York: Columbia University Press, 2015), pp. 15-24.

ingenuity of Europe," as Gibbon put it— and not as a condition of political, social and economic suffering. It thus saddles Ethiopians with fake problems and wrong solutions.

The hegemony of Gibbonism in the social sciences on Ethiopia is the root of the Ethiopian failure to develop an emancipatory theory immanent to Ethiopian history and society that could grasp Ethiopians historically, politically, ethically and psychologically, and galvanize them to engage in the social transformation of Ethiopia. Bound by Gibbonism, Ethiopian Studies have not been since their inception a discourse of Ethiopians for themselves. That is, they have not been a process of self-questioning, self-critique, dialogue between the Ethiopian past and the present, and lateral dialogue between Ethiopia's intellectual and cultural traditions and practices. Consequently, they have failed to unpack and account for the richness and challenges of the Ethiopian life-world and have thus undermined the possibility of constituting the Ethiopian self as a reflective subject and of developing an emancipatory understanding of Ethiopia's conditions. Gibbonism has made Ethiopia increasingly opaque and unable to cope with this self-created social and political opacity, Ethiopians have slid into the thoughtless clarity of ethnic thinking: the reduction of Ethiopian history to ethnic struggles against the Ethiopian state which was identified," in terms of the uncritically borrowed concept of "colonialism, as a "colonial state" run by the "Amhara." [29]

Though ethnic politics has since 1991 undermined the possibility of establishing a democratic, prosperous, knowledge-producing Ethiopia, the underlying issue Ethiopians face is not, however, the rise of ethnic politics. The fundamental issue is the decomposition and disorientation of Ethiopia's democratic forces without which ethnic politics would not have triumphed. It is more important for the future of Ethiopia to know why democratic forces failed than to see why ethnic-identity politicians succeeded in gaining power. To put it differently, we will be able to understand and act in ways that defeat, politically and cognitively, anti- emancipatory forces whose current form is ethnic authoritarianism only if we understand why and how Ethiopians created an intellectual void that anesthetized democratic ideas, norms and forces, and

---

29 This was the dominant view espoused by the Ethiopian Students Movement. Walleligne Mekonnen, "On the Question of Nationalities in Ethiopia," *Arts IV* (Addis Ababa: November 17, 1969). Available at https://www.marxists.org/history/erol/ethiopia/nationalities.pdf. Bonnie K. Holcomb and Sisai Ibssa, *The Invention of Ethiopia* (Trenton: The Red Sea Press, 1990); Asafa Jalata, *Oromia and Ethiopia: State Formation and Ethnonational Conflict, 1868-2004* (Boulder, CO: Lynne Reiner publishers, 1993); Abbas Gnamo, *Conquest and Resistance in the Ethiopian Empire, 1880-1974: The Case of the Arsi Oromo* (Leiden: Brill, 2014).

created a political vacuum into which rushed ethnic authoritarianism without meeting much resistance.

The intellectual vacuum that led to the decomposition and disorientation of emancipatory ideas, values, norms, and forces could be traced in important ways to the erosion of Ethiopia's intellectual traditions, one of which is the *qiné* hermeneutical tradition.[30] It is an erosion that stripped away Ethiopia's intellectual independence and epistemic autonomy. One could say that there was a premonition among some Ethiopian intellectuals of the early twentieth century of the dangers of the loss of epistemic autonomy if Ethiopians embarked on an uncritical embrace of Western knowledge.[31] They were apprehensive that the loss of epistemic autonomy could lead to the intellectual and political decline of Ethiopia.[32]

Epistemic autonomy is a "good" comparable to moral and political autonomy. One does not have moral autonomy when one's choices are driven by internal or external compulsions. Nor does one have political autonomy when a country's choices and actions are dictated by external forces or by internal anti-democratic forces. In both moral and political autonomy, autonomy is a "good" and assumes the equality of subjects as well as their interdependence: it excludes moral and political hierarchy and servility as well as moral and political isolation. Similar considerations apply to epistemic autonomy: equality among knowing subjects and interdependence as equals, and it excludes epistemic hierarchy and servility.[33] By epistemic autonomy I do not mean intellectual autarchy or self-reliance that cuts off the bridges with the knowledge and knowledge-producing processes that the West or others have created. Rather, by epistemic autonomy, I mean epistemic self-governance, that is, governing oneself according to a rational norm such that one is free from internal and external compulsions, epistemic vassalage, as well as from epistemic isolation in the production of knowledge.

The lack of epistemic autonomy has stifling and distorting consequences on our study of Ethiopian society, development, democratization, and education of and knowledge production by Ethiopians. The lack of epistemic autonomy

---

30 Maimire Mennasemay, *Qiné Hermeneutics and Ethiopian Critical Theory* (Los Angeles: Tsehai Publishing, 2021).
31 Bahru Zewde, *Pioneers of Change in Ethiopia* (Addis Ababa, Addis Ababa University Press, 2002), p. 35-99.
32 Ibid.
33 On epistemic autonomy, see Linda Zagzebski, *Epistemic Authority: A Theory of Trust, Authority, and Autonomy in Belief* (New York: Oxford University Press, 2012); Jonathan Matheson and Kirk Lougheed, eds. *Epistemic Autonomy* (New York: Routledge, 2022).

and the reliance on borrowed knowledge has generated, to use Ulrich Beck's terms, "zombie" concepts and a "science of unreality" in which "distorted beliefs and notions about what constitutes the real world remain on their feet, shuffling about and causing all kinds of intellectual havoc," and political calamities, as we could see in the repeated failures of Ethiopia's reforms and revolutions, all based without exception on an uncritically borrowed knowledge about development and democracy.[34]

An important aspect of the absence of epistemic autonomy is the domination of methodological Westernism in Ethiopian Studies. The basic characteristic of methodological Westernism is "methodological individualism."[35] It asserts that social facts are constituted by facts about individuals, and that explanations of social phenomena are derived from facts about individuals. It treats facts as mono-vocal, discrete, ahistorical, quantifiable and neutral entities, and method as a non-hermeneutical, context-transcendent standardized procedure that reduces the studied reality to the results of its mechanisms of observation, measurement, and calculation. It reduces Ethiopian society into discrete units that it inserts into its conceptual boxes, and subjects them to measurement standards and calculating procedures that the West has developed in the process of its critical reflection on its own practices, problems, interests, and needs. Since these conceptual boxes, measurement standards, and calculating procedures lead to the exclusion of all that which cannot enter or does not fit the conceptual boxes, and does not meet the criteria for being measurable and calculable, subjecting Ethiopian social practices to these borrowed concepts, measurements, standards, and methods make her appear as a deficient society that has to meet the criteria of these borrowed intellectual tools if she wants to "develop." That is, the criteria of development are teleological and external to Ethiopian society. For example, autopoietic Ethiopian institutions such as *iddir*, *iqqub*, *däbo* are excluded from the borrowed concept of "civil society" precisely

---

34 Mads P. Sorensen and Allan Christansen, *Ulrich Beck: An Introduction to the Theory of Second Modernity and the Risk Society* (New York: Routledge, 2013), pp. 2, 69, 83, 192. Zombie ideas are ideas that will not die, no matter how often they are disproved, write Brainard G. Peters and Maximilian L. Nagel, *Zombie Ideas* (New York: Cambridge University Press, 2020); John Quiggin, *Zombie Economics: How Dead Ideas Still Walk among Us* (Princeton: Princeton University Press, 2012).

35 Lars Udéhn, *Methodological Individualism. Background, history and meaning* (London: Routledge, 2001); John Gerring, *Social Science Methodology: A Criterial Framework* (New York: Cambridge University Press 2001).

because they do not meet the criteria of the borrowed intellectual tools used to identify and analyse "civil society."[36]

The absence of epistemic autonomy has confined the study of Ethiopian society, politics, economics, and knowledge production by Ethiopians to the logic of "repeat after me" where the commanding "me" is the (epistemology and methodology of) West. This means how we conceptualize Ethiopian issues, the kind of topics we raise, the sort of questions we ask, and the methods we follow, and what counts as knowledge are already fashioned for us by the borrowed social sciences. The upshot is that Ethiopian issues are treated as "givens" rather than as issues that must be problematized, conceptualized, and interpreted from within Ethiopian history and social practices. One could thus call the borrowed social sciences somnambulist knowledge for they manipulate Ethiopian social practices without being conscious of the historicity and polysemy of these practices. Consequently, they end up producing representations and conceptualizations of Ethiopian issues that have tenuous connections to Ethiopian reality. The logic of "repeat after me" that the zombie concepts and methods of the borrowed social sciences impose on Ethiopian studies replace epistemic autonomy with epistemic vassalage, an epistemological condition that Quijano calls "coloniality."[37]

Knowledge is not just a neutral and a-historic construct; it is the outcome of the ways social structures and relations are organized under certain historical conditions. One cannot have the concept of "modern" in 12th century Ethiopia, 12th century Europe, or 12th century China. The particular concepts such as "development," "democratization," "civil society," "participation," "poverty," "nationalism," "ethnicity," "people," "nation" that one finds in the social science theories that dominate Ethiopian Studies are not the outcomes of Ethiopia's history, social practices, and critical reflections rooted in Ethiopia's conditions, emancipatory aspirations, and intellectual traditions. They are parachuted from outside as *prêt-à-porter* concepts. The concepts the West developed through its own critical reflections on its historical processes, social practices, interests, and needs are used in Ethiopian Studies as neutral, ahistorical, and universal discursive instruments for observing and analysing Ethiopian conditions,

---

36   Jeffery Clark, *Civil Society, NGOs, and Development in Ethiopia* (Washington: The World Bank, 2000); "Many Ethiopians are members of *iddir*, for example, but few participate in civil society institutions." Dessalegn Rahmato, "Investing in Civic Tradition: Civil Society and Democratization in Ethiopia, 2004," http://www.fssethiopia.org.et/civdemo.htm#Civic Tradition or Social Capital. Accessed 04/03/ 2010.

37   Aníbal Quijano, "Coloniality and Modernity/Rationality," in Walter Mignolo and Arturo Escobar, eds. *Globalization and the Decolonial Option* (New York: Routledge, 2010), pp. 22-32;

identifying and circumscribing issues, and formulating solutions. These concepts are used in ways that assume that Ethiopia is a purely empirical object devoid of concepts and that imported ready-to-wear concepts are adequate for understanding her. Inevitably, the results of these analyses do not mesh with Ethiopian realities, as one could see in the failures of "liberal" and "socialist" political reforms and the rise of ethnic politics. Riffing off of Mbembe's concept of "necropolitics," one could say that uncritically borrowed Western ideas and practices have engendered necro-democracy and necro-development: governmentality as the systemic political and economic production of death, transforming Ethiopia into what Mbembe calls a "death-world," as one could see in the transformation of vast areas of the Oromo, Amhara, Tigray, Benishangul-Gumuz, and Southern *kilils* into fields of ethnicity-based abjection and selective elimination under the Prosperity Party regime.[38]

Qiné hermeneutics objects to Gibbonism. It tells us that all social practices are *nägär* (internally complex and tensioned phenomena, see Chapter 1, #1). They are neither atheoretical, nor value neutral and mute empirical objects. Thus, to assume that Ethiopian social practices could be reduced to "data" that are transparent, monosemous, neutral, immediately accessible to and manipulable by borrowed concepts and methods is, on the hand, to de-historicise and de-socialize Ethiopian social practices and, on the other, to hypostatize the borrowed Western concepts and methods as self-contained autonomous accessories in a universal tool box. This divorce between Ethiopian reality and the hypostatized concepts and methods transforms the latter into zombie or "living-dead" concepts and methods—"living" in the Western context, but "dead" in the Ethiopian context—with no connections with the living forces and processes that constitute the world Ethiopians have created and live in. Thus, they systematically distort our understandings of Ethiopian society and our self-understanding as Ethiopians. Inevitably, development whose policies and projects are elaborated through zombie concepts and methods have put Ethiopia on the fast lane of self-destruction.[39]

The reduction of Ethiopia to a mere empirical object manipulated transcendentally by zombie concepts and methods has led to both objective

---

38 On necropolitics, see Achille Mbembe, *Necropolitics* (Durham: Duke University Press, 2019); on necrocapitalism, see Bobby Banerjee, "Necrocapitalism", *Organization Studies* 29 (2008), pp. 1541-1563. Since 1974, Ethiopia has become a repository of suffering, terror, and death. Political violence and man-made famines have subjected Ethiopians to selective eliminations based on ethnicity, religion, and region.

39 Fragile state index, https://fragilestatesindex.org/. Accessed 6/16/2023. Ethiopia is between Haiti (more fragile) and Myanmar (less fragile.)

and subjective failures. Objectively, the changes brought about in 1974 (the DERG), 1991 (EPRDF), and 2019 (Prosperity Party) have all failed to meet the aspirations of Ethiopians to be free from political, economic, social, and epistemic unfreedoms, inequalities, and injustices.[40] Subjectively, modern educated Ethiopians are captives of Gibbonist knowledge that has transported them to a state of "contemplation without knowledge" of Ethiopia, a phenomenon that has given birth to free-floating Ethiopian intellectuals who, because of the historical groundlessness of their knowledge of Ethiopia, easily change their ideological and political camps and as easily transform themselves from "socialists" to "ethnic nationalists," from "liberals" to practitioners of "ethnic segregation," euphemistically called "ethnic federalism," bringing endless turmoil to the country. In light of these failures, we could say that the borrowed social sciences in Ethiopian Studies have become "epistemological obstacles" that prevent the generation of an emancipatory knowledge that could drive the political, economic, social, and intellectual transformations of Ethiopia.[41] An epistemological obstacle is not external to the theory we bring to our study; it does not arise from observational limitations.[42] That is, the epistemological obstacles that have led to the harmfulness of Ethiopian Studies are internal to the borrowed social sciences that articulate Ethiopian Studies.

Despite their failures, the borrowed concepts, standards and measurements of political and economic development are still the tools by which we evaluate Ethiopian conditions. But, one cannot recognize a world nor act effectively on it if one does not supply, from within one's own history/society, aspirations and interests, the measure by which one sets the standards for what one chooses and

---

40 *Prosperity Party Program*, https://aapp.gov.et/resources/manifesto/; Prosperity Party *Constitution*, https://aapp.gov.et/resources/manifesto/. Accessed 6/13. 2022. These documents have an uncontestable democratic content. But the distance between what the democratic contents of these documents and the actions of the Prosperity Party, which have been since 2020 anti-democratic, is astronomical, as we shall see in various references in this book.

41 On "epistemological obstacle", see Gaston Bachelard, *Formation of the Scientific Mind,*, trans. Mary McAllester Jones (Manchester: Clinamen Press, 2006), pp. 24-32. "An epistemological obstacle will encrust any knowledge that is not questioned. Intellectual habits that were once useful and healthy can, in the long run, hamper research." p.25. The borrowed social sciences may be "useful and healthy" in the context of the West for they are the outcomes of the West's critical self-reflection. In the context of Ethiopia, however, they constitute what Bachelard calls a "counter-thought" (27) for they do not emerge from the critical self-reflection of Ethiopians. They are "zombie" social sciences.

42 Gaston Bachelard, *Formation of the Scientific Mind, supra*, pp 24-32.

accomplishes. Almost a century of development experience shows that the imported standards themselves are part of the problem in which Ethiopia is mired. This implies that we have to develop emancipatory theories and concepts immanent to Ethiopian history that articulate methods, measures and standards that meet the emancipatory aspirations of Ethiopians. This task demands epistemic autonomy.

It is important to note that the epistemic vassalage of Ethiopian Studies to the borrowed social sciences does not take place in a historical vacuum. It is rooted in the material dependence of Ethiopia on the West such that we can say Ethiopia is subject to a triple domination—economic, political, and epistemic—exercised by the forces that possess the political, economic, and epistemic powers that enable them to impose their understanding of the world and of their interests on others.

However, epistemic autonomy does not exclude Western ideas or those of other civilizations. As one could see in the *qiné* hermeneutical practice of *andemta* (አንድምታ)—"fusion of horizons of diverse understandings"–(Chapter 1, #26)–an understanding of epistemic autonomy as self-rule means not only rejecting epistemic servility, but also rejecting epistemic isolation. Epistemic autonomy does not mean excluding learning from others, provided that the learning is a critical process. Given the epistemic complexity of the world and one's own epistemic limitations arising from the fact that each is formed by particular historical and social conditions, one cannot practice epistemic autarchy and reject the outcomes of the intellectual labours of others. Rather, the perspective of epistemic autonomy embedded in the practice of *andemta* demands a critical external journey into the knowledge and practices others have created.

A critical external journey based on epistemic autonomy treats the knowledge others produce as "raw material" that we should subject to what *qiné* hermeneutics calls *zäräfa* (Chapter 1, # 20). *Zäräfa* enables us, to use the words of the Brazilian poet Oswald de Andrade, to cook, masticate, digest, transform and subject the knowledge the West (other) produces and to dislocate it and subject it to *détournement* in light of the emancipatory needs and interests of Ethiopians that we have elucidated through our critical internal journey. We appropriate the "nutritive" outcomes of this critical external journey and reject the "excremental" (anti-emancipatory) contents and forms. Moreover, to ensure epistemic egalitarianism, the critical external journey must be rooted in the emancipatory questions, ideas, and interests elicited by our critical internal journey. The aim is to develop an *andemta* or a fusion of horizons of the ideas and practices produced through these two critical journeys, which responds to the political, economic, and intellectual challenges Ethiopia faces internally and externally.

Qiné hermeneutics considers all human beings to have comparable epistemic powers and holds that it is incumbent on each to demand first-order reasons in order to accept a claim as true or as having the status of knowledge. Hence the *qiné* hermeneutical *andemta* comment: "The certification of being a scholar is research (ምርምር, *mirmära*, see Chapter 1 # 9), not learning (መማር, *mämar*) by itself."[43] Thus, the *qiné* hermeneutical acerbic critique of the person who does not conduct critical internal and external journeys and does not practice *andemta*, and who, instead, "breathes from the air his master breathes, … rests where he [his master] rests, and … preserve[s] the teaching as he has received it.…"[44] The *andemta* practice articulates a critique *avant la lettre* of epistemic servility and of the logic of "repeat after me."

The failures of Ethiopian Studies to throw light on Ethiopia's conditions in ways that enable Ethiopians to engage freely and with fidelity in emancipatory political, economic, and intellectual activities suggest the need for an alternative approach: one that recognizes Ethiopians as the imaginers, creators, thinkers, and actors of the ideas and practices of democracy, social transformation, and knowledge production. *Qiné* hermeneutics opens up the possibility of developing such an approach and of enucleating an emancipatory theory that is immanent to Ethiopian society and social practices, past and present.[45] *Qiné* hermeneutics is not only about interpreting texts; it is also about engaging the world through the *säm ena wärq* appropriation of experiences, social practices, events, institutions, discourses and knowledge; it does not aim to reinforce the hegemonic order, but to question and subvert it by considering it as *säm ena wärq*. (see Chapter 1 #2).

This short book proposes *qiné* hermeneutical reflections with the hope that the epistemic autonomy that *qiné* hermeneutics exudes and articulates will exemplify the importance of epistemic autonomy if we are to develop an emancipatory understanding of Ethiopian conditions and of ourselves. The book shows that a *qiné* hermeneutical approach enables us to conduct a critical internal journey into Ethiopian history and social practices, vertically (temporally) and laterally (trans-regionally or trans-ethnically) and elicit their unthought, repressed, or excluded emancipatory meanings and possibilities. I

---

43 Roger W. Cowley, "Old Testament Introduction in the Andemta Commentary Tradition," *Journal of Ethiopian Studies* 12, 1 (1974), p. 165.
44 Ibid., p. 170.
45 Maimire Mennasemay, *Qiné Hermeneutics and Ethiopian Critical Theory, supra*, pp. 49-185..

18 Surplus History and Emancipation: Another Ethiopia is Possible

call the outcome of this reading "surplus history" (*säwrä tarik*, see Chapter 2 below): the repressed emancipatory questions, aspirations, ideas, concepts, ideals, interests, norms, goals, and practices that throb in the interstices of the vertical and lateral dimensions of Ethiopian history and society.

As Debebe Seyfu notes in his *qiné* given in the exergue above—ሩቅ ነው ጉዛችን / ድንቅም ነው ጉዛችን ("Our destination is distant, But our journey is glorious")—the transition from epistemic vassalage to epistemic autonomy and the liberation from the triple domination under which Ethiopians currently labour is a long and difficult "journey." Nevertheless, it is a "glorious" one for it affirms Ethiopians as free historical agents, taking their destiny into their own hands and creating an emancipated Ethiopian society in which they recognize themselves as its thinkers, architects, and builders.

1

Critical *Qiné* Hermeneutical Concepts

አዲስ ቃል፤ አዲስ ዓለም
(A new concept, a new world.)
a *sineñ* from a *hibrä qiné*[46]

"A tree without roots does not bear fruits."
          A Gurage aphorism.

The *qiné* line—*A new word, a new world*—in the exergue tells us that the concepts we use constitute our understanding of the world we live in. In this chapter, I enucleate the important critical concepts of *qiné* hermeneutics. A knowledge of these concepts is indispensable for critically reading Ethiopian social practices, past and present, and for identifying and generating *säwrä tarik* or "surplus history"—the emancipatory surplus meanings (*säwrä fitch* / ሰውረ ፍች) of Ethiopian history and social practices, past and present, vertically and laterally. They provide the concepts and vocabularies (*lissan*, see below # 22) we Ethiopians need to develop our political imaginary and critical reflection from within Ethiopian history and social practices on political, cognitive, social and economic emancipation, There is an important truth in the saying, "A tree without roots does not bear fruits," which to a great measure explains the fruitlessness of modern Ethiopian thinking, for it has severed itself from Ethiopia's intellectual roots. The *qiné* hermeneutical concepts discussed here could provide some roots that could enhance the fruit production capacities of the modern Ethiopian knowledge tree.

---

46 *sineñ* means line; a *hibrä qiné* is a *qiné* exemplar, usually an old *qiné*, used for teaching in *qiné* schools.

These concepts are:
1. *Nägär* (ነገር);
2. *Säm ena wärq* (ሰም እና ወርቅ) / wax and gold;
3. *Ena* (እና) / "and" or conflictual interinvolvement;
4. *Gädl* (ገድል) / struggle;
5. *Ewnät* (እውነት) / truth or "the hidden good";
6. *Ewqät* (እውቀት) / knowledge;
7. *Enkän* (እንከን) / incompleteness;
8. *Qisäla* (ቅጸላ) / propaedeutic to *mirmära* (research);
9. *Mirmära* (ምርመራ) / research;
10. *Säwrä bahil* (ሰውረ ባሕል) / non-tradition;
11. *Säwrä hiywät* (ሰውረ ሕይወት) / surplus life;
12. *Säwrä ras* (ሰውረ ራስ) / surplus self;
13. *Säwrä tarik* (ሰውረ ታሪክ) / surplus history;
14. *Arnät* (አርነት) human emancipation;
15. *Hiss* (ሂስ) / critique;
16. *Zäybé* (ዘይቤ) / symptom, signal, way;
17. *Hibrä qal* (ሕብረ ቃል) / harmonizer;
18. *Andem* (አንድም) / and one;
19. *Arat ayn* (አራት ዓይን) / "four-eyed";
20. *Zäräfa* (ዘረፋ) / decentering and diverting;
21. *Quanqua* (ቋንቋ) / language as a discourse of domination;
22. *Lissan* (ልሳን) / language of emancipation;
23. *Tsinsä hassab* (ፅንስ ሓሳብ) / concept;
24. *Admas* (አድማስ) / horizon;
25. *Wihdät* (ውህደት) / unity;
26. *Andemta* (አንድምታ) / "fusion of *wärq* horizons";
27. *Silt* (ስልት) / method-approach;
28. *Mädämamät* (መደማመጥ) / critical dialogical dialogue;
29. *Minab* (ምናብ) / utopianism without utopia;
30. *Yäwäl* (የወል) / the commons;
31. *Dagmawi Tinsa'e* (ዳግማዊ ትንሳኤ) / The Second Resurrection;
32. *Bähig amlak* (በሕግ አምላክ) / the God of Law, ፍትህ (*fithe*) justice;
33. *Tirgum* (ትርጉም) / critical translation;
34. *Antsar nibab* (እንፃር ንባብ) / distanciation reading;
35. *Wistä wäyra nibab* (ውስጠ ወይራ ንባብ), symptomatic reading;
36. *Säwrä fitch* (ሰውረ ፍች) / surplus meaning.

Below, I discuss the 36 entries separately, and develop more extensively four of these—*säwrä tarik, arnät, minab,* and *yäwäl*—in two separate chapters.

1. *Nägär* (ነገር)

The Amharic term *nägär* (ነገር) is derived from the Ge'ez ነገር (*nägär*) which covers a wide semantic field. In Ge'ez, it means "speech, talk, language, saying, pronouncement, discourse, statement, thing, affair, subject, matter, account."[47] Leslau translates *nägär* as "word, thing, affair, matter, item, subject, fact."[48] The 1993 Amharic Dictionary gives thirteen meanings that expand Leslau's translation.[49] Interestingly, one of the meanings of *nägär* is በስም ያልተጠቀስ እቃን (*bäsim yältätäqäsä eqan*), which means the "unnamed."[50] A social practice, a fact, an act, an idea, a belief, an identity, an activity, a norm, an institution, an event, a relation, knowledge, a conflict, in brief, all that is the creation of men, women, and society, be it material or non-material, concrete or mental, cognitive or affective, or has no name or is not nameable is *nägär*. All things, being *nägär*, are internally heterogeneous, self-conflicted, and incomplete. *Nägär* is a semantically rich concept that grasps the world and experiences in their contradictions, tensions, and complexity.

A *qiné* hermeneutical interpretation of two *qiné* derived fragments (*sineñ*, ስነኝ) used as aphorisms could help us understand the complex concept of *nägär*. These two aphorisms must be treated as brachylogia, formulations of excessive brevity that must be interpreted together to grasp their full meaning:

> ነገሩ ነገር ነው ውስጡ ጥቅጥቅ ነው (*Nägäru nägär näw wustu tiqtiq näw*): That which is *nägär* is *nägär*, for it is internally crowded; or, a thing is a thing, but is internally dense.
>
> ነገሩ ነገር ነው ውስጡ ጉራንጉር ነው (*Nägäru nägär näw wustu gourangur näw*): That which is *nägär* is *nägär*, for it is diverse / of different colors inside; or, a thing is a thing, but is internally heterogeneous and tensioned.

The word ጥቅጥቅ (*tiqtiq*) means, depending on the context, complexity, tension, pressure, density, or crowdedness. The word ጉራንጉር (*gourangur*) means, depending on the context, internally heterogeneous, self-conflicted, or contradictory. The meaning of *nägär* combines *tiqtiq* and *gourangur*. The aphorisms intimate that *nägär* is internally complex, heterogeneous, tensioned,

---

[47] Wolf Leslau, *Comparative Dictionary of Ge'ez (Classical Ethiopic)* (Wiesbaden: Otto Harrassowitz, 1991), p. 128; Kidane Weld Kifle, መጽሐፈ ሰዋስው ወግስ ወመዝገበ ቃላት ሐዲስ (Addis Ababa: Artistic Printing Press, 1978 E.C.), p. 626.

[48] Wolf Leslau, *Concise Amharic Dictionary: Amharic-English, English-Amharic* (Berkeley: University of California Press, 1976), p.115.

[49] የአማርኛ መዝገበ ቃላት (Addis Ababa: Addis Ababa University, 1993), p. 284.

[50] Ibid.

dynamic, non-transparent, incomplete, open-ended, and inhabited by antagonisms and contradictions. Note how each line starts with "ነገሩ ነገር ነው / *Nägäru nägär näw*," i.e. "A thing is a thing." This seemingly tautological phrase intimates that the folding of the predicate *nägär* over the subject *nägär* is a signal that indicates its incompleteness and the presence of internal contradictions, of the presence of unsaid determinations of *nägär*, intimating that *nägär* does not exist harmoniously with itself, and that it has surplus meanings (*säwrä fitch*, see # 36 below) that need to be excavated. At the same time, it bears a critique of the law of identity. The identity of *nägär* is mediated by the negations that articulate it. Eliciting the surplus meanings of *nägär* thus requires recognizing *nägär* as a site of contradictions and seeking what it is not within what it is, and what it is in what it is not. Enucleating its "unsaid" or "repressed" dimensions (በስም ያልተጠቀሰ እቃን / *bäsim yältätäqäsä eqan*) is crucial for understanding *nägär*.

The concept of *nägär* rejects the empiricist myth that there are bare facts. For *qiné* hermeneutics, *nägär* is simultaneously dialectical and historical; no *nägär* is atheoretical and devoid of a value dimension. There are neither naked nor atomic *nägär*. *Nägär* is, as we shall see below, a *säm ena wärq* in that it is always polysemous. Because no *nägär* exists in isolation, it cannot be understood independently of its explicit and implicit internal and external contexts. Therefore, *nägär* cannot be simply used as a discreet theory and value-free data to test a concept, as is done in the borrowed social sciences in Ethiopian Studies.

A critical understanding of *nägär* requires going beyond social science empirical observations and generalizations, for these two are framed by the "hegemonic" criteria of intelligibility, which in various ways are shaped by the interests that inform the triple domination.[51] It thus demands questioning the hegemonic understanding of *nägär*, unpacking its internal relations and the social processes that produced it, disclosing its inner split and the antagonisms that are constitutive of it, and revealing the questions and answers that are repressed by the manifest questions to which the empirical *nägär* appears as an answer.

---

51 I submit to *zäräfa* (see # 20, below). Raymond Williams' definition of "hegemony." Raymond Williams, *Marxism and Literature* (New York: Oxford University Press, 1977), p. 110. He writes. "hegemony" refers to a "whole body of practices and expectations, over the whole of living: our senses and assignments of energy, our shaping perceptions of ourselves and our world. It is a lived system of meanings and values-constitutive and constituting-which as they are experienced as practices appear as reciprocally confirming. [Hegemony] thus constitutes a sense of reality for most people in the society."

2. Säm ena wärq (ስም እና ወርቅ) / wax and gold

Säm ena wärq is an intellectual tradition that exists since at least the sixth century, when Saint Yared (505-571 AD) took the first steps in the systematization of *qiné* composition in addition to his systematization of *zema* (religious chants).[52] *Säm* means wax and *wärq* means gold. At first flush, *säm ena wärq* means appearance and reality, with appearance commonly understood as illusion and discovering the gold understood as peeling away the wax or the illusion that hides it. This is the *azmari* (አዝማሪ, minstrel) interpretation of *säm ena wärq* in the context of circumstantial *qiné*. The latter does not have much to do with the understanding of *säm ena wärq* in classical *qiné*, the source of *qiné* hermeneutics..

In *qiné* hermeneutics, *säm ena wärq* has a radically different meaning. It is a master metaphor for the contradictory Ethiopian conditions and the deadlocks and antagonisms of Ethiopian life. The *säm*, in *qiné* hermeneutics, is not an illusion; nor is the *wärq* a Platonic essence. The *säm* is as real as the *wärq*. *Säm ena wärq* is an approach that considers that there is interaction between living and thinking, and that knowledge production about Ethiopian life is a struggle (*gädl*, see entry # 4 below) against and a critique (*hiss*, see entry # 15 below) of the given: beliefs, ideas, ideals, norms, values, institutions, and practices.

Säm ena wärq is rooted in the idea that reality—all that is the product of human beings, be it social, political, economic, material, intellectual, affective, or belief—is *nägär*, and that therefore reality must be interpreted to be understood adequately. Since reality is *säm ena wärq*, there are no self-evident truths. Every social fact (*nägär*) is polysemous and theory and value-laden. *Säm* and *wärq* do not coincide with each other; nor do they belong to unconnected realities, for they are connected antagonistically. *Säm ena wärq* harbours a critique of identity. As we have seen above in the discussion of *nägär*, the folding of the predicate *nägär* over the subject *nägär* signals a critique of the law of identity (see also # 3 below).

Säm ena wärq spells disunity and mutual dependency between *säm* and *wärq* as well as an antagonistic unity of the disunity of the two. The opposition *säm / wärq* is not distributive. *Säm ena wärq* is a knot of conflicting meanings that express the antagonism between reality's (*nägär*'s) external face or appearance (*säm*) and its internal face or repressed meaning (*wärq*). That is, *säm / wärq* are interinvolved: the understanding of each is dependent on the

---

52 Maimire Mennasemay, *Qiné Hermeneutics and Ethiopian Critical Theory* (Los Angeles: Tsehai Publishing, 2021), Chapter 2.

interpretation we operate on both. Through *säm ena wärq* formulation, *qiné* hermeneutics enables us to decipher the contradictions of reality (*nägär*) and to make possible the transition from the "thought" to the "unthought" or *wärq*, from an inadequate to an adequate (*wärq*) understanding of reality. According to *qiné* hermeneutics, one cannot grasp the *wärq* or the true potential or meaning of *nägär* directly; it has to be unpacked as *säm ena wärq*. The path to *wärq* always traverses the *säm*

Säm ena wärq problematization of issues assumes that Ethiopian reality cannot be understood and changed without resolving the deadlocks that inhabit it. *Säm ena wärq* articulates these deadlocks as antagonistic relations between *säm* (appearance, the given, the self-evident) and *wärq* (the repressed or gestating truth). Interpreting the given reality requires treating it as *säm ena wärq*, and interpreting it, not only on the basis of what it is, but also on the basis of what it denies or represses. According to *qiné* hermeneutics, to grasp the true meaning or *wärq* of reality or *nägär*, one must make a detour and go interpretatively through the *säm* and its contradictions on pain of failing to understand adequately the true meaning of the *nägär* we are studying. That is, an indirect approach to reality is necessary to understand it adequately, because reality, being internally complex, tensioned and contradictory, cannot deliver its *wärq* or true meaning if we try to grasp it directly.[53] *Säm ena wärq* is in a sense a venue for resistance to the hegemonic discourse according to which Ethiopia's problems are limited only to the empirically given and are directly observable and understandable. This hegemonic understanding occludes the forces and structures that generate the empirically given. *Säm ena wärq* as resistance means that thinking is asking questions in order to flush out the "more" or the *wärq* that the given distorts, hides, obscures, dissimulates, or represses but whose presence is intimated by the *zäybé* (symptoms, see # 16) that are present in the given or the *nägär* as disturbances, glitches, anomalies, inconsistencies, or contradictions.

Neither the *säm* nor the *wärq* are homogeneous and complete. Both are always incomplete or *enkän* (see # 7). Both are traversed by antagonisms that hold them together and render them unstable, making them subject to interpretations. The labour of interpretation of the *säm ena wärq* of Ethiopian reality or *nägär* involves examining, searching, and bringing to light new ways

---

53 That is why, often, contemporary Ethiopian novels help us to understand the present Ethiopian crisis more adequately than the unmediated empirical observations and generalizations that the borrowed social sciences of Ethiopian Studies do. For a succinct description of the life and works of some of the major Ethiopian novelists, see Reidulf K. Molvaer, *Black Lions: The Creative Lives of Modern Ethiopian Literary Giants and Pioneers*, (Lawrenceville, NJ, Rede Sea Press, 1997).

of comprehending our lives, others, the world and our relations to it. It makes possible new ways of thinking as well as new thoughts. The *säm ena wärq* process of elucidation assumes that the path to *wärq* is a moment of *wärq*, or, to put it differently, the error(s) or appearances that *säm* embodies is also a moment of the path to *wärq*. The influential *qiné* scholar Kebede G/Medhin compares the path of *säm ena wärq* hermeneutics as a process of smelting, separating, hammering, purifying, and producing gold from ore.[54] One finds in *säm ena wärq* hermeneutics something analogous to Marx's comment, "All science would be superfluous if the form of appearance of things directly coincided with their essence."[55]

Wärq stands for the "hidden good"— the unthought emancipatory surplus meanings—that *säm* distorts, dissimulates, represses, or hides.[56] The *wärq* is immanent to Ethiopian reality but transcends it in ways that reveal the *säm* interpretation as inadequate to understand it. The *wärq* however is not identical to itself, for it is always incomplete or *enkän* (see # 7, below) and therefore it incubates a new *säm ena wärq* that harbours its own internal antagonisms and is thus subject to further interpretation. The quest for *wärq* through the practice of *säm ena wärq* expresses the desire to change life and oneself. The *qiné* hermeneutical tradition, with its innumerable compositions on the sorrows and sufferings of life (*hazan*, ሓዘን; *tkazie*, ትካዜ) and its deeply rooted desire for an alternative way of being and living, expressed in *zäläsäña* (ዘለሰኝ) *qiné* and *minab* (ምናብ, concrete utopian desires, see Chapter 3 below), intimates that the quest for *wärq* or emancipation (*arnät*, see Chapter 3 below) must take place in the here and now.[57]

Säm ena wärq is the organizing spirit of *qiné* hermeneutics. Aläka Imbakom Kalewold, the *qiné* scholar, draws our attention to the depth, intensity, and complexity of *qiné* hermeneutics driven by *säm ena wärq*. He describes it as an intellectual activity that embraces "መማር መመራመር ማወቅ መረቀቅ መጥላቅ መውለድ መፍጠር መፈልሰፍ" (*mämar, mämaramär, mawäq, märaqäq, mättläq, mäwläd, mäftär,*

---

54 Kebede G/Medhin, ሳይንሳዊ የቅኔ አፈታት ስልት (Addis Ababa: Birana Matëmia Bet, 1992), p.7.
55 Karl Marx, *Capital* Vol. 3 (London: Penguin Books, 1981) p. 956.
56 The "hidden good," see Claude Sumner, *Classical Ethiopian Philosophy* (Los Angeles: Adey Publishing Company, 1994), p. 186. The "hidden good" is the emancipatory surplus meaning or "surplus history" (*säwrä tarik*, see Chapter 2, below) that is immanent in Ethiopian social practices and history.
57 Emancipation as *arnät* (አርነት) covers and articulates political, economic, and epistemic liberation from oppression, exploitation, and epistemic domination or Gibbonism. See Chapter 3 below. On *zäläsäña* (ዘለሰኝ) *qiné* Balambaras Mahtem Selasse Welde Mesqel, "ዘለሰኝ አማርኛ ቅኔ (Addis Ababa: Artistic Printing Press, 1955 E.C.), pp. 93-284.

mäfälsäf).⁵⁸ That is, *qiné* hermeneutics embraces "learning, exploring, examining, knowing, abstracting, analyzing, questioning, critiquing, philosophizing, and gestating or giving birth to new ideas." It deals with personal, social, spiritual, philosophical, and political issues and raises questions that pertain to *hassabä ewen*, ሃሳበ አውን (metaphysics), *sinä ewen*, ሥነ አውን (ontology), *sinä ewqät*, ሥነ አውቀት (epistemology), and *sinä migbar*, ሥነ ምግባር (ethics), and all life activities. This is the sense of *säm ena wärq* in what Mengestu Lemma calls "classical *qiné*" that is foundational of *qiné* hermeneutics.⁵⁹

One must not conflate *säm ena wärq* in classical *qiné* with *säm ena wärq* in circumstantial *qiné*. Classical *qiné* is the source of *qiné* hermeneutics; it is reflexive, critical, and dialectical. Circumstantial *qiné* is the stock in trade of the *azmari*; it is based on a mechanical interpretation of *säm ena wärq*. The *azmari* use the *säm ena wärq* trope by stripping it of its philosophical exigencies and reducing it to a play on the polysemy of words to praise, insult, express commentaries on events and practices. *Azmari qiné* is circumstantial *qiné*. Once we know the circumstances of its composition, its meaning is self-evident and limited. The mechanical interpretation is adequate for *azmari qiné*, because *azmari qiné* deals with a straightforward dualism of appearance (*säm*) and essence (*wärq*) and treats the *ena* in *säm ena wärq* as *wäyim* (ወይም, or): a disjunctive. The mechanical interpretation considers *wärq* as if it were already there, to be discovered by peeling the wax (*säm*) that is assumed to wrap the "gold" (*wärq*). An advocate of the mechanical interpretation of *säm ena wärq* is Donald Levine whose social science inspired dualistic view has been uncritically adopted in Ethiopian Studies: he treats *ena* as if it meant ወይም (*wäyim*) meaning "or" and reduces all *qiné* to circumstantial *qiné* and writes that *säm ena wärq* is "a form built of two semantic layers. The apparent figurative meaning of the words is called wax; their more or less hidden actual significance is the "gold."⁶⁰ Donald Levine adopts the *azmari* or mechanical interpretation of *säm ena wärq*, primarily because he pays no attention to the historical and intellectual roots of *säm ena wärq*. He thus empties the *qiné* intellectual tradition of its critical hermeneutical content. The mechanical interpretation of *säm ena wärq* is inapplicable to classical *qiné*. In classical *qiné*, *wärq* is not an already formed thing, present inside the *säm* envelope; rather, it is produced, as the *qiné* scholar Kebede G/Medhin, quoted above, explains through a complex labour of interpretation that he

---

58 Aläka Imbakom Kalewold, ቅኔ ትምህርት ና ስለ ጥቅሙ, Proceedings of the Third International Conference of Ethiopian Studies (Addis Ababa, 1966), p. 136.
59 Menghestu Lemma, "Appendix: Ethiopian classical poetry" in Aläka Imbakom Kalewold, *Traditional Ethiopian Church Education*, trans. Menghestu Lemma (New York: Teachers College Press, 1970), p. 33.
60 Donald N. Levine, *Wax and Gold* (Chicago: University of Chicago Press, 1972), p. 5.

compares to the process of smelting, separating, hammering, purifying, and producing "gold" from ore.[61] The interpretation of the *säm ena wärq* deploys *zäräfa, tirgum, andem, arat ayn,* and *hiss* (see for these concepts, # 20, 33,18, 19, 15) to elucidate the tension and complexity that informs the *säm ena wärq* and produce the *wärq*. In *qiné* hermeneutics, *säm ena wärq* is the weapon of the weak, of those who have no other weapon to wield against oppression except their emancipatory ideas.

3. Ena (እና) / "and" as conflictual interinvolvement

The *"ena"* in the *säm ena wärq* of classical *qiné* does not separate categorically the *säm* from the *wärq*. Rather, it intimates a reciprocal antagonistic determination between the two and articulates the idea that *säm / wärq* neither coincide with each other nor pertain to mutually exclusive realities. It indicates the presence of antagonisms and contradiction (*t'mir,* ጥምር) internal to the *säm ena wärq* and its *nägär*, and the necessity to engage in *gädl* / struggle (see # 4) to resolve the contradictions that arise from the internal complexity of *nägär* and its *säm ena wärq* existence. Thus, *ena* is a critical concept that points to the non-identity of *säm* and *wärq*, of their entanglement and struggle with each other, opening up possibilities of something new. *Ena* ushers in a hermeneutics of contradictions. In *qiné* hermeneutics, *ena* in *säm ena wärq* is not a mere conjunction. It expresses the recognition of the conflicted nature of the subject matter of the *säm ena wärq* by indicating that the subject of the *säm ena wärq* is not identical to itself: it is what it is and what it is not, or it is *säm* and not *säm* at the same time. *Ena* thus signals the inadequacy of identity and self-identify in understanding the *säm*, the *wärq*, and the *säm ena wärq*.

Ena expresses the rejection of dualism and monism. It indicates that *säm* and *wärq* constitute a duality without dualism: an inclusive duality where each, in some sense, requires the other for its existence. The concept of "ex-timate"— the idea that the center of a social practice or the center of the individual (be it consciousness or the unconscious) is inside and outside it, breaking down the interior / exterior dualism—comes close to catching the idea of duality without dualism that informs *qiné* hermeneutics.[62] *Ena*, in the *säm ena wärq* formulation of *nägär*, indicates that *wärq* is inside and outside the *säm*, as the *säm* is inside and outside the *wärq*, and these internal relations are antagonistic. *Ena* thus indicates that *säm ena wärq* is neither reductive nor dualistic and that *säm ena wärq* is held

---

61 Kebede G/Medhin, ሳይንሳዊ የቅኔ አፈታት ስልት (Addis Ababa: Birana Matëmia Bet, 1992), p.7.
62 A *zäräfa* of "ex-timacy," see Dylan Evans, *An Introductory Dictionary of Lacanian Psychoanalysis* (London: Routledge, 1996), p. 59. The concept of ex-timacy overcomes the apparent, superficial duality between the interior and the exterior.

together by the antagonism that *ena* refers to. It shows the necessity to consider both the internal and external contexts and processes that produce the *nägär* that is the subject matter of the *säm ena wärq*. *Ena* in *säm ena wärq* conveys the processual nature of both *säm* and *wärq*. Thus, *säm ena wärq* is not *säm wäyim wärq*. *Wäyim* is a disjunctive term that sets up mutually exclusive and jointly exhaustive relations and is associated with dualism. The understanding of *ena* as *wäyim* is characteristic of circumstantial *qiné* and of the mechanical interpretation of *säm ena wärq*.

4. Gädl (ገድል) / *struggle*

Gädl means in Ge'ez "strife, striving, conflict, contending, combat, mortification, spiritual battle, life of a saint."[63] It is a term that one finds in the title of the hagiographies of Ethiopian Orthodox saints. When one speaks of the *gädl* of holy men (*Gädlä Täklä Haimanot, Gädlä Abew WeAhaw*, and so forth), one refers to their "struggle" against falsehoods, injustice, sinful acts, and evil temptations; to their ironclad discipline to follow the right path and accept all sufferings that arise from following it; to their striving to do good in the eyes of God and persuade people to follow the right path; and to their determination "to stand up" against earthly powers who commit injustices.[64]

The Amharic term *gädl*, derived from Ge'ez, also means struggle, but in a secular sense.[65] It means to struggle against injustice, wrongdoing, corruption, oppression, falsehood, inequality, unfreedoms, false claims, wrong arguments, and so forth. *Gädl* is driven by the desire to expose and overcome the political, economic, social, and epistemic sufferings of Ethiopian life. In its operation, *gädl* engages the mind and the body, spirit and passion. Defying the conventional and eliciting the contradictions of social practices and trying to overcome them are inherent to *gädl*. In Amharic, the defiant aspect of the secular *gädl* is partly expressed in the term *wäné* (ወኔ). A person who has *wäné* is one who lives by the conviction that nothing changes without struggle, that emancipation is not available without combat, be it political, social, or intellectual. The core idea of *gädl* is active struggle for the sake of the "the hidden good" or emancipation.

---

63 Wolf Leslau, *Concise Dictionary of Ge'ez (Classical Ethiopic)* (Wiesbaden: Otto Harrassowitz, 2010). Kidane Weld Kifle, መጽሐፈ ሰዋስው ወግስ ወመዝገበ ቃላት ሐዲስ (Addis Ababa: Artistic Printing Press, 1978 E.C.).
64 Getatchew Haile, ደቂቀ እስጢፋኖስ በሕግ አምላክ, trans. from Ge'ez (Collegeville, MN. 2004), pp. 102, 105-9, 112, 120, 122-7, 207.
65 አማርኛ መዝገበ ቃላት (Addis Ababa: Addis Ababa University, 1993); Kidane Weld Kifle, መጽሐፈ ሰዋስው ወግስ ወመዝገበ ቃላት ሐዲስ (Addis Ababa: Artistic Printing Press, 1978 E.C.).

Without *gädl*, the apparent (*säm*) or the hegemonic understanding of *nägär* reigns uncontested.

Gädl is a struggle that shines light on alternative ways of becoming and living. It challenges the frontier between the possible and the impossible established by the hegemonic order, opening the door for going beyond the hegemonic order and knowledge and unveiling that which is impossible in terms of the criteria of intelligibility and possibility of the hegemonic order and its knowledge discourse, but that which becomes possible once we discard these criteria. *Gädl* brings to light non-tradition (*säwrä bahil* / ሰውረ ባሕል), surplus life (*säwrä hiywät* / ሰውረ ሕይወት), surplus self (*säwrä ras* / ሰውረ ራስ), surplus history (*säwrä tarik* / ሰውረ ታሪክ), and surplus meanings (*säwrä fitch*, ሰውረ ፍች) (see below # 10 to 13, and #36 for these terms). In *qiné* hermeneutics, *gädl* leads to an emancipatory conception and practice of knowledge (*ewqät*, እውቀት, see # 6 below) whose form and content are guided by *ewnät* (*ewnät*, እውነት, see # below) or *wärq*.

5. *Ewnät* (እውነት) / truth, *wärq*, or "the hidden good"

Ewnät means "truth." It is the "hidden good." *Wärq* (ወርቅ) is *ewnät* (እውነት). *Ewnät* is emancipatory knowledge that discloses the presence of the other reality that the hegemonic discourse represses: the emancipatory surplus meanings that *gädl* produces through the *säm ena wärq* interpretation of *nägär*. *Ewnät* links causality (*säbäb*, ሰበብ) and reason (*miknyat* / ምክንያት) in that it shows that identifying a cause presupposes that the elements that enter in the causal explanation (*fitch*, ፍች) are subject to *säm ena wärq* interpretation. *Ewnät* subsumes explanatory reasoning to the rational *qälb* (ቀልብ) interests of emancipation. According to *qiné* hermeneutics, a means-end rationality that is not subject to *ewnät* is a rationality of domination.

The process of acquiring *ewnät* has a performative character. It is a process that lays bare that which is in *nägär* more than *nägär* by eliciting the internal tensions and contradictions that unite and destabilize the given *nägär* and point to the emancipatory possibilities that gestate in it; at the same time, it is a process that transforms the agent who is struggling to produce *ewnät*. *Ewnät* is universal (*huläntänawi*, ሁሉንተናዊ) because it is emancipatory. In exposing *nägär*'s contradictions, *ewnät* discloses the possibilities of going beyond them. *Ewnät* is critical of the hegemonic order and its legitimating discourse. Though universal, *ewnät* is not, however, immutable; nor is it transcendentally guaranteed. Being inhabited by new tensions and contradictions, it is always incomplete (*enkän*, እንከን, see # 7 below). It is not free from new internal tensions and contradictions. In this sense, *ewnät* incubates its own *säm ena wärq*, indicating that there is no final and closed *ewnät*.

Ewnät is not thinkable in terms of the coordinates of the hegemonic parameters of knowledge and of knowing. It "bursts through the shackles," to use an expression from the *qiné* hermeneutical *andemta* (አንድምታ, see #26 below.) tradition, of the hegemonic knowledge, be it Ethiopian or Western (or other).[66] *Ewnät* creates its own coordinates of intelligibility and possibility, of knowing, feeling, conviction, evaluation, and action. The telos of *ewnät* (*wärq*) is emancipation (*arnät*, አርነት, see Chapter 3) from powerlessness: epistemic, political, social, and economic. *Ewnät* throws light retroactively on *nägär* and its hegemonic interpretations, brings out their distortions, reorders the relation of the *säm* (the particular) to the universal (*wärq*). In the process, it creates new parameters of intelligibility, normativity, and possibility. It discloses *säwrä bahil* (non-tradition), *säwrä hiywät* (surplus life), *säwrä ras* (surplus self), and *säwrä tarik* (surplus history), all of which are invisible in terms of the parameters of intelligibility and normativity of the hegemonic order (for the above terms, see # 10 to 13 below). Epistemic autonomy is indispensable for the production of *ewnät*.

6. *Ewqät* (እውቀት) / knowledge

Literally translated, *ewqät* means knowledge. Insofar as it imparts an effective understanding of the mechanisms and processes of the world, knowledge/ *ewqät* is crucial in the interpretation, explanation, and understanding of *nägär*. *Ewnät* (*wärq*) requires knowledge/*ewqät* (እውቀት) for its production. The relation between *ewnät* and *ewqät* is not a relationship of similarity or equivalence; the quest for *ewnät* is the quest for *wärq* / truth, a quest for emancipatory knowledge; the quest for *ewqät* is a quest to understand how the given world is organized and functions. However, *ewnät* and *ewqät* are not mutually exclusive. In *qiné* hermeneutics, knowledge/*ewqät* is amphibolic. Depending on the role it plays in *säm ena wärq*, it could be a path to either the empirical understanding of *nägär* or to its *wärq* or to both. As a path to empirical understanding, *ewqät* embodies the instrumentalist understanding of *nägär* and thereby could serve to hide, neglect, or repress tensions and contradictions and play a role in the practices of oppression and exploitation: consider the use of the knowledge/*ewqät* of evolutionary theory, biology, psychology, neoclassical economics, and so forth, to implement or rationalize oppression, exploitation, racism, sexism, and inequalities. However, when subordinated to *ewnät*, *ewqät* could be a path to *wärq* or emancipatory ideas.

---

66 On "bursting through the shackles of tradition," see Roger W. Cowley, "Old Testament Introduction in the Andemta Commentary Tradition," *Journal of Ethiopian Studies* 12, 1 (1974), p.170..

Ewqät is external to the *nägär* it studies, while *ewnät* is practical in the sense that it changes its very object and the agent engaged in producing it. Once peasants have *ewnät* (*wärq*) that they are exploited, they are no longer peasants who know (*ewqät*) that they are exploited but continue to live their exploitation as a natural order; rather, with *ewnät* of their exploitation, the peasants undergo a subjective transformation that brings out their *säwrä ras* (surplus self, see # 12), produces *säwrä bahil* (non-tradition, see #10), and changes the meaning of the experience they live such that they act differently and try to overthrow the conditions that make them exploited peasants. Before 1968, the Gojjam peasants knew (*ewqät*) they were exploited, but they lived with it. It is only in their uprising in 1968-9 that the *ewnät* of their condition manifested itself, an *ewnät* that transformed them and their *ewqät*, leading them to emancipatory acts articulated as a peasant uprising expressive of *säwrä ras* (surplus self, see # 12) and *säwrä hiywät* (surplus life, see # 11).[67]

Ewqät by itself does not bring emancipation. It could serve emancipation only if it subsumes itself to *ewnät* (*wärq*). There could be "unity" (*wihdät*, ዉህደት, see # 25)—in the *qiné* hermeneutical sense of "without mixture or separation," as we shall see below—between *ewnät* (*wärq*) and *ewqät* (knowledge) only when *ewnät* guides *ewqät*. The unity embraces both factual truth and moral rightness and mobilizes *ewqät* in the interest of emancipation, making *ewqät* self-reflexive, critical, prescriptive, productive, and emancipatory. *Ewnät*'s guidance of *ewqät* discloses the emancipatory potential of *ewqät* (knowledge), and enables *ewqät* to engage in *gädl* against its appropriation for the purposes of oppression and exploitation. Skendes, one of the founders of Ethiopian classical philosophy, writes, "Wisdom is the light that fills the soul. It is everywhere; it has no end and it cannot be found.... It calls knowledge conscience."[68] It is the submission to *ewnät* that gives *ewqät* "conscience." Knowledge without conscience is part of the hegemonic order and a tool of domination.

7. *Enkän* (እንከን) / *incompleteness*

Enkän (እንከን) means incompleteness in that *nägär* and the understanding we have of it is always incomplete.[69] The idea of *enkän* is central to *qiné* hermeneutics and points to the historicity of *nägär* and its interpretation. Every *nägär* is

---

[67] Gebru Tareke. *Ethiopia: Power and Protest: Peasant Revolts in the Twentieth Century* (New York: Cambridge University Press, 1991), pp. 168ff.

[68] Claude Sumner, *Classical Ethiopian Philosophy* (Los Angeles: Adey Publishing Company, 1994), p. 198.

[69] Kidane Weld Kifle, መጽሐፈ ሰዋሰው ወግስ ወመዝገበ ቃላት ሐዲስ (Addis Ababa: Artistic Printing Press, 1978 E. C.), p. 302.

enkän or incomplete in that it is opaque, internally complex, contradictory, and subject to change and transformation without ever reaching completeness. It is contingent, historical, and transformable. *Ewqät* and *wärq/ ewnät* are also *enkän* in that each is a *nägär*. Indeed reality (*ewen*, እውን) itself is incomplete and contradictory, an idea encapsulated in the following *qiné* lines.

ቸሩ ወልደ እግዚአብሔር ሽማኔ ነህ አሉ	/ Benevolent God, it is said that you are a cloth weaver.
ያንተ ሽማኔነት ምኑ ይደነቃል	/ But who could admire your skill?
ካንድ ወገን ስትሠራ ካንዱ ወገን ያልቃል[70]	/ While you are weaving the cloth at one end, it comes undone at the other end.

The *qiné* has multiple meanings, which point to the secular and critical spirit that informs *qiné* hermeneutics. The *qiné* compares the "Son of God" to a weaver whose work does not merit praise, because while he is weaving the cloth at one end it comes undone at the other end, contradicting the purpose of the weaving. In referring to God's work as always "unfinished" and "self-negating," *qiné* hermeneutics gestates the idea of ontological (*sinä ewen*, ሥነ እውን) incompleteness and openness. The *qiné* hermeneutical idea of *enkän* does not mean that the world cannot be known. Rather, it means no *nägär*, including *ewqät* and *wärq/ewnät*, is a self-harmonizing and a self-totalizing system. Every *nägär* is *enkän* because it has tensions and contradictions, limits and openness, and possibilities for the emergence of something new or for change. For the *qiné* hermeneutical tradition, *enkän* is not a deficiency. Rather, it fosters questioning and change.

For *qiné* hermeneutics, *enkän* intimates not only that Ethiopian reality incubates its own emancipatory aspirations but it also contradicts them. Ethiopian society is, as *säm ena wärq*, *enkän*; that is, it is always already incomplete and contradictory, and so is our understanding of it. The incompleteness of Ethiopian reality and of our understanding of it does not lead to a dead-end; on the contrary, it invites and makes possible a search for new coordinates of the possible and feasible understandings. Thus, *enkän* does not paralyze Ethiopians: it provides the ground for the emergence of a social and political thinking and imagination that shows that the future is not limited to what the hegemonic order projects; it opens the door for critical inquiries and signals new possibilities for identifying the possible subjective and objective sites of emancipatory struggle and thereby the possibility of bringing forth new coordinates of social becoming.

---

70 Balambaras Mahteme Selasse Welde Mesqel, አማርኛ ቅኔ (Addis Ababa: Artistic Printing Press, 1955 E. C.), p. 156, no. 400.

Though universal (*huläntänawi*), the *wärq* of *qiné* is also *enkän* and is thus a "situated universality."[71] It is incomplete and tensioned, nevertheless it transcends its time and place and speaks to the past and to future issues in new ways. For *qiné* hermeneutics, there is no complete universal (*huläntänawi*) understanding of what counts as universal or rational (*qälb*). This does not imply relativism. Rather, it implies that all understandings of what counts as universal or rational are *enkän* and are not the prerogative of a particular language, culture, horizon, epistemology, or method. This means three things. First, what counts as universal or rational is itself *nägär*, therefore *enkän*. And as *nägär*, it is subject to the operation of *säm ena wärq*, which means that a criticism of a particular conception of the universal or of the rational is not a denial of universality and of rationality but a recognition of the *enkän* of the particular conception of the rational and the universal. Second, from the perspective of *enkän*, to claim the universal or rational is *enkän* is to invite a "critical dialogical dialogue" or *mädämamät* (see below # 28) between the diverse understandings of the rational and universal, and of the statements or practices that are claimed to be universal or rational. *Enkän* thus opens the door for critical dialogical dialogue expanding the interlocutors' understanding of the universal and rational. Nevertheless, the new understanding emerging from the critical dialogical dialogue is still *enkän*, though at a more comprehensive level. Third, to say that *nägär* is *enkän* or incomplete means that what is considered impossible could emerge as a possibility that breaks through the given order. *Enkän* makes possible the practice of *zäräfa* (*détournement*), *andem* (alternative interpretation), *tirgum* (critical translation), *arat ayn* (four-eyed view), *hiss* (critique), and *tähägagari hiss* or *mädämamät* (see below entries #20, 18, 33, 19, 15, 28, for discussion of these terms).

Given the Ethiopian debate, sometimes violent, regarding the Ethiopian past, the *qiné* idea of *enkän* intimates that the Ethiopian past is not something that is given as a complete oeuvre; it is a *nägär*: unfinished, complex, internally contradictory. It is *enkän*. It harbours non-synchronous, super-imposed, and entangled processes manifesting discordances of temporalities and spaces. The *enkän* of the Ethiopian past makes possible "thinking backward" in order to look forward. First, it points to the existence of failed emancipatory aspirations—the "future in the past"—and thus introduces the openness of the future into the Ethiopian past, exposing its repressed emancipatory

---

71 On the idea of situated universality, Alain Badiou, *Ethics* (London: Verso, 2001), 72–7; Alain Badiou, *Theoretical Writings*, ed. and tr. by R. Brassier and A. Toscano (London: Continuum, 2005), 143–52.

possibilities.[72] Second, it allows us to put ourselves back in time, identify a decision in the Ethiopian past that actualized one of the possible alternative paths and crushed the other alternatives inhabiting the situation, and imagine how, at that moment, a different decision may have put Ethiopian history on a different or emancipatory path. Thus, the *enkän* of the Ethiopian past enables us to disclose the emancipatory surplus meanings that the hegemonic past repressed but that haunt contemporary Ethiopia and which we could retrieve from the perspective of the emancipatory interests of the present. The point of backward thinking is not to search for origins. The thinking backward that the *enkän* of the past makes possible unveils the aleatory and disjointed processes by which an aspect of the past wins and becomes the present. The recognition of the past as *enkän* and the backward thinking it makes possible liberates the past from its givenness, shows the contingency of the present, and the undecidedness of the future. It thus reveals the past's dynamism and repressed alternative futures, and enables us to conjugate theoretical thought with political imagination so that we can engage with the present historical crisis in Ethiopia from the perspective of our emancipatory projects whose roots are also in the past. Thinking backward and the *enkän* of the past that is its premise do not mean we invent facts about the past; rather, it means not essentializing the practices, institutions and identities we have inherited from the past, and liberating its hidden, forgotten, or repressed forward-looking emancipatory alternatives (*säwrä tarik* / ሰውረ ታሪh, see Chapter 2). The *enkän* of the Ethiopian past shows that there is neither teleology nor linear causality in Ethiopian history. What appears to be linear causality is what the hegemonic present order produces by its retroactive ideological appropriation of a specific past as its sufficient cause.

8. *Qisäla* (ቅጸላ) / *propaedeutic to mirmära (research)*

A critical interpretation that unpacks the tensions and contradictions of *nägär* and brings out its surplus meanings demands a preliminary process of preparation. This process is what *qiné* hermeneutics calls *qisäla* (ቅጸላ). *Qisäla* is the first step in the conduct of *mirmära* (ምርመራ) or research (see # 9 below). The persons engaged in *qisäla* strive to liberate their intellect and imagination through

---

72 On "thinking backward, see" Stephen R. L. Clark, *G. K. Chesterton: Thinking Backward, Looking Forward* (West Conshohocken, PA: Templeton Press, 2006). As we will see below, *zäräfa, andem, tirgum,* and *arat ayn* (entries # 20, 18, 33, 19) make possible "thinking backward."On "future in the past," Ernst Bloch, *The Principle of Hope*, vol. I., trans. Neville Plaice, Stephen Plaice and Paul Knight (Cambridge, Mass.: The MIT Press, 1986), pp. 9, 154, 298.

a deconstruction of the conventional limits of the possible and the imaginable to reveal or see what the domesticated intellect and imagination cannot. Those who succeed to liberate their intellect and imagination from the hegemonic parameters of the possible and imaginable achieve epistemic autonomy and are said to have an *absho* (አብሾ) mind, i.e., an explosive, transgressive, and creative intellect / imagination.[73] The person practicing *qisäla* engages in critical reflection upon the hegemonic ideas, assumptions, questions, and judgements as well as on those that one brings along as part of one's intellectual, cultural, and belief baggage.[74]

The articulation of critical self-questioning with the questioning of and reflection upon the subject matter provides freedom to the scholar, which allows him /her to throw new light on the subject matter in the sense that it liberates the subject matter from the hegemonic biases and prejudices that repress its complexity and contradictions as *nägär* and limit its possible interpretations. The scholar explores the relevant existing field of knowledge and raises questions as to the adequacy of already existing interpretations to grasp the subject matter in its complexity. He /she explores new perspectives and interpretations, and demarcates his /her work from the previous ones. The effort to bring to light the unsaid, the unquestioned, and the unknown of the subject matter is what drives *qisäla*. It is important to note that *qisäla* is a process that problematizes *nägär*. The problematization of *nägär* prepares the ground for ምርመራ (*mirmära*) or research.

9. Mirmära (ምርመራ) / research

Qisäla is the first step in *mirmära* (ምርመራ). The problematization of the subject matter and of the researcher through *qisäla* initiates a process of exploration of the subject matter or *nägär*. The scholar, known as *leeq* (ሊቅ), *däbtära* (ደብተራ) or *mämhir* (መምህር) in the *qiné* hermeneutical tradition, explores the subject matter through questioning (ጥያቄ, *tiyaqé*), observation (ማስታወል, *mastawäl*), critique (ሂስ, *hiss*, #15), alternative interpretations (*andem*, አንደም #18), critical translation (*tirgum*, ትርጉም, #33), and *arat ayn* አራት አይን, four-eyed view, #19). According to *qiné* hermeneutics, "The certification of being a scholar is research

---

73 *Absho* (አብሾ) is a drink made from a plant that is believed to enable one to break through inhibitions, liberate one's intellect and imagination, and make them creatively productive. The word *absho* is used metaphorically to indicate that a person has a rich and creative intellect/imagination.
74 For a beautiful and instructive literary rendition of the demanding mental labour *qisäla* requires, see Hiwot Teferra, ገለሳ (Addis Ababa: Eclipse Printing Press, 2009).

(ምርመራ, *mirmära*), not learning by itself."⁷⁵ *Mirmära* is indispensable because, according to *qiné* hermeneutics, there are no self-evident truths, and *nägär* and the *ewqät/ewnät* we have of it is always *enkän* (incomplete). Thus, the *qiné* hermeneutical tradition asserts, "the teachers of former times… *never felt that they had learned enough.*"⁷⁶ One cannot grasp the surplus meanings of *nägär* by analysing it in terms of procedures that reduce *nägär* to its observables or quantifiable dimensions, though knowledge of these dimensions is necessary. There is more to *nägär* than, to paraphrase a *qiné*, what the eye could see, the ear could hear, the hand could grasp, and the heart could feel, requiring thus *mirmära*, which means not only asking questions but also unveiling unasked or repressed questions related to the *nägär* under *mirmära*. *Mirmära* and its outcome are always incomplete (*enkän*). Consequently, further research (ምርመራ, *mirmära*) is always possible and even indispensable.

The *absho* (አብሾ) mind, which, as we saw, plays a crucial role in *qisäla*, also plays the same crucial role in *mirmära*. The practice of *mirmära* demands epistemic autonomy and the *absho* intellect and imagination to deconstruct the limits convention establishes regarding the knowing process, the object of *ewqät/ewnät*, and what counts as *ewqät/ewnät*. It liberates these from what the *qiné* hermeneutical tradition calls the *"shackles of tradition."* *Mirmära* means going beyond mere learning, for it requires *strik[ing] off in various directions,"* opening new paths, new orientations, and new horizons.⁷⁷ In *"strik[ing] off in various directions,"* the practitioner of *mirmära* transgresses *"the grammatical form of the original"* and challenges the co-ordinates and boundaries of the hegemonic discourse.⁷⁸ In the process, the practitioner of *mirmära* triggers new questions, develops critical alternatives, discloses surplus meanings (*säwrä fitch*), and makes possible a transformative, more comprehensive, and open-ended understanding of *nägär*.

The aim of *mirmära* is to help us understand not only what we are seeing and thinking as *nägär*, not only how we are seeking and thinking *nägär*, but also how and what we exclude in our way of seeing and thinking *nägär*. *Mirmära* is not a simple application of a concept to a fact for the purpose of identifying and classifying it. Given that from the perspective of *qiné* hermeneutics, every *nägär* is complex, incomplete (*enkän*), and internally tensioned, *mirmära* involves the intellectual effort to grasp *nägär* in its specificity and complexity with a view to

---

75 Roger W. Cowley, "Old Testament Introduction in the Andemta Commentary Tradition," *Journal of Ethiopian Studies* 12, 1 (1974), p. 165.
76 Roger W. Cowley, "Old Testament Introduction..," p. 169. Emphasis added.
77 Roger W. Cowley, "Old Testament Introduction..," pp. 169-170.
78 Roger W. Cowley, "Old Testament Introduction..," pp. 169-170, emphasis added.

eliciting its *wärq* or surplus meaning. *Mirmära* expresses the conviction deeply rooted in *qiné* hermeneutics that, given the complexity of *nägär*, it is necessary to develop multiple perspectives (*andem*, see # 18) to map out more adequately the various dimensions—the different and the contradictory, the familiar and the unfamiliar, the new and the old, the given and the repressed, the questioned and the unquestioned, the answered and the non-answered—of the *nägär* under inquiry. This is a point that the seventeenth-century thinker Zära Yacob expressed in a different way. He claimed, "We cannot, however, reach truth through the doctrine of men, for all men are liars."[79] Zära Yacob is not making a moral judgement. Rather, he is referring to the fact that *ewqät/ewnät* is *enkän* and that it cannot produce the "hidden good" or "*wärq*" without unpacking the various dimensions of *nägär*. For him, those who deny that *ewqät/ewnät* is *enkän* "are liars."

10. *Säwrä bahil* (ሰውረ ባህል) / *non-tradition*

Säwrä bahil (ሰውረ ባህል) means "non-tradition." *Bahil* (ባህል) means tradition; *tzärä-bahil* (ፀረ ባህል) means anti-tradition. Non-tradition (*säwrä bahil*) is, in *qiné* hermeneutical terminology, an *andem* (see below # 18), a new meaning that steps aside from both tradition (*bahil*) and anti-tradition (*tzärä-bahil*) and opens a new horizon. There is a homeomorphic similarity between the "non" in non-tradition and the "non" in non-Euclidean geometry.[80] Non-Euclidean geometry goes beyond Euclidean geometry without rejecting it, but it shows also its limits. Similarly, non-tradition goes beyond tradition without erasing it, but it also discloses its limits. The word "tradition" refers to the norms, beliefs, structures, relations, and ideas—be they "traditional" or "modern"—that are hegemonic in Ethiopian society. In this sense, there are two traditions in Ethiopia: the local and the "imported". Whereas the first tradition originates in Ethiopia, the imported one originates in the West: the tradition of "development" and "democracy." The "non" refers to both traditions' repressed surplus meanings, meanings that are neither traditional nor anti-traditional but could be elucidated through a critical internal journey into Ethiopian traditions and through a critical external journey into the Western imported tradition. The "non" reflects the *qiné* hermeneutical rejection of dualism and monism and points to an emancipatory horizon that reveals the

---

79 Claude Sumner, *Classical Ethiopian Philosophy* (Los Angeles: Adey Publishing Company, 1994), p. 240.
80 Marvin Jay Greenberg, *Euclidean and Non-Euclidean Geometries Development and History* (New York: W. H. Freeman and Company, 1993).

unthoughts of both the local and the imported traditions from within their silences and blind spots.

One can understand tradition (*bahil*) and anti-tradition (*tzärä-bahil*) in terms of the hegemonic coordinates of understanding. Non-tradition (*säwrä bahil*), however, is a meaning or a practice that is unavailable within the hegemonic order's parameters of meanings, practices, and possibility. It is thus not part of the given social reality (*ewen* / አሙን). However, it is not anti-tradition (*tzärä-bahil*). The "non" in non-tradition indicates the presence of an unthought alternative to both tradition and anti-tradition. However, non-tradition is not something halfway between tradition and anti-tradition. It is the repressed part of tradition (*bahil*) and anti-tradition (*tzärä-bahil*) that goes beyond both tradition and anti-tradition and opens a new space of meanings, norms, and practices. To understand the meaning of "non" in non-tradition let me use an example I have used elsewhere. One could say, (a) the Ethiopian state is an ethnic state; (b) the Ethiopian state is an anti-ethnic state; and (c) the Ethiopian state is a non-ethnic state. Now, (b) is just the negation of (a), whereas (c) affirms a non-predicate, which is neither ethnic nor anti-ethnic, and thus occupies the space that qualitatively differs from (a) and (b). Note that 'a' and 'b' are within the same horizon, that of ethnic identity; the first affirms it, and the second negates it. The third option (c) bores through (a) and (b) and produces a surplus meaning and a new horizon that is free from the dualism of 'ethnic' and 'anti-ethnic'. For example, the state that the TPLF (1991-2018) created and the Prosperity Party (2019…) maintained is an ethnic state; the state that Ethiopian monarchists want to create is an anti-ethnic (centralizing) state; the state Ethiopian democracy activists want to create is non ethnic: a federation based on citizenship (political non-ethnicity), and that organizes the Ethiopian space in terms of regions (spatial non-ethnicity) and the Ethiopian economy in terms of criteria that enhance prosperity for each and all Ethiopians (economic non-ethnicity). In general the *qiné* hermeneutical concept of "non" overcomes unproductive dualisms such as tradition and modernization, individualism and communalism, Ethio-centrism and Euro-centrism. Each of these is a false duality in that a "non" of each always exists in another dimension as an *andem* (see # 18).

Säwrä bahil expresses "local critique" and "subjugated knowledge" directed by the oppressed against the hegemonic order. Local critique is "an autonomous, non-centralized kind of theoretical production, one … whose validity is not dependent on the approval of the established regime of thought."[81] And "subjugated knowledge" is made up of "knowledges that have been disqualified

---

81   Michel Foucault, *Power/Knowledge: Selected Interviews and Other Writings, 1972-1977*, Colin Gordon, ed. (New York: Pantheon Books, 1980), pp. 81

as nonconceptual knowledges, as insufficiently elaborated knowledges: naive knowledges, hierarchically inferior knowledges, knowledges that are below the required level of erudition or scientificity."[82] *Säwrä bahil*, subjugated knowledge and local critique, could take the form of aphorisms, songs, stories, spirit possessions, heretic movements, and autopoietic organizations such as *däbo*, *iddir*, *iqqub*, and other local visions of a possible alternative society such as Awra Amba.[83] Ethiopia's local critiques and subjugated knowledge and the practices, particularly autopoietic organizations, they engender are expressions of local ruptures in the hegemonic order and are pointers to the possibility of an alternative way of becoming and living. Not only does *säwrä bahil* signal the presence of epistemic autonomy among the oppressed, enabling them to break through the wall of hegemonic ideas and beliefs, but it also discloses the necessary link between epistemic autonomy and emancipatory knowledge and practice.

Säwrä bahil is not just a different interpretation of tradition or *nägär*. Whereas "tradition" considers norms as pre-given independently of our agency and are there to be discovered by us, the "non" of *säwrä bahil* discloses that tradition, be it local or imported, is of our own creation and therefore something that we could change.[84] *Säwrä bahil* challenges the hegemonic order not only by proposing a different meaning but also by signalling the presence of an active agent (*säwrä ras*, see below # 12) capable of thinking and implementing alternative coordinates of intelligibility and legitimacy.

11. *Säwrä hiywät* (ሰውረ ሕይወት) / *surplus life*

Säwrä hiywät (ሰውረ ሕይወት) means surplus life in the sense of the "good life" or "good living," which, as we shall see in Chapter 5, is opposed to "poor living." The great majority of Ethiopians know hardly anything other than a life of labouring that never meets their needs. As *nägär*, the Ethiopian subject is formed by the complex self-experiences arising from his/her daily struggles for living, his/her experiences of powerlessness, his/her efforts, failures, and occasional

---

82   Michel Foucault, *Society must be defended*, trans. David Macey (New York: Picador, 2003), pp. 7-8;.
83   Maimire Mennasemay, *Qiné Hermeneutics and Ethiopian Critical Theory*, supra, Chapter 6.
84   That "norms are pre-given independently of our agency" is true not only for "traditional" societies, but also for "modern" societies. Neoliberal economics, hegemonic in the West, treats capitalism as a natural order. Hence the claim that there is no alternative to it. Anthony Giddens, *The Third Way: The Renewal of Social Democracy* (Cambridge: Polity Press, 1999).

but short-lived successes to overcome hardships. Out of these experiences of oppression and exploitation emerges a hopelessness that triggers and nourishes a resistance to unbearable life and opens up the possibility of the impossible: an emancipated life, a vision of a better life that could have been realized, but exists now only as defeated struggles and unfulfilled hopes, experiences captured in many *zäläsäña* (ዘላሰኛ) *qiné*. *Zäläsäña qiné* laments bare existence and expresses the haunting but unfulfilled presence of an alternative Ethiopian life, one that is liberated from unfreedoms, inequalities, and injustices.[85] *Säwrä hiywät* points to an idea that is persistent in *zäläsäña qiné*. It intimates that human life does not coincide with the life that Ethiopia's rulers call "life," that a human life is larger than this "death" we call life in Ethiopia, to paraphrase Abe Gubegna (አይሻልም ይሆን ሐይወት ከሚሉት ሞት?/ is there something better than the death they call life?)[86] *Säwrä hiywät* points to this alternative life yet to be experienced.[87]

Säwrä hiywät makes visible through the cracks of the oppression of the lives of Ethiopians the flickering light of the absent and desired alternative life, one that is free from the hegemonic order's oppressive coordinates of actions, meanings, normativity, and possibility. Its symptoms are the silent resistance or "murmur" against the ruler (the Chronicles of Lalibela[88]), the revolts, rebellions, uprisings, heretic movements (such as the *Däqiqä Estifanos*[89]), internal and external exile, and violent conflicts.[90] It also expresses itself as oppositional art, mainly as *qiné* (ቅኔ), novels and stories.[91] *Säwrä hiywät* signifies life's openness to emancipatory transformations. It rejects the practice dominant in Ethiopia wherein ሰው (*säw* / humanity) exploits and oppresses ሰው (*säw* / humanity), a rejection expressed in the *sineñ* (a fragment from a *hibrä qiné* or an old *qiné*): ሰው ለሰው መድሃኒቱ / *säw läsäw mädhanitu* (*säw*/

---

85 On *zäläsäña* (ዘላሰኛ) *qiné* Balambaras Mahtem Selasse Welde Mesqel, "ዘላሰኛ" አማሪኛ ቅኔ (Addis Ababa: Artistic Printing Press, 1955 E.C.), pp. 93-284.
86 Abe Gubegna, ስብስብ ሥራዎች, (Addis Ababa Ezop Publishing, 2010), p.255.
87 "Surplus life" refers to the idea that life has excesses that are a source of resistance to hegemonic power and knowledge. Michel Foucault, *Power. Essential Works of Foucault 1954-1984.* Edited by J. Faubion, Vol. 3. (New York: The New Press, 2000), pp. 403-417.
88 On "murmur" as resistance, Richard Pankhurst, *The Ethiopian Royal Chronicles* (Los Angeles: Tsehai Publishing, 2010), p. 12.
89 Getatchew Haile, ደቂቀ እስጢፋኖስ በገግ አምላክ, trans. from Ge'ez (Collegeville, MN: 2004).
90 *Säwrä hiywät* / surplus life manifests itself in peasant uprisings. See, Gebru Tareke, *Ethiopia: Power and Protest* (Cambridge University Press, New York 1991).
91 Consider the *efita* / እፍታ collection, Maaza Mengiste's *Beneath the Lion's Gaze*, Addis Alemayehu's *Yälm Zjat*), the painting of Eshetu Tiruneh's "victim of famine", and Betty G.'s song, አዲስ ሰማይ, *Addis Semay*, Teddy Afro's ናዕት, *Na'et*, and the oft interpreted old classical song, *tizita* meaning nostalgy.

humanity is the cure for *säw*/humanity). Given that Christianity and Islam have profoundly penetrated and shaped Ethiopian culture—Christians and Muslims constitute the overwhelming majority of Ethiopians—one could see here the transformation into secular ethics the injunction to "love your neighbor as yourself" made in Leviticus 19:18, Mark 12:30-31, and The Holy Qur'an, al-Nisaa 4:36.

In *säwrä hiywät*, *säw läsäw mädhanitu* does not refer to a utilitarian understanding of happiness (*dästa*, ደስታ) that one may get from helping another. Rather, *säwrä hiywät* sees in the idea of *säw läsäw mädhanitu* the possibility of *fissiha* (ፍስሃ, joy). *Fissiha* is different from and is beyond *dästa*, for unlike the latter, which is an individualistic experience, *fissiha* is a joy that embraces the individual and the community. The Ethiopian monastic tradition, which is one of the roots of *qiné* hermeneutics, describes the person who experiences *fissiha* as one who "grows angelic wings or gains a heavenly crown."[92] *Fissiha*, secularly understood, expresses a commonly shared social life without unfreedoms, inequalities, injustices, and loneliness. *Säwrä hiywät* considers secular life is human when it is lived as a life of *fissiha*. Only humans who pursue a commonly shared aim and act freely, rationally, and in shared solidarity could experience *fissiha*. Such an experience of the world is what *säwrä hiywät* expresses.

Among the social signals of the presence of *säwrä hiywät* are autopoietic collective activities such as *däbo* (ደቦ), *iddir* (ዕድር), *iqqub* (ዕቁብ), and communities such as Awra Amba wherein Ethiopians organize themselves as autonomous beings, enjoying equality, solidarity, fraternity, epistemic autonomy, creating non-oppressive social relations, and consciously and collectively pursuing the common good for the good of each member and of the association.[93] We see in these autopoietic associations an intimation of an idea central to *säwrä hiywät*: that freedom requires a thick background of equality—social, economic, political, and epistemic. Otherwise, freedom could be instrumentalized to serve domination, as one could see in the practice of freedom under capitalism in liberal democratic societies.[94] According to *säwrä hiywät* the decline in freedom leads to the decline

---

92 Getatchew Haile, "Ethiopian Monasticism" in Aziz S Atiya, ed., *Coptic Encyclopedia*, vol. 3 (New York: Macmillan, 1991), pp. 993-94; Joachim Persoon, "Ethiopian monasticism" *International Journal for the Study of the Christian Church*, Volume 7, 3, 2007. Addis Ababa Diocese of the Ethiopian Orthodox Tewahido Church, ልሳነ ጥበብ ዘ ቅድስት ሥላሴ መንፈሳዊ ኮሌጅ መጽሐፍ (Addis Ababa : Theological College, undated photocopy).

93 On *däbo*, *iddir*, and *iqqub*, see Maimire Mennasemay, *Qiné Hermeneutics and Ethiopian Critical Theory* (Los Angeles: Tsehai Publishing, 2021), Chapter 10. On Awra Amba, ibid., Chapter 6.

94 Pierre Dardot and Christian Laval, *The New Way of the World: On Neo-liberal Society*, trans. Gregory Elliot (London: Verso: 2013); Peter Kelly, *The Self as Enterprise* (New

in equality and fraternity, and the decline in equality leads to the decline in freedom and fraternity; and the enhancement of each leads to the enhancement of the other. The struggle for *säwrä hiywät* is indissociable from the agency of *säwrä ras* (ሰውረ ራስ) / surplus self.

12. *Säwrä ras* (ሰውረ ራስ) / *surplus self*

Säwrä ras (ሰውረ ራስ) means surplus self. *Säwrä ras* (surplus self) is that part of Ethiopian subjectivity that escapes the hegemonic order's "interpellation" of Ethiopians as obedient beings for whom the existing society is something like a natural order.[95] From the perspective of *qiné* hermeneutics, every Ethiopian is *nägär*: internally complex and contradictory. He/she has therefore a heterogeneous self that is internally split and tensioned. The *säwrä ras* expresses the active presence of an internal self-difference. Ethiopians are constituted through the subjectivization process produced by the reigning Ethiopian political, legal, cultural, and economic order. This process produces the "official self," the self that abides by the hegemonic beliefs, ideas and practices. Nevertheless, Ethiopians are also beings whose self-identification is formed by the contradictory self-experiences arising from their exploitation and oppression, from their overt and covert resistance to these, and from their failed emancipatory efforts and unfulfilled hopes. These complex and contradictory self-experiences open a space for the formation of *säwrä ras* (surplus self): a relation to oneself which resists oppression and exploitation and hopes for and imagines an alternative life, and could act to bring it about.

Säwrä ras emerges from the contradictory unity of the Ethiopian individual and Ethiopian society. It is the dimension of the Ethiopian self that embodies the critical and context-transcending capacity for emancipation that inhabits each Ethiopian, even if it is repressed, and is in tension with one's "official self": the identity formed by the hegemonic society's subjectivization process. Though repressed by the official self, the *säwrä ras* is a decentered emancipatory self that lives life as resistance, escapes the regime's effort to absorb it entirely into its hegemonic representation of Ethiopians. As such, *säwrä ras* is that which is in the given Ethiopian more than the given Ethiopian. It is non-synchronous with the one's "official self" that the hegemonic order defines and projects as the "law-abiding citizen": the official self and the *säwrä ras* live "at the same time"

York: Routledge, 2013).
95 On interpellation, see Louis Althusser, *Lenin and Philosophy and Other Essays* (London: NLB, 1971), p.174.

but "not *in* the same time."⁹⁶ *Säwrä ras* is the internal antagonist of the "official self."

Säwrä ras is what one could call an "excessive subjectivity," an agent that questions, subverts, and resists oppression and exploitation and imagines a future society whose coordinates render oppression and exploitation unfeasible.⁹⁷ Popular protests, uprisings and revolts indicate the awakening of *säwrä ras*, even if it is for a short time. The *qiné* aphorism የኔ ቢጤ (*yäne bitie*) discloses the presence of *säwrä ras*. It means "he/she is like me or I am like her/him. It is an expression that is uttered only and only when one sees a person who is suffering and recognizes the other in oneself, and the self in the other, and thus the concrete universality of each. The universality to which *yäne bitie* points is rooted not in something positive Ethiopians share but in the commonly shared traumas of oppression, exploitation, and sufferings that traverse their lives. As Buck-Morss puts it, "human universality emerges…at the point of rupture," in the experiences of oppression and exploitation, creating "subterranean solidarities" despite ethnic, cultural and historical differences.⁹⁸ የኔ ቢጤ (*yäne bitie*) is the voice of *säwrä ras* expressing these "subterranean solidarities" and "human universality" in the face of oppression.

The *säwrä ras* is the agency that produces *säwrä bahil* or "subjugated knowledge," and the "local critique" of the domination weighing down on Ethiopians. It is grounded in "struggles and the raw memory of fights."⁹⁹ The hegemonic order considers local critique naïve (ደደብ, *dädäb*), uninformed (ደንቆሮ, *dänqoro*), inferior (መናኛ, *mänaña*), or vulgar (ብልግና, *bilgena*). However, local critique is a symptom (*zäybé* / ዘይቤ, # 16 below) of the presence of the *säwrä ras* who rejects the social, political, economic, and epistemic sufferings that the hegemonic order inflicts on Ethiopians.

Säwrä ras is an idea that one finds explicitly formulated in the 15th century movement of the *Däqiqä Estifanos*. In their resistance to the diktats of Emperor Zära Yacob, the *Däqiqä Estifanos* point out that "People tend to resemble their rulers," but then suggest that the Ethiopian self is not totally captured by the

---

96 On "non-synchronicity," see Ernst Bloch, *Heritage of Our Times*, trans. Neville Plaice and Stephen Plaice (Oxford: Polity Press, 1991), p. 97.
97 Dominik Finkelde, *Excessive Subjectivity: Kant, Hegel, Lacan, and the Foundations of Ethics,* trans. Deva Kemmis and Astrid Weigert (New York: Columbia University Press, 2017), pp. 5, 77. He gives the example of Rosa Parks's refusal to give up her seat to a white passenger to illustrate the idea of "excessive subjectivity" or what *qiné* hermeneutics calls *säwrä ras* as that which enables the subject to produce an extraordinary action with incalculable consequences.
98 Susan Buck-Morss, *Hegel, Haiti, and Universal History* (Pittsburgh: University of Pittsburgh Press, 2009), p. 133.
99 See Michel Foucault, *supra*, *Power/Knowledge…*, and *Society must be defended…*.

subjectivization process of the reigning order, and that it has uncaptured resources embodied in the *säwrä ras* that give Ethiopians the capacity to "stand upright," "to follow their mind," and to become masters of their own lives.[100]

13. *Säwrä tarik* (ሰውረ ታሪክ) / *surplus history*

Säwrä tarik (ሰውረ ታሪክ) could be translated as surplus history. *Säwrä tarik* expresses and articulates the emancipatory surplus meanings of Ethiopian history and social practices (*nägär*), past and present, that mainstream knowledge, be it popular or social scientific, renders inaudible and invisible. *Säwrä tarik* embraces both the vertical (temporal) and lateral (regional, ethnic, cultural) dimensions of Ethiopian history and *nägär*. It foreshadows an alternative Ethiopia. I discuss *säwrä tarik* more extensively in Chapter 2.

14. *Arnät* (አርነት) *human emancipation*

Arnät (አርነት) means human emancipation. It embraces political, economic, social, cultural, and epistemic emancipation. It is the continuous minimization of political, economic, social, and epistemic powerlessness and the continuous maximization of political, economic, and cognitive "capabilities."[101] I discuss *arnät* more extensively in Chapter 3, below.

15. *Hiss* (ሂስ) / *critique*

Hiss (ሂስ) means immanent critique. It names the practice of questioning and unpacking the complexities and dynamics of Ethiopian conditions, disclosing the tensions and contradictions (*t'mir* / ትምር) that articulate them, eliciting the critical ideas and norms that incubate in them, and producing the *wärq* or the possibility of *wärq* that are immanent in them. In its operation, *hiss* (immanent critique) calls upon *tichit* (ትችት, extended interpretations or "*commentaire de texte*"), *tintena* (ትንተና, analytical interpretation, exposition, demonstration), and

---

100 Maimire Mennasemay, *Qiné Hermeneutics and Ethiopian Critical Theory* (Los Angeles: Tsehai Publishing, 2021), Chapter 8.
101 On "capabilities," see Amartya Sen, *The Idea of Justice* (Cambridge: Harvard University Press, 2009), pp. 225-317. Sen's innovation, the "capabilities approach," though it injects ethics into economics and rescues the idea of welfare from a narrow utilitarian understanding, is nevertheless individual-centric and consistent with the logic of capitalist accumulation. It is not certain that capabilities developed within the framework of capitalism could be sufficient for the pursuit of *arnät*. They could even be obstacles, given that success in the capitalist context of life is what makes acquired skills, know-hows, ways of acting and relating to others and to one's life "capabilities" that facilitate one's integration into the hegemonic order.

hatäta (ሐተታ, dialectics) or disclosing the contradictions (*t'mir*) and the possibilities for change and transformation. In the process, it produces different kinds of understanding (አገባብ, *agäbab*): ጠቅላላ አገባብ (täqlala agäbab) referring to comprehensive or synthetic understanding; ዓቢይ አገባብ (*abiy agäbab*) referring to contradictory or subversive or reflexive understanding; ደቂቅ አገባብ (*däqiq agäbab*) referring to analytical or inferential understanding; and ንዑስ አገባብ (*n'oos agäbab*) referring to subtractive understanding.[102] Since *tichit*, *tintena*, and *hatäta* are part of *hiss*, I will unpack the meaning of *hiss* and clarify these terms in the process.

According to *qiné* hermeneutics, *hiss* is an intellectual activity that has a diagnostic and normative-evaluative function; it is reflexive. It makes possible the self-clarification of the emancipatory struggles and aspirations of Ethiopians through an immanent critique of Ethiopian society. *Hiss* enucleates and reconstructs from within Ethiopian social reality the critical concepts that gestate in it. It discloses the political, economic, epistemic, and cultural processes of the pathologies of Ethiopian society—unfreedoms, inequalities, injustices, economic deprivations, epistemic servitude—and unpacks the repressed emancipatory possibilities and paths that incubate in it. Unlike "method" in Gibbonist Ethiopian Studies, which applies external theories and methods to Ethiopian reality, *hiss* is attentive to the inner life of Ethiopian society—its tensions, contradictions, latencies, tendencies, aspirations and possibilities, and develops its analytical and interpretative methods from within these. *Hiss* does not reject empirical methods. However, it subsumes them to its goal of elucidating the triple domination—political, economic, and epistemic—and the ways of overcoming it.

The practice of *hiss* embraces *tichit* (ትችት), which is an extended interpretation or a *"commentaire de texte"* that unfolds the various meanings that gestate in *nägär*. *Tichit* articulates itself with *tintena* (ትንተና). What *tichit* lays out, *tintena* subjects to analytical work. It clarifies the range and limits of the various meanings that *tichit* exposes and clarifies complexities and ambiguities. *Hatäta* (ሐተታ) puts these in motion by bringing out the historical and social processes that produce them, the contradictions, latencies and tendencies they are pregnant of, and the possibilities and potentialities of transformations they project. We could say that *tichit* is interpretative, *tintena* is analytical, and *hatäta* is dialectical. The meanings of these terms are internal to the operation of *hiss*.

---

102 Liqä Siltanat Habtä Mariam Werqneh, ጥንታዊ የኢትዮጵያ ትምህርት (Addis Ababa: Berhan ena Selam Printing Press, 1962 /63/ 70), pp. 210-1; Hiruie Ermias, *The Issues of 'Aggabāb (Classic Gə'əz Grammar) According to the Tradition of Qəne Schools*, PhD Dissertation in Ethiopian Studies, Faculty of Humanities at the University of Hamburg, (2019).

Hiss practices and is indissociable from *zäräfa, andem, tirgum,* and *arat ayn* (see below entries # 20, 18, 33, 19 respectively for these terms).

An important species of *hiss* is *täshägagari hiss* (ተሸጋጋሪ ሂስ) or *mädämamät* (መደማመጥ, see entry # 28 below), which means "transcritique" or critical "dialogical dialogue." It is a critique or *hiss* that moves back and forth between the different understandings of Ethiopian conditions past and present, of Ethiopia's cultures and intellectual traditions, and of Ethiopia's cultural and intellectual traditions and those of the West (or other's). *Täshägagari hiss* elucidates the contradictions that inhabit these various *nägär*, and the emancipatory possibilities that gestate in them. The aim of *täshägagari hiss* is to develop an *andemta* or "fusion of horizons" (see *andemta,* entry # 26 below) of emancipatory ideas. Inevitably, *hiss*, as an immanent critique of Ethiopian society, also engages in a critique of its own concepts and practices to prevent it from being coopted by the dominant discourse or *quanqua* (see entry # 21 below).

16. *Zäybé* (ዘይቤ) / *symptom, signal, way*

Zäybé (ዘይቤ), sometimes also called *mängäd* (መንገድ, meaning way), is a rich and complex concept.[103] In *qiné* hermeneutics, it has multiple interrelated meanings: trope, symptom, signal, or way. Some *zäybé* refer to logical categories. *Zäybé* means symptom in that *zäybé* function in *qiné* hermeneutics as symptoms of the unsaid, unrecognized, hidden, occluded, and repressed. Understood as symptom, *zäybé* is a signal of the presence of more fundamental questions, processes, or meanings at a non-given level. In this sense, *zäybé* indicates the "way" (መንገድ, *mängäd*, the other name of *zäybé*) that leads to the unsaid, unrecognized, unseen, unheard, hidden, occluded and repressed questions, meanings, contents, or processes of *nägär*. The types of *zäybé* in *qiné* hermeneutics are numerous.[104] Liqä Siltanat Habtä Mariam identifies more than a hundred *zäybé*.[105]

---

103 On *zäybé* as *mängäd* (መንገድ), see Liqä Siltanat Habtä Mariam Werqneh, ጥንታዊ የኢትዮጵያ ትምህርት (Addis Ababa: Berhan ena Selam Printing Press, 1962 /63/ 70), pp. 183ff. Sergew Hable Selassie, የአማርኛ የቤት ክርስቲያን መዝገበ ቃላት ፣ ረቂቅ, 13 volumes (Addis Ababa: Hand-written manuscript, 1977-1990). pp. 138-141.

104 Liqä Siltanat Habtä Mariam Werqneh, ጥንታዊ የኢትዮጵያ ትምህርት (Addis Ababa: Berhan ena Selam Printing Press, 1962 /63/ 70), pp. 183-205. For a brief and selective modern discussion of *zäybé*, see Ngusse Nagaw Dagaga, የቅኔ አፈታት ዜዴዎች ና የምርጥ ቅኔዎች ስብስብ, Second edition (Addis Ababa: Mega, 1993), pp. 4-6; Birhanu Gebeyhu, የአማርኛ ስነ ግጥም (Addis Ababa: Alfa Printing, 2003), pp. 88-151; Alemayhu Mogess, መልከ ኢትዮጵያ, *Mälkea Ethiopia* (Asmara: Graphic Printing Press, 1952 E. C.), pp. 7-35. Maimire Mennasemay, *Qiné Hermeneutics and Ethiopian Critical Theory* (Los Angeles: Tsehai Publishing, 2021), Chapter 2.

105 Here, I will very briefly present the major ones. As there are no exact English equivalents, the English translations give only the approximate meanings of these *zäybé*. Though one could see a certain measure of homeomorphic equivalences between some

Zäybé expresses the *säm ena wärq* founding idea that there are no self-evident truths, that *nägär* is internally complex and tensioned, and that to understand it, one must approach it indirectly and mediately. It is important to note that two

---

zäybé and English rhetorical tropes and logical categories, *zäybé* often have a different reach; they intersect with each other in different ways, and sometimes have meanings that do not have counterparts in English. They are: *Täläwach zäybé* (ተለዋጭ ዘይቤ) alludes to indirect meanings; *misät zäybé* (ምጸት ዘይቤ) refers to contraries. *Antsar zäybé* (አንጻር ዘይቤ) refers to distanciation. In addition *antsar zäybé* also combines with *t'mir* (ጥምር) to refer to *antsar t'mir* (አንጻር ጥምር), which means "determinate negation." *Tänätsatsari zäybé* (ተነጻጻሪ ዘይቤ) refers to expressions where each is in opposition to the other or becomes the mirror of the other. *Afrash zäybé* (አፍራሽ ዘይቤ) refers to negation and plays a crucial role in *hatäta*. *Tässalqo zäybé* (ተሳልቆ ዘይቤ) conjoins opposing terms or expressions and looks for meanings in the crack between the two. *Säwigna zäybé* (ሰውኛ ዘይቤ) denotes anthropomorphism. *Mäsiya zäybé* (መሲያ ዘይቤ) signifies the virtual or hidden dimension of reality—the unsaid, the unseen, and the unheard. The understanding of the virtual here is different from the understanding of the virtual that one finds in the expression "virtual reality." The virtual that *mäsiya zäybé* (መሲያ ዘይቤ) refers to is as real as the actual. *Tämssalit zäybé* (ተምሳሊት ዘይቤ) compares similarities and dissimilarities, and *entsarawi gälätsa zäybé* (አንጻራዊ ገለጻ ዘይቤ) is comparable to metaphor; it also covers "double entendre" and catachresis. *Afla zäybé* (አፍላ ዘይቤ) is comparable to metonymy. *Qulqul zäybé* (ቁልቁል ዘይቤ) designates something like synecdoche. Given the role of polysemy and homonyms in *qiné* hermeneutics, *afla zäybé* and *qulqul zäybé* have a wide range of use, mainly to express ideas economically. *Gädlo madän zäybé* (ገድሎ ማደን ዘይቤ) expresses an affirmative by negating or denying its opposite. *Gädlo madän zäybé* intimates the idea of the negation of the negation and plays an important role in *hatäta*. *Zimd zäybé* (ዝምድ ዘይቤ) is like analogy and requires unveiling the similarities and dissimilarities of the compared as well as whether these similarities and dissimilarities are trivial or essential. *Filatsa zäybé* (ፍላጻ ዘይቤ, *filatsa* means arrow) is comparable to an allegory and requires developing a framework of interpretation to deliver its meanings. *Wistä wäyra zäybé* (ውስጠ ወይራ ዘይቤ) alludes to the idea that there is an invisible discourse embedded in the visible discourse. Related to *wistä wäyra zäybé* are *säm läbäs zäybé* (ሰም ለበሰ ዘይቤ), *wärqa wärq zäybé* (ወርቃ ወርቅ ዘይቤ), and *libsä wärq zäybé* (ልብሰ ወርቅ ዘይቤ). They form a class of their own. *Säm läbäs zäybé* (ሰም ለበሰ ዘይቤ) refers to statements that appear to be *säm* in that their meanings appear to be transparent. Consequently, understanding or interpreting them requires formulating a framework of interpretation that discloses how the transparency of the *säm* functions as a hiding or repressive mechanism. *Wärqa wärq* zäybé (ወርቃ ወርቅ ዘይቤ) and *libsä wärq zäybé* (ልብሰ ወርቅ ዘይቤ) indicate that the *wärq* (the "hidden good") is seemingly there in the open for everybody to see. These *zäybé* point to the necessity of conducting a critique of spontaneous consciousness, of the practice of accepting the given and the actual as self-evident. The idea behind these *zäybé* is that what appears to be self-evident may not after all be self-evident once we release ourselves from its power to enchant, fascinate, or blind us. These *zäybé* point to the importance of unmasking or debunking what appears as *wärq*. *Wistä wäyra zäybé, wärqa wärq* zäybé, *libsä wärq zäybé,* and *säm* läbäs zäybé play significant roles in the analysis of beliefs, symbols, discourses, and social practices. Crucially, they point to the idea of unveiling. They have meanings that suggest the ideas of demystification, dereification, and defetishization. All the above *zäybé* are crucial in the practice of *hiss*, the production of *säwrä tarik*, and of the "non" that informs *säwrä bahil*, *säwrä ras*, and *säwrä hiywät*. Maimire Mennasemay, *Qiné Hermeneutics and Ethiopian Critical Theory, supra.*

zäybé, namely, *antsar zäybé* (አንጻር ዘይቤ, distanciation) and *wistä wäyra zäybé* (ውስጠ ወይራ ዘይቤ, a symptom of the hidden or of the invisible), are indispensable elements of all *zäybé* and mobilize almost all of the major *zäybé* in their operations.[106] As such, they serve as strategies of reading (ንባብ, *nibab*, see #34 and #35 below) *nägär*. Kebede G/Medhin, the *qiné* scholar, points out that the role of *zäybé* in *qiné* hermeneutics is so important that one could describe it as "limitless" (ወሰን የለህ, *wäsän yäläh*).[107]

17. *Hibrä qal* (ሕብረ ቃል) / harmonizer

Hibrä qal (ሕብረ ቃል) means "harmonizer." Whereas *zäybé* indicate the presence of repressed meanings, frictions, negations, and tensions, *hibrä qal*, which means harmonizer of words, occludes or neutralizes these tensions, frictions, and contradictions; it normalizes and integrates them as surface glitches of the situation, which the hegemonic parameters could remedy or explain away. *Hibrä qal* functions as a rhetorical tool that ensures that the interpretation or explanation of a *nägär* does not escape the horizon of meanings of the hegemonic order.

Take the use of quantification as a *hibrä qal*. Ethiopian regimes regularly produce numbers regarding economic growth, poverty reduction, and decline in illiteracy rates. Under the TPLF, statistics showed increases in the GNP, in the number of primary schools, high schools, universities (the regime has created over 30 public universities), hospitals, people who vote at elections, and so forth. These numbers function as *hibrä qal* in that they appear to be clear, precise, transparent, objective, and above political and ideological divisions and criticism. They seem to show that the country is developing, although poverty, unemployment, homelessness, undernourishment and food scarcity, undereducation (the degradation of educational standards), the inadequacy of health care, and the wealth gap between the miniscule ruling elite and most Ethiopians are increasing. The *hibrä qal* of quantification reduces qualitatively different issues to quantities that are measurable, and harmonizes them through numbers and graphs.[108] For example, educational statistics reduce education to enrollment and thus equate an increase in enrollment to an increase in education, though students finish their schooling without acquiring basic literacy and numeracy.

---

106 For the names and meanings of the major *zäybé*, see supra.
107 Kebede G/Medhin, ሳይንሳዊ የቅኔ አፈታት ስልት (Addis Ababa: Birana Matëmia Bet, 1992), p. 6; Berhanu Gebeyhu, የአማርኛ ስነ ግጥም (Addis Ababa: Alfa Printing, 2003) also draws our attention to the same point, pp. 88-151.
108 World Bank Group, Open Knowledge Repository, *Ethiopia Poverty Assessment 2014* https://openknowledge.worldbank.org/handle/10986/21323.; The Africa Report, *Ethiopia: The Addis millionaire's club* (Monday, March 9, 2015), www.theafricareport.com/East-Horn-Africa/ethiopia-the-addis-millionaires-club.html. Accessed 11/26/2015.

Quantification in Ethiopia is a *hibrä qal* that conceals qualitative issues and masks inequalities, injustices, contradictions, and failures. The Prosperity Party government is continuing the practice of using quantification as *hibrä qal*.[109]

Besides quantification, there are other *hibrä qal* concepts in contemporary Ethiopia: elections, democracy, development, ethnic self-determination, and so forth. They all serve to occlude the failures, tensions and contradictions that permeate Ethiopian regimes. Thus, the alienation of large tracts of land to foreign agro-business companies, the forced displacement, resettlement and villagization of the inhabitants of the Omo Valley and the Gambella region, the repression of journalists, the persecution of political opponents, the PP regime's pervasive state violence in the Tigray, Amhara, and Oromo *kilils* are all harmonized through the *hibrä qal* of 'democracy,' 'peace,' and 'development.'[110] Interestingly, Ethiopian regimes have used 'elections' as a *hibrä qal* to mask their authoritarianism as politics based on representation. The various Ethiopian regimes—from 1957 (without political parties) to the present PP regime (2022)—have marshalled elections as *hibrä qal* thirteen times. Officially, these regimes use elections to claim that their rule is based on popular consent. However, in practice, elections are used for occluding the tensions, contradictions, injustices, inequalities, oppression, and exploitation that characterize Ethiopian regimes and for legitimating the power of the ruling elites. It is important to note that elections under Ethiopian regimes, though used as *hibrä qal*, have failed to mask the *zäybé* (the contradictions) of Ethiopian political life, as one could see from the political turmoil that followed the elections of 1957 (the failed *coup d'état* of 1960), 1973, 1987, 2005, 2010, 2015, and 2021.The TPLF regime declared a state of emergency in 2016, just one year after an election (2015) in which it "won" all the seats of parliament. The PP regime engaged in military campaigns in the Tigray, Oromo, and Amhara *kilils* after its "landslide" electoral victory in 2021 and declared a state of emergency twice.

What *hibrä qal* presents as technical problems solvable administratively, *zäybé* discloses as political problems that are unsolvable within the existing political and economic parameters. *Hibrä qal* naturalizes the hegemonic order, while

---

109 On the unreliability of Ethiopian economic data, United Nations, *Census of Economic Establishments in Ethiopia*, https://unstats.un.org/unsd/economic_stat/Economic_Census/Ethiopia/ Census%20of%20Economic%20Establihments%20in%20Ethiopia.pdf . Accessed 7/26/2023.
110 On land alienation to foreign companies through the forceful appropriation of land and the displacement of its inhabitants, see The Oakland Institute, "Unheard Voices the Human Rights Impact of Land Investments on Indigenous Communities in Gambella" (2013). https://www.oaklandinstitute.org/sites/ oaklandinstitute.org/files/OI_ Report_ Unheard_Voices.pdf. Accessed 1/2/ 2010. On political violence, see Ethiopian Human Rights Commission Reports from 2020 to the present. www.ehrc.org.

zäybé problematizes it, exposes its contradictions, and invites an immanent critique of the given conditions with the aim of transforming them.

18. *Andem* (አንድም) / *and one*

Andem (አንድም) means "and one." It serves for marking every new interpretation of a *nägär* as "and one" instead of saying, first, second, third, and so forth, as if each interpretation opened a new horizon of meaning, and to avoid a hierarchization of the interpretations. In *qiné* hermeneutics, the practice of *andem*, whose origin is in Ethiopian Biblical exegetes, plays an important role in the struggle against dogmatism, obscurantism, intellectual sclerosis, and in the quest for alternative interpretations that bring clarity and enlightenment. Discussing the Ethiopian exegetical tradition, Cowley writes,

> The interpretation called the *andem* interpretation is that in which, after the text has been interpreted once, a chain of successive comments is given, as many as 10 or 15, each one being introduced by '*andem*' ('and one'). ...This is equivalent to saying that in addition to this meaning, there is a commentary like this, and presenting the reader with a choice. But in Amharic, it does not say 'secondly' or 'thirdly' but goes on saying 'and one' [*andem*], as many as 16 times.[111]

Abba Paulos Tzadua gives a succinct description of the *hiss* (critique) character of the *andem* (አንድም) approach. He writes,

> Where a sentence is complicated or its meaning was equivocal or unintelligible, as happens very often, the professor would resort to the famous አንድም [*andem*] system, interpreting the *equivocal or obscure passage or sentence in two, three, or even more different ways*. These interpretations might be made by *inserting words*, by *dropping words*, by *changing a sentence from the negative to the affirmative or vice versa*, by *changing the syntax* of the sentence.[112]

Andem is a practice where the interpreter develops "*two, three, or even more different*" interpretations and evaluates each to provide the best possible intelligibility to "*equivocal or unintelligible...or obscure*" *nägär*. The interpretative process in the *andem* tradition is radical, for it does not shun "*inserting words*, ... *dropping words*, ... *changing a sentence from the negative to the affirmative or vice versa*, ... *changing the syntax* of the sentence." The practice of referring to each commentary as *andem* ("and one") indicates that each new interpretation has an autonomous standing that projects an alternative meaning. Each interpretation requires a new count, i.e., "and one" or *andem*, because it opens a new perspective. The practice of *andem* introduces the necessity of practicing *täshägagari hiss* or

---

[111] Roger W. Cowley, "Old Testament Introduction in the Andemta Commentary Tradition," *Journal of Ethiopian Studies* 12, 1 (1974), pp. 169-170.

[112] Abba Paulos Tzadua, "Foreword," *The Fetha Nägäst: The Law of the Kings*, Trans. Abba Paulos Tzadua, ed. Peter L. Strauss (Addis Ababa: Haile Selassie I University, 1968), Abba Paulos Tzadua, p. xx. Emphasis added.

transcritique before one makes a judgement as to which interpretation or which combination of interpretations adequately grasps the *wärq* of the *nägär* under study. *Andem* also opens the possibility of transiting from the possible to what the hegemonic order of meaning considers impossible, given that *andem* does not shirk "*inserting words, ... dropping words, ... changing a sentence from the negative to the affirmative or vice versa, ... changing the syntax* of the sentence." This radical practice of interpretation also offers a path for dealing with hopelessness, for exiting from crises and dead ends, and for resolving antagonisms.

The practice of *andem* intimates that there is no final interpretation, that every interpretation is marked by *enkän*, that grasping the matter at hand in its completeness is not possible, and that a new *andem* is always possible. The *qiné* hermeneutical idea of *enkän* makes the practice of *andem* necessary, not with the intention of resolving the tensions and incompleteness that characterize *nägär* and its interpretations, but with the aim of deepening our understanding of *nägär* and its *enkän*, and the unexpressed or repressed alternatives it harbours. *Andem* makes it possible to experiment with divergent and contradictory interpretations, and offers a critical way of opening alternative paths for questioning and thinking. *Andem* subverts the idea of teleology (*sinä mädräsha*, ሥነ መድረሻ) that drives development and democratization theories. It brings into play the possibility of going in unexpected directions and leapfrogging to new ideas and practices. *Andem* rejects linearism, monism, relativism, evolutionism, and dualism.

19. *Arat ayn* (አራት ዓይን) / "four-eyed"

Arat ayn (አራት ዓይን) means "four-eyed." It is a critique of two-eyed vision—knowledge limited to empirical observations and generalizations—which it considers inadequate for understanding *nägär*. Speaking of an *andem* practicing scholar, an *andemta* commentary states,

> As we have explained above, this man, although he was *blind*, was known as "four-eyed" because of the depth of his knowledge and the extent of his researches. The certification of being a scholar is research, not learning by itself. To do research it is necessary to read, and because of this he [the blind] felt himself constrained to read so many books.[113]

Traditionally, calling a scholar "four-eyed" means that he knows The Old Testament, The New Testament, The Books of the Scholars (*Fetha Nägäst Qerellas, Yoahnnes Afä* Wärq, *Haymanotä Abäw, Mäsheftä Qeddaséeyat*), and The Book of Monks. "[T]hose who knew all four departments used to be called 'four-eyed' out

---

113 Roger W. Cowley, "Roger W. Cowley, "Old Testament Introduction in the Andemta Commentary Tradition," *Journal of Ethiopian Studies* 12, 1 (1974), p. 165.

of sheer amazement."[114] However, the text on "four-eyed" approach articulates a contradiction that allows us to subject it to an *andem* interpretation or to *zäräfa* (decentering and diverting, see #20 below) and redirect it in a direction other than the original one. It speaks of a "blind" person who "reads so many books." The contradiction (*t'mir*) lodged in the claim that a "blind man" reads "many books" makes "blindness" a force of negativity and creativity that challenges the two-eyed vision. "Blindness" is a *zäybé* that refers to the deficiencies of two-eyed vison and to the existence of the repressed, the invisible, the unsaid, and the undone that inhabit *nägär* and that, though inexistent to the "two-eyed" vision, one has nevertheless to render visible, sayable, and understandable. Simultaneously, "blindness" is a *zäybé* that functions as a ladder for the "two-eyed" to reach the "four-eyed" level of knowledge that shows the necessity of rejecting the "two-eyed" vision and kicking away the ladder and interpreting *nägär* in a way that shows its complexity, contradictions, and the potentialities that simmer in it requires *arat ayn*. This means treating *nägär* as *säm ena wärq*, and interpreting it, not on the basis of the hegemonic understanding, but in terms of what it is not, and reading it against the grain of the hegemonic understanding,

The idea of the "blind" reading books intimates that there is something more than what the "two-eyed" vision shows us: its surplus meanings that are invisible to the "two-eyed" vision but are available to *arat ayn* vision. Observation framed by the hegemonic understanding or "two-eyed" vision has a "blindness" that shuts out the *enkän*, the antagonism, conflict, and possibilities lodged in *nägär*. To overcome the "epistemic fallacy" or the "two-eyed" vision that reduces our knowledge of reality to the empirical observations we have of it, one must have *arat ayn* ("four eyes").[115] That is, one must consider *nägär* as a process and in its historical and social breadth, depth and complexity, and go beyond empirical observations and generalizations. That is, *arat ayn* discloses *nägär*'s internal antagonisms, its incompleteness (*enkän*) and historicity, its apparent and repressed questions and meanings, and the hegemonic coordinates that frame its intelligibility. In doing so, *arat ayn* discloses at the same time the alternative coordinates of visibility and intelligibility that are unavailable to empirical observations and empirical generalizations. *Arat ayn* reveals the possibility of what the two-eyed vision or hegemonic order considers impossible. It opens paths for resolving antagonisms and for exiting from crises and dead ends. The concept of *arat ayn* leads to the *qiné* hermeneutical idea that our knowledge of

---

114 Ibid., pp. 168-9.
115 The epistemic fallacy reduces reality to our observations of it. In *qiné* vocabulary, it reduces *nägär* to *säm* or to a "two-eyed" view. On epistemic fallacy, see Roy Bhaskar, *A Realist Theory of Science* (London: Verso, 1997), p. 36.

nägär is always *enkän* ("...*the scholars never felt that they had learned enough*...."[116]). Hence, the primacy of critical questioning over settled knowledge and the *andemta* commentary's claim that "The certification of being a scholar is research, not learning by itself."[117] *Qisäla, mirmära, zäräfa* (next entry), *andem, tirgum* (entry # 33), and *hiss* are inseparable from the *arat ayn* approach to *nägär*.

20. *Zäräfa* (ዘረፋ) / *decentering, dislocating, and diverting*

The conventional meaning of *zäräfa* (ዘረፋ) is "robbery, plunder, pillaging."[118] In the practice of *qiné* hermeneutics, it means decentering, dislocating, diverging, purging, and subjecting ideas, norms and practices to *détournement*.[119] *Zäräfa* always harnesses *hiss, andem, arat ayn, tirgum* (critical translation, see entry #33), and *täshägagari hiss* or *mädämamät* (entry # 28) in its operation. *Zäräfa* is in fact inseparable from these in practice, and its principal reading strategies are *antsar nibab* (distanciation reading, see entry # 34) and *wistä wäyra nibab* (symptomatic reading, see entry # 35). *Zäräfa* is made possible and necessary by the fact that all *nägär* and its interpretations are *säm ena wärq* and *enkän*. Importantly, *zäräfa* is a manifestation of epistemic autonomy. *Zäräfa* plays an indispensable role in critical internal and external journeys and in the elaboration of *andemta* ("fusion of *wärq* horizons", see # 26).

The source of the practice of *zäräfa* is *qiné zäräfa*: the critical reformulation of an already existing *qiné*, be it new or old, to generate a more comprehensive *qiné*, a more comprehensive *säm ena wärq*, and a more comprehensive *wärq*. Critical *qiné* hermeneutics appropriates the concept of *zäräfa* from *qiné zäräfa* and puts it to work for subverting hegemonic meanings, the naturalization of

---

116 Roger W. Cowley, "Old Testament Introduction in the Andemta Commentary Tradition," *Journal of Ethiopian Studies* 12, 1 (1974), p. 169. Emphasis *added.*
117 Ibid.
118 Kidane Weld Kifle, መጽሐፈ ሰዋስው ወግስ ወመዝገበ ቃላት ሐዲስ (Addis Ababa: Artistic Printing Press, 1978. E. C.), pp. 429-430. Wolf Leslau, *Concise Amharic Dictionary* (Berkeley: University of California Press, 1976), p. 182.
119 *Détournement* is a term that Guy Debord defines as: "le contraire de la citation, [....] le détournement est le langage fluide de l'anti-idéologie...Le détournement n'a fondé sa cause sur rien d'extérieur à sa propre vérité comme critique présente." Guy Debord, *La société du spectacle* (Paris: Buchet Chastel, 1967), sec.208. However, I subject Debord's term itself to *zäräfa* from the perspective of *qiné* hermeneutics to mean the act of dislocating and diverting. I use the word dislocation to signify both.

language, the homogenization of the past and of the present, the reduction of the future to an evolutionary outcome of the present, the reification of meanings and practices, the ontologization of identity, the objectification of knowledge, and the feshitization of social practices. Because *zäräfa* always mobilizes *andem*, *tirgum*, *hiss* and *täshägagari hiss / mädämamät*, and *arat ayn* in its operations, it makes possible the creation of new questions and concepts (*tsinsä hassab* / ፅንሰ ሐሳብ, # 23 below), and the formulation of alternative coordinates of interpretation and alternative metrics of evaluation. It opens the door for transgressing the hegemonic order of meanings and brings into the realm of the possible what the hegemonic order considers impossible.

The goal of *zäräfa* is to produce a more critical and more compelling *wärq* or emancipatory ideas and norms, thereby opening a new horizon (*admas*, see #24 below) for understanding the subject matter. Though *zäräfa* is made possible because *nägär* and its interpretations are *enkän*, it does not resolve *enkän*. Rather, *zäräfa* enriches our understanding of the incompleteness and contradictions of *nägär* by making it possible to raise new questions for exploring that which was not visible from the perspective of the parameters of intelligibility and possibility of the reigning discursive and material order.

Zäräfa plays a determinant role in critical internal and external journeys. It enables us to make what one could call "overreading," which often leads to "productive misreading," or "productive misunderstanding" of knowledge produced by others, be they Ethiopians or foreigners.[120] The critical external journey guided by the emancipatory questions resulting from our critical internal journey uproots through *zäräfa* Western theories and practices from their context and re-contextualizes them in terms of the emancipatory problematics of our critical internal journey and gives them new meanings that have no relation of direct filiation to their original meanings. The result is the dislocation of Western theories and practices.[121] The *andemta* (# 26 below) or

---

120 On overreading, see Colin Davis, *Critical excess: overreading in Derrida, Deleuze, Levinas, Žižek and Cavell* (Stanford: Stanford University Press, 2010).

121 Productive misreading or overreading is not in itself a new practice. Consider for example Maoism. Mao "misread" or "overread" Marxism. He uprooted Marxist theory for the Western industrial society and re-contextualized it within a peasant society and in the process dislocated major elements of Marxist theory such that his concepts of dialectics and contradictions are new contributions to political theory. Stuart Schram *The Thought Of Mao Tse-Tung* (Cambridge, Cambridge University Press, 1989); Enfu Cheng, "Marxism and Its Sinicized Theory as the Guidance of the Chinese Model: The "Two Economic Miracles" of the New China ," *World Review of Political Economy* , Vol. 9, No. 3 (2018), pp, 296-314. The same could be said of Amilcar Cabral. Amilcar Cabral, *Resistance and Decolonization* (New York: Rowman & Littlefield Publishers). Also consider Fanon's productive

the fusion of horizons that results from this articulation of the two critical journeys dislocates the Western social sciences and practices such that they find themselves transformed and in a context that differs radically from the context out of which they emerged. They are inserted in an *admas* (# 24, below) or a symbolic universe that confers upon them new meanings that respond to the emancipatory needs and interest of Ethiopians,

Zäräfa's practice of "overreading" treats ideas as raw material, reworks, transforms, and dislocates them, and, in the process, generates new questions, new concepts, new formulations, and new understandings. Even if the outcome of *zäräfa* appears to be a dislocation, distortion or a misunderstanding of what is being interpreted when seen from the perspective of hegemonic knowledge or of the originators of the knowledge, it is nevertheless a practice that is necessary for producing the emancipatory *ewqät/ewnät* that established knowledge represses or is unthinkable to it. What is important is not the misreading and the dislocation, but the productivity of the misreading or of the dislocation. A misreading could expose the repressed or the unthought of the misread knowledge / *nägär*. If the misreading is a source of a more comprehensive understanding that enables us to actualize the emancipatory interests of Ethiopians, it is not a misreading when seen from the perspective of Ethiopians. Rather, it is an emancipatory *andem* or a *tirgum* (# 33, below)), made possible by *zäräfa* of the given knowledge / *nägär*. *Zäräfa* transforms what it reads into something different and novel. *Zäräfa* unveils the "unthought," the hidden and suppressed beliefs, assumptions and implications of knowledge / *nägär*, be it Ethiopian or Western (or other).

One may still argue that the *zäräfa* practice of overreading will lead to erroneous interpretations of what others—Ethiopians or foreigners—have produced. However, several reasons neutralize this objection. First, the *qiné* hermeneutical tradition is critical of the person who "breathes from the air his master breathes, ... rests where he [his master] rests, and ... preserve[s] the teaching as he has received it, without the slightest change, or difference of opinion," intimating that *zäräfa* of the knowledge / *nägär* produced by others is indispensable for acquiring critical knowledge.[122] Second, the objection assumes that the knowledge / *nägär* the other produces is monosemous. Given that one

---

misreading of Hegel's master-slave dialectic to develop a powerful critique of racism. Frantz Fanon, *Black Skin, White Masks*, trans. C. L. Markman (London: Pluto Press, 1986). These over-readings are productive mis-readings, for they open new horizons of reflection, new understandings, and new possibilities of actions..

122 Roger W. Cowley, "Old Testament Introduction in the Andemta Commentary Tradition," *Journal of Ethiopian Studies* 12, 1 (1974), p. 170.

cannot totally insulate knowledge / *nägär* from the historical / social context in which it is produced and the multiple meanings that traverse it, one cannot accept the claim that *nägär* is monosemous. For *qiné* hermeneutics, knowledge / *nägär*, being a *säm ena wärq*, could have meanings that its authors may not perceive. Thus, one cannot exclude the possibility that the proposed knowledge / *nägär* could have blind spots and distortions that *zäräfa* could expose.[123] That is, knowledge / *nägär* is always *enkän* and a candidate for *zäräfa*. Third, to subject to *zäräfa* the knowledge / *nägär* the other has produced is not to downgrade it. To paraphrase Foucault, to "deform" the ideas and theories of others to serve our emancipatory interests and make them "groan and protest" in the process is to pay tribute to their importance.[124] Finally, if the misreading of knowledge / *nägär* resulting from *zäräfa* furthers the emancipatory interests of Ethiopians, what is a misunderstanding and distortion from the point of view of the originators of the knowledge / *nägär* counts as *andem* or *tirgum* (see # 33) that is productive and emancipatory for Ethiopians. As Karl Mannheim notes, "productive misunderstanding is often a condition of continuing life."[125] The treatment of knowledge / *nägär* others produce through *zäräfa* is indispensable for historicizing and Ethiopianizing it, because one cannot go to the roots of Ethiopian issues with a social science that has no roots in Ethiopian history and society.

Importantly, in a multi-cultural or multi-ethnic society such as Ethiopia, *zäräfa* is indispensable for harnessing the multiplicity and complexity of Ethiopian cultures and intellectual traditions—vertically and laterally—for practicing *täshägagari hiss* or *mädämamät* (መደጋገም ፕ, transcritique, see # 28)—between the knowledge / *nägär* of different Ethiopian regions, cultures, and so

---

123 Richard Bookstaber, *The End of Theory: Financial Crises, the Failure of Economics and the Sweep of Human Interaction* (Princeton, NJ: Princeton University Press, 2017). Recent history shows that misunderstanding is internal to social science knowledge, despite the use of sophisticated methodologies and mathematical modeling. Paul Krugman, the Noble Prize economist, points out that just a year before the financial collapse, economists believed that "the battles of yesteryear were over," that the "central problem of depression-prevention has been solved" and that "Few economists saw our current crisis coming." Paul Krugman, "How Did Economists Get It So Wrong?" *New York Times Magazine* (September 6, 2009).

124 Foucault notes, "The only tribute to thought…is precisely to use it, to deform it, to make it groan and protest." Michel Foucault, *Power/Knowledge: Selected Interviews and Other Writings, 1972-1977*, ed. Colin Gordon, trans. Colin Gordon, Leo Marshall, John Mepham, Kate Soper (New York: Pantheon Press, 1980), pp. 53-4.

125 Kurt H. Wolff, ed., *From Karl Mannheim*, (New Brunswick: Transition Publishers, 1993), p. 380.

forth, in order to produce an *andemta* (አንድምታ, fusion of horizons, see # 26) that makes the emancipatory interests and needs of all Ethiopians accessible and understandable, and makes them a shared grammar of emancipation for all Ethiopians. For example, a *zäräfa* of the Oromo practices of *luba*, *butta*, eight-generation rule, and *moggaasa* generate the ideas of the "common good," of a "common economy," and of "secondary identification" and an understanding of Ethiopians as a "people" who have a commonly shared destiny and are active historical agents.[126]

The practice of *zäräfa* makes the issue of language, especially the creation of concepts, central to its practice (see below #21 *quanqua*, #22 *lissan*, #23 *tsinsä hassab*). From here onwards, I will use the term *zäräfa* to include *andem*, *arat ayn*, *hiss*, *täshägagari hiss*, *mädämamät* (entry # 28), and *tirgum* (# 33) and its two main reading strategies: *antsar* reading and *wistä wäyra* reading (see # 34 and 35).

21. *Quanqua* (ቋንቋ) / language as a discourse of domination

Quanqua (ቋንቋ) means language in the sense of a linguistic practice that frames, articulates, and generates the meanings and understandings that are hegemonic in Ethiopian society. *Quanqua* takes social reality as a given, expresses the hegemonic system of practices, values and beliefs, and is a communication medium that presents the ruling order as normal, legitimate, and unchangeable. Consequently, it anaesthetizes critical questioning and *hiss*. It represses *zäräfa* and considers the existing system of oppression and exploitation as if it were a natural order such that the possibility of an alternative Ethiopian reality is rendered unthinkable, or thinkable only as an impossibility. *Quanqua* is what enables the hegemonic power to represent itself as something permanent and without an alternative.

An example of *quanqua* is development and democratization discourse in Ethiopia. The *quanqua* of development and democratization is a language of domination. It tacitly assumes "development" and "democratization" are the only goals Ethiopians must pursue, and that these two have been already achieved in the West, intimating that "development" and "democratization" for

---

126 Maimire Mennasemay, *Qiné Hermeneutics and Ethiopian Critical Theory* (Los Angeles: Tsehai Publishing, 2021), Chapter 9. On "secondary identification," Slavoj Žižek, *The Ticklish Subject* (London: Verso, 2000), p. 90.

Ethiopians is a process of evolving eventually into a liberal democratic capitalist society, making the latter the *terminus ad quem* of Ethiopian history. The DERG, the TPLF, and the Prosperity Party regime have extrapolated on and expanded this modern *quanqua* of domination by conjugating the *quanqua* of "ethnic-self-determination" with the *quanqua* of liberal democracy and capitalism. In all these regimes, *quanqua* is the language of subjugation, exploitation, and indoctrination, even when it speaks of elections, democracy, development, and self-determination.

Language as *quanqua* does not have the vocabulary Ethiopians need to name the unfreedoms that masquerade as freedom, the oppression that masks itself as "democracy" and "ethnic self-determination," and the exploitation that disguises itself as "development." Language as *quanqua* is a "prison house" that blocks Ethiopians from venturing beyond the given order of thoughts, knowledge, normativity, and practices. To free oneself from *quanqua* is to free oneself from the language of political, economic, and epistemic servitude. When *Gudu* Kassa, one of the main characters in Addis Alemayhu's *Fiqer eskä Mäqaber* (ፍቅር እስከ መቃብር) muses, "Why do people prefer to believe what the powerful tell them rather than believe what they experience?," he is raising the issue of freeing oneself from *quanqua* and the "voluntary servitude" it cultivates.[127] On the other hand, there is no meta-language to which we could resort to escape *quanqua*. What the critique of *quanqua* shows is that we cannot naively rely on it for thinking about Ethiopian issues. Rather, we have to subject it to *zäräfa*, violate the rules of *quanqua*, and think against it. This critical alternative to *quanqua* is what *qiné* hermeneutics calls *lissan*. It is an approach that produces a language of emancipation.

22. *Lissan* (ልሳን) / *language of emancipation*

Lissan (ልሳን) is the negative and transformative power of language that emerges from a *zäräfa* of *quanqua*. *Lissan* is a linguistic practice that goes against the grain of *quanqua*, subverts its rules and usages, and develops an alternative emancipatory discourse. The quest for and the development of *lissan* animates the practice of *qiné* hermeneutics. The critical conception of language as *lissan* is best formulated by a question raised in an *andemta* commentary: "In what

---

127 Addis Alemayhu, ፍቅር እስከ መቃብር (Addis Ababa: Mega, 1992, first published in 1965), pp. 370-2. Etienne de la Boétie, *Discourse on voluntary servitude*, trans. James B. Atkinson and David Sices (Indianapolis: Hackett, 2012). De la Boétie asks why people accept voluntarily to make the interests of their oppressors their own. A question that *Gudu* Kassa also raises in ፍቅር እስከ መቃብር..

language did God say, 'let there be light?'"[128] In this question, the importance of language in making the world is highlighted. We see in the question the significance *qiné* hermeneutics gives to the relations between language and reality, language and power, language and action, language and *ewqät,/ewnät*, and language and creativity.

Language as *lissan* is the *wärq* of language: the outcome of the problematization of language as *quanqua* through *zäräfa*. *Zäräfa* mobilizes all its resources to struggle against *quanqua's* instrumentalization of language in the service of power, and its normalization or naturalization of the existing practices of domination. Language as *lissan* strips *quanqua* of its anaesthetizing properties. It enables us to invent new concepts and expressions that point to an alternative way of being: socially, politically, economically, cognitively, affectively, and culturally. Language as *lissan* enables us to think critically about the existing order, to elicit its economic, political, social, cognitive, affective, and cultural pathologies, break through its pacifying descriptions and anesthetizing self-justifications. It enables us to develop emancipatory parameters of interpretation, intelligibility, evaluation, and action. *Lissan* discloses the performativity of language and its force as a world-making activity. The *qiné* line አዲስ ቃል፣ አዲስ ዓለም (*Addis qal, addis aläm /* a new concept, a new world) given as an exergue, expresses the world-constituting power of *lissan*. *Lissan* provides us with the semantic and syntax we need to name correctly the unfreedoms, inequalities and injustices that weigh down on Ethiopians, and to conceptualize the paths they must follow and the actions they must carry out to actualize their emancipation. The answer to the question of the *andemta* commentary— "In what language did God say 'let there be light'?"—is then: *lissan*. *Qiné* hermeneutics draws several implications from this question and its answer.

First, *qiné* hermeneutics sees in *lissan* the power to disclose the transformability of the world. *Lissan* considers the given as something Ethiopians have created and could question, undo and change. *Lissan* makes us realize that there is something yet to be articulated, yet to be known, yet to be understood, yet to be undone, yet to be constructed, and yet to be invented and created. Unlike *quanqua*, *lissan* is open-ended and knows itself to be *enkän* (incomplete and tensioned) and treats reality as always open-ended and as a realm of emancipatory possibilities. In *lissan*, Ethiopians are the active agents that give form, content, and meaning to the world they inhabit.

---

128 Roger W Cowley, *Ethiopian Biblical Interpretation: A Study in Exegetical Tradition and Hermeneutics* (Cambridge: Cambridge University Press, 1988), p. 245.

Second, *qiné* hermeneutics interprets the very pithiness of the question, "In what language did God say 'let there be light'?" as an indication that the productive "light" of language as *lissan* resides in the economical rather than in the inflationary use of language. One sees this in the distinctive austereness of *lissan* in *qiné* as opposed to the pedestrian volubility of *quanqua* in hegemonic discourse. Note the anesthetizing and inflationary uses of terms such as democracy, development, participation, civil society, ethnic self-determination, and so forth, in Ethiopia. These terms exist as *quanqua*, as tools of domination and deception. They obscure rather than bring "light" to Ethiopian conditions.

Third, "Let there be light" serves as an injunction that continuously repeats itself in the practice of *qiné* hermeneutics, because, given *enkän* characterizes all *nägär*, there can never be a light that reveals all. *Lissan* is always *enkän*. Coping with each new endeavor, with each new situation, with each new problem, *lissan* must obey the demand of "Let there be light," for every light creates its own dark corners and its own incompleteness and tensions. "Let there be light" acknowledges that there is no final light that reveals all; there is no final interpretation, and no final *wärq*. To believe otherwise is to reduce *lissan* to *quanqua* and integrate it into the hegemonic power's language of domination.

Finally, the development of *lissan* draws its emancipatory vocabulary, questions, ideas, and methods not only from our critical internal journey but also from our critical external journey which we conduct in terms of the emancipatory needs we have disclosed through our critical internal journey. That is, the development of *lissan* takes place through the operations of *zäräfa* and *tähägagari hiss* during our critical internal and external journeys.

It is important to note that *qiné* hermeneutics does not see *quanqua* and *lissan* in a binary manner. Rather, *quanqua* as language is *nägär* whose *wärq*—*lissan*—is repressed by the hegemonic order's material and discursive practices. *Lissan*, as the repressed of *quanqua*, gestates in *quanqua* as an antagonism whose resolution discloses the emancipatory possibility that could be brought to existence through the *zäräfa* of *quanqua*. *Quanqua* and *lissan* are thus internally related dynamically and contradictorily. *Lissan*'s struggle (*gädl*) with *quanqua* is endless, because the two are intertwined such that what is part of *lissan* at one moment could evolve into part of *quanqua*, requiring a permanent *zäräfa* of *quanqua* to maintain *lissan*'s critical, productive, performative, and emancipatory power.

23. *Tsinsä hassab* (ፅንሰ ሐሳብ) / *concept*

Tsinsä hassab (ፅንሰ ሐሳብ) means concept. Though translated as concept, the meaning of *tsinsä hassab* is in important respects different from the meaning of concept in the borrowed social sciences in Ethiopian Studies. Let me first consider *tsinsä hassab* and then show how it differs from the understanding of concept in social science Ethiopian Studies.

For *qiné* hermeneutics, *tsinsä hassab* (concept/s) are formulated during the problematizing of *nägär* as *säm ena wärq*, during *zäräfa, andem, qisäla* and *mirmära*, while developing *andemta* (see entry #26 below), during *antsar nibab* (አንፃር ንባብ / distanciation reading, see #34 below) and *wistä wäyra nibab* (ውስጠ ወይራ ንባብ / symptomatic reading, see # 35 below). *Tsinsä hassab* (concept/s) are not congruent with the studied *nägär*, nor are they totally cleansed of it. *Tsinsä hassab* bear within themselves aspects of the heterogeneity of the studied *nägär*. Ethiopian facts are *nägär* and therefore resist totalizing objective descriptions, are traversed by an internal antagonism that prevents them from being identical to themselves, and are polysemous and *tsinsä hassab*-laden. Concepts / *tsinsä hassab* are not immediately accessible through empirical observations. *Tsinsä hassab* dwell in and circulate through *nägär*, that is, through the repressed or unexpressed dimensions of the understandings Ethiopians have of their conditions and actions, of their failures and successes, of their hopes and desires. A *tsinsä hassab* rarely stands alone. It is part of a network that brings into play other *tsinsä hassab* to more adequately understand *nägär*.

There is an internal connections between *tsinsä hassab* and *nägär* such that one could say that the process of developing *tsinsä hassab* is a process of conceptualization that articulates what is active in *nägär*: its tensions, contradictions, incompleteness (*enkän*), and potentials. *Tsinsä hassab* are thus active moments of the *nägär* they conceptualize, but they also transcend it. They have substantive connotations, are performative, open-ended, and *enkän* (incomplete). They enable us to make new connections within and through *nägär*. Given *enkän*, the outcomes of these new connections open the door to more *qisäla, mirmära,* and *zäräfa* that could lead to the development of new, more comprehensive but still incomplete *tsinsä hassab*. Recall for instance the *tsinsä hassab* of *säwrä bahil* (non-tradition), *säwrä ras* (surplus self) , *säwrä hiywät* (surplus life), and all the others discussed in this chapter. *Tsinsä hassab* have *säm ena wärq* features and are battlegrounds of ideas and are thus subject to *zäräfa*.

The borrowed epistemology and methodological Westernism that dominate Ethiopian Studies operate with a radically different understanding of concepts. These concepts are ready-made concepts that are mostly borrowed or derived from the West, and are as such external to Ethiopian reality (*nägär*). They are used to categorise, order, rank, label, organize, and quantify *nägär* as an aggregate of discrete facts. These concepts do not have any internal connection with *nägär*. They do not articulate what is active in *nägär* and thus do not go beyond the observables of *nägär* in that they do not grasp the historical singularity and dynamic of *nägär's* becoming: its internal and external contexts, tensions, processes, and potentialities. Unlike *tsinsä hassab*, the borrowed concepts are hypostatized and become self-sufficient entities that function as real facts irrespective of what Ethiopians say, think, and do.

The problem of the borrowed social science concepts in Ethiopian Studies is not only that they limit us to a "two-eyed" vision, but also that they stipulate *a priori* what counts and does not count as a "datum" or "evidence" in terms of the Western experiences, supplanting thus the experience of Ethiopians. The borrowed concepts silently posit the Western experience as the indispensable grid for interpreting Ethiopian *nägär*. Thus, one could say that, from the *qiné* hermeneutical perspective, the borrowed social science concepts do not enable us to move beyond the experience of the West. The Ethiopian experience thus remains in the dark. The borrowed concepts determine how we perceive and conceive Ethiopian issues and conditions, and thus silently frame the questions we raise and the answers we look for.

Western social science concepts are a closed and fixed system of meanings that hide or exclude essential aspects of Ethiopian reality and thus disable Ethiopians from understanding and creatively transforming their reality in terms of their emancipatory aspirations. They deprive Ethiopians of their epistemic autonomy. In social science Ethiopian Studies, Ethiopians are subject to the "panoptic gaze" of Western social science concepts that deny the historical agency of Ethiopians and reduce them to being "interpassive" audiences of development and democratization experts who become "eyes that see" Ethiopians "without being seen," and "powers" that tell Ethiopians what is and is not "democracy," and what is and is not "development."[129] These concepts

---

129 On panopticon, Jeremy Bentham, *Panopticon: Or The Inspection House* (1791) (Whitefish: Kessinger Publishing, 2009); On panopticon gaze, Michel Foucault, *The Foucault Reader*, ed. Paul Rabinow (New York: Pantheon, 1984), pp. 189, 217. On "interpassive," see Slavoj Žižek, *The Plague of Fantasies* (London: Verso, 1997), pp. 109-112, 144-7. An interpassive experience is one where Ethiopians outsource their "enjoyment" of thinking on "development" and "democracy" to the other, i.e., the development and democratization experts who do the problematizing of our conditions for us and theorize for us how we "develop" and "democratize." If true freedom lies in our power to problematize our conditions ourselves, then our interpassive participation in "development" embodies our epistemic servility. Thus the fetishization of Western social sciences and its Western practitioners in Ethiopia.

are thus epistemological obstacles to understanding Ethiopian conditions and issues in terms of the emancipatory dynamics that gestate in Ethiopian history, both vertically and laterally. Inevitably, in the realm of development and democratization in Ethiopia, the borrowed concepts function as part of the *quanqua* of control and domination. *Tsinsä hassab* make Ethiopians themselves the "eyes" and the "ears" that see and hear Ethiopians. They give Ethiopians the epistemic autonomy that enables them to conceive and create democracy and development that respond to their emancipatory interests.

24. *Admas* (አድማስ) / *horizon*

Admas means horizon. The *admas* of the hegemonic order circumscribes the range, types, and limits of *ewqät*, *ewnät*, norms, values, practices, institutions, expectations, and possibilities, and so forth, that are available to Ethiopians. Each Ethiopian regime moves within a given *admas* (horizon). For example, the feudal *admas* that dictated the topography, processes, and orientations of life in the pre-1974 regime coloured and shaped all activities and institutions; and the *gada admas* shaped and oriented the institutions and life of the Oromo in the 16th century. The 1995 Constitution made ethnicity the *admas* of Ethiopian life. Consequently, practices, institutions, relations, organization, norms, values, aims, conflicts, goals, and so forth became overdetermined by the ethnic *admas*.[130] The *admas* of the hegemonic regime determines the "specific gravity," as it were, of Ethiopian society and social practices under that regime.

From the perspective of *qiné* hermeneutics, *admas* is *nägär* which means it is internally tensioned, contradictory, and incomplete. Its claimed closedness is a *zäybé* of what it excludes and represses. Given that every *admas* is a *nägär*, it is internally split into a *säm admas* (its manifest/hegemonic horizon) and a *wärq admas* (the *säwrä tarik* or *wärq admas* repressed in the *säm admas*). The articulations of the vertical and the horizontal dimensions of Ethiopian history thus generate internal splits within each hegemonic *admas* between their manifest (*säm*) *admas* and their repressed (*wärq*) *admas*. The Ethiopian *wärq admas* is the horizon or the *admas* of emancipation that gestates in the two dimensions—vertical and horizontal—of Ethiopian history. The Ethiopian *wärq admas* is discernable only through a critical internal journey that traverses the *admas* as *nägär* of the lateral and vertical dimensions of Ethiopian history. As well, the *wärq admas* of the West (or another society) is educed through a

---

130 A capitalist *admas* overdetermines all relevant structures, relations, norms, etc. in the USA, as the Stalinist *admas* did in the Soviet Union. Changing the *admas* of a society is engaging in a revolution.

critical external journey. The question here is how to produce an *andemta* (fusion of horizons, # 26 below) of the *wärq admas* produced from the two dimensions, vertical and lateral, of Ethiopian *nägär*. The same question applies in the construction of *andemta* with the outcomes of our internal and external journeys into Ethiopia's and the West's (or others) *admas*, when it is necessary to advance the emancipatory interests of Ethiopians. *Qiné* hermeneutics has a concept of "unity" that deals with this issue as well with the issues of the relation between diversity and unity.

25. *Wihdät (ውሕደት) / unity*

Wihdät (ውሕደት) means unity or totality but not in the sense of an organic whole.[131] This *qiné* hermeneutical concept of unity or totality has its source in the monophysite *Täwahedo* theology. According to this theology, "the divinity and the humanity" of "Christ" continues "in Him *without mixture or separation, confusion or change.*"[132] *Qiné* hermeneutics subjects to *zäräfa* the conception of unity as *"without mixture or separation,"* discards its theological baggage, and secularizes it to mean unity of the same [*"without separation"*] and the different [*"without mixture"*], overdetermined by that which unites it. The secularized concept of *wihdät* is a critical and not an affirmative concept. It sees the relation between the "same" and the "different" as a relation of antagonism or contradiction and not as a relation of opposition.

---

131 Kidane Weld Kifle መጽሐፈ ሰዋስው ወግስ ወመዝገበ ቃላት ሐዲስ (Addis Ababa: Artistic Printing Press, 1978 E. C.), page 383.

132 Archbishop Mekarios et al., eds., *The Ethiopian Orthodox Täwahedo Church Faith, Order of Worship and Ecumenical Relations* (Addis Ababa: Tinsae ZeGubae Printing Press, 1996); Archbishop Gabriel, ትምህርተ ሃይማኖት ኦርቶዶክሳዊ (Addis Ababa: Addis Printers, 2001); Mebratu Kiros Gebru, *Miaphysite Christology: An Ethiopian Perspective* (Piscataway, NJ: Gorgias Press, 2010). According to Liqä Siltanat Habtä Mariam Werqneh, "the Ethiopian Church maintains that Christ is perfect God and perfect man, at once Unsubstantial with the Father and with us; the divinity and the humanity continuing in Him *without mixture or separation,* confusion or change. He is one and the same person both in his eternal pre-existence and also in the economy, in which he performs the redeeming work of God on behalf of man, from the indivisible state of union of Godhead and manhood." *Doctrine of the Ethiopian Orthodox Täwahedo Church* (undated manuscript). Also available at http://www.dskmariam.org/artsandlitreature/ literature/pdf/doctorinoftheethiopianorthodoxchurch.pdf. Accessed 21/5/2013; Abba Hailemariam Melese Ayenew, *Influence of Cyrillian Christology in the Ethiopian Orthodox Anaphora* (Pretoria: The University of South Africa, 2009), pp. 255-300; Italics added. Abba Hailemariam Melese Ayenew, *Influence of Cyrillian Christology in the Ethiopian Orthodox Anaphora*, Doctoral Thesis (Pretoria: The University of South Africa, 2009).

Wihdät is "diversity-in-unity," an internally differentiated and tensioned unity, with diversity understood as internal differences bound by antagonistic relations, rather than as external relations of hermetic or independent units. It is not a seamless totality; rather being a unity of "without separation" and "without mixture," it is internally complex and traversed and stitched by internal antagonisms.

The conception of *wihdät* (unity) as diversity-in-unity is what one finds in *säm ena wärq*. The *ena* in *säm ena wärq* is the marker of the *"without mixture or separation"* that characterizes the contradictory *wihdät* (unity) of *säm ena wärq*. As we have already seen, every *nägär* is *a säm ena wärq*. This implies that any *wihdät* (unity), be it the "unity" of an idea, a norm, an action, a social practice, a discourse, a social institution, and so forth, is fraught with constitutive contradictions arising from the *"without mixture or separation"* inter-relations of its parts. It is a *wihdät* (unity) or a totality of the same ("without separation") and the different ("without mixture"). The antagonism between these two is internal to *wihdät*. However, this antagonism is not only a relationship of conflict, it is also a relationship of mutual interpenetration and dependency of the antagonistic parts, and thus of unity.

Wihdät, as a complex and internally variegated historical reality understood as diversity-in-unity, is the context for enucleating and understanding Ethiopia's repressed emancipatory possibilities of the past and the undisclosed emancipatory possibilities of the present and the future, and for understanding how the possibilities of the past and the future throw light on the present and its immanent possibilities. *Wihdät* or diversity-in-unity is always incomplete (*enkän*), because the past is incomplete and bears the scars of defeated hopes and unrealized dreams, the present is shot with antagonisms that make it open-ended, and the future is undecided, which means that *wihdät* is a provisional, internally tensioned, dynamic, and unfinished historical totality that enables us to conceive its transformability. *Wihdät* and its conceptualization as diversity-in-unity is essential for thinking about Ethiopian emancipation (*arnät*, see Chapter 3).

The alternative to *wihdät* (diversity-in-unity) is unity-in-diversity, an understanding of unity according to the hegemonic order. The concept of unity-in-diversity in Ethiopia has a specific historical meaning that is rooted in the ethnic politics that gained hegemony in 1991 and was enshrined in the 1995 Ethiopian Constitution and the ethnic federalism it created. It means an Ethiopia wherein ethnic groups are, according to the 1995 Constitution, sovereign (Article 8) and have the right of self-determination including secession (Articles 39, 47). That is, diversity has primacy over unity, making unity an aggregation of externally related units: thus, unity-in-diversity, which is the expression used in the regime's *quanqua*.

To understand the meaning and implications of unity-in-diversity, let me consider the example of international organizations. The exemplar of unity-in-diversity is an international organization such as the League of Nations or the United Nations. An important aspect of such international organizations is the possibility each state has to externalize its internal antagonisms into an opposition between itself and another state and to create an external enemy, when it deems it necessary to advance its interests. Creating an external enemy diverts the people's attention from their society's internal contradictions. The payoff for the state is it can use this "enemy" as a foil for neutralizing internal antagonisms as threats to national security, for strengthening its hold on power, and for bolstering the people's sense of national unity and self-identity. When a multi-ethnic nation adopts the principle of unity-in-diversity to organize its internal units based on ethnic identity, it inevitably reproduces the above logic of inter-state relations. This is the situation that the 1995 Ethiopian Constitution has created by establishing an ethnic federation where each ethnicity is spatially established as a state called *kilil*. These *kilils* see themselves as "sovereign" units, and to avoid facing the internal antagonisms created by the exploitation and oppression the ethnic rulers inflict on their own *kilil's* population, they externalize the antagonisms on another ethnic group, which is held responsible for the problems within the *kilil*. It is a practice that pits one ethnicity against another. The advantages for the *kilil* rulers are multiple: creating a sense of ethnic unity, identity and solidarity that feeds on a putative external threat, and giving a free latitude for the ethnic elites to exploit their own people without meeting much opposition from within. For those who control the federal state, unity-in-diversity institutionalizes ethnic divide-and-rule strategy that gives them a free hand to amass power and wealth, and subverts the emergence of a nation-wide united opposition.

Wihdät (diversity-in-unity) is incompatible with the anti-emancipatory concept of "unity-in-diversity" for the latter conceptualizes ethnic diversity in terms of diversity-as-external-relations, based on the assumption that Ethiopian ethnicities are *only externally* related to each other. It has anti-emancipatory consequences, because it makes it difficult to conceive Ethiopia as a historical totality whose internal antagonisms generate possibilities for system-wide emancipatory changes. Unlike the diversity-in-unity understanding that sees antagonism as a force that pushes towards emancipatory unity, because it sees antagonism as a universality that traverses, stiches, and propels Ethiopian ethnicities towards the recognition of shared common interests and needs, the unity-in-diversity assumes antagonism as an external opposition between ethnicities and gives primacy to conflicts between them and uses this external opposition to occlude internal antagonisms, thus neutralizing struggles for emancipation.

Wihdät or diversity-in-unity enables us to see what unity-in-diversity occludes: that antagonisms traverse all ethnicities diagonally, dividing them as oppressors and oppressed, with members of different ethnicities found on both sides of the divide as oppressors and oppressed.[133] Unity-in-diversity, by subsuming unity to diversity and making the achievement of diversity— "secession" as the 1995 Ethiopian Constitution names it—the goal that uses "unity" as an instrument or a platform to reach it, sets the stage for conflict between the diverse ethnicities. Unity-in-diversity provides neither a critical approach nor a unifying principle that enables a transformation of Ethiopia as a totality. *Wihdät*, on the other hand, enables us to conceive Ethiopia as an internally contradictory social totality, making possible a system-wide unity of the oppressed, irrespective of their ethnicities, to challenge the system-wide oppressors, who in fact hail from all ethnicities. *Wihdät*— diversity-in-unity—incubates emancipatory possibilities, because it enables us to grapple with the systemic pan-Ethiopian internal antagonistic relations.

Wihdät— diversity-in-unity—does not mean either the denial of diversity or the absence of conflicts. It means that diversity is an internal and not an external relation, that conflicts are internal to and constitutive of diversity-in-unity, and that conflicts enrich, complexify, and fortify unity through the *gädl* that produces universality (*wärq*) by resolving internal conflicts in emancipatory ways. *Wihdät* activates the universality that is immanent in the antagonism that traverses the diverse ethnicities diagonally and transcends them without reducing differences to harmonious relations. *Wihdät* is a system-critical concept and not a system-affirmative one. *Wihdät* (diversity-in-unity) is dynamic, dialectical, and bears an emancipatory potential; unity-in-diversity is mechanical, disintegrative, and anti-emancipatory.

26. *Andemta (አንድምታ) / "fusion of wärq horizons"*

Andemta (አንድምታ) means "fusion of horizons" of understandings of the world emerging from different cultures or histories.[134] It is a practice that has deep

---

133 See Chapter 4 below.
134 A *zäräfa* of Gadamer's notion of "fusions of horizons." Hans-Georg Gadamer, *Truth and Method*, Second Revised Edition; translation revised by Joel Weinsheimer and Donald G. Marshall (New York: Continuum, 2004/2006), pp. 301-6, 337, 367, 398, 578. "The concept of "horizon" suggests itself because it expresses the superior breadth of vision that the person who is trying to understand must have.

roots in *qiné* hermeneutics. Claude Sumner notes in his study of Ethiopian philosophical texts from the Axumite period (The *Fisalgwos* or The *Physiologue*) and from the sixteenth and seventeenth centuries,

> Ethiopians never translate literally: they adapt, modify, add, subtract. A translation therefore bears a typically Ethiopian stamp: although the nucleus of what is translated is foreign to Ethiopia, the way it is assimilated and transferred into an indigenous reality is typically Ethiopian. [...] *it is transformed beyond recognition.*[135]

The Ethiopian intellectual tradition has a long history of *täshägagari hiss* / transcritique and critical appropriation of foreign ideas. As we could see in The *Fisalgwos* or The *Physiologue*, the practice of adapting, modifying, adding to, subtracting from, redirecting, that is, subjecting to *zäräfa* the ideas of other civilizations from an Ethiopian perspective is part of the Ethiopian intellectual tradition.[136] An Amharic word, አንደምታ (*andemta*, derived from *andem*) refers to the knowledge produced through the activity of cross-cultural transcritique (*täshägagari hiss*) and the resulting "fusion of horizons of diverse understandings of the world."[137] Negussie Andre Dominic notes in his study on The *Fetha Nägäst and its Ecclesiology*

> [The] word [*andem*] introduces an alternative meaning to a word or concept that needs more than an explanation. This word is notable for having skillfully integrated whatever element it has borrowed from outside into the local culture, frame of mind and language. The አንደምታ [*andemta, i.e., the texts that result from andem interpretations of the thoughts of other cultures*] is an excellent example of *interculturating texts written in foreign languages and in distant contexts into one's own Sitz im Leben* [life setting].[138]

Andemta is an interpretative practice "notable for having skillfully integrated whatever element it has borrowed from outside into the local culture, frame of mind and language" through the practice of *täshägagari hiss* or transcritique that wields *zäräfa*.[139] Does the practice of *andemta* lead to eclecticism and stifle

---

To acquire a horizon means that one learns to look beyond what is close at hand—not in order to look away from it but to see it better, within a larger whole and in truer proportion." p. 304.

135 Claude Sumner, *Classical Ethiopian Philosophy* (Los Angeles: Adey Publishing Company, 1994), p. 51. Emphasis added.
136 Ibid., p. 51.
137 Hans-Georg Gadamer, *Truth and Method*, supra, pp. 301-6, 337, 367, 398, 578
138 Negussie Andre Dominic, *The Fetha Nägäst and its Ecclesiology* (New York: Peter Lang, 2010), p. 13, fn. 2. Emphasis added.
139 On the place and meaning of *andemta* in the Ethiopian intellectual tradition, see Roger W. Cowley, *The Traditional Interpretation of the Apocalypse of St John in the Ethiopian Orthodox Church* (Cambridge: Cambridge University Press, 1983), pp. 46-53; Roger W. Cowley, *Ethiopian Biblical Interpretation: A Study in Exegetical Tradition and Hermeneutics* (Cambridge: Cambridge University Press, 1988).

original thinking? No, on the contrary, it could lead to intellectual and cultural "miracles." An example of *andemta* is what is known as the "Greek miracle"—the rise of philosophy and science in ancient Greece—about which Hegel writes,

> They [Ancient Greeks] certainly received the substantial beginnings of their religion, culture, and social relations more or less from Asia, Syria, and Egypt; but they have so very much obliterated [*getilgt*] the foreign aspect of this origin, transformed, elaborated, reversed, and made it so thoroughly different, that what they (as we) value, recognize and love in it is essentially their own ... They have, so to speak, ungratefully [*undankbar*] forgotten the foreign origin, put it in the background,..."[140]

In the case of Ethiopia too, what is taken from others, to use Sumner's words, "*is transformed beyond recognition.*" And the result is *andemta*. And *andemta* could create "miracles" such as the "miracle" of Lalibela and of *qiné* culture.[141] The practice of *andemta* enables us to develop an original emancipatory-oriented knowledge by crossing temporal and spatial boundaries. First, it enables us, through the use of *zäräfa*, to cross the boundaries between Ethiopia's past and present *admas* or horizons of experiences and understandings. Its accomplishment necessitates the formulation of concepts (*tsinsä hassab*) and expressions we need to establish a "critical dialogical dialogue" (*mädämamät*, see below #28) between the emancipatory surplus meanings (*säwrä fitch*, ሰውረ ፍች, see # 36) that connect the past, the present and the future, elicit their *wärq*, and see how we could overcome the crisis of the present, with our questions and concerns planted in the present. In doing so, the practice of *andemta* enables us to open new horizons, invisible to the official past, present, and projected future. The practice of *andemta* rejects the reduction of the relation between the past and the present to a linear narrative of events that simply follow each other.

Second, the practice of *andemta* enables us to cross the boundaries via *zäräfa* between the diverse Ethiopian traditions and cultures, discover the incompleteness and contradictions (*enkän*) of each and therefore their openness to each other, and engage them in a transcritique (*täshägagari hiss*) in order to enucleate, develop and expand the *säwrä tarik* (surplus history)—*säwrä bahil* (non-tradition), *säwrä ras* (surplus self), *säwrä hiywät* (surplus life)—that are rooted in the experiences of the commonly shared trauma of oppression and the commonly shared desires and struggles for emancipation. Though these experiences of trauma and quests for emancipation appear empirically to be local and unconnected, *qiné* hermeneutical readings (*antsar* and *wistä wäyra*

---

140 G. W. F. Hegel, *Vorlesungen über die Philosophie der Geschichte*, quoted in Slavoj Žižek, *Absolute Recoil*, (London: Verso, 2014), p.137.
141 On Lalibela, Maimire Mennasemay, *Qiné Hermeneutics and Ethiopian Critical Theory* (Los Angeles: Tsehai Publishing, 2021), Chapter 7.

nibab, see #34 and #35 below) disclose the subterranean vertical (temporally) and lateral interconnections of commonly shared emancipatory aspirations and interests. *Andemta* thus could disclose the "subterranean" relations that exist in the vertical and lateral (ethnic, regional) dimensions of Ethiopian history and develop "interculturating texts" or an *andemta* that articulates a pan-Ethiopian emancipatory *admas*. In the process, it makes possible the creation of vocabularies—*tsinsä hassab* (concepts) and expressions—that enrich *lissan* and enable Ethiopians to name the unfreedoms, inequalities, and injustices they suffer in ways that enable them to overcome these sufferings.

Third, the practice of *andemta* also enables us, through a critical external journey, to cross the boundaries between the Ethiopian and Western (other) *admas* of understanding and create concepts and expressions to articulate the surplus meanings of Ethiopian and Western (or other) horizons of understanding and thus develop "interculturating texts" of *wärq* or emancipatory ideas. The critical external journey is conducted through the *zäräfa* of the Western human and social sciences—their ideas, concepts, theories, questions, methodologies, teleological models, and epistemological standpoints—that are hegemonic in Ethiopian Studies, in terms of the emancipatory surplus meanings that we disclose through our critical internal journey into Ethiopian *nägär*, vertically and laterally. Such a *zäräfa* mediated transcritique enables us to read ideas originating in the West (or elsewhere) against the grain, and dislocate and rework them to respond to our emancipatory interests and needs. One may object that such a practice could lead to a misunderstanding of foreign ideas. The reasons given earlier to counter similar objections to the practice of *zäräfa* as misreading the ideas of others respond to this objection.

Andemta embodies the results of the articulation of the outcomes of our critical internal and external journeys in our quest to give form and content to our emancipatory aspirations, needs, and interests. It could open a path for an emancipatory exit from the crises that afflict Ethiopia, and find answers and solutions to questions and problems the hegemonic order considers unanswerable and unresolvable. The failures of "development" and "democratization" in Ethiopia is in part due to the failure of Ethiopian Studies to develop an *andemta*. This failure reflects the absence of epistemic autonomy and the uncritical dependence of Ethiopian Studies on the borrowed social sciences.

27. *Silt* (ስልት) / *method-approach*

Silt (ስልት) is a "method" proper to *qiné* hermeneutics. Though one could translate *silt* as "method," it does not have the same signification that the term "method" has in the social sciences. Method in the social sciences is a standardized and universal technology of observation, assumed to be value-free, that breaks down human behaviour and social practices, into discrete and quantifiable data, and subjects them to statistical manipulation with the purpose of generating empirical generalizations that are assumed to have a subject-less objectivity and universal validity.[142] It is the application of this method that I called earlier "methodological Westernism." Unlike methodological Westernism, *silt* is not an external method that tries to grasp *nägär* externally as made up of discrete, unidimensional and homogeneous units.

In *qiné* hermeneutics, *silt* (ስልት) is a procedure of investigation that unfolds in the very process of elucidating *nägär*.[143] It uses *säm ena wärq* and *zäräfa* in dealing with *nägär*. *Silt* is not something that is outside the subject matter under study that one could use to manipulate it externally. Unlike the primacy and externality of method in the social sciences, *qiné* hermeneutics puts the emphasis on the idea that to understand a given *nägär* (a subject matter) we need to use an approach that is appropriate to the *nägär* and grasps its specificity. *Säm ena wärq* as *silt* mobilizes *qisäla* and *mirmära* to enable us to grasp the specificity of the subject matter and avoid its homogenization with subject matters that are qualitatively different, as is the case with methodological Westernism in Ethiopian Studies.

One can understand the specificity and the critical nature of *silt* by comparing it to the Cartesian understanding of method which is the foundation of method in the social sciences. The Cartesian understanding operates a split between the observer and the observed, and requires the break down of the object of study "into as many parts as possible," its reduction to the "simplest and easiest to know, in order to ascend little by little...to the knowledge of the most composite things."[144] *Silt*, being rooted in *säm ena wärq* as the master metaphor of the human condition, rejects the idea that *nägär* could be broken down to simple elements without a remainder. Unlike the reductionist Cartesian approach, *silt* starts with the complexity of *nägär* and formulates its complexity as *säm ena wärq*. It considers that the addition of *nägär's* so-called "simple elements" cannot grasp its true meaning, for *nägär* is more than the sum-total of these elements, however "complete" the "enumeration" of *nägär's* elements is. Such a method misses the *säm ena wärq* idea that there is no meaning-free atomic element in

---

142 Michael Hader, *Empirical Social Research* (New York: Springer, 2022).
143 Kebede G/Medhin, ሳይንሳዊ የቅኔ አፈታት ስልት (Addis Ababa: Birana Matĕmia Bet, 1992).
144 René Descartes, *Discourse on Method and Meditations on First Philosophy*, trans. Donald A. Cress (Indianapolis: Hackett Publishing Company, 1998), p. 11. John Gerring, *Social Science Methodology* (Cambridge: Cambridge University Press, 2015).

nägär, for every *nägär* is imbued with interpretation. Precisely because it starts with the complexity of *nägär*, *silt* requires *antsar* reading (reading based on distantiation, see # 34 below) and *wistä wäyra* reading (symptomatic reading, see # 35 below). Both use *säm ena wärq* formulations and *zäräfa* to defamiliarize, contextualize, historicize, and decipher *nägär* and grasp that which makes *nägär* tick and gives it the potential to change—its surplus meaning—making *silt* a critical approach.

In the practice of *silt*, one examines the subject matter recursively, which means the process of understanding *nägär* is neither a linear process nor reductionist, but a process that goes back and forth through *zäräfa* at every stage of the study, revising and refining the interpretation and questions reached at the previous stage. Only through this recursive process could one eventually construct the *wärq* of *nägär*, which retroactively gives us the best possible understanding or explanation of the *nägär* under study. *Silt* unpacks and makes visible the inner contradictions and changeability of *nägär*. It is important to note that such a process does not exclude the use of empirical methods; rather, it subsumes the use of empirical methods to *silt*.

Moreover, unlike the Cartesian mind/body split—"I think therefore I am"—*silt* recognizes the importance of—"I feel therefore I am"—which enables *silt* to recognize the Ethiopian body as a historical thinking body, a *säm ena wärq*, that bears the wounds and scars of exploitation and oppression. This means that unlike the social scientific method that produces disembodied knowledge, *silt* recognizes that knowledge is embodied knowledge.[145] As such, *silt* is social, historical, and political. It is value-loaded for it focuses on producing emancipatory *ewqät/ewnät*, and rejects the possibility of a value-free, and subject-less objectivity and universality. *Silt* does not separate the understanding of Ethiopia from the understanding of the Ethiopian self engaged in understanding Ethiopia.

In the borrowed social sciences that reign in Ethiopian Studies, social scientists apply externally to the subject under study a method claimed to be value-free and universal. Method is presumed to shield them from contaminating with their values and prejudices the subject matter they study or being influenced by it. From the *qiné* hermeneutical perspective, this self-understanding of social scientists dissimulates the norms, values, and expectations that inhabit their intellectual, cultural, historical, class, and political baggage, giving them an unacknowledged influence in the formulation, conduct, and outcome of the study. It transforms social scientists into somnambulist investigators who are

---

145 See the discussion of *säwrä tarik* in Chapter 2 below on embodied knowledge.

oblivious of their surroundings and of the infiltration of their moral and political values into their approaches, perceptions and questions of what they study.

For *silt*, the social scientist is not historically, culturally, and socially "naked." *Silt*, being rooted in *säm ena wärq*, recognizes what Gadamer calls "historically effected consciousness," that is, *silt* recognizes that historical influences affect the interpreters' interests in the topic they choose, the projected meaning they attribute to the interpreted; it sculpts their manner of observing and listening to the interpreted or observed such that one could say the interpreters or observers are present in the interpretation they produce.[146] In its practice, *silt* avoids the moral detachment that methodological Westernism generates.

In addition, from the perspective of *silt*, the social science understanding of method as a value-free, objective, and universal procedure applicable to *nägär* is a non-creative, conformist practice that transforms method into a prison house wherein the interpreter and the subject matter are confined. Whereas *silt* is a process of working through the resistance of *nägär* or the hegemonic understanding of *nägär*, methodological Westernism in Ethiopian Studies is a practice of the uncritical and conformist student who, to quote the *andemta* commentary discussed earlier, "breathes from the air his master breathes, … rests where he [his master] rests, and … preserve[s] the teaching as he has received it, without the slightest change, or difference of opinion."[147] That is, methodological Westernism's "follow me" injunction has a hypnotizing effect that inhibits one from "bursting through", to use the phrasing of *qiné* hermeneutics, the "shackles of tradition"—Western social sciences in Ethiopian Studies—and "striking off" in emancipatory directions."[148]

Argumentation is crucial in the practice of *silt*. One needs to produce arguments in support of the superior comprehensiveness of the alternative formulation and interpretation of *nägär* one proposes. However, it is important to bear in mind that the *qiné* hermeneutical understanding of argument differs from the Western social science understanding. The *qiné* hermeneutical practice does not treat arguments only in an adversarial manner.[149] Rather, in *silt*,

---

146 Hans-Georg Gadamer, *Truth and Method*, Second Revised Edition; translation revised by Joel Weinsheimer and Donald G. Marshall (New York: Continuum, 2004/2006), p. 301.
147 Roger W. Cowley, "Old Testament Introduction in the Andemta Commentary Tradition," *Journal of Ethiopian Studies* 12, 1 (1974), p. 170.
148 For the *qiné* hermeneutical phrasings, *Ibid.*, pp. 165-170.
149 Liqä Siltanat Habtä Mariam Werqneh, ጥንታዊ የኢትዮጵያ ትምህርት (Addis Ababa: Berhan ena Selam Printing Press, 1962), pp. 176-183.

argumentation is also a collaborative and *zäräfa*-based exercise of elucidation and a responsive and critical engagement with and reciprocal attunement of the competing arguments. It is a process of *mädämamät* or critical dialogical dialogue (see below, entry #28) that questions and transforms not only the given interpretations of the *nägär* but also discloses the repressed questions and answers and their parameters that are not visible to the given interpretations and its questions. It is a process of constructing a new, shared hermeneutical space of questioning, inquiry, critique, and understanding, based on the careful and caring listening to and critiquing of the competing arguments. It is within this framework that deductions (*zängä hassab*, ዘንጋ ሐሳብ) and inferences (*zälängä hassab*, ዘለንጋ ሐሳብ) take place.

28. *Mädämamät* (መደጋገሟ) / critical dialogical dialogue

Mädämamät (መደጋገሟ) is a process of mutual active critical listening that takes place between interlocutors, between the interpreter and the interpreted, with the purpose of eliciting the surplus meanings—the hidden questions, assumptions, possibilities and potentialities present in the discourses of the interlocutors, be they individuals, practices, or cultures, as well as in the very form of interlocution. It is a process of oscillation, of moving recursively between various interpretations of *nägär* or discursive systems that differ from or seem to be incompatible with each other. Its purpose is to ferret out the possible *wärq* or emancipatory meanings that traverse them and to construct an *andemta* out of them. *Mädämamät* is critical "dialogical dialogue" or a *tähägagari hiss* and is interwoven with *zäräfa*.[150] However, this does not mean that *mädämamät* is an adversarial relation or a relation of mistrust. On the contrary, to be productive it requires generosity and hospitality to the "other"; that is, *mädämamät* requires a "hermeneutics of trust."[151] To engage in *mädämamät* requires epistemological egalitarianism between the interlocutors, whether these are individuals, communities, societies, discourses, practices, cultures, or civilizations.

---

150 "Dialogical dialogue" is Pannikar's term, Raimon Panikkar, "Cross-Cultural Studies: The Need for a New Science of Interpretation," in *Monchanin* 8:3-5 (1975): 12-15; Raimon Panikkar, *Myth, Faith and Hermeneutics* (New York: Paulist Press, 1979), pp. 8-10.

151 Robert J. Dostal, "The World Never Lost: The Hermeneutics of Trust," *Philosophy and Phenomenological Research*, 47, 3 (1987), pp. 413-434.

Qiné hermeneutics makes a distinction between *madamät* (ማዳመጥ, to listen actively, is the root word of *mädämamät*) and *mäsmat* (መስማት, to hear). *Madamät* demands that we carefully attend to the words and meanings of the interlocutor or of the *nägär* (subject matter) under study. For *qiné* hermeneutics, *madamät* or listening is a hermeneutical activity while *mäsmat* is an involuntary process or an automatic sound perception. If our auditory system functions properly and circumstances allow it, we hear what others say. For example, for a person who is distracted or is asleep, one uses the word *mäsmat* and says አይሰማም (*ay'sämam*), meaning he does not hear, and never the word *madamät*. To say that *mäsmat* is an involuntary process is to say that we hear what people say, follow instructions, respond as socially expected, accept the given as is, and so forth, without distantiating ourselves from our immediate understanding of the issue. That is, *mäsmat* requires neither mutual active critical listening nor questioning what we hear. It takes what the other—a practice, a text, a person, or an event—says at face value or according to the hegemonic understanding. *Mäsmat* is a passive response that reinforces the existing order of meanings. *Quanqua* is the medium of *mäsmat*.

Mädämamät requires a conscious decision to listen attentively, critically, and caringly to the other; it embraces questioning, *tähägagari hiss*, and *zäräfa* as essential moments of listening and *vice versa*. It is important to note that critical questioning (ጥያቄ, *tiyaqé*) and struggling (*gädl*) with old and new meanings are central to the *qiné* tradition and its practice of *mädämamät*. Solomon Gebre Ghiorgis writes,

> In such a school [*qiné* school] discussion and *asking questions* [ጥያቄ / *tiyaqé*, plural ጥያቄዎች, *tiyaqéwoch*] is (sic) encouraged. Since the students in such an atmosphere throughout the Ethiopian tradition have been trained to think rather than believe, they have been dissenters more often than not. Since they tend to rely on reason rather than on mere faith, they tend to be more philosophical than their counterparts the priests are. Indeed, it can be said that Ethiopian philosophy in its true sense, i.e., philosophy based on primacy of reason, originated in the kine [*qiné*] school.[152]

"Asking questions" (ጥያቄዎች, *tiyaqéwoch* / questions) and *zäräfa* animate *mädämamät*. The *qiné* tradition of questioning involves transgressing the given, the accepted, and the boundaries of meanings that the hegemonic order establishes. It gives primacy to questioning over thinking. According to *qiné* hermeneutics, thinking does not necessarily lead to critical questioning, but questioning provokes critical thinking by turning thinking against itself, hence

---

152 Quoted in Claude Sumner, *Classical Ethiopian Philosophy* (Los Angeles: Adey Publishing Company, 1994), p. 224. Italics added.

the importance of *tiyaqé* in *qisäla*, *mirmära*, *zäräfa*, and *mädämamät*. Raising the right question makes possible an adequate problematization of an issue, which is indispensable for making *mädämamät* a productive activity. The activity of *mädämamät* ferrets out the tensions and contradictions, inconsistencies, hidden questions, veiled assumptions, new possibilities, and new directions that inform the activity and the subject of the interlocution. The process of *mädämamät* could lead to critically examining the interlocutors' coordinates of reality, intelligibility, normativity, and possibility with the purpose of generating new coordinates that open up new shared spaces of questioning, intelligibility, normativity, and possibility inaccessible to the coordinates with which the interlocutors started.

Mädämamät does not exclude conflicts of interpretations. The conflicts that arise during the process of *mädämamät* bring in qualitative changes in the *mädämamät* itself in that the process creates new concepts and a richer "hermeneutical circle" that leads to a qualitatively new and shared understanding of the subject matter. This new understanding goes beyond the initial questions, ideas and understandings with which the process started, and discloses new intersubjective conditions and new relations that make an emancipatory transformation possible. *Mädämamät* locates the emergence of new questions and new ideas in the process of critical dialogical dialogue and not in the individual merits of those engaged in *mädämamät*. For *qiné* hermeneutics, critical ideas and questions emerge from *mädämamät* and not from isolated individuals. *Lissan* is the language of *mädämamät*.

29. *Minab* (ምናብ) / *utopianism without utopia*

Minab (ምናብ) is the *qiné* hermeneutical concept that refers to "utopianism without utopia" or "non-utopian utopianism" or "realistic utopia." It conceives ideas and possibilities that go beyond the conventional "two-eyed" vision. I discuss *minab* in more detail in Chapter 3 below.

30. *Yäwäl* (የወል) / *the commons*

Yäwäl (የወል) means the commons. *Yäwäl* "commons" the things necessary for living and of their means of production. It replaces the private or public ownership of such things with their collective-cum-individual use by treating them as a commons. I will discuss *yäwäl* in Chapter 3.

31. *Dagmawi Tinsa'e* (ዳግማዊ ትንሣኤ) / The Second Resurrection

Fassika or *Tinsa'e* (ትንሣኤ, meaning Resurrection) is Easter Sunday. *Dagmawi Tinsa'e* (ዳግማዊ ትንሣኤ), means the Second Resurrection. It is generally celebrated on the Sunday that follows Easter Sunday. Unlike Easter, *Dagmawi Tinsa'e* is a minimally religious holiday in that the activities that characterize it are less religious than those associated with *Tinsa'e* or Easter Sunday. *Dagmawi Tinsa'e* secularizes the religious idea of The Resurrection. It signifies the "resurrection," as it were, of the joys and pleasures of this world, an occasion that dissolves the distinction between "savior" and "saved." We could say that during *Dagmawi Tinsa'e* the savior and the saved form a single subject: Ethiopians creating a joyful life in the here and now, even if the joy lasts only a day. *Dagmawi Tinsa'e* is a *zäybé* of the presence of *säwrä ras* and of the possibility of *säwrä hiywät*.

Dagmawi Tinsa'e is a concept that apprehends life as free from oppression, exploitation, and man-made sufferings. *Dagmawi Tinsa'e* embraces a question and an answer. Whereas *Tinsa'e* (Easter) tells Ethiopians that there is life after death (The Resurrection), *Dagmawi Tinsa'e* indicates the presence of a different question triggered by the endless political, economic, and epistemic sufferings that Ethiopians endure: Is there life before death? *Dagmawi Tinsa'e* germinates an answer to this question: there is life before death only if Ethiopians struggle to transform it into a life that abolishes "social death" by "resurrecting" themselves as a people "standing uprightly," to use the *Däqiqä Estifanos* expression.[153] In the Ethiopian context of generalized immiseration, *Dagmawi Tinsa'e* expresses the desire for the resurrection of that which is dead in everyday life: the freedom and joy (*fissiha*) of "standing uprightly" and living for the good of each and all. *Dagmawi Tinsa'e* thus embodies the aspiration for an Ethiopian life free from the political, economic, social, and epistemic "crucifixions" that the hegemonic regimes inflict on Ethiopians.

In *Dagmawi Tinsa'e*, Ethiopians consider life a right and experience themselves as the "resurrectors" of life as a right. *Dagmawi Tinsa'e* is an idea that has lurked in Ethiopian history since at least the thirteenth century when Lalibela dreamt of and tried to transform Ethiopia into the embodiment of the heavenly Jerusalem here on earth—a permanent *Dagmawi Tinsa'e*.[154]

---

153 Getatchew Haile, ደቂቀ እስጢፋኖስ በገግ አምላክ, trans. from Ge'ez (Collegeville, MN: 2004), pp. 33, 75, 80-81, 87-88, 93, 102-111, 156.
154 Maimire Mennasemay, *Qiné Hermeneutics and Ethiopian Critical Theory* (Los Angeles: Tsehai Publishing, 2021), Chapter 7.

32. *Bähig amlak* (በሕግ አምላክ) / the God of Law / ፍትህ (*fithe*)

Bähig amlak (በሕግ አምላክ) is a concept that embraces two interconnected meanings. It means the "law of God" and "the God of law." Both expressions affirm the supremacy of the "just law." *Bähig amlak* expresses the *säwrä bahil* that a law is a law only if it has both the capacity and the ability to express and serve ፍትህ (*fithe*) or justice. *Bähig amlak* leads to the distinction between the "rule of law" and the "rule of just law."[155] *Fithe* refers to the latter. Accordingly, justice can be achieved only through the reign of the "rule of just law." The "rule of law" would not be up to the task.

Bähig amlak proposes a substantive and not only a procedural conception of justice. From the perspective of *bähig amlak,* the rule of law could be a source of or the embodiment of injustice, for the ruler could enact an unjust law by following procedures of law-making that are legal or constitutional—written or traditional— and apply them through due process, which means that the rule of law does not necessarily exclude committing injustices. The rule of law could be the rule of injustice while being consistently legal. The history of liberal democratic countries offers a multitude of examples of injustice that respect the rule of law.[156] The *qiné* hermeneutical idea of the "rule of just law" that *bähig amlak* conveys is radically different from the liberal idea of "the rule of law." The rule of just law is a *säwrä bahil* that emerges through the *zäräfa* of the rule of law. Once we grasp the meaning of *bähig amlak* as the "rule of just law," we get to the idea that a law proclaimed by a ruler or a government cannot count as law as long as it is not "just" even if it uses the right procedures to pass the law and to implement it. Moreover, the legitimacy of the ruler or the regime is just only if it is founded on the "rule of just law."

One may claim that the distinction between the "rule of law" and the "rule of just law" is comparable to the distinction between the "rule of law" and the "rule by law." The rule of law would imply due process, fairness, and predictability in the application of the law, whereas the rule by law would

---

155 Getatchew Haile, ደቂቀ እስጢፋኖስ በገግ አምላክ, trans. from Ge'ez (Collegeville, MN: 2004), pp. 33, 75, 80-81, 87-88, 93, 156.
156 Elizabeth Kolsky, *Colonial Justice in British India: White Violence and the Rule of Law* (New York: Cambridge University Press, 2009); Kelly McBride, *Colonialism and the Rule of Law* (Oxford: Oxford University Press, 2019); Olivier Le Cour Grandmaison, "The Exception and the Rule: On French Colonial Law," *Diogenes* 53, 4 (2006), pp. 34-53; Michelle Alexander, The *New Jim Crow: Mass Incarceration in the Age of Colorblindness* (New York: The New Press, 2010).

open the door to an unfair and unpredictable application of the law. However, this distinction seems to be more verbal than real. Were we to take the practice of the "rule of law" in the oldest liberal democracies—USA, England, and France—, history shows that the practice of the "rule of law" has legitimated acts that one could describe as unjust, particularly in its application to members of the lower classes, minorities, and, historically, the colonized.[157] Moreover, the relations between "the rule of law" and capitalism have often promoted the interests of capital and not those of justice.[158] From the perspective of *bähig amlak*, the instrumentalization of the "rule of law" to legitimate unjust actions is a real potentiality inscribed in the rule of law precisely because the criterion of the justness of the law—"rule of just law"—is absent. The distinction between the "rule of law" and the "rule of just law" is more substantive, more critical, and more emancipatory than the distinction between the "rule of law" and the "rule by law." The principle of the "rule of just law" renders difficult the instrumentalization of the law in the service of exploitation and oppression, whereas the liberal distinction between the "rule of law" and the "rule by law" does not necessarily exclude such instrumentalization of the rule of law.

Note that unlike liberal democracy where the seat of power is assumed to be "empty" and could be filled by anybody (person or political party) who is elected, for *bähig amlak* the seat of power is not empty.[159] A crucial surplus meaning of *bähig amlak* is that the seat of power is the seat of the "rule of just law," and only he/she who abides by the "rule of just law" has a just claim to sit on the seat of power. Elections as understood in liberal democracy could and indeed have brought anti-democratic politicians to power. According to *bähig amlak*, the ruler is a tenant occupying the seat of power only if he/she respects the obligation to abide by the "rule of just law." Not to abide by this obligation

---

157 Ibid.
158 Randall Holcombe, "Creative Destruction: How capitalism Undermines the Rule of Law," Rule of Law capitalism SSRN-id3942914.pdf; David Barnhizer, Professor Emeritus of Law and Daniel Barnhizer, "Political Economy, Capitalism and the Rule of Law" (Cleveland State University, Cleveland-Marshall College of Law, Research Paper 16-292 January 2016), available at http://ssrn.com/abstract=2716372. Accessed 1/30/ 2020. See the US Supreme Court decision on Citizens United case. https://www.brennancenter.org/our-work/research-reports/citizens-united-explained. Accessed1.20.2019.
159 On the highly influential idea of the "empty seat of power" in contemporary theory of democracy, see Claude Lefort, *L'invention démocratique* (Paris: Fayard, 1994), pp. 172ff.

is to usurp power, even if one is elected according to legally valid procedures.[160] This understanding of the relation between the seat of power and *bähig amlak* was clearly stated by the *Däqiqä Estifanos* in the fifteenth century. They claimed, "If it is true that the Monarch is acting outside the law [in the sense of *bähig amlak*], then he is not a Monarch."[161] He is a usurper.

Bähig amlak requires that all laws, measures, and actions that affect Ethiopians should aim to enhance the life of Ethiopians, and that laws, measures, and actions must be subject to public evaluation to ensure the fulfillment of the just needs of present and future generations. According to the *Däqiqä Estifanos*, one "should not be an insult to the Ethiopian people" in the sense that one must act in ways that enhance the common good of each and all Ethiopians.[162] Moreover, *bähig amlak* makes Ethiopians responsible for the welfare of future generations, thus the *Däqiqä Estifanos* injunction that each and all must "be a witness to those who will come after you."[163] To "be a witness to those who will come after you" means, *inter alia*, that our laws and actions must consider justness to future generations.[164] According to the *Däqiqä Estifanos*, all the above obligations are public in the sense that their fulfillment must be visible and justifiable as "public evidence." Only then could one show that these obligations have been met. Hence, the *Däqiqä Estifanos* claim that each and all must be able to say "behold my evidence," that is, they must be able to provide public evidence to prove that their actions satisfy the "rule of just law."[165]

Only "rule of just law" / *bähig amlak* could enable Ethiopians to be free from political, economic, epistemic oppression, and to "stand uprightly" as

---

160 Two recent examples. Meles Zenawi was "democratically" elected to power repeatedly between 1995 and 2010 in that the legal procedures were followed. Dr Abiy Ahmed was elected "democratically" in 2021. Both could however be considered as usurpers in that their rules are characterized by arbitrary detention of citizens, torture, and forced disappearances of political opponents, journalists, and intellectuals. Both resorted repeatedly to the "state of emergency" despite being "democratically" elected.
161 Getatchew Haile, ደቂቀ እስጢፋኖስ በኅግ አምላክ, trans. from Ge'ez (Collegeville, MN: 2004), p. 156.
162 Ibid., p. 302.
163 Ibid., p. 265.
164 Here we see the relevance of *bähig amlak* as a critique of capitalism and the ecological crisis it has generated, for the former functions in terms of the profit motive that calls for unlimited growth and thus overconsumes the earth's resources in the present, endangering the lives of future generations.
165 Getatchew Haile, *A History of the First Stefanosite Monks*, translated from Ge'ez (Leuven: Uitgeverij Peeters, 2011), p. 9.

individuals and as a community.¹⁶⁶ The demand for ባሕግ አምላክ (bähig amlak) by the oppressed and exploited is present in Ethiopian history since at least the Medieval period—the expression arose during Medieval Ethiopia— and is an important part of *säwrä tarik*.

33. *Tirgum* (ትርጉም) / *critical translation*

In *qiné* hermeneutics, *tirgum* (ትርጉም) is a process of interpretation that is intimately associated with the practice of *andem*. *Tirgum* means critical translation of obscure, difficult, or foreign texts, and clarification of "equivocal or unintelligible…or obscure" meanings. The *qiné* hermeneutical tradition identifies two kinds of *tirgum* or translation: *nätäla tirgum* (ነጠላ ትርጉም) and *yämist'ir tirgum* (የምስጢር ትርጉም). *Nätäla tirgum* is a "direct [literal] translation of what is read." *Yämist'ir tirgum* is a critical translation that discloses the "secret" (ምስጢር, *mist'ir*) the surplus meaning or the *wärq*, the "hidden good," or the repressed of the translated. It is a "translation which preserves the [surplus] meaning only, without needing the text or keeping to its grammatical form."¹⁶⁷ Recall here once again the *andem* process: interpretation … by *inserting words*, by *dropping words*, by *changing a sentence from the negative to the affirmative or vice versa*, by *changing the syntax* of the sentence. One finds the same radical procedure in *yämist'ir tirgum*. *Yämist'ir tirgum* discloses that which *nätäla tirgum* (literal translation) cannot: a "secret" (ምስጢር, *mist'ir*), as Liqä Siltanat Habtä Mariam puts it. It is a *wärq*, a surplus meaning, a hidden or repressed meaning that escapes literal translation.¹⁶⁸ *Qiné* culture often uses brachylogia, formulations of excessive brevity, with words omitted, which are often present as *sineñ* (*qiné* lines) or aphorisms. The missing words are crucial for enucleating the *mist'ir* (secret) or *wärq* of the aphorisms. *Yämist'ir tirgum* treats brachylogia as fragments of a larger non-articulated or hidden discourse. *Qiné* hermeneutics develops these fragments as full sentences by decoding and interconnecting them through *yämist'ir tirgum*. The practice of *yämist'ir tirgum* requires conceptual innovations that decode and broaden the surplus meanings of the translated. It makes possible to *"burst"* what the *andemta* practice calls the *"shackles of tradition"* or the *"shackles"* of hegemonic meanings.¹⁶⁹

---

166 On *bähig amlak*, see Maimire Mennasemay, *Qiné Hermeneutics and Ethiopian Critical Theory* (Los Angeles: Tsehai Publishing, 2021), Chapter 8.
167 Roger W. Cowley, "Old Testament Introduction in the Andemta Commentary Tradition," *Journal of Ethiopian Studies* 12, 1 (1974), p. 171.
168 Liqä Siltanat Habtä Mariam Werqneh, ጥንታዊ የኢትዮጲያ ትምህርት (Addis Ababa: Berhan ena Selam Printing Press, 1962 /63/ 70), pp. 168-171, 219.
169 Roger W. Cowley, "Old Testament Introduction in the Andemta Commentary Tradition," *Journal of Ethiopian Studies* 12, 1 (1974),, pp. 165-70.

It is crucial to understand that in the *qiné* hermeneutical tradition, *tirgum* is always a critical translation or *yämist'ir tirgum* (disclosing the *wärq*, the hidden, the repressed, i.e., the "secret"). *Zäräfa* is indispensable to its practice. It widens and deepens our understanding of the translated, gives voice to its zones of silence and the emancipatory alternatives or surplus meanings simmering therein. *Tirgum* is neither a metaphoric substitute nor a mere reflection of the original. The result of *tirgum* functions as a supplement that "strikes out," in *andem* fashion, in a new direction. It thus situates us in a new horizon of understanding that opens an alternative to hegemonic meanings. *Tirgum* understood as *yämist'ir tirgum* plays a crucial role in the practice of critical internal and external journeys and the production of *andemta*.

34. *Antsar nibab* (አንጻር ንባብ) / distanciation reading

Qiné hermeneutics has two major concepts of reading: they are *antsar nibab* (አንጻር ንባብ, distanciation reading) and *wistä wäyra nibab* (ውስተ ወይራ ንባብ, symptomatic reading). Though both reading strategies observe and gather facts, they avoid the epistemic fallacy that reduces facts to the observational knowledge we have of them. They treat facts as *nägär*. For *nibab*, there is no immutable fact that is known to be the case, as empiricism would have it. As *nägär*, all facts are interpretation-laden. *Nibab* considers that an adequate understanding of *nägär* requires treating it as *säm ena wärq, and arat ayna* vision, eliciting the questions and processes which generated the facts as answers, and unmasking the non-asked and non-said, and the repressed and hidden questions and answers which the observed facts render invisible. I will discuss *antsar* reading (አንጻር ንባብ / *antsar nibab*) in this section, and *wistä wäyra* reading (ውስጠ ወይራ ንባብ) in the following one.

Antsar nibab refers to distanciation-mediated interpretation.[170] *Antsar* reading creates a distance in two senses. The first is in the sense of stepping back from the matter at hand to extricate oneself from the hegemonic understanding of the issue and create a space of critical reflection between interpreter and the subject matter. Such a distance enables the interpreter to identify its *zäybé* and *hibrä qal*, to ascertain the coordinates that make it intelligible within the hegemonic discourse, to disclose how the *hibrä qal* hide or repress the non-said, the non-asked and the tensions and contradictions present in the *nägär* under study, and to conduct *zäräfa* on the subject matter. Distanciation opens a space for *hiss* and *mädämamät*, for raising new questions that go beyond the given questions, and for imagining new coordinates beyond the coordinates of possibility that produced the *nägär* and its hegemonic interpretations.

---

170 I use the term interpretation to include explanation. Interpretation includes explanation in that, for *qiné* hermeneutics, an explanation operates in terms of concepts and procedures that are open to interpretation and whose meanings are subject to *zäräfa*.

Critical *Qiné* Hermeneutical Concepts 83

Distanciation is necessary for the exercise of the creative intellect and imagination (the *absho* mind) and the production of emancipatory "overreading" of texts and practices. Distanciation is not separating oneself from the subject matter; rather, it is a way of being critically present in the subject matter. A critical internal journey into the practices of *qiné* hermeneutics discloses that the distanciation that *antsar zäybé* reading operates has many forms, all of which are forms of struggles (*gädl*) and involve *zäräfa* to overcome *quanqua* and the hegemonic meanings it generates and to develop *lissan*, and emancipatory parameters, ideas, norms and practices.

First, *qisäla* and *mirmära* practice *antsar* reading in that both require exploring the subject matter under study through a process of distanciation of the interpreter from hegemonic knowledge and prejudgements as well as distanciation of the interpreter from him/herself in order to recognize his/her active presence in the process of interpretation and its outcomes. Second, the practice of *andem* is a form of distanciation, in that it involves splitting away from a given interpretation, going in other directions, creating a distance from the original interpretation, and introducing new perspectives and questions. Third, *arat ayn* is a method of distanciation that takes us beyond the "blindness" of the "two-eye" vision and exposes that which is invisible to it. Fourth, the *qiné* hermeneutical understanding of *wihdät* (unity) as "without mixture or separation" makes distanciation an integral part of interpretation by including "without mixture" in the process of developing an interpretation that discloses *wihdät* (unity). Fifth, the very structure of *säm ena wärq* is an invitation to distantiate ourselves from the *säm* and the *hibrä qal* (harmonizer) through the *ena* that articulates the internal contradictions and tensions of the *säm ena wärq* and its subject matter. Sixth, all *zäybé* (symptom, signal, way) use distanciation in that they introduce a *mängäd* (way) that starts from and moves away or "distantiates" from the given and leads to that which the given hides or represses. Seventh, the critical internal journey (vertically and laterally) that enables us to traverse the past and the present and the various Ethiopian knowledge traditions and social practices, and the critical external journey we operate with a view to develop an *andemta* of the *wärq admas* of both journeys is the unfolding of a distance that gets us beyond the *säm admas* (conventional horizon) of each. Eight, *zäräfa* (decentering, diverting, diverging, dislocation, *détournement*) involves distanciation from the given interpretation with the intention to develop an alternative problematization of *nägär* to produce an interpretation that is more potent and more comprehensive. Ninth, the process of *tirgum* (critical translation), as practiced in the *qiné* hermeneutics, involves, as we have seen, distanciation from the matter to be translated and from *nätäla* translation to enucleate the *mist'ir* (*wärq*) of the matter which is being translated. Tenth, *andemta*, as a process that pursues the *wihdät* of various *wärq admas* involves distanciation from the given *admas*. Eleventh, *mädämamät* requires distanciation from self and the other to create a space for questioning and critique in order to allow each to examine the other's and one's own presuppositions, questions, and interpretations. Twelfth, the idea of *enkän* (incompleteness and contradictions) demands distanciation without which one falls into absolutism. Thirteenth, the passage from *quanqua* (language of power) to *lissan* (language of emancipation) requires distanciation from *quanqua* through its problematization. Finally, the practice of *hiss* and *täshägagari hiss* creates distanciation through questioning of the given, the accepted, and the established, be they ideas or practices. In all cases, *antsar* reading liberates through distanciation the creative intellect and imagination (the *absho* mind), makes possible the creation of new concepts, and facilitates raising new questions on and new problematizations of the subject matter. It makes visible and comprehensible that which the hegemonic order considers impossible. Its practice requires epistemic autonomy.

35. *Wistä wäyra nibab* (ውስጠ ወይራ ንባብ) / symptomatic reading

The second concept of reading is *wistä wäyra nibab* or symptomatic reading. *Wistä wäyra* reading has deep roots in *qiné* hermeneutics. Donald Levine considers *wistä wäyra* reading "obscurantist."[171] This is a judgement that arises from the systemic historical and epistemic repression or ignorance of Ethiopian intellectual traditions, particularly *qiné* hermeneutics.

Wistä means interior. *Wäyra* refers to the wood of the wild olive tree, found in Northern and Central Ethiopia. In the past, traditional woodworkers used it for sculpting art works and decorative items and even furniture. It is wood that is hard to work upon but whose interior delivers precious wood if extracted without being splintered. Reaching its interior without fragmenting it requires interpreting and traversing skillfully the different layers and knots of the wood, its *zäybé*, as it were. This is a task that necessitates a great deal of art in reading correctly the texture and knots of the different layers of the wood as symptoms of what is inside or hidden in order to follow the right *mängäd* (መንገድ) to reach its core without fragmenting it. *Wistä wäyra* reading thus intimates a process of reading that requires interpreting symptoms to disclose that which is not immediately visible but nevertheless generates the symptoms and what appears

---

[171] Donald N. Levine, *Wax and Gold* (Chicago: University of Chicago Press, 1972), p. 10.

Critical *Qiné* Hermeneutical Concepts   **85**

as appearance. We could call *wistä wäyra* reading *zäybé*-driven reading or symptomatic reading. It is not the symptoms or the *zäybé* that give meaning to what we unearth. It is what we unearth that retroactively gives meanings to the *zäybé* or symptoms, and the *nägär* we read, meanings that we were not aware of when we started our interpretation.

Wistä wäyra reading is based on the recognition that the hegemonic order and its *quanqua* "can see and hear only what they can see and hear" and "cannot see and hear what they cannot see and hear." To unveil the existence of these structural prohibitions or impossibilities requires *wistä wäyra* reading. *Wistä wäyra* reading unearths the parameters of the hegemonic order that trace the frontiers between what can and cannot be seen and heard, what can and cannot be said and done, and what is possible and impossible. *Wistä wäyra* reading discloses not only the frontiers, parameters, and structures of exclusion but also the alternative parameters of intelligibility and possibility that are excluded and that could break through the frontiers, parameters, and structures of exclusion. It identifies the *zäybé* and follows the ways (*mängäd*) that lead to the "unheard, unseen, unsaid, and not-done" and the conditions that make them so and could overcome them.

To accomplish these tasks, *wistä wäyra* reading marshals, in addition to the other *zäybé*, three particular *zäybé*: *libsä wärq zäybé*, *säm läbäs zäybé*, and *wärqa wärq zäybé*. These three *zäybé*, together with *zäräfa*, serve as different ways (*mängäd*) for disclosing, unveiling, unmasking, and demystifying the forms and contents of the hegemonic practices, processes, discourses, and their parameters.[172] The articulation of these *zäybé* in *wistä wäyra* reading facilitates excavating the unsaid from the said, the unquestioned from the question, the unanswered from the answer, the invisible from the visible, the not-done from the done, the un-conceptualized from the conceptualized, and thus the alternative discourses and practices that are repressed by the manifest discourses and practices.

A crucial aspect of *wistä wäyra* reading is using *zäybé* as trampolines for successively raising new questions that question the previous questions and the answers generated by them during the process of interpretation, and to uncover more questions and answers.[173] Questioning is central at every stage of *wistä wäyra* reading. "Asking questions" is not a single or an isolated moment or event.

---

172 For the meaning of these *zäybé*, see above entry # 16 footnotes above.
173 On the importance of asking questions, Solomon Gebre Ghiorgis quoted in Claude Sumner, *Classical Ethiopian Philosophy* (Los Angeles: Adey Publishing Company, 1994), p. 224. Aläka Imbakom Kalewold, ቅኔ ትምህርት ና ስለ ጥቅሙ, Proceedings of the Third International Conference of Ethiopian Studies (Addis

It is systemic. Each successive question overturns or discloses the previous question as a *säm* or a partially *säm* question. *Wistä wäyra* driven questioning rescues the practice of questioning and questions from being corralled by the hegemonic coordinates of intelligibility and possibility that determine what counts and does not count as questioning and questions. The practice of asking questions recursively in *wistä wäyra* is one that leads to the invention of new metrics that enable us to expose, undermine, and replace the parameters that form and articulate questions that do not question the coordinates of possibility and intelligibility of the hegemonic order. It brings to light alternative understandings that debunk and demystify the hegemonic understanding of the *nägär*.

Concept (*tsinsä hassab*) creation is inherent to *wistä wäyra* reading. The recursive questioning generates new questions, new problems and opens up new directions, requiring the creation of new concepts (*tsinsä hassab*). The new concepts created in the process of *wistä wäyra* reading "burst through the shackles," to use an expression from the *andemta* tradition, of the manifest network of concepts that form a meaning barrier that prevent one from grasping the emancipatory surplus meanings of *nägär*. The new concepts created in the process of *wistä wäyra* reading could render visible questions, problems, and possibilities that are not visible in terms of the hegemonic concepts. Thus the *qiné* dictum: አዲስ ቃል፣ አዲስ ዓለም (*Addis qal, addis aläm* / a new concept, a new world).

A *wistä wäyra* driven critical internal journey into Ethiopia's vertical and lateral history makes possible the elucidation of emancipatory desires, interests and practices, and the creation of new concepts which could open paths to new emancipatory practices. Similarly, a *wistä wäyra* driven critical external journey into the Western (other) intellectual traditions and practices makes it possible to elicit their emancipatory surplus meanings. Of particular interest is a *wistä wäyra* reading of "historical dialectical" approaches and their treatment of reality as a dynamic structure whose political, legal, social and cultural appearances could be read to expose their invisible determinants. These approaches have "family resemblances" with *wistä wäyra nibab*, which means a critical external journey into these approaches could enable us to subject them to *zaräfa* and dislocate them from their Western context and appropriate them through *andemta* as part of *silt* (see above # 27) and emancipatory ideas.[174]

Ababa, 1966), p. 136; Kebede G/Medhin, ሳይንሳዊ የቅኔ አፈታት ስልት (Addis Ababa: Birana Matĕmia Bet, 1992).

174 On "family resemblances," Ludwig Wittgenstein, *Philosophical Investigations* (Oxford: Blackwell Publishing, 2009), p.33 #67.

36. Säwrä fitch / ሰውረ ፍች

Säwrä fitch means surplus meaning. The discussion of the above thirty five concepts indicates that a fact is not an island. Whether it is social, political, economic, cognitive, or personnel, a fact is a condensed *säm ena wärq* that could be considered as an *afla zäybé* (አፍላ ዘይቤ)—something similar to metonymy—and as such, its meaning is not fully given or is not limited to that which *quanqua* bestows on it.[175] That is, a fact is always *enkän* or incomplete, it is decentred and non-monological.

For *qiné* hermeneutics, facts cannot be circumscribed by the correspondence theory of truth, for they have meanings—surplus meanings—that go beyond the social science idea of truth as corresponding with and limited to the observable and quantifiable. Facts are *nägär* and therefore expressive. That is, they are not objective descriptions and identical to themselves as they appear to be in the Gibbonist social science hegemonic in Ethiopian Studies. Because facts are always produced in a particular historical context, they have non-observable meaning and value slopes that, though inaccessible to the "two-eyed" vision, need to be elucidated through *arat ayn* (see # 19 above) to have an adequate understanding of them. To understand facts, one must treat them as *säm ena wärq*, that is, one must contextualize them historically, which means one must go beyond their givenness. For instance, to identify a person as a judge, a mother, a politician, a *näftäña*; or an object as *injera*, a rifle, a chair; or an institution as a *shängo* (parliament), a *chäffe* (a deliberating assembly); or an activity as elections, vote, decision, and so forth, imperceptibly brings into play hidden and latent additional meanings as well as potentialities that indicate that a fact is always a result of a process of becoming. *Quanqua* and Gibbonist social science occlude this historical and expressive nature of facts. An adequate understanding of a fact demands disclosing its hidden and latent meanings and potentialities, that is, its *säwrä fitch* or surplus meaning. For *qiné* hermeneutics, unpacking the *säwrä fitch* or surplus meanings of facts is indispensable for developing a theory of emancipation immanent to Ethiopian history and society.

---

175 On *afla zäybé*, see above # 16.

2

Surplus History / *Säwrä tarik*: Immanent Critique

እንደ ሰው ተወልዶ እንድ ሰው የማይኖር
እንደ ሰው የማይሞት እንደ ሰው ሲቀበር፤
አይተሽ ሰምተሽ ታውቃለሽ ወይ ምድር
ፍረጂኝ ! መስክሪኝ ! .ይህን ክፉ በደል።
Abera Mola, ፍረጂኝ ምድረቱ [176]

(Born human but living as a non-human
Dying as a non-human but human in the grave,
Earth, see and hear this injustice
Be its witness and judge.)

This chapter discusses *säwrä tarik* in five short sections. In the first section, it argues that *säwrä tarik* emerges from a narrative that recognizes and unpacks the complex—the multiple, co-occurring, entangled, contradictory, and interacting—superposed and synchronous strands of Ethiopian history. In the second, it shows that, unlike the subject-less positivist discourse of the social sciences hegemonic in Ethiopian Studies, *säwrä tarik* is embodied knowledge. In the third, it makes a distinction between the "official people" and the "people's people" and elicits the contradictions between the two. In the fourth, it discusses *Oromummaa* as an exemplar of the *official people*'s ideology in post-2019 Ethiopia and proposes an ideology critique of its claims and practices. In the fifth, the text distinguishes "politics as the art of the possible" from "politics as the art of the impossible" and explores both in light of the goal of

---

[176] Abera Mola, ፍረጂኝ ምድረቱ, in Birhanu Gebeyhu, የአማርኛ ስነ ግጥም (Addis Ababa: Alfa Printing, 2003), p. 133.

emancipation or *arnät*. In the concluding section, it argues that *säwrä tarik* embodies the ideal of "standing upright" politically, economically, and epistemically that the radical heretic movements of 15th century Ethiopia defended. I use emancipation or *arnät* to mean political, economic, and epistemic emancipation.[177]

2.1. *Säwrä tarik* and the entangled streams of Ethiopian history

The *qiné* hermeneutical concepts discussed in the previous chapter could be productively used to interpret and understand Ethiopian history/society from the perspective of *arnät* or emancipation. I use the formulation history/society, because from the perspective of *qiné* hermeneutics one has to conjointly treat history and society as a complex and entangled *säm ena wärq* to adequately understand Ethiopian society. The three main questions that the above *qiné* hermeneutical concepts enable us to examine fruitfully are: First, what are the processes, the social and individual practices, and the beliefs that have kept and still keep Ethiopia in a state of triple domination—political oppression, economic exploitation, and epistemic servility? Second, what ideas, actions and practices could rescue Ethiopia from this triple domination and bring about an Ethiopian polity that actively and continuously minimizes unfreedoms, inequalities, injustices and epistemic vassalage, and actively and continuously creates conditions that enhance the capabilities of Ethiopians to flourish politically, materially, cognitively, socially, and culturally? Third, could one elicit an emancipatory theory that is immanent to Ethiopian history/society which could provide adequate answers to the two previous questions?

To answer these questions requires that we conduct a *qiné* hermeneutical reading of Ethiopian history/society in ways that conjugate its vertical (temporal) and lateral entangled and complex streams. By lateral, I mean the histories, practices, cultures, and institutions of Ethiopia's ethnicities. For *qiné* hermeneutics, narrating Ethiopian history/society is incomplete (*enkän*) and our understanding of it half-baked if it does not disclose these temporally and spatially entangled versions and the potentialities for social transformations they incubate. It is only in disclosing the untold narratives of these entangled versions, the numerous ways in which they interact with each other, the antagonisms and traumas that

---

177 For the meaning of *qiné* hermeneutical terms used in this and subsequent chapters, see Chapter 1.

traverse, inflect, interconnect and unite them, and the emancipatory potentialities that simmer in them that we could have an effective understanding of Ethiopian history/society that embraces both its empirical and non-empirical (the transformative potentialities) dimensions. The unpacking of the entangled versions renders visible the traces of past emancipatory possibilities that were thwarted and are haunting and will continue to haunt Ethiopia until they are actualized, and discloses the presence of unique emancipatory desires, needs, and interests as the surplus meanings or *wärq* of Ethiopian history/society. *Qiné* hermeneutics has a name for these emancipatory surplus meanings: *säwrä tarik* (ሰውረ ታሪክ) or surplus history. In short, *säwrä tarik* is the dynamic ensemble of the repressed historical emancipatory potentialities—political, economic, social, cultural, and epistemic—that exist in the present as traces of emancipatory alternatives from the past and continue to incubate in and develop subterraneously in the present. The process of enucleating *säwrä tarik* renders visible the obstacles, deadlocks, and traumas that blocked the past emancipatory possibilities. Importantly, it throws light on the social, material, and knowledge conditions that could overcome similar or new blockages in the present and future. The unpacking of the entangled versions of Ethiopian history/society and the production of *säwrä tarik* are part of the *qiné* hermeneutical practice of critical internal journey.[178] *Säwrä tarik* elicits a counter-history and a counter-knowledge that lay bare the emancipatory potentials immanent to Ethiopian history/society and that past and present hegemonic regimes occlude. It provides Ethiopians with a "cognitive mapping" of their history/society that enables them to render the possibility of emancipation imaginable and thinkable; it makes representable that which is unrepresentable in the hegemonic political, economic, and cognitive order.[179]

The process of developing *säwrä tarik* does not shy away from making counterfactual considerations.[180] For instance, let us assume counterfactually that the Tigrai People Liberation Front (TPLF) had set up in 1991 a non-ethnic, citizen-based democratic federation. Of course, the TPLF did not do so. It decided to create an ethnic federation. But the counterfactual narrative awakens us to the multiple, entangled, contradictory, and interacting alternative versions simmering in the situation of 1991 and were repressed. It thus points to other historically possible paths that were gestating at the time

---

178 Maimire Mennasemay, *Qiné Hermeneutics and Ethiopian Critical Theory* (Los Angeles: Tsehai Publishing, 2021), pp. 151-9.
179 On "cognitive mapping," Fredric Jameson, *Postmodernism, Or The Cultural Logic of Late Capitalism* (Durham: Duke University Press, 1991), p. 51.
180 Lucian Hölscher, "Virtual Historiography: Opening History Toward the Future," *History and Theory* 61, no. 1 (2022), pp. 27–42; Niall Ferguson, ed. *Virtual History: Alternatives and Conterfactuals* (New York: Basic Books, 1999).

in Ethiopian history/society. The purpose of such an exercise is not to re-write Ethiopia's history. Rather, it is to show that developing a narrative that explores the entangled and antagonistic alternative strands that are constitutive of Ethiopian history/society as a *wihdät* is necessary to grasp both its empirical and non-empirical (potentialities) dimensions, without which we fail to understand Ethiopian history/society and its immanent emancipatory possibilities. Such an understanding rescues us from three obstacles that block Ethiopia's transformations into a society that continuously minimizes unfreedoms, inequalities, injustices, and epistemic servility. First, it enables us to overcome what Addis Alemayehu calls ጥራዝ ነጣቅ (*traz nätäq*, uncritical appropriation) knowledge through a process Wiredu names "conceptual decolonization," which one could characterize, combining Addis and Wiredu, as the emancipation from the epistemic servility that we have internalized through Gibbonism and that "remain in our thinking owing to inertia rather than to our own reflective choice."[181] Second, it rescues us from a linear and monochromatic understanding of Ethiopian history/society that is blind to the alternative possibilities of transformation that are at hand but are invisible and inaudible to narratives that limit themselves to what has happened or is happening. Third, it liberates us from reducing the future to that which is possible according to the coordinates of the existing order.

Qiné hermeneutics does not limit itself to an internal critical journey into Ethiopian history/society. It also conducts an "external critical journey" into the political, social, economic, and knowledge practices of the West (and others, if need be) and critically digests them in light of the emancipatory interests and needs we produce through our critical internal journey. That is, it re-interprets, overreads and dislocates them, and appropriates the outcome from the perspective of the emancipatory interests and needs that *qiné* hermeneutics enucleates in its critical internal journey. The articulation of the internal and external critical journeys from the perspective of the emancipatory interests and needs we enucleate from our critical internal journey provides us with an *andemta* that helps us reflect on the emancipatory possibility immanent to Ethiopian history/society, the internal and external obstacles that block its materialization, and how to overcome these blockages and actualize emancipation (*arnät*, see Chapter 3).

---

[181] Addis Alemayehu, የልም ዣት (Addis Ababa: Kuraz Printing Press, 1980), p. 373, pp. 369-383; Kwasi Wiredu, "Conceptual decolonization as an imperative in contemporary African philosophy : some personal reflections," *Rue Descartes*, 36, (2002), p. 56.

Zäräfa is the principal interpretative procedure for developing *säwrä tarik* or surplus history. It marshals the various interpretative concepts discussed in Chapter 1 and conducts an *antsar nibab* (reading through distanciation) and *wistä wäyra nibab* (symptomatic reading) of *nägär*. According to *qiné* hermeneutics, *nägär* has, as we have already seen, a double dimension: its empirical aspects and its non-empirical aspects or potentialities; and both its empirical aspects and potentialities are real. Produced through *qiné* hermeneutical readings of *nägär*, *säwrä tarik* expresses and articulates the repressed emancipatory surplus meanings (*säwrä fitch*): the questions, ideas, ideals, norms, needs, aspirations, beliefs, goals, aims, interests, latencies and tendencies, potentialities and possibilities, and utopian impulses that gestate in the interstices of Ethiopia's history/society.

It is important to recognize that Ethiopian history/society is *enkän*: unfinished, contradictory, contingent, and open-ended, and accessible to thinking backward. We can interpret Ethiopian history/society to retrieve from it the emancipatory potentialities it incubated but failed to actualize. From the *qiné* hermeneutical perspective, failures of emancipatory efforts have to be considered as sources of future success in that each failure is a *säm ena wärq* that could help us grasp the why and how of the wrong decisions and actions that generated the failure, and transform these failures into conditions for generating the right decisions and actions that could actualize our emancipatory aspirations, making past failures retroactively predecessors and part of a successful actualization of the present projects of emancipation. In liberating Ethiopia's past from its failures through the enucleation of the emancipatory ideas and hopes lodging in these failures, we open the way for historically rooted forward-looking emancipatory thinking in the present, and for liberating Ethiopia's present and future from the inherited and the new political, material and intellectual adversities. For *säwrä tarik*, disavowing the emancipatory potentialities of the past and not mobilizing its failures as trampolines for reflecting on emancipation in the present leads to disavowing the possibility of emancipation in the future.

Säwrä tarik is an immanent critique of Ethiopian society that exposes Ethiopia's inner contradictions and antagonisms, identifies the emancipatory potentialities available to Ethiopians, and the agents (*säwrä ras*, surplus self) that can concretize the emancipatory potentials. It discloses the *säwrä bahil* (non-tradition), *säwrä ras* (surplus self), *säwrä hiywät* (surplus life), *yäwäl* (the commons), *minab* (concrete utopia), *arnät* (emancipation) that gestate in Ethiopian history/society. It makes the uncounted and nameless Ethiopians emerge from the shadows of Ethiopia's history/society, and throws light on the conditions that could make them the authors and actors of their history/society. At the same time, it identifies the forces and obstacles that stand in the way of emancipation (*arnät*). *Säwrä tarik* subverts the hegemonic order in that it opens the door to make possible what the hegemonic order considers impossible. It does so by exposing the unfinishedness, contradictoriness, contingency, entangled multiplicity, and open-endedness of the Ethiopian past and present, and thus of the undecidedness of Ethiopia's future, making thinkable and feasible what the extant order deems impossible: *arnät* or emancipation.

Qiné hermeneutical readings of the processes and practices of Ethiopia's history/society unearth the cognitive blind-spots in the hegemonic political, economic and epistemic practices and discourses, in the understandings and self-understandings that inform them, and the repressed emancipatory questions that inhabit them. Unearthing these cognitive blind-spots enables us to develop a *säwrä tarik* that articulates a critique of the triple internal and external domination—political, economic, and epistemic—that has shackled Ethiopians to a life of unfreedoms, inequalities, injustices, and systematically distorted knowledge of themselves and of Ethiopia's historical and social conditions and processes. Subjecting Walzer's ideas to *zäräfa*, we could say that without the political and "moral revulsion" against oppression and without the new questions and ideas on emancipation that *säwrä tarik* unveils, *arnät* is not possible.[182]

2.2. *Säwrä tarik* as embodied knowledge

> "I said: Pain and sorrow.
> He said: Stay with it. The wound is the place where the Light enters you."
> Molānā Jalāl ad-Dīn Muḥammad Rūmī, "Rūmī Quotes,"[183]

The imported social sciences in Ethiopian studies espouse a Cartesian conception of value-free and disembodied knowledge understood as data articulated in semantically defined propositions whose content corresponds to a reality assumed to be independent of the knower.[184] *Säwrä tarik* rejects the idea of a value-neutral, subject-less, disembodied and abstract knowledge.[185] Consider the following *qiné*.

---

182 A *zäräfa* of Michael Walzer, *Exodus and Revolution* (New York: Basic Books, 1986), p.40.
183 Goodreads Inc, accessed December, 11, 2019. https://www.goodreads.com/quotes/1299504-i-said-
184 Christopher G. A. Bryant, *Positivism in Social Theory and Research,* (London: Palgrave Macmillan, 1985).
185 On knowledge and the body, see entry # 27, *silt*, in Chapter 1. The idea of embodied knowledge in *qiné* hermeneutics is the outcome of a *zäräfa* that secularizes the deeply

ነፍሴ ያለዋል ደንግጣ / My soul is anxious/frightened
ከግድግዳ ሥር ተሸጉጣ / Hiding furtively under a wall
አወጣትም ብል ቾገረኝ / I could not release her
ተሥጋ እንቢ አለችኝ.[186] / Worried /being flesh, she resists.

The *qiné* speaks of the tumultuous relations between the soul (ነፍስ, *näfs*) and the body (*siga*). Amharic makes a distinction between soul (ነፍስ, *näfs*) and mind (አእምሮ, *aemero*), but it considers both to be embodied. Consider the Amharic expression for a murderer, "ነፍስ ገዳይ," *näfs gädy*. It literally means the "killer of a soul." Also consider the expression ገባኝ (*gäbañ*) meaning "I understand." It has a physical connotation in that it signifies that "what I understand enters me."[187] That is, the *siga*/body and the *näfs*/*aemero* are in "unity" in the *qiné* sense of *wihdät*, (diversity in unity). The above *qiné* develops the idea that the *siga*/body and *näfs*/*aemero* are interinvolved, that they form a *wihdät* and that their internal conflict is a *zäybé* (ዘይቤ, symptom) of their entanglement and antagonistic codependence. Each needs the other for its existence. The *qiné* brings to light the *säwrä bahil* that rejects the mind-body dualism and adopts a duality without dualism that discards the monopoly of the mind over knowledge and says that for better or worse, *näfs*/*aemero* and body/*siga* form *wihdät*; though in conflict with each other, they depend on each other to know the world and themselves, even if it is the case, as the *qiné* points out, that the communion between the two is turbulent.

According to *säwrä tarik*, the body of the Ethiopian is not a mere physical body, but a living and suffering body—the site of social, political, economic, epistemic relations, oppressions, sufferings, and contradictions—as *zäläsäña qiné* (ዘለሰኛ ቅኔ) reminds us.[188] The Ethiopian body bears the scars of past injustices

---

held belief in *qiné* culture derived from the statement: "ቃል ስጋ ሆነ / The word became flesh." (The New Testament, John 1:34). It is an idea often articulated in ዘለሰኛ *qiné*. Balambaras Mahtem Selasse Welde Mesqel, "ዘለሰኛ" in አማሪኛ ቅኔ (Addis Ababa: Artistic Printing Press, 1955, E. C.), pp.93-284. Also on embodied knowledge, Maurice Merleau-Ponty, *The phenomenology of Perception*, trans., Colin Smith (London: Routledge & Kegan Paul, 1962); Richard Kearney and Brian Treanor, eds. *Carnal Hermeneutics* (New York: Fordham University Press, 2015); G. Lakoff and M. Johnson, *Philosophy in the Flesh: The Embodied Mind and Its Challenge to Western Thought* (New York: Basic Books. 1999).

186 Balambaras Mahteme Selassie, አማርኛ ቅኔ (Addis Ababa: Artistic Printing Press, 1955 E.C.), p. 49, # 118

187 It is derived from the infinitive መግባት / *mägbat* which means to enter through a door.

188 *zäläsäña qiné* (ዘለሰኛ ቅኔ) deals with the sufferings and sorrows of life Balambaras Mahteme Selassie, አማርኛ ቅኔ (Addis Ababa: Artistic Printing Press, 1955 E.C,), pp. 92-184.

and the wounds of the present. In this sense, Ethiopian society is written in the Ethiopian body, and its sufferings are expressed in *säwrä tarik*.[189] As we have seen, *säwrä bahil*, which is subjugated knowledge expressed in local critiques, emerges as an effort to construct an alternative to the lived experience of dominated life. It is embodied knowledge and is part of *säwrä tarik*. *Säwrä tarik's* idea of embodied knowledge intimates that Ethiopian Studies cannot be separated from knowledge of the suffering Ethiopians.

The Oromiffa aphorism—*Qaroo nafti ila*, "The whole body of a person is like his eye"— catches *säwrä tarik's* idea of a body who sees the world and him/herself in the world and has knowledge of these that are in a sense constitutive of who he/she is and of the world in which he/she moves. This embodied knowledge embraces not only the observables but also, the felt, the unsaid, the undone, the invisible, and the unthought dimensions of Ethiopian realities. It thus demands a *qiné* hermeneutical approach to disclose them and unravel their meanings. Unlike the imported epistemology hegemonic in Ethiopian Studies, the Oromiffa aphorism and *qiné* hermeneutics have a carnal conception of knowledge that tells us that the "whole" Ethiopian body is an active "eye": it is a knowing body. The effable and ineffable sufferings of the Ethiopian body call for knowledge that recognizes the Ethiopian not only as a suffering body but also as a knowing agent that mobilizes the body and the mind, reason and affects via its sufferings as sources for producing knowledge that discloses the political, economic, and epistemic causes of the agent's sufferings and the possibilities and ways of overcoming them. As Rumi put it in the exergue above, *"I said: Pain and sorrow / He said: Stay with it. The wound* [the suffering] *is the place where the Light enters you."*

For *säwrä tarik* or surplus history, knowledge (*ewqät* / ዕውቀት) cannot be reduced to cognition free from values, affects and conatus or a striving towards action. Subjecting Adorno to *zäräfa* from the perspective of *zäläsaña qiné* (ዘለሰኛ ቅኔ), we can say that for *säwrä tarik*, "to lend a voice to suffering is a condition of all truth," which means that *säwrä tarik* registers as knowledge (*ewqät* / ዕውቀት) "the smallest trace of senseless suffering in" the lives of Ethiopians, and that this senseless suffering "ought not to be, that things should be different."[190] In this sense, knowledge (*ewqät* / ዕውቀት) cannot be dissociated from truth (*ewnät* /

---

189 I am subjecting Pierre Bourdieu's idea to *zäräfa*, "Habitus" is "society written into the body...." *In Other Words: Essays Towards a Reflexive Sociology*, trans. Matthew Adamson (Stanford, CA: Stanford University Press, 1990), p. 63.
190 Theodor W. Adorno, *Negative Dialectics*, trans. E. B. Ashton (London and New York: Routledge, 2005), pp. 17, 203.

ሰውነት). The importance of giving cognitive value to suffering is not, however, to cultivate something like the "ethics of compassion" that reduces Ethiopians to moral patients or targets of the moral responsibilities of moral agents. This kind of ethics seems to motivate international and national NGOs in Ethiopia, hence the failures of NGOs to tackle and eliminate the sources of social sufferings, for the ethics of compassion fails to recognize that the suffering body is also a knowing body and a history/society making agent.

From the perspective of *säwrä tarik*, these NGOs, immersed in their disembodied knowledge about poverty, pretend to combat it after having reduced it to discrete aggregated abstract data. But such an approach fails to understand that poverty is only the tip of suffering in Ethiopia, and to reduce poverty alleviation to providing services and employable skills is as futile as teaching a person on his deathbed how to earn his/her living. Poverty alleviation programs and the NGO approaches occlude and leave intact the carnal, the political, economic, and cognitive *nägär*—structures, processes, and relations—that in their very functioning necessarily generate the suffering of Ethiopians. I discuss the issue of poverty in Chapter 5.

Knowledge of suffering Ethiopians as *ewqät/ewnät* that recognizes their agency as knowers and doers awakens and mobilizes the *säwrä ras* of suffering Ethiopians and liberates the emancipatory energies and the history making capabilities that inhabit them. For *säwrä tarik*, knowledge, being embodied, is political in that the question of how we know what we know cannot be separated from the interests that are served by how we, as embodied beings, know what we know, why we want know, and how we implement what we know. We live knowledge and its consequences as embodied beings and not as disembodied minds. *Säwrä tarik* rejects the reduction of knowing Ethiopia to the production of mere propositional knowledge, the treatment of the Ethiopian body as a mere physical object, and the reduction of its actions and discourses to disembodied atomic data to be aggregated and manipulated by statistical and mathematical procedures. *Säwrä tarik* considers the emancipation of the body, reason and affects, and their mobilization indispensable dimensions of the emancipation of Ethiopian society.

Ethiopia is rich with social practices and autopoietic institutions: mutual aid associations such as *iddir, kire, zakat, iqqub and ezen*; labour-sharing associations such as *däbo, wänfal, dafo, läfenty, jigge, mol'a, säddaka* and *bayto*; conflict resolution institutions such as *araaraa, jaarsummaa, biyyaas, afärsata, shimgelina, ayyanaa*; women's associations such as *ateetee, siiqqee, sänbäte, mahibär*, and so forth. These associations intimate the existence of emancipatory aspirations, embodied knowledge, and epistemic autonomy that simmers in the actions of the powerless, for these associations are local creations that are based on the problematizations of daily problems and of possible solutions by the dispossessed. They gestate emancipatory surplus meanings that express the desire for an alternative way of life, free from the political, economic, and epistemic injustices of the extant order.[191] However, these institutions are not based on systemic problematization of and systemic answers to the existing structures of domination. They are at best partial resolutions of the immediate and particular materializations of the generalized powerlessness Ethiopians encounter on a daily basis; they leave untouched the structures and mechanisms that produce their powerlessness. *Qiné* hermeneutical readings consider these local institutions as *zäybé* (symptom) of the Ethiopia-wide structures and relations of oppression and exploitation.[192] *Qiné* hermeneutical readings elucidate them as practices of resistance whose surplus meanings are part of Ethiopia's "tradition of the oppressed" that express "subjugated knowledges" and articulate "local critiques" of the daily traumas of oppression and exploitation: they express the desire for and the effort to create an alternative way of life.

However, the failures of local actions and critiques to bring about transformative social changes, despite the desire for and the effort to create an alternative way of life, point to the importance of understanding Ethiopian issues from the perspective of totality (*wihdät*) and not as individual or non-systemic issues or as aggregates of discrete value-free empirical data. The totality (*wihdät*) of the Ethiopian condition embraces both the empirical existence of this condition and the emancipatory potentialities that simmer in the antagonisms that articulate this condition. For *säwrä tarik*, reality is not limited to the empirically given; emancipatory potentiality, conceived as the *antsar t'mir* (አንጻር ትምር) or the "determinate negation" of the historically specific Ethiopian society, is as real as the empirically given. *Säwrä tarik* considers the local conditions and issues, the local critiques and subjugated knowledge as *zäybé*, and digs out from them and the lived experiences of Ethiopians the social structures and processes that generate the systemic nation-wide network of oppression and exploitation, the systemic contradictions that characterize them, and the systematic aspirations and possibilities for emancipation.[193]

---

191 For a study of these associations from a *qiné* hermeneutical perspective, see Maimire Mennasemay, *Qiné Hermeneutics and Ethiopian Critical Theory* (Los Angeles: Tsehai Publishing, 2021), Chapter 10.
192 *Zäybé* means also *mängäd* (መንገድ, the way) in the sense of the "way" or the symptom that leads to the real cause. See Chapter 1 #16 above.
193 Given Ethiopia's induction into the global capitalist process as a subaltern society located at the level of the extractive, cash crop production, and manufacturing of

Overcoming meaningfully oppression and exploitation thus requires going beyond the local practices of resistance and overcoming the general causes that generate the diverse local sufferings and local critique and subjugated knowledge.

2.3. *Säwrä tarik* and the *people's people* and the *official people*

Unlike the linear temporality that structures the narratives of the hegemonic discourse in Ethiopia, *säwrä tarik* has a triple temporal *andem* or a triple temporality—the repressed alternative "future of the past" that thinking backward reveals, the alternative future of the present gestating in the present, and the alternative future to the future the hegemonic order projects.[194] *Säwrä tarik*'s temporality is non-synchronous with official time; it constitutes an alternative temporal *andem*, that of emancipation and therefore of social transformation, while the official time articulates the temporality of domination and of the naturalization of this domination. The repressed alternatives of the past and the failed attempts to create a better Ethiopian society leave traces of emancipatory possibilities as indicators of a possible alternative future that exists in the present. They haunt the Ethiopian present as deferred emancipatory possibilities and are waiting for the intervention of Ethiopians to conjure the unfulfilled emancipatory hopes into reality. For *säwrä tarik*, one cannot disavow the past without disavowing the future.

The Oromiffa proverb—*Kan darbe yaadatani, isa gara fuula dura itti yaaddu*, which translates, "in remembering the past, the future is remembered"—draws

---

the global capitalist supply chain, *säwrä tarik* calls for a *zäräfa* and *antsar* and *wistä wäyra* readings of Marxism to expand its interpretative range without loosing its rootedness in Ethiopian history/society. Note that the structure of *säm ena wärq* intimates the idea of an appearance (the *säm* articulated in *quanqua*), and of a hidden or repressed presence of another level (the *wärq* articulated in *lissan*), that, when unveiled, developed, and applied to the *säm*, transforms the *säm* and gives it form and content radically different to that which appears as appearance (the *säm*) in the first place. The practice of *qiné* hermeneutics intimates that the relation between the two—the *säm* and the *wärq*—is dialectical and not mechanical in that the relation between the two is mediated by *zäybé* that are themselves historically formed.

194 The formulation is a *zäräfa* of Ricoeur's reflection on temporality. Paul Ricoeur, *Time and Narrative*, vol. 1, trans. Kathleen McLaughlin and David Pellauer (Chicago, IL: University of Chicago Press, 1984), pp. 7-30. On "future in the past," Ernst Bloch, *The Principle of Hope*, vol. I., trans. Neville Plaice, Stephen Plaice and Paul Knight (Cambridge, Mass.: The MIT Press, 1986), pp. 9, 154, 198-205.

our attention to the important point of the emancipatory link *säwrä tarik* makes between past and present emancipatory aspirations. This idea can be described by a *zäräfa* of Marx to whom the issue of emancipation "is not a question of drawing a great mental dividing line between past and future, but of *realising* the thoughts of the past."[195] The emancipatory "thoughts of the past" embedded in the non-synchronous temporality of *säwrä tarik* live in the emancipatory hopes and dreams of the present as unfulfilled promises to be redeemed, as challenges to the limits of the present, as traces of doors waiting for Ethiopians to make them visible and push them open.

Säwrä tarik's non-synchronous temporality implies that, politically considered, there are two people in Ethiopia: the "official people" (ገዥ ሕዝብ / *gäzi hizb*) and the "people's people"(ተራ ሕዝብ / *tära hizb*).[196] Though the two "peoples" live together "externally" *at* the same time, they do not all live, however, "*in* the same time."[197] Each has its own temporal dimension: the first, the temporality of domination; the second, the temporality of suffering and emancipation. The *official people* or the *gäzi hizb* is made up of the Ethiopian ruling elites, organized on ethnic lines since 1991. The Ethiopian ruling elites or the *official people* are composed of those who are part of the state institutions and control the powers of the state, and those who are in the economic arena, politics, the media, religious institutions, academics, the organic intellectuals and fellow travelers, and so forth, and support the existing political system. The *official people* universalize their interests as the interests of all Ethiopians.

Since the 1995 Constitution that made ethnicity the constitutive identity of every Ethiopian, the *official people* see Ethiopians not as citizens but as "ethnicities" or as ethnic populations, hence, the reference to Ethiopians in the plural as peoples (ሕዝቦች, *hizbotch*) in the 1995 Constitution and official

---

195 Letter from Marx to Arnold Ruge. https://www.marxists.org/archive/marx/works/1843/ letters/ 43_09.htm. Accessed 6/27, 2019.
196 A *zäräfa* of Badiou's discussion of the concept of "people." Alain Badiou, "Twenty-Four Notes on the Uses of the Word "People "," in Alain Badiou, et.al., *What is a People?* , trans. Jody Gladding, (New York: Columbia University Press, 2016). He writes on page 17, "But isn't there also the "people" in the sense that, even without ever activating an assembled detachment, is nevertheless not truly included in the contingent of "the sovereign people" as constituted by the state? We will answer "yes." It makes sense to speak of "the people's people" as they are *what the official people, in the guise of the state, regards as nonexistent.*" Italics in the text..
197 On the distinction between "living at the same time" and "living in the same time," see Ernst Bloch, *Heritage of Our Times*, trans. Neville and Stephen Plaice (London: Polity Press, 1991), p. 97.

discourse.[198] The 1995 Constitution has made, through its articles 8, 39, and 47, ethnic identity the "black hole" of Ethiopian society into which every question and answer, every problem and solution is sucked and crushed into ethnic issues; it has established ethnicity as the "event horizon" that has captured political, legal, economic, and educational rights, institutions and practices and made them subservient to ethnic interests.

The post-1991 *official people*, made up of ethnic elites, have confiscated the question of identity and defined it as a question of "being" or "essence," and established a Constitution (1995) that articulates political, legal, economic, social, educational, religious and cultural issues in terms of ethnic categories, thus de-historicizing identity. The *official people* articulate all experiences as ethnic experiences and all rights as primarily ethnic rights. Under the pretext of enforcing the ethnic rights established in articles 8, 39, and 47 of the Constitution, all individual rights and freedoms are flouted systematically. Thus, all the post-1995 Ethiopian governments, The EPRDF (1995-2018) and Prosperity Party (2019…), carry out systematic arbitrary arrests, detentions, enforced disappearances, imprisonment, torture, abduction of critics and opponents of their policies, use the armed forces to settle political issues (the war in Tigray, 2020-2022) and in Amhara (2023…), and repeatedly resort to rule by "state of emergency" under the pretext of ensuring "peace," with peace reduced to maintaining the ethnic political order.[199] As we shall see below in the discussion of *Oromummaa* and the critique of *kilil* in Chapter 4, the 1995 Constitution has instituted an ethnic federalism made up of ethnic *kilils* that generates and legitimates "necropower": the deployment of abjection, humiliation, violence, social and physical death as expressions of ethnic sovereignty and governmentality,

---

198 There is no other country in the world whose Constitution refers to its people in the plural "peoples," even though there are African and Asian countries that are as, if not more, multi-ethnic than Ethiopia. In fact, Ethiopia is the only ethnic federation in existence at the present time, and seems to be proving that an ethnic federation has political disintegration and authoritarianism built into it.

199 See the regular reports of the Ethiopian Human Rights Commission (EHRC), of Amnesty International and Human Rights Watch since 1991 and particularly since 2020. https://ehrc.org/. https://www.ohchr.org/en/press-releases/2023/05/un-committee-against-torture-publishes-findings-brazil-colombia-ethiopia. Ethiopian Human Rights Commission, Press Release on Enforced Disappearance, June5, 2023, https://www.ehrc.org/. Accessed 6/6/2023. The Prosperity Party, the governing party, was founded in 2019 by Dr. Abiy Ahmed who, after the demise of the TPLF, was chosen by the EPRDF in 2018 as the Prime Minster of Ethiopia, replacing PM. Hailemariam Desalegn.

directed against another ethnic group a given *kilil's official people* consider an existential threat to their power.[200]

The *people's people* or the *tära hizb* are the oppressed, the exploited, the poor, the marginalized, and the uncounted. They are, irrespective of their ethnicity, religion and region, against the exclusions, oppression and exploitation that afflict their lives. One could see this in transethnic organization such as the Confederation of Ethiopian Trade Union (CETU). In CETU, class interests trump ethnic identity, despite the ethnic regimes' efforts to ethnicize it since the proclamation of the 1995 Constitution.[201] *Iddir* and *iqqub*, which are mutual aid associations organized by the *people's people*, are trans and multi-ethnic in urban areas.[202] The demand of the *tära hizb* to be recognized as "citizens" or *zega* (ዜጋ) is inscribed in their efforts to create "secondary communities" such as *iddir* and *iqqub* to partially alleviate their social suffering.[203]

The demands of the *tära hizb* cannot be met by the 1995 Constitution and the legal, political, educational, and economic institutions and practices that implement it, because these treat the *tära hizb* as an aggregate of ethnicities wherein each Ethiopian is defined as a sample of his or her ethnicity and not as a citizen or *zega*. Thus, each Ethiopian is expected to accept and put ethnic interests above class and individual interests. Those who refuse to do so are accused of undermining the ethnic constitutional order and are subjected to

---

200 On necropower, Achille Mbembe, *Necropolitics* (Durham: Duke University Press, 2019), pp. 66-92.
201 Alarmed by the transethnic nature and demands of the CETU, The Prosperity Party government prevented it from holding its planned May 1, 2023 Labour Day march.
202 According to a Report by the Ministry of Capacity Building, *iddirs* have nationally around 39 million numbers, and Addis Ababa alone has around 7,000 *iddirs*, and *iqqubs* have some 21 million members. Ministry of Capacity Building, *Civil Society Organizations' Capacity Building Program*, (Addis Abeba,2004). http://www.crdaethiopia.org/PolicyDocuments/MCB%20CSO-CBP%20Program%20Document%20 (Zero%20Draft).pdf. Accessed 7/ 14/2022. See also on *iddir*, Desalegn Amsalu, Laura Bisaillon, Yordanos Tiruneh, *I Have Risen from the Place I Always Used to Be': An Annotated Bibliography of the Ethiopian Iddir* ,https://papers.ssrn.com/sol3/papers. On *iqqub*, see Temesgen Teshome, *Role and Potential of 'Iqqub' in Ethiopia*, http://etd.aau.edu.et/handle/123456789/26579. Accessed 7/15/2022.
203 The surplus meaning of these associations—the transition from a primary to a secondary community—resides in the fact that there is a move towards individualization insofar as membership is not based on primary identities but on the individual's decision to become a member and act for the good of the association with the other members. CETU is the modern example of this. On secondary community, Slavoj Žižek, *The Ticklish Subject* (London : Verso, 1999), p. 90.

oppressive measures such as arrests, detentions, enforced disappearances.[204] It is important to note the political cynicism of the *official people* in the post-1991 period: they oscillate between the identity of Ethiopian citizenship or *zega* and their ethnic identity, depending on the interests and power positions they pursue, while forcefully confining the *tära hizb* to their ethnic identities. Official history and politics in Ethiopia are the history and politics that cater to the *official people*'s representation of Ethiopian history, reality, and interests. Though the 1995 Constitution (article 8) claims that "sovereign power resides" in ethnicities (it uses the euphemisms "Nations, Nationalities and Peoples"), in practice, "sovereign power resides" in the ethnic rulers of each ethnic *kilil* and not in the people of the *kilil*. The *official people* mobilize ethnic identity to garner the economic and political benefits of "modernization," and to enhance their social status, wealth and power.[205] They mask their oppressive and exploitive practices as ethnic self-determination, development, and democracy.

The 1995 Constitution and the establishment of a federation based on ethnic separation has radically altered the Ethiopian political *admas* or *zeitgeist* by replacing citizenship with ethnic identity as the foundation of rights and by creating political arrangements and spatial configurations (ክልል / *kilil*) wherein an ethnic group is made to overlap with an ethnic space, generating atavistic ethnic nationalism, ethnic exclusivism, and the sacralization of ethnic space. Inevitably, the 1995 Constitution and its ethnic federation have made ethnic "othering" a permanent feature of the political life of Ethiopians such that one could say that the Constitution has transformed Ethiopia into a "society of enmity," to us Mbembe's expression.[206] One could say the *official people* have politically, culturally, and legally set up Ethiopians "to give up thinking for the sake of being" (ethnic identity), precipitating them into the thoughtless comfort of the closed horizon of their ethnic wombs, from where the demonizing and persecution of the ethnic other appear indispensable for surviving.[207] The establishment of ethnic identity as the bedrock of political, social, economic, educational, cultural and intellectual life has allowed the *official people* to project and universalize their interests and needs as the

---

204 https://www.ohchr.org/en/press-releases/2023/05/un-committee-against-torture-publishes-findings-brazil-colombia-ethiopia. EHRC, Press Release on Enforced Disappearance, June 5, 2023, https://www.ehrc.org/. Accessed 6/6/2023.
205 For a list of the new millionaires in Ethiopia, https://accgroup.vn/top-20-ethiopian-richest. Accessed 8/9/2023.
206 Achille Mbembe, *Necropolitics* (Durham: Duke University Press, 2019), pp. 42-65.
207 As Žižek points out, subordinating thinking to being leads to fascism. Slavoj Žižek, *The Ticklish Subject. The absent centre of political ontology* (London: Verso, 1999), pp. 9-22.

interests and needs of the *people's people* and thus mask the exploitative practices they inflict on the *people's people*.

The ethnic *official people* have plunged the *people's peoples* into a "naked crisis." I say a "naked crisis," because the displacement of the universal principles of freedom, equality, knowledge, justice, and citizenship and their replacement with ethnic politics, ethnic closure, ethnic hierarchy, ethnic purity, ethnic justice, ethnic knowledge, and ethnic identity has triggered a vertiginous downward spiral towards the emergence of a "failed state."[208] The seeds of a "failed state" were sown in 1991 with the formation of the TPLF-dominated EPRDF regime and its ethnicization of Ethiopian politics and life.[209] The fall of the TPLF regime in 2018 sparked the hope of a transition to a citizenship-based democracy that will give voice to the *people's people* and recognize individual rights and liberties as the foundation of political life. However, despite the eviction from power of the TPLF, the ethnicity-centred Constitution and the ethnic federation it imposed on Ethiopians remained in force. The government that succeeded the TPLF—the Prosperity Party (PP) government—kept not only the TPLF-penned Constitution and ethnic federation, but also the TPLF/EPRDF's organizational criterion: ethnic identity. The new governing national political party, the PP, formed in 2019 to replace the EPRDF, adopted a political party system similar to that of the EPRDF in that it is a collection of ethnic parties, each appending the epithet Prosperity Party to its ethnic name.

The transition from the EPRDF to the PP regime was simply a transition from one group of ethnic *official people* to another. In the same way that the TPLF dominated the EPRDF regime, it became clear with time that the Oromo Prosperity Party, a major ethnic member of the PP, dominates the ruling party (the PP) and the new Ethiopian government. Consequently, the ethnic conflicts inherited from the TPLF reign intensified in new forms, leading to war in Tigray (2020-2022), in Amhara (2023…), and ethnic cleansing in Oromo areas, Beni Shangul Gumuz, Gambella, and the Southern Nations, Nationalities, and Peoples' Region. The shoots of state failure that sprouted

---

208 According to the Fragile State Index of 2023, Ethiopia (100.4) is among the eleven failed states, boxed in between two other failed states, Haiti (102.9) and Myanmar (100.2). The higher the score, the more failed a state is. https://fragilestatesindex.org/. Accessed 6/16/2023.

209 EPRDF is the acronym for Ethiopian Peoples Revolutionary Democratic Front. Meles Zenawi passed away in 2012 but the EPRDF survived until 2019. The Prosperity Party replaced it.

under the TPLF, which Ethiopians thought were nipped in the bud in 2018, multiplied and developed under the PP regime.[210]

2.4. *Säwrä tarik*, ideology critique, and *Oromummaa*

One of the ideological tools that the ethnic *official people* use to impose their hegemony over the *people's people* is "the invention of tradition" in the sense that Eric Hobsbawm has discussed.[211] An exemplar of an "invented tradition" under the Prosperity Party (PP) regime is *Oromummaa*.[212] I treat it as an exemplar because, first, it is the ideology of the most important ethnic Prosperity Party—the Oromo Prosperity Party (OPP)—that currently dominates the national PP

---

210 Ethiopian Human Rights Commission, በኢትዮጵያ እየጨመረ የመጣው ሰዎችን አስገድዶ የመሰወር (Enforced Disappearance) ድርጊት በአፋጣኝ ሊቆም ይገባል June 5, 2023 https://www.ehrc.org/ Accessed 6/15/2023. Ethiopian Human Rights Council, መንግስት እየተፈጸሙ ላሉ የስብዓዊ መብቶች ጥሰቶች በቂ ትኩረት ይስጥ! . Accessed 6/24/2023.

211 Eric Hobsbawm, "Introduction: Inventing Traditions," pp. 1-14, in *The Invention of Tradition*, eds., Eric Hobsbawm and Terence Ranger (Cambridge: Cambridge University Press, 1983), pp. 1-14.

212 For the constitutive elements of the *Oromummaa* ideology, see Asafa Jalata, "The Concept of Oromummaa and Identity Formation in Contemporary Oromo Society" (2007); https://trace.tennessee.edu/cgi/viewcontent.cgi?article=1009&context=utk_socopubs. Asafa Jalata, "Promoting and Developing Oromummaa" (2012). https://trace.tennessee.edu/utk_socopubs/83. Accessed 6/5/2014. Asafa Jalata, *Oromia and Ethiopia: State Formation and Ethnonational Conflict, 1868-2004* (Trenton, NJ: Red Sea Press, 2005); Asafa Jalata, *The Oromo Movement and Imperial Politics: Culture and Ideology in Oromia and Ethiopia* (Lexington Books, 2005). Asafa Jalata, *Oromo Nationalism and the Ethiopian Discourse: The Search for Freedom and Democracy* (Trenton, NJ. ʃRed Sea Press, 1998). Professor Asafa Jalata, an Ethiopian Oromo who teaches at the University of Tennessee, is the progenitor and articulate and prolific voice of *Oromummaa*. Gemetchu Megerssa & Aneesa Kassam, *Sacred Knowledge Traditions of the Oromo of the Horn of Africa* (Fifth World Publications, 2020). Bonnie K. Holcomb, "Oromummaa as a Construct or Peace Through Balance: Oromummaa in the Twenty-First Century," *Presentation prepared for the Oromo Studies Association Conference Roundtable*," Washington, DC, July 27-28, 2002. Gemetchu Megerssa & Aneesa Kassam, *Sacred Knowledge Traditions of the Oromo of the Horn of Africa* (Fifth World Publications, 2020). P.T.W. Baxter, Jan Hutlin and Alessandro Triulzi, eds., *Being and Becoming Oromo* (Lawrenceville, NJ.: The Red Sea Press, 1996). In a way comparable to the studies of Belgian colonial "social scientists" who pinpointed and accentuated the minor differences between the Tutsi and Hutu, some Western scholars appear to be engaged in a comparable enterprise that pinpoints and accentuates differences between the Oromo and the Amhara. Mahmood Mamdani, *When Victims Become Killers: Colonialism, Nativism, and The Genocide in Rwanda* (Princeton: Princeton University Press, 2001).

and the government led by PM. Dr. Abiy Ahmed, and, second, many ethnic elites from other *kilils* have resorted to adopting aspects of *Oromummaa*'s ideas and practices of exclusive ethnicity. I will conduct an ideology critique of *Oromummaa* using the concepts of *säwrä tarik*. I draw *Oromummaa*'s main constitutive ideas to understand the inordinately intense ethnic political violence that has befallen Ethiopia since 2019—the year the Oromo Prosperity party and the national Prosperity Party were formed.

Oromummaa was first formulated at the beginning of the twenty-first century by Western-educated Oromo ethno-nationalist intellectuals residing in the West.[213] *Oromummaa*—an "invented tradition" from afar—is the Oromo *official people*'s ideological bricolage made up of claims about Oromo ethnic purity, homogeneity, hermetic identity, and narratives of victimization. It asserts an Oromo monolithic group identity essentialism—an essence that *Oromummaa* calls "Oromoness" and that Oromos supposedly share and makes the Oromo a single undifferentiated collectivity.[214] It proposes to cleanse the Oromo *kilil* and other areas *Oromummaa* claims to have been the land of the Oromo from non-Oromos and alien religions, Christianity and Islam, which it considers to have polluted the purity of the Oromo identity, culture and soul.[215] The true religion of the Oromo is claimed to be *Waaqeffannaa*. As Addisalem Bekele Gemeda puts it, *Waaqeffannaa* is not an "imported" religion and belongs to the "Cush" people, implying the unfounded and controversial differentiation and categorization of Ethiopian culture in terms of Cushite and Semite. He writes,

> The source of Waaqeffannaa religion is the culture, philosophy, knowledge and civilization of the Cush people. It is not imported from other's culture, philosophy and civilization just like other modern religions which were introduced to the Oromo people in different times (Orthodox Christianity in the 4th century and Islam in the 7th century). Orthodox Christianity is originated from Israeli culture and civilization whereas Islam from Arab culture and civilization. The very simple evidence here is to look at the name of the followers of these respective religions.[216]

---

213 Asafa Jalata, "The Concept of Oromummaa, *supra*; Asafa Jalata, ""Promoting and Developing Oromummaa," *supra.*
214 Anders Berg-Sørensen, Nils Holtug & Kasper Lippert-Rasmussen, (2010) "Essentialism vs. Constructivism: Introduction," *Distinktion: Journal of Social Theory*, 11:1, (2010), pp. 39-45.
215 There is no historical record of a country or an Ethiopian province called Oromia, and for that matter, Amhara. But inventing a name for a non-existent country is quite common among atavistic ethno-nationalists.
216 Addisalem Bekele Gemeda, "Indigenous religion and being human: The case of 'Waaqeffannaa' religion of the Oromo people," *International Journal of Academic Research and Development*, Vol. 3, 2 (2018}) pp. 566-574. Quoted text, p. 571.

The above statements about *Waaqeffannaa*, Christianity, and Islam are articles of faith for the followers of *Oromummaa*. Leaving aside "the simple evidence" the writer leans on to make such a sweeping generalization, one must note that Christianity and Islam are present among the Oromos for centuries and the absolute majority of Oromos adhere to these two religions.[217] *Oromummaa* entertains the fantasy of turning the historical clock back and resurrecting the putatively lost ethnic, cultural, and spiritual purity and homogeneity of the Oromo. *Oromummaa* claims the existence of a primordial connection that ties Oromos together and transcends class, religion, gender and region; it asserts that it "eliminates differences" among the Oromos, and that it "goes beyond culture and history," and projects a quasi-impermeable identity boundary between the Oromo and other ethnicities.[218] There is a kind of mysticism running through *Oromummaa* that banishes doubt and uncertainty about the assertions it makes and excludes a rational discussion of its claims. As we shall see below, whether one is an Oromo or not, to question *Oromummaa*'s claims is to be *ipso facto* an enemy of the Oromo.

Oromummaa laments that the ethnic purity and unity of the Oromo and their culture have been polluted and stunted by "Ethiopian colonialism" whose agents are claimed to be the "Amhara," hence the Oromo *official people*'s pursuit of ethnic cleansing in the Oromo *kilil*, and the pursuit of "ethnic self-determination" as a venue to secession from Ethiopia in the sense of article 39 of the 1995 Constitution. In the mean time, *Oromummaa* is wielded by the Oromo *official people* to accrue power and wealth at the expense of the Oromo *people's people* by diverting the latter from their emancipatory needs and by focusing their attention on the necessity of evicting non-Oromos from areas inhabited by Oromos as a necessary measure to ensure a better future for the Oromo. Given its monolithic identity essentialism and the mystical way it conceives Oromo unity and identity, it is not surprising that *Oromummaa* entertains a political ideal that projects politics among the Oromos as a process without agonism and antagonism.[219] This has two political implications, fully

---

217 Asafa Jalata, "The Concept of Oromummaa, *supra*; Asafa Jalata, ""Promoting and Developing Oromummaa," *supra*.
218 Jalata, Asafa, "The Concept of Oromummaa, *supra*.
219 "Oromummaa as an intellectual and ideological vision rejects the position of Ethiopianists, collaborationists, modernists, and mainstream Marxists and places the Oromo man and woman at the center of analysis and at the same time goes beyond Oromo society and aspires to develop global *Oromummaa* by contributing to the solidarity of all oppressed peoples and by promoting the struggle for national self-determination, statehood, sovereignty, and multinational democracy. Hence, *Oromummaa* is a complex and dynamic national and global project and opposes the ideologies of racism, classism, and sexism from without and from within."

assumed by the followers of *Oromummaa*. Any conflict within the Oromo community is considered to have been fomented by outsiders, always identified as the Amhara; second, Oromos who reject the *Oromummaa* depiction of exclusive Oromo identity are considered collaborators with the enemy—the Amhara being the figure of the enemy in *Oromummaa*—and subjected to exclusion, to social and even physical death.[220] From the perspective of *Oromummaa*, to be an Oromo who does not believe in the claims and goals of *Oromummaa* is to become an existential threat to the Oromo, with all that such a characterization entails.

The Oromo *official people*, within and outside the state, present *Oromummaa* as the essence of Oromo culture that provides a political prescription for the present and the future. From the perspective of *säwrä tarik*, one must however make a distinction between the "invented tradition" of *Oromummaa* and the historically existing culture of the Oromo. The "invented tradition" of *Oromummaa* does not have much to do with the history and culture of the Oromo. Oromo society has a historically formed cultural aquifer that is deep, contradictory and complex, and which expresses itself variously and partially in institutions, practices, ideas, and beliefs. It is historical, multi-dimensional, and pluri-vocal.

Säwrä tarik intimates that this historical cultural aquifer serves as a source of ideas on how to cope with a changing world. In the process of coping with historical changes, the cultural aquifer is fed with new questions, new practices, new ideas and new possibilities that influence and modulate its composition, viscosity, contact angles, capillary actions, internal tensions and contradictions, and movement. Historical vagaries thus bring about certain changes to the cultural aquifer even if it is the case that the changes appear to be slow and even imperceptible empirically, though there could also be bursts of change. Like all historical cultural aquifers, Oromo culture has universalist and emancipatory dimensions, though the Oromo *official people* routinely repress these. That is, Oromo culture is not static. Beliefs, practices, questions, and interpretations that were once dominant either change or fade away, as is the case with the waning of *gada*, and new questions, practices, ideas, and interpretations emerge, albeit, slowly. The intentional simplification of the Oromo historical cultural

---

Asafa Jalata, "Promoting and Developing Oromummaa" *supra*. The distance between the rhetoric of democracy and the practice of Oromummaa in Ethiopia by its followers reminds one of the distance between the rhetoric of socialist democracy and the practice of actually existing socialism in the former communist regimes. The former communist regimes also talked a lot about "the solidarity of all oppressed peoples."

220 Asafa Jalata, "Promoting and Developing Oromummaa" *supra*.

aquifer by the inventors of *Oromummaa* has devastating consequences for Ethiopians, and, particularly, the Oromos. For example, the inventors of *Oromummaa* have radically impoverished the complex historical *gada* by funneling it into their makeshift and one-dimensional invented tradition. Though *gada* has faded away as a living and functioning institution—precisely the reason why the inventors of *Oromummaa* were able to caricature it so brazenly—the historical *gada* has a depth and complexity from which one could enucleate emancipatory surplus meanings through a critical hermeneutical labour, a task that is yet to be undertaken and which requires recognizing the wealth of the Oromo cultural aquifer as well as the empirical death of *gada* in order to save its spirit.[221] From the perspective of *säwrä tarik*, eliciting the emancipatory potential of the Oromo cultural aquifer requires questioning its empirical manifestations and treating them as *säm ena wärq* or *nägär*, not taking them at their face value and subjecting them to a critical internal journey. This need for questioning and critical hermeneutical labour is what the Oromo tradition intimates in part in its "eight generation rule."[222] It is a rule that could be interpreted to mean that we should not de-historicize and fetishize either the historical cultural aquifer or its empirical expressions. The empirical expressions are historically contingent and are systematically moulded by *the official people* to serve their interests. On the present lack of questioning and absence of critical hermeneutical labour in understanding Oromo culture, and the ensuing simplification and fetishization of Oromo culture, I agree with Eshete Gemeda's remark that in the study of Oromo culture, "scholars provide surface level explanations…" only.[223] *Oromummaa* is the outcome of this lack of questioning and critical hermeneutical labour, of the prevalence of "surface level explanations," and of the de-historicization, simplification, ossification and fetishization of Oromo culture for the purpose of gaining power over the Oromo *people's people*.

Historical events and processes indicate the fantasy nature of the claims of *Oromummaa*. Mohammed Hassen shows in his historical studies of the Oromo in Ethiopia that, since at least the thirteenth century, the Oromo have been an

---

221 A critical internal journey into *gada* generates important emancipatory surplus meanings that are part of *säwrä tarik*. For a tentative exploration of the surplus meanings of gada, see Maimire Mennasemay, *Qiné Hermeneutics and Ethiopian Critical Theory* (Los Angeles: Tsehai Publishing, 2021), Chapter 9.
222 Asmarom Legesse, *Oromo Democracy: An Indigenous African Political System* (Trenton, NJ: The Red Sea Press, 2006), p.232.
223 Eshete Gemeda, *African Egalitarian Values and Indigenous Genres: A Comparative Approach to the Functional and Contextual Studies of Oromo National Literature in a Contemporary Perspective* (Berlin: LIT Verlag Muster, 2012), p. 136.

integral part of the historical process that led to the formation of present-day Ethiopia.[224] In addition to commercial relations and peaceful inter-regional demographic movements, the conflicts of the 13th, 14th, 15th centuries, and particularly the one of the 16th century, opened the door for important population movements from South to North and eventually from North to South.[225] From at least the 13th century on, the intermingling of the Oromo and the inhabitants of northern, central, and southern Ethiopia have led to trans-ethnic cultural diffusions, cultural cross-pollinations, political upheavals, political and cultural oscillations, changing political alliances, economic exchanges, and interpersonal relations that led the Oromo and other ethnicities—the Amhara, the Somali, the Sidama, the Afar, the Tigrayans, and the inhabitants of central and southern Ethiopia—to be jointly active agents in the conflicted creation of the Ethiopian political and cultural landscape embracing the territory we now call Ethiopia.[226] These historical processes had effects on the cultural aquifer of Ethiopia's ethnicities and contributed to the development of a commonly-shared Ethiopian cultural aquifer. The shared cultural commonality of the latter is reflected empirically in the overlapping affinities, "family resemblances," and the contiguity of practices, values and beliefs one finds between many Ethiopian ethnic cultures.[227] These practices relate to modes of communication, beliefs and ideas, mutual aid institutions, family practices (*gudifecha*), labour-sharing practices, conflict resolution mechanisms, music and dance, cuisine and clothing, magical practices and superstitions (spirit possessions), myths, hopes and aspirations, and religions, particularly Christianity and Islam to whom the quasi-totality of Ethiopians adhere. It is the commonly-shared Ethiopian cultural aquifer that helps us understand the strong

---

224 Mohammed Hassen, *The Oromo and the Christian Kingdom of Ethiopia 1300–1700* (Oxford: James Currey, 2015); Mohamed Hassen, *The Oromo of Ethiopia: A History 1570-1860* (Cambridge: Cambridge University Press, 1990).

225 Sihab ad-Din Ahmadbin' Abd al-Qader bin Salem bin Utman, *The Conquest of Abyssinia (16th Century)*, trans. Paul Lester Stenhouse, annotations by Richard Pankhurst (Los Angeles: Tsehai Publishing, 2003). Harold G. Marcus, *A History of Ethiopia* (Berkeley: University of California Press, 2002), p. 15. See also Chapter 4 below.

226 Mordechai Abir, *The Era of the Princes: The Challenge of Islam and the Re-unification of the Christian empire, 1769-1855* (London: Longmans, 1968); Bilaten Geta Hiruy Welde Selassie, የኢትዮጵያ ታሪh (Addis Ababa: Central printing Press, 1999); Harold Marcus, A *History of Ethiopia* (Berkeley: University of California Press, 2002); Bahru Zewde, *A History of Modern Ethiopia, 1855-1974* (London: James Curry, 1991); Pauk Henze, *Layers of Time: A History of Ethiopia* (London: Hurst & Company, 2000).

227 On "family resemblances," Ludwig Wittgenstein, *Philosophical Investigations* (Oxford: Blackwell Publishing, 2009), p.33 #67.

family resemblances between many of the cultural *nägär* or social practices of various Ethiopian ethnicities. It also makes possible the eliciting of *säwrä tarik* both vertically and laterally.

The Oromo *official people* have invented a tradition—*Oromummaa*—that denies this rich entangled, and complex historical, political, and cultural formation of Ethiopia and its constituent ethnicities, including the Oromo. From the perspective of *säwrä tarik*, *Oromummaa* scotomizes the historical, political, economic, and cultural mutual interactions, often mediated by conflicts, and the numerous cross-fertilizations among Ethiopian ethnic cultures. It occludes the historical, multi-dimensional and polysemous nature of Oromo culture, of the other ethnic cultures with which it interacted, and of the multi and trans-ethnic outcomes that constituted in various ways the Ethiopian cultural aquifer. From the perspective of *säwrä tarik*, *Oromummaa* operates a dangerous simplification, ossification, and impoverishment of Oromo culture and history, of the history and cultures of other ethnicities with which it interacted for centuries, and of Ethiopian history, politics, and culture which are the outcome of these interactions.

The Oromo *official people*'s politics of ethnic self-determination is rooted in the rhetorical use of the concept of "colonialism" that fallaciously and ahistorically projects onto the pre-1974 Ethiopian feudal history the material (political, economic, legal) and ideological practices of capitalist European colonialism.[228] Only Gibbonism or epistemic colonialism justifies the projection of a historical characteristic of capitalist Europe onto feudal Ethiopia. A counter-factual proposition shows the absurdity of such a projection. Consider projecting the practices and beliefs of Feudal Ethiopia on European capitalist society of the 19th century to explain the workings of the political economy of France or England. The absurdity of the conclusion we reach from such an approach is

---

228 The Oromo *kilil* Constitution (*Magalata Oromiya*, 1995) starts with a discourse of victimization. For the rhetorical uses of the concept of colonialism, see Bonnie K. Holcomb and Sisai Ibssa, *The Invention of Ethiopia* (Trenton: The Red Sea Press, 1990); Asafa Jalata, *Oromia and Ethiopia: State Formation and Ethnonational Conflict, 1868-2004* (Boulder, CO: Lynne Reiner publishers, 1993); Abbas Gnamo, *Conquest and Resistance in the Ethiopian Empire, 1880-1974: The Case of the Arsi Oromo* (Leiden: Brill, 2014); Asafa Jalata, ed, *Oromo Nationalism and the Ethiopian Discourse* (Lawrenceville NJ: The Red Sea Press, 1998); P.T.W. Baxter, Jan Hutlin and Alessandro Triulzi, eds., *Being and Becoming Oromo* (Lawrenceville, NJ.: The Red Sea Press, 1996). Meles Zenawi, the one-time leader of the TPLF and Prime Minister f Ethiopia (1991-2012) was a militant promoter of the idea of Ethiopian colonialism to advance his agenda of dividing Ethiopia ethnically in order to grasp and monopolize power through ethnic divide and rule. Abrham Yayeh, የኤርትራ ህዝብ ትግል ከየት ወዴት (Washington, 1992).

self-evident. The spurious use of the concept of colonialism in the context of Ethiopia's feudal history may have a political payoff for the Oromo *official people* in that it allows them to render the putative colonizer, "the Amhara" or the "Abyssinians" responsible for the miseries that the they—Oromo *official people*—inflict on the Oromo *people's people*.[229] The political and ideological payoff of the vacuous claim of Amhara colonialism, the organizing grammar of *Oromummaa* discourse, is that it obfuscates the class conflicts that openly wrack Ethiopian society and therefore Oromo society by recasting and masking them as ethnic conflicts.[230] The claim of Abyssinian colonialism allows the Oromo *official people* to be oblivious of the historicity of Ethiopia's state formation and of the intertwined, heterogeneous and contradictory alternative processes constitutive of the Ethiopian state formation, vertically and laterally. It thus allows them to preemptively repress the Ethiopian commonly inherited emancipatory aspirations and struggles of the Oromo *people's people* and to reduce these struggles to ethnic problems created by outsiders: the Amhara.

Both in practice and theory, *Oromummaa* has not much to do with either Oromo culture and history or the emancipatory needs and interest of the Oromo *people's people*. It is essentially an ideological-political bricolage that serves as a "panopticon" from where the Oromo *official people* permanently survey the authenticity of one's "Oromoness" in order to protect their power.[231] First, it is a mechanism of exclusion of all those who are identified as non-Oromo. Second, it is a mechanism for excluding those Oromos deemed to behave in ways that do not conform with the "Oromoness" precepts of *Oromummaa*. Oromos who are caught in default of "Oromoness" by the *Oromummaa* panopticon are condemned as "collaborators" of Ethiopia,

---

229 Bonnie K. Holcomb and Sisai Ibssa, *The Invention of Ethiopia* (Trenton: The Red Sea Press, 1990); Asafa Jalata, *Oromia and Ethiopia: State Formation and Ethnonational Conflict, 1868-2004* (Boulder, CO: Lynne Reiner publishers, 1993); Abbas Gnamo, *Conquest and Resistance in the Ethiopian Empire, 1880-1974: The Case of the Arsi Oromo* (Leiden: Brill, 2014).

230 A *qiné* hermeneutical reading of Ethiopian history generates a *säwrä tarik* which intimates that, given Ethiopia's induction into the global capitalist process and its effects on contemporary Ethiopian society, a class analysis of Ethiopians society is an indispensable aspect of the production of *lissan* and for disclosing the emancipatory potentials that lurk in Ethiopian society. But a class analysis must be rooted in *säwrä tarik* without which it floats over the concrete political, economic, epistemic, and cultural experiences of Ethiopians and becomes a dead-end discourse.

231 On "panopticon," Jeremy Bentham, *Panopticon: Or The Inspection House* (1791) (Whitefish: Kessinger Publishing, 2009). On the panopticon gaze, Michel Foucault, *The Foucault Reader*, ed. Paul Rabinow (New York: Pantheon, 1984), pp. 189, 217.

"de-Oromized," "hopeless liability of the race," "biologically and culturally assimilated," suffering from "slave psychology" and "self-hatred and self-contempt," and practitioners of "borrowed religions," referring to Islam and Christianity, though the overwhelming majority of Oromos have adhered to them for centuries.[232] *Oromummaa* is a mortal threat not only to the Amharas and the non-Oromos but also to the Oromo *people's people* and to those Oromos who put citizenship above ethnic identity.

What *Oromummaa* aims at in its claim of going "beyond culture and history" and "eliminat[ing] differences," and in its preaching of Oromo ethnic purity and homogeneity, is the denial of the internal antagonisms that challenge the assumed primordial unity of Oromo society. What this denial forgets is that Oromo society is *nägär*, thus historical, and is wracked by social antagonisms; it is internally complex, tensioned, contradictory, and *enkän*. The social antagonisms that traverse Oromo society have multiple sources. They emerged in its interactions through war and commerce with other Ethiopian ethnicities since at least the 13th century, in its transition of [Oromo societies] from pastoralism to sedentary agriculture, in the rise of the Gibe states (ca. 1800), and in the gradual subsumption of Ethiopians, therefore of the Oromos, to the global capitalist process as a subaltern people.[233] *Oromummaa* scotomizes these historical processes and their outcomes.

How does *Oromummaa* scotomize this history and occlude the internal antagonisms of Oromo society and assert a non-antagonistic Oromo identity? A *säwrä tarik*-based critique of self-identity could help us cast a critical eye on *Oromummaa*'s claims of the organic unity and self-identity of Oromo society and the accompanying denial of its internal antagonisms.[234] *Oromummaa*

---

232 All the quotes are from Asafa Jalata, "Promoting and Developing Oromummaa" *supra*.
233 Mohammed Hassen, *The Oromo and the Christian Kingdom of Ethiopia 1300–1700* (Oxford: James Currey, 2015); Mohamed Hassen, *The Oromo of Ethiopia: A History 1570-1860* (Cambridge: Cambridge University Press, 1990), p.88ff; Kenneth A. Reinert, "Ethiopia in the World Economy: Trade, Private Capital Flows," *Africa Today*, Vol. 53, No. 3 (2007), pp. 65-89.
234 I conduct here a *zäräfa* of the Hegelian critique of identity based on the idea that *nägär* and *säm ena wärq* harbour a critique of identity, as discussed in Chapter 1 # 1, and # 2. Hegel is a critique of the law of identity, i.e., A=A. For Hegel, every identity bears within itself its own contradiction, a claim that is interesting to subject to *zäräfa* to explore the idea pregnant in *säm ena wärq* that every *säm ena wärq* and its *säm* and *wärq* are *enkän* and therefore harbour their own contradictions as part of their identity. G.W.F. Hegel, *Science of Logic* (Cambridge: Cambridge University Press, 2010). The discussion in the following two paragraphs draws on a *zäräfa* of the following studies. Todd McGowan, *Emancipation After Hegel*

grounds Oromo identity in a monolithic collective identity essentialism and the establishment of a hard identity border with non-Oromos. In the process, it transforms internal contradictions into external oppositions and aims to give the Oromo an external enemy on which to direct the anger and aggression stemming from the oppression and exploitation that the Oromo *official people* inflict on the Oromo *people's people*. That is, the internal social contradictions are externalized in order to provide "an external enemy to fight." The payoff of this operation is the artificial creation of a coherent sense of Oromo identity that occludes the conflicts of interests between the exploiting Oromo *official people* and the exploited Oromo *people's people* and universalizes the interest of the *official people* as the universal interest of the exploited Oromo *people's people*.[235] The function of *Oromummaa* is not then to liberate the Oromo. It is to deny the internal antagonisms arising from the exploitation of the Oromo *people's people* by their *official people* and to direct the anger that arises from this exploitation on an external enemy so as to protect the power, wealth and interests of the Oromo *official people* from the fury of the exploited Oromo *people's people*. In this ideological operation, *Oromummaa* designates the Amhara as the "external enemy," and as the "enemy within" (the Oromos who reject *Oromummaa*) that has to be externalized.[236]

The ideological fantasy of the Amhara as a figure of evil who intrudes into Oromo society, robs it of its ethnic purity and harmony, and creates the internal antagonisms of Oromo society is a constitutive element of the invented tradition of *Oromummaa*. It is a fantasy that is articulated through a network of symbolic "overdetermination," condensed in the term *näftäña*, which makes the Amhara the locus of heterogeneous negative attributes—exploiter, colonizer, aggressor, polluter of Oromo purity, destroyer of Oromo religion (*Waaqeffanna*), divider of the Oromos, seducer of "Oromo women," making the Amhara some kind of "unfathomable X."[237] Thus, for *Oromummaa*, to be an Amhara is to become the object of abjection and ineligible to the right of existence.

Oromummaa thus makes the Amhara— fantasized as a force of corruption, destruction, and pollution of Oromo society—the embodiment of the phantasmatic figure of disruption that prevents Oromo society from achieving

---

(New York: Cambridge University Press, 2019), pp. 11-36; Slavoj Žižek, *The Sublime Object of Ideology* (London: Verso, 1989), pp. 124-28; Slavoj Žižek, *Interrogating the Real*, eds. Rex Butler, Scott Stephens (London: Continuum, 2005), pp. 249-70.
235 Ibid.
236 Ibid.
237 "Protect Oromo women," in Asafa Jalata, "Promoting and Developing Oromummaa" *supra*.

its full and unadulterated organic unity. *Oromumma* needs an enemy, and thus creates one, in order to define Oromo identity, as if being denied to have an enemy is being denied to exist. *Oromummaa* is a "fantasy," in the political sense, that represses "the traumatic impossibility" of having an Oromo society as a closed, frictionless, and homogeneous entity.[238] To mask "the traumatic impossibility," internal conflicts among the Oromos are displaced to an external cause—the Amhara, the fantasized enemy created by *Oromummaa*. The Amhara, the fantasized enemy, is not only external, it is also a screen on which Oromos who oppose *Oromummaa* are projected as the "internal enemy." They are seen as a foreign body to be expunged. To requote Asafa Jalata, they are "collaborators," "de-Oromized," "hopeless liability of the race," "biologically and culturally assimilated," suffering from "slave psychology" and "self-hatred and self-contempt."

The displacement of internal antagonisms onto a fantasized external enemy gives Oromo identity a spurious unity and mystical dimension that the Oromo *official people* use to promote a religious-like investment in Oromo identity and ethnic purity: The Oromo *official people* fantasize the Oromo as a self-sufficient, homogeneous, harmonious, and insular people. They see Oromo ethnicity as an identity that transcends human rights, civic rights, and individual liberties, hence their quasi-messianic engagement in ethnic-cleansing of Amharas, pan-Ethiopian Oromos, and non-Oromos from Oromo areas. What *Oromummaa* promises is the dystopia of a perfect society without antagonisms. A critical external journey shows that this is the utopia of fascism.[239] Heidegger, one of the great German philosophers of the twentieth century, whose sympathies for Nazism have been well documented, expresses the fascist idea of creating a society without antagonisms by annihilating the putative cause of these antagonisms. He writes

> it is a fundamental requirement to find the enemy, to expose the enemy to the light, *or even first to make the enemy*.... [The challenge is] to bring the enemy into the open, to harbor no illusions about the enemy, to keep oneself ready for attack, to cultivate and intensify a constant readiness and to prepare the attack *looking far ahead with the goal of total annihilation*.[240]

---

238 Jason Glynos, "Fantasy and Identity in Critical Political Theory," *Filozofski vestnik*, XXXII: 2 (2011), pp. 65-88.; J.H.Behagel, Aysem Mert, "The political nature of fantasy and political fantasies of nature," *Journal of Language and Politics*, 20:1(2021), pp. 79-93. Žižek, Slavoj, *The Plague of Fantasies* (London: Verso, 1997).
239 Alfred Rosenberg, *Der Mythos des zwanzigsten Jahrhundert* (Hoheneichen-Verlag, 1942).
240 Martin Heidegger, *Being and Truth* (Bloomington: Indiana University Press, 2010), p. 73. On the link between Heidegger nad Nazism, see Richard Wolin, *Heidegger*

These anti-human and anti-democratic words have found a new home in *Oromummaa*. *Oromummaa*'s monolithic group identity essentialism and its use of "Oromoness" as a panopticon make "a fundamental requirement to find the enemy, to expose the enemy to the light, *or even first to make the enemy*," and once it has fabricated the enemy—and the enemy *Oromummaa* has fabricated is the Amhara— *Oromummaa* expects that each Oromo "keep oneself ready for attack, to cultivate and intensify a constant readiness and to prepare the attack looking far ahead with the goal of total annihilation." In the unrelenting ethnic-cleansing from Oromo areas of the Amhara, other non-Oromos, and the Oromos who are targeted as failing the test of "Oromoness," the Oromo *official people* are implementing *Oromummaa*'s "goal" of "annihilation" of the fantasized "enemy." Thus, the Oromo *official people*, be they in power or waiting to assume power, disregard the rights of the Amhara, other non-Oromos, and Oromos who put universal rights above ethnic belonging.

Oromummaa discourse asserts "the number of Amharas, Tigres, Adares, Gurages, and Somalis in Oromia has increased *at the cost of* the Oromo population."[241] *Oromummaa*'s anti-historical claim that the Oromos were harmed (" *at the cost of*") by the historical intermingling of the Oromo and various ethnicities is currently used as a justification by the Oromo *official people* to claim that there is nothing to be shared with these ethnicities, that the only solution is the eviction of the "enemies of *Oromummaa*" from Oromo areas in order to restore Oromo ethnic purity and supremacy. *Oromummaa* is telling Amharas, other non-Oromos, and pan-Ethiopian Oromos, whose ancestors have lived in Oromo areas for centuries, "You have lived for centuries among us, but you are not one of us." *Oromummaa* thus reduces all historical relations between Ethiopian ethnicities to relations of enmity. It excludes the Amharas, other non-Oromos, and democratic Oromos in the Oromo *kilil* from the social realm and renders them abject things that are socially dead to the Oromos. They thus become disposable people in Oromo areas and potential targets of ethnic and political cleansing. Their life is thus what Mbembe calls "death-in-life."[242] For *Oromummaa*, the "social death" of the Amhara, other non-Oromos and of Oromos critical of *Oromummaa* becomes the foundation of the social life of the Oromo.[243] Not surprisingly, *Oromummaa* believers oppose inter-ethnic marriages

---

    in *Ruins: Between Philosophy and Ideology* (New Haven: Yale University Press, 2022).
241 Jalata, Asafa, "The Concept of Oromummaa and Identity Formation…" *supra*.
242 Achille Mbembe, *Necropolitics* (Durham: Duke University Press, 2019), p. 75.
243 Ibid, on "social death."

in their pursuit of ethnic purity and a politics of *Blut und Boden*.[244] One is not surprised then to see the claim that one of the tasks of *Oromummaa* is "to protect Oromo women," a topos often present historically in fascist discourse.[245] Indeed, one is struck by certain similarities between the ideas and practices defended in the name of *Oromummaa* and some of the ideas that Alfred Rosenberg defended in 1934.[246]

Yet, the Oromos and the "Amharas, Tigres, Adares, Gurages, and Somalis" that *Oromummaa* considers as anti-Oromo intruders have been living together for centuries. As Mohammed Hassen's historical studies show, the Oromos were present in almost every part of Ethiopia since at least the thirteenth century. Indeed, one could legitimately point out that the "Amharas, Tigres, Adares, Gurages, and Somalis in Oromia" and the other ethnicities that *Oromummaa* considers harmful intruders have intermingled and lived together with Oromos for centuries in a commonly shared political and cultural space and time, to the benefit of the Oromos, the other ethnicities, and Ethiopians in general.[247]

If it is the case that ideology is in the sphere of *doing* and not in the realm of *knowing*, that ideology expresses itself in what is done and not in what is said, the ideology of *Oromummaa* resides also in what its practitioners do.[248] The protagonists of *Oromummaa* claim it is "democratic." However, it brews its "democracy" in a casserole of paranoia whose ingredients are exclusion, humiliation, and ethnic-cleansing, spiced with a sauce of mystical devotion to

---

244 At a celebration of the International Women's Day organized by the Oromo Federalist Congress on Sunday march 8, a participant declared that the Oromo should not marry Amharas and those who are already to Amharas should divorce them. Present were the leaders of the party, who were nodding approvingly this proto-fascist statement. Source, Oromo Media Network. March 8, 2020, cited in https://borkena.com/2020/03/09/a-woman-calls-for-an-end-to-interethnic-marriage-for-oromo-struggle/. Given the repeated calls by some Oromo leaders to make marriage an instrument of Oromo ethnic purity, it is of interest to note the affinity of such calls with the Nazi use of marriage to promote Aryan purity. Lisa Pine, *Nazi Family Policy, 1933-1945* (New York: Berg, 1997),

245 Asafa Jalata, "Promoting and Developing Oromummaa…." *Supra*. Protecting one's ethnic women from the other ethnic men is a common theme of fascist ideologies.

246 Alfred Rosenberg, *Der Mythos des zwanzigsten Jahrhundert* (Hoheneichen-Verlag, 1942).

247 Mohammed Hassen, *The Oromo and the Christian Kingdom of Ethiopia 1300–1700* (Oxford: James Currey, 2015); Mohamed Hassen, *The Oromo of Ethiopia: A History 1570-1860* (Cambridge: Cambridge University Press, 1990).

248 A *zäräfa* of Žižek's discussion of ideology Slavoj Žižek, *The Sublime Object of Ideology* (London: Verso, 1989), Chapter 5.

the primacy of Oromo ethnic identity, purity and homogeneity.[249] It is a "democracy" that devalues the lives of Amharas, other non-Oromos, and citizenship-minded Oromos and treats them with abjection, that is, it perceives them as "death infecting [the] life" of the Oromo and thus as an existential threat that must be eliminated, either socially or physically.[250]

One sees in *Oromummaa* some kind of a religious like belief: it sacramentalizes what it calls the land of the Oromo, considers it defiled by the presence of Amharas and other non-Oromos, and argues for measures of purification through ethnic cleansing; it considers Oromo identity as if it were a destiny rooted in something like a doctrine of grace and predestination—an Oromo follows and acts the *Oromummaa* way because he/she is an Oromo. *Oromummaa*'s religious-like investment in Oromo identity expresses the withering of the historical, cultural, and political imagination of the Oromo *official people* and the destructive impact of Gibbonist education that creates a culture of "believing" rather that a culture of questioning and thinking. The idea of the emancipation of the *people's people* from the triple domination—political, economic, and epistemic—that weighs on them is outside the horizon or *admas* of *Oromummaa*. From the perspective of *säwrä tarik*, one can say that *Oromummaa* rejects the universalist and civilizing surplus meanings of Oromo culture that a critical internal journey into Oromo culture and history elicits, for example, in the practice of *moggaasa, siiqqee* and *ateetee*, and regresses to the pre-*moggaasa* notion of primordial identity.[251]

If, as I have indicated earlier, ideology resides in what one does and not in what one says, then one must recognize that *Oromummaa* is an ideology of inhumanity and destruction. In light of this, why the Oromo *official people*, its supporters, and its organic intellectuals and fellow travelers do not see the inhumanity and destructive nature of such an ideology is an interesting question. One possible answer is that they engage in a "fetishist disavowal": "I know very well, but all the same…." [252] Subjecting Mannoni to *zäräfa*, one could

---

249 Ibid.
250 Kristeva defines the "abject": "It is death infecting life." Julia Kristeva, *Powers of Horror: An Essay on Abjection*, trans., Leon S. Roudiez (New York: Columbia University Press, 1982), p.4.
251 On the civilizational aspects of *moggaasa*, see Maimire Mennasemay, *Qiné Hermeneutics and Ethiopian Critical Theory* (Los Angeles: Tsehai Publishing, 2021), Chapter 9.
252 Octave Mannoni, *Clefs pour l'imaginaire ou l'autre scène* (Paris: Seuil, 1969), pp.12-13, 32. "*je sais bien, mais quand même* . . ." ("I know very well, but all the same…"); Slavoj Žižek, *Violence: six sideways reflections* (New York: Picador, 2008), pp. 52, 124

say that the "fetishist disavowal" of the practitioner of *Oromummaa* runs: "I know very well *Oromummaa* is destructive, but all the same I believe as true what I know not to be true: that *Oromummaa* is democratic"; or in the words of Žižek, the fetishist disavowal runs: "I know [that *Oromummaa* is destructive], but I don't want to know that I know [that *Oromummaa* is destructive], so I don't know."[253] Inevitably, such a fetishist disavowal expels moral consciousness and liberates destructive inhibitions from the psychological and ethical fetters that keep them at bay, The political and ethical blindness that inevitably afflicts the *Oromumma* believer firmly shuts the door to the ideas of dialogue, mutual recognition and reconciliation. *Oromummaa* perceives politics as an ethnic struggle to the death with those identified as the "enemies" of Oromos.[254] Being an invented tradition constructed through fantasies of ethnic purity and homogeneity, there is no place for rational argument in *Oromummaa*.

For the first time in Ethiopian history, we see in the practice of *Oromumma* the presence of what Alan Wolfe calls "political evil," which he defines as "the willful, malevolent, and gratuitous death, destruction, and suffering inflicted upon innocent people by the leaders of movements and states in their strategic efforts to achieve realizable objectives."[255] What makes the *official people* who wield the political evil of *Oromummaa* utterly frightening is "their very rationality; they engage in political activity to achieve their ends much as other kinds of leaders do."[256] They speak of elections, democracy, development, peace, and ethnic self-determination, but they wield these as tools of "political evil," thus transmogrifying them into killer zombie concepts.

The 1995 Constitution has set up a federation of ethnic archipelago that has triggered among many *official people* of Ethiopia's ethnicities a frenzy of "invented traditions" that imitate many elements from *Oromummaa*, including the externalization of internal contradictions into an external opposition of enmity between the given ethnie and another ethnic group, and the discourse

---

253 Slavoj Žižek, *Violence: six sideways reflections, supra.*
254 Wollega, Northern Shoa, and Sheger, the newly-created Oromo city that surrounds Addis Ababa, are some areas where Amhara-cleansing take place. https://www.amnesty.org/en/latest/news/2022/07/ethiopia-authorities-must-investigate-massacre-of-ethnic-amhara-in-tole/; https://www.hrw.org/world-report/2023/country-chapters/ethiopia#407c75 Accessed 6/23/2023; https://ehrc.org/download, የኢትዮጵያ ሰብአዊ መብቶች ሁኔታ ዓመታዊ ሪፖርት (ከሰኔ ወር 2014 ዓ.ም. እስከ ሰኔ ወር 2015 ዓ.ም.). Accessed 7/15/2023.
255 Alan Wolfe, *Political Evil: What It Is and How to Combat It* (New York: Alfred A. Knopf, 2011), pp.4-5.
256 Ibid. p. 26.

of victimization. The result is 6 million internally displaced people.²⁵⁷ Given that Ethiopia has more than 80 ethnic groups, the pursuit of *Oromummaa* and its imitation by the *official people* of other ethnicities will engulf Ethiopia in a naked crisis, which is already unfolding in acts of ethnic-cleansings in many parts of Ethiopia.²⁵⁸ The silver lining in this *Oromummaa* instigated crisis is that, though *Oromummaa* has become the *Codex Gigas* of the Oromo *official people*, the great majority of Oromos have no truck with this political evil, for they know well that its serves only the interests of the Oromo *official people* and has total disregard for the emancipatory needs of the Oromo *people's people*. ²⁵⁹ Consequently, a concerted action that brings together anti-*Oromummaa* Oromos, who are the majority, and the rest of the Ethiopian population —non-Oromos and Amharas—to liberate Ethiopians from this political evil is necessary and possible.

From the perspective of *säwrä tarik*, it is clear that it is the eviction of the *people's people* or the *tära hizb* from political, economic, and cognitive power that has delivered Ethiopia into the hands of the *official people*. Inevitably, the current naked crisis is plunging Ethiopia into an economic crisis, and she is in 2023 on the cusp of collapsing into a failed state. ²⁶⁰

---

257 https://data.unhcr.org/en/documents/details/92844. Accessed 8/6/2022.

258 United Nations High Commissioner for Refugees, https://data.unhcr.org › documents› download. https://www.amnesty.org/en/latest/news/2022/07/ethiopia-authorities-must-investigate-massacre-of-ethnic-amhara-in-tole/ Accessed 1,15 / 2023. Sheger, the city that surrounds Ethiopia is being forcefully cleared of non-Oromo residents with the intention of making it a city inhabited only by the Oromo, creating as a result thousands of homeless people. https://addisinsight.net/the-demolition-and-forced-resettlement-of-houses-in-sheger-city-in-oromia-region-has-exacerbated-homelessness/

259 The *Codex Gigas* is also known as the Devil's Bible, composed during the thirteenth century.

260 UNDP, https://report.hdr.undp.org/intro (2021-2022). Ethiopia is 175th (out of 191) on the Human Development index, below poor countries such as Sudan, Equatorial Guinea, Benin, Togo. The exchange value of the Ethiopian money (*birr*) is collapsing, the inflation rate is galloping, and poverty is on the rise. https://reliefweb.int/report/ethiopia/wfp-ethiopia-market-watch-march-2023. Accessed 5/13/2023. https://countryeconomy.com/countries/ethiopia. The *official people* are oblivious to the economic crisis that has made the daily life of the *tära hizb* a struggle for bare survival. Ethiopians). https://www.lemonde.fr/afrique/article/2023/02/06/en-ethiopie-un-palais-pharaonique-pour-abiy-ahmed-pris-par-la-folie-des-grandeurs_6160783_3212.html. Accessed 7/4/2023. Fragile state index, https://fragilestatesindex.org/. Accessed 6/16/2023. Ethiopia is between Haiti (more fragile) and Myanmar (less fragile.)

2.5. *Säwrä tarik* and politics as the art of the impossible

The emancipatory ideas that constitute *säwrä tarik* create a vantage point immanent to Ethiopian history/society. We could, from this vantage point "suspend our beliefs" in the hegemonic order's desire, will, and capacity to bring about an Ethiopian society of freedom, equality, justice, knowledge, and prosperity, and "suspend our disbelief" that another Ethiopia is possible.[261] We can cast from *säwrä tarik* a critical glance on Ethiopia's present reality, exposing its harmfulness, wrongness, and contingency; revealing it as an obstacle to political, economic, social, and cultural flourishing of Ethiopians. At the same time, we could see from this vantage point the emancipatory potentialities gestating within Ethiopian history/society, These potentialities could be actualized if Ethiopians were to liberate them from the repressed zones of Ethiopian history/society, develop them, and struggle to concretize them.

Säwrä tarik provides the epistemic, practical, and affective resources for the emergence of new parameters of knowing, evaluation, standards, affect, interpretation, commitments and actions, enabling us to go beyond the idea and practice of "politics of the art of the possible" that the hegemonic order and development and democratization theories and practices promote. When politics is confined to the art of the possible, policies and actions are guided and constrained by the constitutive political, economic, and knowledge coordinates of the hegemonic order, and the future is a projection of the present with changes, if any, that maintain the parameters of the extant regime. To put it differently, politics as the art of the possible limits politics to that which is analytically possible within the parameters that define the hegemonic regime. Things change only within the parameters of the overarching political space, which in the case of Ethiopia is authoritarianism. The changes from the Haile Selassie regime to Colonel Mengestu's, to Meles Zenawi's, and to Abiy Ahmed's are changes that maintained and modernized the authoritarian tradition of Ethiopian politics—known as the "Zara Yacob Syndrome," after the 15th century Ethiopian emperor who was known for his cruelty and despotism.[262] These changes espoused different forms of authoritarianism: absolute monarchy (up to 1974), military authoritarianism (the DERG, 1974-1991), TPLF's ethnic

---

261 A *zäräfa* of the ideas of suspending belief and disbelief in Paul Ricoeur, *Lectures on Ideology and Utopia*, ed. G. H. Taylor (New York: Columbia University Press, 1986), p. 16.

262 On the Zāra Yacob syndrome, Maimire Mennasemay, *Qiné Hermeneutics and Ethiopian Critical Theory* (Los Angeles: Tsehai Publishing, 2021), pp. 460-464.

authoritarianism (1991-2018), and the Prosperity Party's emerging necropower (2019...).[263] Despite their organizational differences, these regimes practice extensive repression internally and pursue externally a policy of anti-democratic integration of Ethiopia into the global economic order as a subaltern state.[264]

Säwrä tarik contests the internal and external limits that the politics as the art of the possible imposes on what Ethiopians could do to change the present situation. Politics as the art of the possible prevents questioning the foundational internal and external coordinates of the Ethiopian political, economic, and epistemic regime; it excludes the transformation of the totality (*wihdät*) of Ethiopian society into a system whose functioning renders impossible the triple domination that the current political, economic, and knowledge regime generates as normal conditions and outcomes of its functioning. Politics as the art of the possible limits economic development, democracy, and knowledge production to the interests of the *official people* of Ethiopia.

Säwrä tarik rewrites the coordinates of the thinkable, possible, knowable, and feasible such that what are analytically, politically, and epistemically unthinkable and impossible in terms of the parameters of the regime of the *official people* become possible, thinkable, knowable, and feasible from the perspective of *säwrä tarik*. *Säwrä tarik* opens to Ethiopians the possibility of making a qualitative change of direction or *andem*—by activating the emancipatory potentialities gestating in the present political, economic, social, and epistemic deadlocks—from the "politics as the art of the possible" to the "politics as the art of the impossible," from a regime of oppression and exploitation to a regime of *arnät*, that is, to a regime of emancipatory democracy, emancipatory economic transformation, and emancipatory knowledge production. We can subject here Milton Friedman's idea of the "impossible" becoming "inevitable" under certain circumstances to *zäräfa* to illustrate the importance of keeping *säwrä tarik* alive for making a qualitative and emancipatory *andem* from "politics as the art of the possible" to "politics as the art of the impossible" in order to actualize the emancipatory interests of the *people's people*. Friedman writes,

> Only a crisis—actual or perceived—produces real change. When that crisis occurs, the actions that are taken depend on *the ideas that are lying around*. That,

---

263   The PP regime seems to be increasingly committed to the biopoitical ordering of life based on ethnic differences and is steadily subjugating the life of non-Oromos and particularly of the Amharas to the power of death in the name of the ethnic self-determination of the Oromo. On necropower, Achille Mbembe, *Necropolitics* (Durham: Duke University Press, 2019), pp. 66-92.

264   https://www.imf.org/en/Countries/ETH. https://www.worldbank.org/en/country/ethiopia/overview Accessed 6/19/2023.

I believe, is our basic function: *to develop alternatives to existing policies, to keep them alive and available until the politically impossible becomes politically inevitable.*²⁶⁵

Though Milton Friedman, a Nobel Prize economist, is a theorist of neoliberal capitalism and is writing here about supplanting Keynesianism with his theory of market supremacy, we can nevertheless subject his idea "to keep them [qualitatively different ideas] alive and available until the *politically impossible* becomes *politically inevitable*" and subject it to *zäräfa*. We can thus overread and dislocate it to serve the interests of emancipation.²⁶⁶ Thus, we could say that were we to develop *säwrä tarik* by going against the political and the intellectual grain of Ethiopia's hegemonic regimes and the theories and practices of development and democratization that subtend them, and keep it "alive and available *until the politically impossible becomes politically inevitable,*" we could eventually make an *andem* or a qualitative transition from "politics as the art of the possible" to "politics as the art of the impossible" and make *arnät*—the political, economic, and epistemic emancipation of Ethiopians—possible. Politics as the art of the impossible is the politics of the *people's people*. One finds this idea in Abera Mola's *qiné* lines,

> እንደ ሰው ተወልዶ እንድ ሰው የማይኖር / Born human but living as a non-human
> እንደ ሰው የማይሞት እንደ ሰው ሲቀብር / Dying as a non-human but human in the grave,
> አይተሽ ሰምተሽ ታውቃለሽ ወይ ምድር / Earth, see and hear this injustice
> ፍረጂኝ ! መስከሪኝ ! ይህን ክፉ በደል²⁶⁷ / Be its witness and judge

The *qiné* lines intimate that the Ethiopian, though born human, lives and dies as non-human (እንድ ሰው የማይኖር ... እንደ ሰው የማይሞት), but recovers his/her humanity only when he/she is in the grave (እንደ ሰው ሲቀብር). The *qiné* raises the question that is at the heart of *Dagmawi Tinsa'e* (secular resurrection), a question triggered by the endless political, economic, social, and epistemic sufferings of Ethiopians: Is there life before death for Ethiopians?²⁶⁸ The answer to this question, which is far from simple, lies in *säwrä tarik*. From the perspective of *säwrä tarik*, one could say that there is "life" before death only if Ethiopians act

---

265 Milton Friedman, *Capitalism and Freedom* (Chicago: Chicago University Press, 1982), p. ix. (Emphasis added).

266 On "overreading" or "productive misreading," see Maimire Mennasemay, *Qiné Hermeneutics and Ethiopian Critical Theory*, supra, pp.33-5; Colin Davis, *Critical excess: overreading in Derrida, Deleuze, Levinas, Žižek and Cavell* (Stanford: Stanford University Press, 2010).

267 Abera Mola, ፍረጂኝ ምድሩቱ, in Birhanu Gebeyhu, የአማርኛ ስነ ግጥም (Addis Ababa: Alfa Printing, 2003), p. 133.

268 On *Dagmawi Tinsa'e*, see Maimire Mennasemay, *Qiné Hermeneutics and Ethiopian Critical Theory* (Los Angeles: Tsehai Publishers, 2021) pp. 183-5

freely and bring about their emancipation and "resurrect" as "humankind" from the social death in which they live. To achieve this "resurrection," they have to see themselves as symbolically or socially dead vis-a-vis the existing order and to its politics of the possible. In seeing themselves as socially dead vis-a-vis the existing order, they open their eyes and recognize themselves as history/society making humans in *säwrä tarik*. Only in *säwrä tarik* are the *people's people* present as agents who discover their humanity in their social death (እንደ ሰው ሲቀበር) and in their resurrection from it as the authors and actors of Ethiopian society/history. The *qiné* alludes to the fact that "politics as the art of the possible" in Ethiopia amounts to live and die as a "non-human," suggesting that Ethiopians have to conduct "politics as the art of the impossible," or as the "art of political, economic, epistemic resurrection," as it were, to recover their humanity. We can say that Ethiopians can transform *"the politically impossible"* into the *"politically inevitable"* only when they appropriate their *säwrä tarik* and act on it, for only then can they recognize themselves as "humankind [that] can do the impossible."[269] *Säwrä tarik* does not consider the impossible an absolute barrier; rather, it considers it an enabling and productive test whose goal is the actualization of *arnät* or emancipation..

The idea that to be free, we need to transgress the limits of the possible and create the political, economic, and epistemic coordinates that enable us to do that which appears impossible for the hegemonic order is an idea that is also explored by the greatest modern Ethiopian author, Addis Alemayehu, in his now classical novel, *Fiqer Eskä Mäqaber / ፍቅር እስከ መቃብር* (Love Unto Crypt).[270] As I have discussed *Fiqer Eskä Mäqaber* elsewhere from a *qiné* hermeneutical perspective, I will limit myself here to a very short discussion to show how emancipation is associated in the transition from the possibility of the possible to the possibility of the impossible.[271]

Addis uses love (ፍቅር / *fiqer*) as the *zäybé* of *arnät* or emancipation. Säble, the central character of the novel is the daughter of a feudal lord. She meets Bäzabeh and they fall in love with each other. Bäzabeh, though highly educated, was from the lowest class, and thus subject to the hegemonic order's prohibition from having social relations with members of the upper class. Both Bäzabeh and Säble realize that the limits of the possible of their society make their love for each

---

269 One finds a similar idea in Goethe: "Nur allein der Mensch / Vermag das Unmögliche" ("Only humankind / Can do the impossible"), Goethe, *Das Göttliche* (1783). Available at https://prezi.com/p/kpshvu0tvv3j/das-gottliche-johann-goethe/. Accessed 1/24/2018.
270 ሀዲስ ዓለማየሁ፣ ፍቅር እስከ መቃብር (Addis Ababa: Mega Press, 17th edition, 2007).
271 Maimire Mennasemay, *"Fiqer Eskä Mäqaber:* A *Qiné* Hermeneutical Reading," *International Journal of Ethiopian Studies*, Vol. 10, No. 1 & 2 (2016), pp. 1-34.

other impossible, but they react to this injustice differently, he with resignation, she, with asking why. The third character, *Gudu* Kassa, is an intellectual from the upper class who is keenly aware of how society represses emancipatory needs, and makes it known that there is an alternative way of living. His ideas transgress the limits of the possible verbally. The inhabitants of the locality are shocked by his views, and consider him a "mad person." hence the epithet *Gudu* (crazy) attached to his name. Addis suggests the "madness" of Kassa is the *zäybé* of emancipatory reason that appears as "madness," because irrational / impossible from the perspective of hegemonic reason, but signifies the possibility of the impossible: changing society from root to fruit.

Bäzabeh, an intellectual like Kassa, submits to society's hegemonic reason and leads an empty life, despite *Gudu* Kassa's advice and encouragement to transgress the limits of the possible and fulfil his emancipatory needs—the fulfillment of his love for Säble. But Bäzabeh recoils from doing what hegemonic reason characterizes as "madness." Säble, on the other hand, though without education, listens to *Gudu* Kassa's "mad" ideas. They trigger in her questions and doubts about her society, but it is her lived experience of discovering that she is not the master of her own life that slowly puts her on the path of resistance and finally revolt. She eventually did what the intellectual *Gudu* Kassa did not dare to do, despite his radical ideas. She awakens her *säwrä ras* and rebels against tradition: she cuts her family ties completely and totally, "exiles" herself to a "new land," and starts a "new life" as the author and actor of her own life. Addis intimates that change must be total (*wihdät*) in his depiction of Sable's rejection of her society as an "exile" to a "new land" and a "new life," that is, Säble dies symbolically vis-a-vis the existing order, while Bäzabeh accepts to live as the "living dead" of the same existing order. Addis makes the fulfillment of the emancipatory needs of Bäzabeh and Säble coincide with death, interestingly with the physical death of Bäzabeh, for they do fulfill their emancipatory need: they tie the knot with Bäzabeh on his deathbed. Addis ends his novel in a way that suggests that acceptance of the hegemonic order leads to real death—the death of Bäzabeh—whereas rejecting the hegemonic order and starting a new life—the case of Säble — fulfills the emancipatory needs of the person who revolts and inaugurates a "new life," but also of those who do not revolt against injustice in that it emancipates them, even if retroactively, which is the case of the dying Bäzabeh. Whereas Bäzabeh's natural death has no redemptive value, Säble 's symbolic death vis-à-vis the existing social order liberates both of them. Addis expresses a view that is similar to Abera Mola's poem we saw above: it is by considering themselves symbolically dead to the existing order, which Säble did, that Ethiopians could succeed to transgress the inner and external limits of the existing order and bring about the emancipation that appears impossible from within the coordinates of the hegemonic order. This means that it is only when one sees oneself politically as symbolically dead to the existing order that one could grasp politics as the art of the impossible, i.e., politics as the art of emancipation. According to *säwrä tarik*, the *säwrä ras* (the surplus self) is the Ethiopian historical subject, the "excessive subject," that is capable of transiting from the possibility of the possible to the possibility of the impossible.[272]

From the perspective of *säwrä tarik*, Ethiopia is a "not yet," because the Ethiopia that existed and exists is not the Ethiopia that *säwrä tarik* gestates.[273] In this sense, Ethiopians are yet to "become Ethiopians": a people free from unfreedoms, inequalities, injustices, and epistemic servility. From the perspective of *säwrä tarik*, we cannot rely on the eschatology of the emancipation-to-come. The choice is between others opening the future for we Ethiopians, an idea central to Gibbonism and that leads to the strengthening of the triple domination, or we ourselves open it in ways and purposes that are of our own choosing. Since the future does not yet have a definite form and content, its very undecidedness makes possible the practice of politics as the art of the impossible. Such a practice requires engaged agents (*säwrä ras*) who intervene and give Ethiopian society emancipatory form and content and render possible that which the hegemonic order and its development, democracy, and Gibbonist social sciences consider impossible. The emergence of *säwrä ras* is precisely what the *official people* try to prevent by narratives such as Oromummaa, which means that only the struggle (the *gädl*) against the regime of the *official people* could lead to the emergence of *säwrä ras*: the only agent that can wield "politics as the art of the impossible" and build *arnät*.

From the perspective of *säwrä tarik*, one could say that in Ethiopia, the practice of politics as the art of the possible has led to the "Ptolemization" of democracy, development, and knowledge production through *hibrä qal* (ሕብረ ቃል) that are used as "epicycles."[274] Ptolemization narrates the practice of

---

272 See Chapter 1 # 12. As György Lukács puts it, "Only he who is willing and whose mission it is to create the future can see the concrete truth of the present." György Lukács, *History and Class Consciousness* (Cambridge, MA: MIT Press, 1971), p. 204. The "he who is willing…" is the *säwrä ras* of Säble.

273 On the concept of "not yet," Ernst Bloch, *The Principle of Hope* I, trans. Neville Plaice, Stephen Plaice and Paul Knight (Cambridge, MA: MIT Press, 1986), pp, 196-205.

274 On *hibrä qal*, Maimire Mennasemay, *Qiné Hermeneutics and Ethiopian Critical Theory*, supra, pp.195-201. *Hibrä qal* (ሕብረ ቃል) facilitate Ptolemization by smoothing over contradictions, inconsistencies, and lacks in what are claimed to be

oppression as democracy through the *hibrä qal* epicycles such as ethnic self-determination (the 1995 Constitution and the Prosperity Party regime) or as "multi party" elections—(the 1995, the 2021 general elections)—though the parties are based on ethnic identity and the outcome is decided before the election starts. The predatory economic practices, the frenzied race for riches of the *official people*, and the massive corruption of the state apparatus that have flung the majority of Ethiopian into destitution are Ptolemized as "development" through the *hibrä qal* epicycles such as prestige and extraverted projects: palaces, parcs, export-oriented industrial parcs, cash crop production, while more than 20 million Ethiopians depend on international fool aid, and schools and hospitals are deteriorating.[275] Inflated numbers about economic growth, education, health, and so forth, are used as *hibrä qal* epicycles to Ptolemize economic and social failures as development. Epistemic servility is Ptolemized as knowledge on Ethiopia through the *hibrä qal* epicycles of studies of development projects, civil society, cultures, politics, the economy. and so forth, though none of these studies are rooted in the emancipatory interests of the *people's people*. This Ptolemized knowledge rationalizes, under the claim of scientificity, the existing order and the oppression and exploitation of the *people's people*, not directly, but by limiting itself to the given and by not making emancipation the guiding thread of knowledge production. This triple Ptolemization—of politics, of the economy, and of knowledge production—is the defence mechanism of "politics as the art of the possible" in Ethiopia. It normalizes unfreedoms, inequalities, economic miseries, hunger, undereducation, deficient health services, homelessness, predatory exploitation, and epistemic subjugation.

---

development, democracy, and knowledge production in Ethiopia. On *hibrä qal* (ሕብረ ቃል), see above Chapter 1 # 17. On Ptolemy's use of epicycles to save the phenomenon, A. Pannekoek, *A History of Astronomy* (New York: Interscience Publishers, 1961), pp.133-144. "When a discipline is in crisis, attempts are made to change or supplement its theses within the terms of its basic framework - a procedure one might call 'Ptolemization'." Slavoj Žižek, *The Sublime Object of Ideology* (London: Verso, 2008), p. viii.

275 On prestige projects: Le Monde, https://www.lemonde.fr/afrique/article/2023/02/06/en-ethiopie-un-palais-pharaonique-pour-abiy-ahmed-pris-par-la-folie-des-grandeurs_6160783_3212.html.; Africa Confidential, https://www.africa-confidential.com/article-preview/id/12584/Abiy_dining_dangerously Addis Standard, https://addisstandard.com/news-pm-abiys-signature-park-inaugurates-today/ Accessed 7/4/2023. Prestige projects and corruption go hand in hand. On the high rate of corruption in Ethiopia, https://www.transparency.org/en/countries/ethiopia. Accessed 4/13/2023. Ethiopia Insider, "በኢትዮጵያ ካሉ ትምህርት ቤቶች ውስጥ "ከፍተኛ" የሚባለውን ደረጃ ያሟሉ፤ አራት ብቻ መሆናቸውን ትምህርት ሚኒስቴር አስታወቀ" https://ethiopiainsider.com/2023/11020/, Accessed, 7/1/2023.

2.6. *Säwrä tarik* and "standing upright"

For *säwrä tarik*, the way Ethiopians perceive Ethiopia and themselves depends on the emancipatory practical projects they pursue to concretize these aspirations. It is precisely these emancipatory projects that define the obstacles Ethiopians have to overcome as a people and their commitment to making the impossible possible, a point that is strongly intimated by the 15th century heretic movements: the Estifanosites, the Ewostatewosites, and the Zamika'elites.[276]

According to the *Däqiqä Estifanos*, one's "question" must reflect "[one's] judgement" and not be "a repetition of what others [the imported social sciences and the experts of the IMF, the World Bank, and so forth, in our case] say."[277] The *Däqiqä Estifanos* assert that "you" must "stand upright" and "[c]ontinue with full determination and without interruption until you reach the summit" of "what you have decided to do" (ከደብሩ ከጫፉ እስከተደርሱ ድረስ ትጉ እንጂ ከጭሉ ቁጭ አትበሉ / *Kädäbru kächafu esktdärsu dräs enji kächinu quch atbälu*).[278] In other words, for the *Däqiqä Estifanos*, our actions must be commanded by our decision to "reach the summit." The obstacles we encounter in our effort to "reach the summit" are not obstacles independent of what we decide to accomplish. They compel us to affirm our freedom by overcoming the objective resistance of reality and the subjective resistance that restrains or inhibits us from assuming and exercising our freedom. It obliges us to uphold our commitment to achieve what the *Däqiqä Estifanos* call "standing upright," to overcome the internal and external obstacles that block our way, and to bring our decisions to fruition. This idea, expressed in different forms and couched in religious language by the various heretic movements of the 15th century, is present in *säwrä tarik*. "Standing upright" is also what informs the daily struggles of the *people's people*, their "subjugated knowledge," their "local critiques," and their mutual aid, labour-sharing, and conflict resolution institutions.

From the perspective of *säwrä tarik*, we do not start, as the *official people* have been doing since 1951, from Ethiopia as described and conceptualized by the borrowed theories of democracy and development, and then tailor Ethiopian

---

[276] Taddesse Tamrat, *Church and State in Ethiopia, 1270-1527* (Oxford: Clarendon Press, 1972); Getachew Haile, "Ethiopian Heresies and Theological Controversies" in Coptic Encyclopedia, vol 2, ed. Aziz S. Atiya (New York: Macmillan, 1991), 984a-987b; Teweldeberhan Mezgebe Desta, *Gädlä Abäw wä-Aḥaw [Fourth Part]: Edition and Annotated Translation with Philological and Linguistic Commentary* (Addis Ababa: Addis Ababa University Dissertation, 2019).

[277] Getatchew Haile, ደቂቀ እስጢፋኖስ በገነ አምላክ, trans. from Ge'ez (Collegeville, MN: 2004)., pp. 23, 44, 70, 94.

[278] Ibid., p. 268; see also pp. 70, 232, 241, 250, 274.

society to fit the description and conceptualizations of the imported theories through Ptolemization.²⁷⁹ Rather, we start by "standing upright," that is, by recognizing ourselves as the authors and actors of the political, economic, and epistemic impasses into which we have driven Ethiopia, critically reflecting in terms of the questions, aspirations and interests that we have enucleated through our critical journey into our vertical and lateral history and practices, conducting an *andemta*, and conceiving and implementing the actions necessary to exit from these impasses of our creation. From the perspective of *säwrä tarik*, one can say that the political and economic errors that have dogged Ethiopia are also theoretical errors that arise from the lack of thinking and acting "standing upright." That is, our political and economic errors are the offspring of Gibbonism: the absence of modern Ethiopian thinking rooted in the emancipatory surplus meanings immanent to Ethiopian history/society.

Tsegaye G/Medhin, the poet laureate and master of Amharic *qiné*, articulates a crucial idea of *säwrä tarik* when he writes, "ይሕ ሕዝብ፡ / መሪዎቹን የሚፈራ- መሪዎቹን የሚጠላ /መሪዎቹ የሚፈሩት-መሪዎቹ የማይወዱት ፡፡ / ሠምና ወርቅ የሆነ ሕዝብ ነው፡፡"²⁸⁰ "The [Ethiopian] people / fear their rulers but loath them / feared and disliked by its rulers / it is a *säm ena wärq* people." The Ethiopian people—the *people's people*— "fear their rulers," the *official people*, but "loath" them; and the rulers "hate them" (the *people's people*) but also "fear" them. That is, the *people's people* and their conditions of existence are *säm ena wärq*. They and their conditions of existence are *nägär*, triggering both fear and hatred, internally split, conflicted, and bearing heterogeneous potentialities. Tsegaye's *qiné* implies that emancipation requires that the *people's people* engage in *gädl* (struggle), which includes self-*gädl* (self-struggle). This means "standing upright" and engaging with the antagonisms of their conditions of existence as well as of themselves, hence the need to practice, together with *gädl*, self-*gädl* which includes self-*zäräfa* (self-*andem*, self-*tirgum*, self-*arat ayn*, and self-*hiss*) in order to awaken successfully *säwrä ras* (surplus self) as an active historical agent of *arnät* or emancipation.

Säwrä tarik has diagnostic and normative functions, but it eschews the idea of teleology. It intimates that the decision of the *people's people* to enucleate and

---

279 1951 because it is the year that marks the official beginning of the westernized idea and project of development articulated in the Point Four Program signed between the Ethiopian Imperial Government and the United States. U.S.A. Operations Mission to Ethiopia, *Point Four Agreements between the Imperial Ethiopian Government and the Government of the United States* (Washington: Information, Mission to Ethiopia Subject Files, 1954).
280 Thanks to Hibrat Agonafir for drawing my attention to this composition of the Poet Laureate Tsegaye G/Medhin.

put to work the *wärq* or the emancipatory potentialities of their history/society is a necessary condition for emancipatory action. Such a decision involves "standing upright." This implies going beyond politics as the "the art of the possible," which is the politics of "prostration" (to use the critical term of the 15th century heretics) to the triple domination, and grasping politics as the "art of the impossible, "which is the politics of "standing upright," in order to bring about a historical *andem*—a lateral move, a historical skipping and catapulting, and a new historical orientation. "Politics as the art of the impossible" is the politics that can enable the *people's people* to "stand upright," to emerge from their nameless existence, overcome their "fear" and "loathing" of their rulers, and convert their negative sentiments into a productive transformative emancipatory force that will liberate all Ethiopians. The *people's people* can then break through the hegemonic order's oppressive interpellations—currently as ethnic beings under the 1995 Constitution and the regimes founded on it—and shatter the practical, normative, conceptual shackles with which the hegemonic order fetters them, thus making possible the emancipation (*arnät*) of both the *people's people* and the *official people*.

Säwrä tarik does not have causal powers of its own, although it provides the political, social, ethical, epistemic, and affective criteria and motivations to enable Ethiopians to act in ways that promote emancipation (*arnät*). *Säwrä tarik* is graspable only from the site of an Ethiopian who is committed to emancipation, that is, who is "standing upright." This committed agent is *säwrä ras* (surplus self) who knows that ideas exist only through our fidelity to them and their implementation in practice. *Säwrä ras* discovers through *säwrä tarik* what Ethiopians have failed to become, what they could have become, and what they could become were they to grasp the emancipatory potentialities that simmer in Ethiopian history/society, past and present, vertically and laterally, and act to concretize them. Without political thinking that is nourished by *säwrä tarik* and the emancipatory energy, conceptual imagination, and political creativity it generates, Ethiopians will not be able to construct a society that is liberated from the unfreedoms, inequalities, injustices, and epistemic servility from which they have suffered under the various regimes of "development" and "democratization," and "ethnic self-determination." It is precisely the presence of *säwrä tarik* in Ethiopian history that provides the ground for not excluding *a priori* that which the extant order considers impossible: *arnät* or political, economic, and epistemic emancipation.

Säwrä tarik posits that freedom and equality are inseparable in the sense that they are directly proportional to each other: a decline in one leads to a decline in the other; an increase in one leads to an increase in the other. In *säwrä tarik*, these ideas are expressed in two statements from the *qiné* tradition. የኔ ቢጤ (yäne *bitie*), and ሰው ለሰው መድኃኒቱ / *säw läsäw mädhanitu*. These two extremely concise aphorisms must be treated as brachylogia. They are incomplete fragments that appear separately though they have subterranean connections. When subjected to a *qiné* hermeneutic reading, we see that they are fragments of a complex discourse. I will thus unpack them and disclose their connections and show the crucial meanings they generate. የኔ ቢጤ (*yäne bitie*) means he/she/they are like me, and I am like him/her/them, expressing the importance to see oneself in the others, and the others in oneself as acts of freedom, equality and justice. ሰው ለሰው መድኃኒቱ / *säw läsäw mädhanitu* means each is the cure for the other, intimating the idea that one must go beyond merely recognizing the other; one must affirm in what he/she does the freedom and equality of the other. የኔ ቢጤ (*yäne bitie*) and ሰው ለሰው መድኃኒቱ / *säw läsäw mädhanitu* express the acknowledgment in the *qiné* hermeneutical tradition that no Ethiopian is a "social atom" or a bounded self. The *säm ena wärq* conception of the individual sees the self as decentered, as trans-subjective, and constituted through the mediation of the other, hence የኔ ቢጤ (*yäne bitie*) and ሰው ለሰው መድኃኒቱ / *säw läsäw mädhanitu*. These two fragments express, when conjoined, the idea that one finds oneself outside oneself and is therefore essentially "ex-timate," that life and society, in all their vicissitudes, are always shared life and shared society, and that each is responsible (*mädhanitu*) for the welfare, freedom, equality and justice for the others, as the others are for him/her.[281]

These two fragments bring out something essential. Unlike the Gibbonist conception of identity that is rooted in the Western idea of "being" (the ontologization of ethnicity as in "Oromoness") that Ethiopian ethno-nationalists have adopted uncritically, the two fragments show that identity is not fixed: it is relational, plastic, and involves reciprocal implications. When conjoined, የኔ ቢጤ (*yäne bitie*) and ሰው ለሰው መድኃኒቱ / *säw läsäw mädhanitu* are acts of "standing upright," not only individually but also collectively. They intimate that the individual and society are constituted through the mutual mediation of one and the other, and both are decentered in the other. These fragments point to the necessity of conjugating critical reflection with "doing." They signal the concrete universality of each Ethiopian: the belief that the other—irrespective of ethnicity, status, gender, or faith—is immanent in me as I am in the other, that the other's need is mine, as mine is the other's, that the other's suffering is mine as mine is the other's. and that I find my concrete universality in the other as the other meets his/her concrete universality in me. These two fragments jointly

---

281 A *zäräfa* of "ex-timacy," see Dylan Evans, *An Introductory Dictionary of Lacanian Psychoanalysis* (London: Routledge, 1996), p. 59. The concept of ex-timacy overcomes the apparent, superficial duality between the interior and the exterior.

express the idea that freedom and equality are universal only as shared freedom and equality. *Säwrä tarik* discerns these as surplus meanings of the *people's people* local critiques, subjugated knowledge, overt and covert struggles against oppression and exploitation. When taken together the fragments express the inseparability of freedom, equality, justice, and epistemic autonomy not only conceptually but also practically. They form a *wihdät* and are central to *säwrä tarik* and its three constitutive dimensions—*arnät* or emancipation, *minab* or concrete utopia, and *yäwäl* or the commons. The following chapter deals with each of these separately.

3

Säwrä tarik: Overcoming the Triple Domination

አርነት ያለው ሕዝብ ማለት... ለብቻው መንግሥት ያለው ሕዝብ ማለት ብቻ አይደለም... ራሱንም የቻለ ሕዝብ ማለት ነው.[282]

(To have *arnät* or to be an emancipated people is more than having an independent state, it is also being a master of one's own destiny.)

Negadras Gebre Hiywet Baykedagn, ሥራዎች

3.1 *Säwrä tarik* and *arnät*: beyond Potemkin democracy

A critical internal journey into Ethiopian history/society discloses that the telos of *säwrä tarik* (surplus history) is *arnät* (አርነት). Usually translated as "emancipation," *arnät* has a wider significance. It embodies the idea of political, economic, social, intellectual, and cultural flourishing of every Ethiopian, and of Ethiopia as a context of living. It expresses the aspiration of the *people's people* for a society whose structures, relations, and functioning *continuously minimize* powerlessness: unfreedoms, inequalities, injustices, material deprivations, social sufferings, and epistemic repression, while at the same time *continuously maximizing* "the expansion of human capabilities" of all the members of Ethiopian society, irrespective of their ethnic, religious, political, or ideological affiliation.[283] These two dimensions of *arnät* (emancipation)—minimizing powerlessness and maximizing capabilities—are inseparable; achieving one cannot be

---

282 Negadras Gebre Hiywet Baykedagn, ሥራዎች (Addis Ababa: Addis Ababa University Press, 2007), p. 102.
283 On the concept of capability and on the capabilities approach, Amartya Sen, *The Idea of Justice* (Cambridge: Harvard University Press, 2009), pp. 225-252. See Chapter 1, above, *supra*.

dissociated from achieving the other. To describe *arnät* negatively as the uninterrupted *minimization* of powerlessness signifies that *arnät* is not made up of static ideas, practices, and institutions; it is a process of a collective self-emancipation that is always a *gädl* in progress, whose outcomes are always *enkän* (incomplete and contradictory), and require *zäräfa* of what *arnät* has already achieved to prevent its sedimentation into a new system of domination and to resolve the inevitable antagonisms that the functioning of *arnät* produces. In *säwrä tarik*, *arnät* is the means and end of all political, economic, social, and intellectual activities, projects, policies, and organizations. Unlike liberal democracy that limits democracy to politics, facilitates the annexation of society by capitalism, and shields the latter from the effects of emancipatory politics, *arnät* considers democracy as inseparable from the liberation of the economy from the interests and forces of domination. *Arnät* gives power to the *people's people* to know, say, and act in ways that continuously enhance political, economic, social, and epistemic capabilities and justice.

It is important to note, as we have seen in the discussion of *säwrä hiywät*, that freedom and equality are, according to *arnät*, internally related. This means that a thick background of equality—political, economic, epistemic, and social—is a necessary condition for the exercise of freedom, and *vice versa*. Without such a background, freedom loses its power to enhance the individual and the community and becomes a tool of domination.[284] *Arnät* weaves relations between equality and freedom that are critical of and incompatible with non-reciprocal relations between equality and freedom and of the inequalities of powers and life conditions that these non-reciprocal relations produce. One could use Balibar's term "equaliberty" to name the directly proportional relations that exist between freedom and equality.[285] *Arnät* demolishes down the partition between freedom and equality that liberalism

---

284 We could see the instrumentalization of freedom as a tool of domination in the rise of the "security state," the "carceral state," the "surveillance state," the "indebted man," and the multi-dimensional inequalities that thrive in liberal democracies, all in the name of freedom. Maurizio Lazzarato, *The Making of the Indebted Man: An Essay on the Neoliberal Condition*, trans. Joshua David Jordan (Amsterdam: Semiotext (e), 2012). Stuart Croft and Terry Terriff, eds., *Critical Reflections on Security and Change* (London: Frank Cass, 2000); Jackie Wang, *Carceral Capitalism* (South Pasadena, CA: Semiotext(e) Intervention Series, 2018). Shane Harris, *The Watchers: The Rise of America's Surveillance* (New York: Penguin Books, 2011).
285 Étienne Balibar, *Equaliberty*, trans. James Ingram (Durham: Duke University Press, 2014).

erects and makes one's responsibility for the flourishing of the "other" a dimension of one's freedom and equality: an issue examined in the previous chapter in the discussion of የኔ ብጤ (*yäne bitie*) and ሰው ለሰው መድሃኒቱ / *säw läsäw mädhanitu*. It creates a *wihdät* that embraces politics and economics. *Arnät* dismantles the barriers between politics and economics and treats the two as "diversity-in-unity" with emancipation as their shared goal. This shared goal mediates and unifies them in the sense of *wihdät*. However, like all *wihdät*, it is *enkän* and traversed by tensions between politics and economics. In all cases, *arnät* is a critique of and incompatible with development and democratization that are wedded to the structures and relations of the triple internal and external domination—political, economic, and epistemic—that one finds in contemporary Ethiopia. It challenges the hegemonic beliefs of development and democratization theories that capitalism and liberal democracy are the ultimate framework for a better society in Ethiopia. Nor could *arnät* be reduced to *nätsanät* (ነጻነት, freedom in the sense of an independent state). As the early twentieth century writer Negadras Gebre Hiywet Baykedagn noted in the exergue above,— "አርነት ያለው ሕዝብ ማለት... ለብቻው መንግሥት ያለው ሕዝብ ማለት ብቻ አይደለም... ራሱንም የቻለ ሕዝብ ማለት ነው" / "To have *arnät* or to be an emancipated people is more than having an independent state, it is also being a master of one's own destiny." Being an independent state is not enough, as the contemporary history of Africa, Asia, and South America shows, to enjoy *arnät*. A country could be independent and yet be politically, economically, and epistemically non-autonomous. To enjoy freedom, equality, justice, and epistemic autonomy, Ethiopians need much more than an "independent" state. Negadras Gebre Hiywet Baykedagn considered that Ethiopians will be committing a grave mistake to conflate, as Ethiopians often do, *arnät* with *nätsanät* and reduce the former to the latter. *Arnät* is all encompassing, while *nätsanät* is limited in that it means independence from foreign rule. For Negadras, an indispensable element of *arnät* was intellectual autonomy without which we can neither have a correct diagnosis of our conditions nor generate knowledge and policies that bring about political, economic, and epistemic emancipation. He characterized the lack of epistemic autonomy and the uncritical borrowing of "knowledge" as "broken words" (*yätäsäbabäru qalat*, የተሰባበሩ ቃላት), which he considered obstacles to *arnät*.[286]

From the perspective of *säwrä tarik*, democracy and development enhance the lives of Ethiopians only and only if they are emancipatory in the sense of *arnät* and not in the sense that democracy and development have in the

---

286 Negadras Gebre Hiywet Baykedagn, *supra*, ሥራዎች, p. 104.

borrowed social sciences. The borrowed social sciences limit democracy to the political sphere, which they reduce to procedures such as multi-party competitive elections. Economic issues are reduced to technical matters and their political contents occluded. These two reductions of democracy to formal procedures and of the economy to technical issues transform democracy and development into vehicles for serving the interests of the *official people*. Arnät's conception of democracy and development as interconnected processes that must work together to minimize powerlessness and maximize capabilities is alien to the hegemonic theory and understanding of democracy and development. What we have currently in Ethiopia is Potemkin democracy: an elaborate façade of fake multi-party elections, though the results of the elections are already pre-determined, to hide the oppressive reality of ethnic authoritarianism and to deceive outsiders.[287] Potemkin democracy is anti-emancipatory or anti-*arnät*.

The concept of *arnät* has a wider range and reach than the Western concept of emancipation. The modern Western concept of emancipation first appeared in the Enlightenment and the Declaration of the Rights of Man and of the Citizen (1789), which asserted that "men" are born and remain free. Kant described it as the "emergence" of "man...from his self-incurred immaturity."[288] The understanding of emancipation that emerged from the Enlightenment and that liberal democracy has endorsed is individualistic. One must note that the Enlightenment understanding of emancipation is limited to politics. Moreover, it is, right from its beginning, contaminated with racism, sexism, class and colonial exploitation.[289] In light of the continued structural presence of class, racial, and gender injustices in contemporary liberal democracies, the history and practice of the individualistic understanding of emancipation suggests that it does not have the conceptual resources to go to the roots of the relations and

---

287 On Potemkin village, see Jennifer Murtoff, "Potemkin village". *Encyclopedia Britannica*, https://www.britannica.com/topic/Potemkin-village. Accessed 14 September 2023.

288 *Kant's Political Writings*, ed. Hans Reiss (Cambridge: Cambridge University Press, 1970), p. 54.

289 Kant, the philosopher of freedom, could reasonably be seen as one of the founders of scientific racism. Robert Bernasconi, "Who Invented the Concept of Race? Kant's Role in the Enlightenment Construction of Race," in Robert Bernasconi, ed. *Race* (New York: Blackwell Publishing, 2001), pp. 11-36; Damien Tricoire, *Enlightened Colonialism: Civilization Narratives and Imperial Politics in the Age of Reason* (New York: Palgrave Macmillan, 2017). Michelle Alexander, *The New Jim Crow: Mass Incarceration in the Age of Colorblindness* (New York: The New Press, 2010).

structures of the triple domination that weigh on Ethiopian society and which must be tackled in order for *arnät* to prevail.[290]

Emancipation gets a new meaning in the nineteenth century, primarily in the works of Marx and various socialist writers, as collective emancipation. This understanding of emancipation arises from the recognition of the modern (capitalist) form of collective domination—those (the class) who own capital over those (the class) who own only their labour power—as systemic oppression and exploitation of one class by another. The Marxist tradition founds emancipation on the class struggle that ensues from this systemic exploitation. The advocates of class struggle justify it in terms of the knowledge of the accumulation process and of the "laws of motion of history" that would describe the movement from capitalism to communism. This knowledge, they claim, provides the theoretical ground for revolutionary actions, capable of transforming the class society of capitalism into a classless society. The transformation would be led by an enlightened elite, the "vanguard party," that organizes the working class and acts to free society from the fetters of capitalism and its supporting political institutions.[291] However, historically, the outcome has been a ruthless dictatorship of the "enlightened" elite over the rest of the population.

Despite the goals of equality and autonomy to which both currents of Western theories of emancipation—liberal (the individualistic) and Marxist (collective)—are committed, both pursue emancipation in a manner that maintains, in differing ways to be sure, structures and relations of inequality between the emancipators and the to-be-emancipated. Note that one of the influential philosophers of freedom of the individualistic tradition, Kant, wrote that "progress" must be from *"the top downwards"* and not *"from the bottom*

---

[290] It is the Haitian Revolution, not the French and American Revolutions, that universalized egalitarianism, political emancipation, and human rights unconditionally and for the first time. C. L. R. James, *The Black Jacobins: Toussaint L'Ouverture and the San Domingo Revolution* (New York: Vintage Books, 1963); Susan Buck-Morss, *Hegel, Haiti, and Universal History* (Pittsburgh: University of Pittsburgh Press, 2009). Note that it is Napoleon, the champion of the French Revolution, who reinstated slavery in the French colonies in 1802 by revoking the Law of 1794 that abolished slavery. Robert Giacomel, *Le code noir : autopsie d'un crime contre l'humanité* (Nîmes : Lacour, 2003).

[291] Tom Bottomore, ed. *A Dictionary of Marxist Thought, Second Edition* (Oxford: Blackwell Publishers, 2001), p. 54. "The party was to be composed of militant, active Marxists committed to the 'socialist revolution', while those who merely sympathized with the socialist idea, and inactive members, were to be excluded from membership."

upwards."[292] The liberal tradition limits emancipation to political rights and allows the development of inequalities in the economic and social spheres.[293] The practitioners of the Marxist theory of emancipation usually resort to the use of force and repression to "emancipate" the "oppressed." In all cases, the emancipators—political leaders, the intelligentsia, politicians, the vanguard party, revolutionaries, and so forth—claim to have emancipatory knowledge that throws light on how a given political and economic system oppresses people, how it could be reformed or overthrown, and by whom. This knowledge is assumed to be unavailable to the oppressed, thus requiring those who have this knowledge to lead the emancipatory struggle.

The emancipators tell the to-be-emancipated the meanings of their experiences as oppressed people, how degrading these experiences are, and why they should accept and follow the path of emancipation—competitive multi-party elections, say the liberals; a proletarian or a peasant revolution, claim the Marxists—that the emancipators have worked out for them. The emancipators separate themselves from the to-be-emancipated not only epistemologically but also politically, in that they appropriate for themselves the power to organize and lead the to-be-emancipated towards a putatively better and enlightened society. In general, one could say that Western theories—liberal and Marxist—articulate emancipation in terms of what Jeremy Gilbert calls "Leviathan Logic" or "verticalism."[294] It is part of their internal logic that an emancipatory organization requires vertical structures that establish hierarchical relations between the self-proclaimed emancipators and the to-be-emancipated, and imposes the obligation on the latter to submit to the epistemological and political authority of the former. The process of emancipation *à la* West, be it liberal or Marxist, keeps the to-be-emancipated in a state of inequality and "immaturity," despite the understanding of emancipation as the overcoming of inequality and immaturity.

In their ideas and policies of development and democracy, Ethiopian politicians of all ideological persuasions and development experts adopt "verticalism" as their *modus operandi*. They treat the *people's people* as political patients and not as political agents, as subordinates rather than as equals. Often, those in power or seeking power use them as pawns in political struggles, "wars

---

292 *Kant's Political Writings*, ed. Hans Reiss. (Cambridge: Cambridge University Press, 1970), p. 188. Italics in the original.
293 Larry Bartels, *Unequal Democracy: The Political Economy of the New Gilded Age* (Princeton: Princeton University Press, 2008); Branko Milanovic, *Global Inequality* (Cambridge: Harvard University Press, 2016).
294 Jeremy Gilbert, *Common Ground: Democracy and Collectivity in an Age of Individualism* (London: Pluto Press, 2014), pp. 69-70.

of liberation," "ethnic self-determination," and winning "elections". None of the modern Ethiopian regimes and political parties see the *people's people* as autonomous beings capable of critically evaluating their conditions of existence and taking their destinies into their own hands.[295] The last EPRDF Prime Minister Hailemariam Dessalegn (2012-2018), stated, "due to poor education and illiteracy, the Ethiopian public is too underdeveloped to make a well-reasoned, informed decision"; therefore, the "enlightened leaders" have "to lead the people."[296] The late Prime Minister, Meles Zenawi, saw himself as a political, social, economic theoretician and spoke down to Ethiopians. The Prosperity Party Prime Minister, Dr Abiy Ahmed (2019…) has a pastoral approach in his communication with Ethiopians, whoever they may be, and dissertates on subjects ranging from military science, the social sciences, religion, to philosophy.[297]

There is a radical difference between the Western traditions of emancipation and emancipation understood as *arnät*. *Säwrä tarik* rejects the split between the emancipators and the to-be-emancipated, for both are *nägär* and thus *säm ena wärq*. The split between the emancipators and the to-be-emancipated create conditions that make power relations immune to democratization and makes *arnät* unattainable. *Säwrä tarik* conceives *arnät*/emancipation as the work of those who are oppressed and exploited. Consider the following *qiné* that speaks of the *people's people* and of their awareness of oppression, and of their desire for *arnät* or emancipation.

---

295 EPRDF documents: *Our revolutionary democratic goals and the next step* (Addis Ababa, 1993); *Strategy of revolutionary democracy, tactics and the question of leadership* (Addis Ababa, 2007).
In 2018, a self-described liberal regime, led by Prime Minister Abiy Ahmad, came to power. His political thinking articulated in his book መደመር (*Mädämer*) exudes a pastoral relation between the leader and the people, with the latter seen as coming together (*Mädämer*) through the guidance of the political pastor. *Mädämer* intimates a kind of "pastoral" verticalism.
296 Quoted in René Lefort, "The 'Ethiopian Spring': Killing is not an answer to our grievances" opendemocracy.net/ren-lefort/ethiopian-spring-killing-is-not-answer-to-our-grievances. September 2016 (2016-09-09T10:31:50+01:00). Accessed 8/26/2017.
297 Abiy Ahmed, መደመር (Los Angeles: Tsehai Publishers, 2019); Abiy Ahmed, እርካብና መንበር https://www.scribd.com/document/460179655/Erkab-Ena-Menber. The attitude of knowing it all is also the central feature of his books. Government employs are obliged to buy his books and are supposed to consult them as a source of wisdom for guiding their activities. Abiy Ahmed seems to be in the process of incarnating himself as the new embodiment of the Zära Yacob syndrome. Maimire Mennasemay, *Qiné Hermeneutics and Ethiopian Critical Theory* (Los Angeles: Tsehai Publishing, 2021), pp. 460-464.

> ድንጋይ ተጫኖኛ ከበላይ / A rock is weighing on my shoulders
> ላወርደው ሳስብ ከትክሻዬ / I am thinking of throwing it down
> የሚረዳኝ ሰው አጣሁኝ / I could not find a person to help me
> ሁሉም እኔን ተጫነኝ / Everybody weighs on me. [298]

The person in the *qiné* says the "rock" (ድንጋይ, *dingay* meaning "rock," used here as a *zäybé* for oppression) weighs on his shoulders. The first line clearly states that the oppressed not only lives but also experiences oppression as oppression, and is thus cognizant of oppression as something wrong that needs to be overcome. The person does not attribute the awareness of oppression as a wrong nor the desire to get rid of it to another entity or to knowledge derived from an outside source. The first three lines suggest that the oppression or *dingay* is both subjective and objective. Though the oppressed try to unburden themselves of it, they find themselves in a quandary on how to do it. The oppressed have to overcome their own internalized resistance to change the order of things and the temptation to look to others to get rid of the *dingay* for them. The last two lines introduce the idea of an external help; however, they question it at the same time. The tensions between the four lines suggest skepticism about any "help" from "outside" to emancipate oneself. The fourth line—ሁሉም እኔን ተጫነኝ (*hulum enén tächanän*) / everybody weighs on me—points to the danger of depending on an external emancipator. It intimates that external help, even if its intent is benevolent, transmutes itself eventually into a new *dingay*. The *wärq* of the *qiné* is that only the *people's people* have the experience of oppression and the desire for emancipation existentially deep enough to bring about emancipation that is free from the kind of political regression (the fourth line) that the split between emancipators and the to-be-emancipated inevitably produces. This means a number of crucial things from the perspective of *säwrä tarik* in the pursuit of *arnät*.

First, the means for achieving *arnät* must be consistent with the goal that is sought, i.e., *arnät*. Second, it means that *arnät* cannot be granted from above; it is the achievement of the *people's people*: those who are oppressed, exploited, and uncounted. Third, *arnät* demands that knowledge be a commons (*yäwäl*, see below 3.3), because knowledge as a commons ensures *arnät*-driven knowledge production that involves the active consideration of the emancipatory interests and needs of the *people's people* and of their active participation in the production of knowledge. It becomes knowledge (*ewqät/ewnät*) based on epistemic autonomy and epistemological egalitarianism between those who claim to

---

[298] Ngusse Nagaw Dagaga, የቅኔ አፈታት ዜዳዎች ና የምርጥ ቅኔዎች ስብስብ, Second edition (Addis Ababa: Mega, 1993), p. 131.

know and those who are claimed to benefit from this knowledge, thus avoiding the emergence of intellectual and political "verticalism." Finally, as the above *qiné* intimates, Ethiopian history / society will always be *säm ena wärq*, thus it will always be traversed by social antagonisms. The *qiné* implies that the process that actualizes *arnät* could create new social antagonisms that could transform it into its opposite and make it a new *dingay*. The implication is that *arnät* must continuously be subject to *zäräfa* to prevent it from sedimenting into a new order of domination.

Säwrä tarik shows that *arnät* has deeper roots in Ethiopian history than the liberal conceptions of democracy and development. Moreover, it is difficult to imagine how liberal capitalist democracy could rescue Ethiopians from unfreedoms, inequalities and injustices when even the richest liberal capitalist democracy is mired in cumulative social injustices.[299] Unlike the "backward-looking" and unthinking conception of "democracy" and "development" that Gibbonism has installed in Ethiopia, *arnät* offers a "forward-looking" conception of democracy and social transformation whose forms and content Ethiopians must actively imagine, theorize, and implement in terms of the emancipatory aspirations, ideas, ideals, possibilities, needs and interests articulated in the *andemta* worked out through critical internal and external journeys.

3.2 *Säwrä tarik* and *minab*: beyond adaptive preferences.

ሜዳ አድርጎት ዳጉቱን	/ Others have flattened the escarpments
ወዴት ላርገው ጉልበቴን	/ How could I test my strength?
ኩሉ በላይ ሽንፈት	/ I am filled with pride
ያልተዘጋ በር መክፈት	/ Though I open the doors others have opened
ባሁ ላከልኝ ፈተና	/ Please put me to the test
አቅሜን ይነግረኛልና	/ So that I would know my powers.

Bäewqätu Siyum, ስብስብ ግጥሞች[300]

The composer of the *qiné* in the exergue laments his (the composer being the stand in for Ethiopians) current place in the world as a passive being: others have flattened "escarpments" and unlocked doors. "Escarpments" and "closed doors" are *zäybé* for adversities, obstacles, and challenges. Since others are solving his problems—flattening escarpments and opening closed doors—he has become a

---

299 (United Nations General Assembly, Human Rights Council, *Report of the Special Rapporteur on extreme poverty and human rights on his mission to the United States of America*, A/HRC/38/33/Add.1. Accessed 4 May, 2019.
300 Bäewqätu Siyum, ስብስብ ግጥሞች (Addis Ababa: Hitmat, 2001), p. 134.

squatter in a world he has not created. He sees in this condition a loss of himself and of the world he lives in and entreats God to put him to the test so that he could discover and affirm his powers by flattening escarpments and unlocking closed doors. He would then be creating the world through his own active agency, recognize himself in the world he has made and affirm himself as an active and free being.

To submit Ethiopia to Gibbonist knowledge and practices, as is the case in the areas of development and democratization, is in fact to let others flatten our "escarpments" and to limit ourselves to entering through "doors" that others have "already opened." It is thus to avoid confrontations with our political, economic, social, and intellectual problems as issues of our own making and to evade resolving them through our own questions, critical reflection, and actions grounded in our history (vertical and lateral) and our own emancipatory interests. Letting others open the "door" to and flatten the "escarpments" of "development" and knowledge production is what Ethiopians have been doing. The result has been the intensification of the opacity of Ethiopia's conditions, leading Ethiopians into the false clarity of ethnic thinking, and the unthinking politics of ethnic identity and its inevitable consequence: political violence.

To be able to understand the world in which we live and recognize ourselves in it, we need to grasp and overcome the opaqueness and resistance of the world as well as of ourselves through our own intellectual, affective, and material struggles (ወዴት ላድርገው ጉልበቴን / *Wädet ladergäw gulbäten*). The *qiné* intimates that we know ourselves only retroactively through the world we ourselves have made or have failed to make through our own agency or lack of it. Given the present condition of Ethiopia as a subaltern nation in the world, the *qiné* articulates the demand that Ethiopians venture beyond what they have made of themselves: squatters vegetating in a globalized capitalist world in which they are potentially disposable beings whose fate hangs on the interests of global capital's accumulation.[301] Without exerting the necessary epistemic, material, and affective efforts to "flatten escarpments" and "unlock doors," Ethiopians cannot know what their powers, opportunities, and possibilities are. The *qiné* expresses the *minab* (ምናብ) that inhabits Ethiopian history as part of its *säwrä tarik*. *Minab* is utopianism without utopia or a "concrete utopia."[302]

---

301 Ethnic self-determination will not save Ethiopians from this fate. It is a distraction from the real issue.
302 "*Concrete utopia stands on the horizon of every reality; real possibility surrounds the open dialectical tendencies and latencies to the very last.*" Ernst Bloch, *The*

Before I discuss *minab*, I will clear the ground by eliminating the common understanding of utopia as a blueprint of a perfectly functioning society. This is what the *qiné* hermeneutical tradition calls *yählm injera* (የሕልም እንጀራ). It means literally "the bread of dreams" or "bread made from dreams." *Yählm injära* designates an abstract utopia. In Ethiopia, where food scarcity and hunger are historically endemic, the expression "the bread of dreams" conveys precisely the notion of an abstract utopia, for no amount of bread produced in dreams or out of dreams can fend off hunger. A utopian blueprint is a *yählm injära* with no roots in reality (*ewen*, እውን). Unlike *minab*, which is a utopianism without utopia that articulates its ideas of an alternative Ethiopia from within *säwrä tarik*, *yählm injära* offers a blueprint of the ideal society detached from *säwrä tarik* and the concrete problems it articulates. Unlike *minab*, which arises immanently out of Ethiopia's historical and social conditions, *yählm injära* is an abstract utopia imposed transcendentally in order to change the coordinates of Ethiopian society from above. Unlike *minab* that is traversed by antagonisms arising from its functioning, *yählm injera* offers a society without antagonisms. *Yählm injära*, because it has no roots in *säwrä tarik*, leads to a dystopian society. *Minab* is radically different from *yählm injera* in that its ideas and images of the better society are immanent to Ethiopian history/society and does not promise a flawless society. It is rooted in *säwrä tarik*.

Minab covers a complex semantic field. First, it means *lib wäläd* (ልብ ወለድ), which one could translate as "that which originates in the heart," referring to the desire and fidelity that inhabit it. Second, it means *aynä hileena* (ዓይነ ሕሊና), which translates as the "eye of the mind" or of the intellect and the imagination. *Minab* conjugates what the "heart" (ልብ, *lib*) desires with what the "eye of the mind" (*aynä hileena* / ዓይነ ሕሊና) sees or what the intellect and imagination disclose as possible. *Minab* is not an escape from reality. Rather, it conceives and imagines new possibilities through *arat ayn* in that it goes beyond the conventional "two-eyed" vision—which is limited to the empirically given—and prefigures an alternative Ethiopia that is already germinating in the struggles and sufferings of Ethiopians and the hopelessness of their conditions. *Säwrä tarik* sees in hopelessness the limitations of the possible, the birth of militant hope, and an opening up of the impossible in the form of *minab*. *Minab* operates in terms of what Jean-Pierre Dupuy calls "enlightened catastrophism."[303] To realize the necessity of *minab* in present-day Ethiopia,

---

Principle of Hope, trans. Neville Plaice, Stephen Plaice and Paul Knight (Cambridge, MA: The MIT Press, 1986), p. 223. Emphasis in text.
303 On forestalling a catastrophe, Jean-Pierre Dupuy, *Pour un catastrophisme éclairé, Quand l'impossible est certain* (Paris : Seuil, 2004).

one must see *as if* Ethiopia has already come to its catastrophic end—the collapse into ethnic dictatorship or the fragmentation of Ethiopia into an archipelago of ethnic tyrannies— so that we could realize, looking at Ethiopia retroactively from this catastrophic end to come, the futility of putting our hope in the existing order and recognize the necessity of taking emancipatory actions in the present to prevent from happening the coming real catastrophe. *Minab* springs from the hopelessness that the catastrophe to come triggers, a hopelessness that *säwrä ras* transmutes through its actions into an opening for the possibility that the extant order considers impossible: an Ethiopia constituted through and expressive of *arnät*. *Minab* is not and does not propose a blue print of an ideal society; rather, it mobilizes the resources of *säwrä tarik* and concentrates on the obstacles (the "escarpments," the "locked doors") to overcome and excavates the "utopianism without utopia" already simmering in Ethiopian reality. In *säwrä tarik, minab* is both realist and utopian. It is not perfectionist, but a vehicle of the passionate desire of Ethiopians for a change that eliminates the triple domination that has made social suffering a daily staple food for the *people's people*.

Minab could be disclosed through *antsar* and *wistä wäyra* readings of Ethiopian reality. *Minab* develops in the interstices of the conflicts and contradictions (ጥምር / *t'mir*) of Ethiopian history/society; it articulates itself in the temporality of the *people's people*, which is the temporality of emancipation, but is absent in the temporality of the *official people*, which is the temporality of domination. To actualize *minab*, we have to appropriate the seeds of emancipation dormant in the past, the present, and the future through a *zäräfa* engaging the past—the emancipatory "future in the-past" that the past has failed to enact, but haunts our present as the possibility of an emancipated Ethiopia—the present and the emancipatory ideas incubating in it, and the alternative future that splits from the future the hegemonic order projects.[304] The *säwrä ras* could awaken to life these dormant seeds of emancipation and make the emergence of what hegemonic society considers impossible: an alternative Ethiopian society free from the current political, economic, and intellectual impasses. *Minab* makes the here and now the ground and time towards which converge the alternative past of the unfulfilled promises and of the failed struggles and the alternative future of an emancipated Ethiopia, making the present the site of emancipatory thinking and actions. *Minab* is incompatible with ideas or approaches that conceive Ethiopia's historical time as homogeneous and linear.

---

304 On the future in the past, Ernst Bloch, *The Principle of Hope* I, trans. Neville Plaice, Stephen Plaice and Paul Knight (Cambridge, MA: MIT Press, 1986), pp.91-3, 116ff, 285ff.

Minab is not an exercise in fabricating a perfect society. It is neither a Kantian regulative idea nor an unrealizable fantasy. It is a concrete expression of a real urgent Ethiopian need, simmering in the Ethiopian conditions themselves, to stop an end to the endless suffering in which the *people's people* are trapped. Unveiling *minab* presupposes a critical internal journey that enables us to assume a critical distance from within Ethiopian history/society so that we could disclose the anti-emancipatory processes, structures and relations constitutive of the hegemonic order. At the same time, this critical distance brings into view a new political *admas* that reveals the possibility of thinking a political *andem*: an alternative to the present order, based on emancipatory ideas and goals, and the kind of possible actions and means that our critical internal and external journeys reveal. Following the *qiné* hermeneutical rejection of dualism, we could say that, in *minab*, there is no dualism between utopia and reality in that there is a *säm ena wärq* relation between the two, which suggests that *minab* is already present in or immanent to Ethiopian reality as a concrete possibility. But it is not present as a place but as a "disturbance that begets clarity," to use Bäalu Girma's words ("ካላረፈስ አይጠራም"), whose *zäybé* are the existing socio-political and economic antagonisms and conflicts.[305]

Minab could be considered as an "extra-territorial" space, a vantage point, in non-synchronous time. It is the space and time of the *people's people*, which has "no place" and "time" in the *official people*'s place and time and narratives of the Ethiopian past, present, and future.[306] It is an extra-territorial place that is immanent and not external to Ethiopian history/society. It offers a vantage point from within Ethiopian history/society which enables one to have a critical stance on Ethiopian history/society, a vantage point from where one could observe and critically examine Ethiopia's political, economic and epistemic pathologies, and its repressed emancipatory potentialities. As a vantage point, *minab* discloses the wrongness and the contingent nature of the extant Ethiopian society as well as the tasks to be pursued if Ethiopia is to take the emancipatory path. It opens a new horizon (*admas*) for thinking beyond the limits of Ethiopia's subaltern political, economic, and epistemic integration into global capitalism.

---

305 Bäalu Girma, ሀዲስ (Addis Ababa: Ethiopia Book Center, 1982), p. 301. From the peasant uprisings in the mid-twentieth century to ethnic conflicts in the present century, contemporary Ethiopia teems with social, political, economic, ideological, and cultural "disturbances," dislocations, and disruptions.

306 I am subjecting some of Ricoeur's ideas on utopia as "extra-territorial space" to *zäräfa*. Paul Ricoeur, *Lectures on Ideology and Utopia*, ed. G. H. Taylor (New York: Columbia University Press, 1986), p. 16.

The new horizon that *minab* opens up defamiliarizes us with the givens of the hegemonic order and makes thinkable the idea that emancipatory social transformation requires grasping politics as the "art of the impossible." It is in engaging in *arat ayn* and conducting a *zäräfa* of what the Ethiopian hegemonic order considers impossible that we could break the regime's ideological and political prohibitions and discover the forbidden possibles. We could then formulate innovative theories and practices that articulate emancipatory problematizations of Ethiopian conditions. *Minab* is the thought vehicle for revealing the "impossibles" that are possible, and thus the repressed possible alternative Ethiopia. *Minab* has the effectiveness of an "enacted utopia" that by virtue of being imagined and conceived allows the disclosure of the presence of *säwrä bahil* (non-tradition), *säwrä ras* (surplus self), *säwrä hiywät* (surplus life), and the possible emancipatory actions that are within the reach of the *people's people*.

Minab emerges from subjugated knowledge, local critiques, and from the various multiple overt and covert struggles of the *people's people* against political and social sufferings. As such, it can be discussed only in ways that negate the acts and processes of existing oppression and exploitation, and not as a vision and a project unrelated to the existing political, economic and epistemic wrongs, nor as a project that tinkers with the hegemonic order without changing its parameters and *admas*. *Minab* is a method for imagining and constructing *arnät*. It has a substantiative content without being a blueprint, in that it articulates the ideas, norms, and practices of *säwrä hiywät* that point to institutions, practices and relations whose contents are the negations of the triple domination—political, economic, and epistemic—that have incarcerated the life of the *people's people*.[307] *Minab* offers an Archimedean point that enables us to make *andem* shifts that render visible, audible, rational, and possible that which the hegemonic order makes invisible, inaudible, irrational, and impossible. That is, *minab* breaks through the given coordinates of the thinkable and doable of the hegemonic order and invents new coordinates of the conceivable and feasible that liberate us from the epistemological, methodological, and teleological prisons of Gibbonist theories and practices of development and democratization. From the perspective of *qiné* hermeneutics *minab* is *enkän* and as such a *nägär* that has its own particular antagonisms that arise from its functioning and is thus open-ended in the sense that its functioning creates new questions, challenges, and possibilities, theoretically and practically.

---

307 On utopia as method, Ruth Levitas, *Utopia as Method: The Imaginary Reconstitution of Society* (New York: Palgrave Macmillan, 2013).

One could say that *minab* shines through the historically and internally generated Ethiopian concepts that *säwrä tarik* excavates: መብት (*mäbit*, rights), ነፃነት (*nätsanät*, liberty as freedom from external domination), አርነት (*arnät*, emancipation), እኩልነት (*equlinät*, equality), አጸፋ (*atsäfa*, reciprocity), ፍትህ (*fithe*, justice), የወል (*yäwäl*, commons), ኅብረት (*hibrät*, solidarity), ምናብ (*minab*, utopianism without utopia), ማዕረግ (*ma eräg*, dignity), ተግባር (*tägbar*, duty), ሰባዊ (*säb'awi*, rights that belong to humans by virtue of being human), ዜግነት (*zegnät*), እውነት (*ewnät*, truth or "the hidden good"), እውቀት (*ewqät*, knowledge), ብልጽግና (*biltsigina*, just prosperity). The emergence of these critical concepts from within and in the Ethiopian context of centuries of oppression signals the existence of resistance to domination that points to the presence of *minab* as a concrete possibility simmering in the very anti-*arnät* conditions that exist in Ethiopia. The concepts exist as negative concepts critical of Ethiopian conditions, but not as parts of a blueprint. Their presence as negative concepts reveals the social, political, economic, and epistemic pathologies of Ethiopian society and projects the need and the possibility of subverting and dismantling the hegemonic order through practices that continuously and unremittingly minimize the oppressions that these concepts make visible as wrong and unacceptable. The presence of these concepts in Ethiopian history/society also shows the error of the claim that Ethiopian history/society is devoid of utopian thinking. It is certainly true, as Messay Kebede claims, that "Ethiopians never created a social utopia."[308] There are no Ethiopian texts specifically focused on providing utopian blueprints comparable to Campanella's *The City of the Sun* or Thomas Moore's *Utopia*.[309] However, the absence of utopian blueprints does not mean the absence of *minab*. That there are no utopian blueprints in the Ethiopian intellectual tradition does not warrant the conclusion that there are no utopian ideas, desires, and impulses in Ethiopian history.

Subjecting to *zäräfa* Žižek's claim that "Every historical situation contains its own unique utopian perspective, an immanent vision of what is wrong with it, an ideal representation of how, with some changes, the situation could be made much better," one could say that every Ethiopian historical situation harbors its

---

[308] Messay Kebede, *Survival and Modernization, Ethiopia's Enigmatic Present: A Philosophical Discourse* (Lawrenceville, NJ: The Red Sea Press, 1999), p. 220. He writes, "It is no surprise, then, that the Ethiopians never created a social utopia. Since each person had an untouchable share, the idea of perfecting the social system from below could only appear as an attempt to cause disorder by questioning the wisdom of God's allotment. What should worry human beings was less the nature of their share than the certitude of being in their apportioned places."

[309] Frank E. Manuel and Fritzie P. Manuel, *Utopian Thought in the Western World* (Cambridge: Harvard University Press, 1979).

own *minab* articulating immanent visions of a better society that overcomes the injustices of the existing society.[310] Thus, the various emancipatory visions: Lalibela's project to construct in Ethiopia an earthly version of the "heavenly Jerusalem"; the struggles of the 15th century Ethiopian heretical movements—the Ewostatewos, the *Däqiqä Estifanos*, the Zamika'elites and their ideal of "standing upright" rather than "prostrating" oneself to power—Emperor Tewodros's effort to create a modern society, the peasant uprisings in Wollo (1928-30), Tigray (1941), Gojjam (1968), and Bale (1963-70), the organization and the functioning of the utopian community of Awra Amba, the Ethiopian Students Movement (1960-74) to bring about a democratic society, the presence of autopoietic mutual aid, labour-sharing, and conflict resolution mechanisms, and the presence of overt and covert "local critiques," though all of these are marked by failures to bring substantive change.[311]

Säwrä tarik does not reject the failures of the past in its pursuit of an alternative Ethiopia. Rather, it considers them as *zäybé* of the emancipatory "futures in the-past" and "futures in the present." It enucleates and uses their emancipatory surplus meanings as ladders for developing theoretical and practical steps for climbing out from the gravity well of oppression and work out the *minab* they gestate. From the perspective of *säwrä tarik*, failures open the door to counter-factual thinking and expose the antagonisms that Ethiopians have failed to identify and confront, the potential actions that Ethiopians have failed to take, and the conditions that the failures themselves have created as indicators of the right decisions to take in the pursuit of *arnät*. If such is the case, it is appropriate that an authentic emancipatory struggle in Ethiopia pursue the goal of unearthing the *minab* that incubates in Ethiopian history/society including its historical failures in order to develop emancipatory thinking in the context of Ethiopian history/society. To deny the existence of a *minab* vision immanent to Ethiopian history/society is to be oblivious of the emancipatory possibilities that are buried in our past failures; it is to be unconscious of the manifold of contradictory and interacting strands of

---

310 Slavoj Žižek, *Disparities* (New York: Bloomsbury Academic, 2016), p.300.
311 Gebru Tareke, *Ethiopia: Power and Protest: Peasant Revolts in the Twentieth Century* (New York: Cambridge University Press, 1991); Bahru Zewde, *The Quest for Socialist Utopia: The Ethiopian Student Movement c.1960-1974* (London: James Curry, 2014); Maimire Mennasemay, *Qiné Hermeneutics and Ethiopian Critical Theory* (Los Angeles: Tsehai Publishing, 2021), Chapters 6, 7, 8, and 10. Getatchew Haile, "Ethiopian Heresies and Theological Controversies" in *Coptic Encyclopedia*, vol 2, ed. Aziz S. Atiya (New York: Macmillan, 1991), 984a-987b. Taddesse Tamrat, *Church and State in Ethiopia, 1270-1527* (Oxford: Clarendon Press, 1972).

Ethiopian history/society that have generated the kind of critical concepts we saw above, the multiple struggles of the *people's people*, and the *säwrä tarik* they produce.

Unlike the European tradition of utopian blueprints *à la* Thomas Moore that limits one to merely implementing an already worked out utopia, *minab* is experimental in its approach to an alternative society. *Minab* is historical, anti-perfectionist, and anti-authoritarian. *Minab* is freedom affirming and cannot be dissociated from *gädl* or struggle. It leaves Ethiopians free to imagine and create an alternative Ethiopian society capable of dealing with the concrete problems of their life conditions in light of their emancipatory interests and needs. *Minab* offers a concrete emancipatory possibility that is beyond the reach of the imported theories and practices of development and democratization. Precisely because development and democratization theories are radically severed from *säwrä tarik* and its *minab*, they have paralyzed Ethiopian thinking, made the interests of the *people's people* invisible, and blocked reflection on how to open a historical path that meets the emancipatory interests and needs of Ethiopians. The abstract utopian (*yählm injera*) nature of development theory and practice, arising from its radical disconnect from Ethiopian history/society and its *säwrä tarik*, has transmogrified development and democratization into the anti-emancipatory and anti-*minab* practices of "adaptive preferences." [312]

Adaptive preferences are the offspring of politics as the art of the possible. Adaptive preferences refer to an "adjustment of people's aspirations to feasible possibilities", and as such prevent the exercise of "autonomous choices."[313] They make one accept less than adequate problematization of the political, economic, and epistemic challenges Ethiopians face, and they normalize the triple domination that weigh down on Ethiopians. They are answers and solutions to Ethiopia's political, economic, and knowledge problems based on the belief that certain options are not available to or appropriate for Ethiopians.

---

312 On adaptive preferences, see Jon Elster, "Sour Grapes - Utilitarianism and the Genesis of Wants," in Amartya Sen, Bernard Williams, eds., *Utilitarianism and Beyond* (Cambridge: Cambridge University Press, 1982), p. 219, Amartya Sen, *Development as Freedom* (New York: Knopf, 2000), pp. 62-3; Martha C. Nussbaum. 2001a, *Women and Human Development: The Capabilities Approach* (New York: Cambridge University Press, 2001), pp. 148-9; Miriam Teschl and Flavio Comim, "Adaptive Preferences and Capabilities: Some Preliminary Conceptual Explorations," *Review of Social Economy*, 63, 2 (2005), pp. 229-247. Though the literature on adaptive preferences refers to the preferences individuals make, I transform it here through *zäräfa* and apply it to the Ethiopian state and its institutions.

313 Jon Elster, "Sour Grapes - Utilitarianism and the Genesis of Wants," *supra*, p.219.

Adaptive preferences are usually formed in contexts of deprivation or powerlessness and are incompatible with preferences that have intrinsic value. In our case, they express the belief that Ethiopia's choices have to be tailored to the options that "globalization without universalization"—via the mediation of the IMF, the World Bank, Western NGOs, foreign public and private investors, and the global market—considers appropriate for Ethiopia.[314]

Globalization without universalization is the current capitalist process that encompasses the globe in a network of "inclusive exclusion" based on the neoliberal ideas of free markets, primacy of contracts, deregulation, privatization, weakened trade unions, less progressive taxation, competitiveness, the elimination of barriers to trade and international financial transactions, and the acceptance of the market as the main order-creating mechanism in society.[315] The inclusive-exclusion takes the form of adaptive preferences. Though it globalizes capitalism, the process does not universalize freedom, equality, social justice, and epistemic autonomy. It is a process of political, economic, and epistemic subalternization of countries such as Ethiopia within a global economic political system that makes the developed capitalist societies the engine of capitalist globalization to whose interests others must submit, blocking the universalization of rights to life without exploitation, oppression, and. epistemic servility. Adaptive preferences are its tools for inducting countries such as Ethiopia into the global capitalist market in terms of the interests that serve the logic of capitalist accumulation. Consequently, development, as articulated in Gibbonist social sciences in Ethiopian studies, international financial institutions, capitalist investors, and the export market promote adaptive preferences that make Ethiopians adjust their aspirations to "feasible possibilities" as defined by the forces and institutions of globalization, preventing Ethiopians to freely pursue their emancipatory aspirations. Politics as the art of the possible means then choosing policies, projects, practices, and

---

314 David Harvey, *A Brief History of Neoliberalism* (Oxford: Oxford University Press, 2007); Graham Harrison, *Neoliberal Africa: The Impact of Global Social Engineering* (London: Zed Books, 2010); Graham Harrison, "Authoritarian neoliberalism and capitalist transformation in Africa: All pain, no gain." *Globalizations* 16, no. 3 (2019), pp. 274-288; Ian Bruff and Cemal Burak Tansel, "Authoritarian neoliberalism: Trajectories of knowledge production and praxis." *Globalizations* 16, no. 3 (2019), pp. 233-244; Ian Bruff, Nana Poku and Jim Whitman, *Africa under Neoliberalism*, (New York: Routledge, 2018; Thomas Biebricher, *The Political Theory of Neoliberalism* (Stanford: Stanford University Press, 2019). Slavoj Žižek, *The Universal Exception* (New York: Continuum, 2006), pp. 193, 341-2. The expression "globalization without universalization" is Žižek's.

315 On "inclusive exclusion," Giorgio Agamben, *Homo Sacer: Sovereign Power and Bare Life* (Stanford: Stanford University Press, 1998), p.21.

institutions whose internal and external limits are dictated by the parameters of adaptive preferences. These work to the detriment of the emancipatory needs and interests of the *people's people* of Ethiopia, though they enable Ethiopia's *official people* to accumulate wealth and power.

In the sphere of politics, the 1995 Constitution and ethnic federalism are the political and legal embodiments of adaptive preferences in that they express the belief that the idea of democracy based on citizenship (*zega*) is not an option that is "feasible" in Ethiopia, despite its intrinsic value. In contemporary Ethiopian politics, the *official people* assume that Ethiopians cannot go beyond their ethnic horizons and participate in politics as citizens and that only ethnicity-based politics is feasible. Therefore, the *official people* practice politics as the art of the possible and opt for a politics based on ethnic identity. They Ptolemize this regression to ethnic politics, which is an adaptive preference, as "*abiyotawi* (revolutionary) democracy," under the TPLF, and as "liberal democracy," under the PP regime, though both are unabashedly ethnic authoritarian regimes. Adaptive preferences are antithetical to *minab*, for they bloc thinking and theorizing about an alternative Ethiopian society that in its very functioning minimizes unfreedoms, inequalities, injustices and epistemic servility, and develops the conditions necessary for cultivating the capabilities necessary for Ethiopians to flourish.

In the economic field, adaptive preferences repress as unfeasible an alternative Ethiopian economy that is oriented to the needs and interest of the *people's people*. Adaptive preferences in the economy make Ethiopians tailor their "aspirations to" what are claimed to be "feasible possibilities" as worked out by the Gibbonist economic sciences and experts: the IMF, the World Bank, Western NGOs, foreign public and private investors. Ethiopia's economic development is calibrated to meet the needs of the capitalist global market making Ethiopia's development dependent on serving the economic interests of external forces. The embodiments of the economic adaptive preferences in Ethiopia are, among others, industrial parks for manufacturing goods for the export market and the production of cash crops to the detriment of food security.[316] This economic

---

316 One of the development faces of adaptive preferences in Ethiopia is "The industrial Park" geared toward the export market at the cost of meeting local needs. The works in these industrial parks receive wages that barely keeps them above the poverty line. On industrial parks, see the reports by the Ethiopian Investment Commission, Ethiopia plans to have 15 industrial parks by 2018. See the reports by the Ethiopian Investment Commission, http://www.investethiopia.gov.et/about-us/how-we-can-help?id=485; Accessed 5/9/2021. Laura Dean, "Ethiopia Touts Good Conditions in Factories for Brands Like H&M and Calvin Klein, but Workers Scrape By on $1 a Day." *The Intercept* (July 8 2018) https://theintercept.

vassalage, dubbed development benefits the *official people* in that they draw from it the wealth and power they need to dominate the *people's people*, while more than 20 million Ethiopians depend on food aid. Adaptive preferences subvert and occlude *minab* and thereby the possibilities of the political, economic, and epistemic emancipation that *säwrä tarik* articulates and proposes. It is crucial to bear in mind that the present ethnic politics in Ethiopia is compatible with economic vassalage in that the ethnic fragmentation of Ethiopia facilitates the servicing of the interests of globalized capital through the creation of weak states that have no choice but to submit to its interests in the form of adaptive preferences masked as "democratization," "development," and "ethnic self-determination."[317]

In the area of knowledge production in Ethiopian studies, adaptive preferences are the rule. Epistemic autonomy exists as an inaccessible goal and is replaced by the Gibbonist conception of knowledge production that considers knowledge produced in the West as the standard and measure of what knowledge is and that Ethiopians must follow. Ethiopia's conditions, problems, issues, and interests are conceptualized, problematized, analysed, and given discursive forms through intellectual processes grounded in epistemic and methodological servility. In addition, adaptive preferences in knowledge production promote the internalization of the interests, knowledge and values that inform the global market, international financial institutions, international NGOs, and the discourses of Western development and democratization experts on Ethiopia as the only available interests, values, and knowledge. These cognitive adaptive preferences repress *säwrä tarik* and the emancipatory knowledge it yields, and

---

com/2018/07/08/ethiopia-garment-industry/. Laura Dean notes, "In the Hawassa Industrial Park, factory operators make 750 Ethiopian *birr*, or about $27 a month. Out of this sum, workers must pay for rent and food." Accessed 20/7/2018. "The severity of food insecurity in Ethiopia is among the worst globally." Reliefweb, "Ethiopia Food Security Outlook June 2022 to January 2023," https://reliefweb.int/report/ethiopia/ethiopia-food-security-outlook-june-2022-january-2023. Accessed, 6/8/2023. On adaptive preferences, see Maimire Mennasemay, *Qiné Hermeneutics and Ethiopian Critical Theory* (Los Angeles: Tsehai Publishing, 2021), pp.425-30.

317 On globalization without universalization and ethnic conflicts, see Arjun Appadurai, *Modernity at Large: The Cultural Dimensions of Globalization* (Minneapolis, MN: University of Minnesota Press, 1996); Susan Olzak, "Does Globalization Breed Ethnic Discontent?" *Journal of Conflict Resolution* 55,1, (2011), pp. 3–32; Amy Chu, *World on Fire: How Exporting Free Market Democracy Breeds Ethnic Hatred and Global Instability* (New York: Doubleday, 2003); Margit Bussman and Gerald Schneider, "When Globalization Discontent Turns Violent: Foreign Economic Liberalization and Internal War." *International Studies Quarterly* 51,1, (2007), pp.79–97.

the *minab* it articulates. Cognitive adaptive preferences impede the exploration and development of emancipatory theories, standards, and methods immanent to Ethiopian history/society that could challenge the structures and processes that produce and reproduce the conditions of triple domination: economic, political, and epistemic. Whereas "knowledge is power" in the West, cognitive adaptive preferences have made "knowledge" in Ethiopia a process of servility to the West and an instrument of self-repression.

That political, economic, and cognitive adaptive preferences will lead to democracy and prosperity that serves the *people's people* is a perfect example of *yählm injera* or abstract utopia. Adaptive preferences are in the process of making Ethiopia a "prosthetic nation" made up, metaphorically speaking, of foreign organs—ideas, institutions, projects, practices—that have not grown out of the Ethiopian body or history/society. They are as such disarticulated appendages that require political, economic, and epistemic vassalage to the West in order to maintain them and give them a semblance of coordinated functioning. Adaptive preferences thus trap Ethiopians into a state of permanent political, economic, and epistemic serfdom, masked as national sovereignty. They sabotage the very idea of thinking about an alternative Ethiopia, leech the self-esteem of Ethiopians, and make them accomplices of their own subjugation and exploitation. Adaptive preferences have shackled knowing Ethiopia to Gibbonist knowledge, development to cash crop production and sweat shops, and democracy to electoral despotism with voting taking place under the "pastoral" gaze of foreign "election observers." *Minab* is the antidote to the adaptive preferences that pass for development, democratization, and knowledge in Ethiopia.

We cannot imagine a *qiné* without *wärq*, nor could we imagine an emancipated Ethiopian society without *minab*. As the 15th century *Däqiqä Estifanos* put it, "ከደብሩ ከጌፉ እስክትደርሱ ድረስ ትጉ እንጇ ከጭኑ ቆጭ አትበሉ / Continue with full determination until you reach the summit."[318] The summit—*minab*—may never be reached, but pursuing it gives Ethiopian society a goal: creating a society of *arnät*. The pursuit of *minab* enables us to be the authors and actors of our history and empowers us to understand ourselves and our history. As Karl Mannheim notes, "We cannot imagine... a society without Utopia [*minab*], because this would be a society without goals. [W]ith the relinquishment of Utopias [*minab*], man would lose his will to shape history and therewith his ability to understand it."[319] A society that does not have a vision of the good

---

318 Getatchew Haile, ደቂቀ እስቲፋኖስ: በሕግ አምላክ (*Däqiqä Estifanos: BäHeg Amlak*), translated from Ge'ez by (Collegeville, MN. 2004), p. 268.
319 Karl Mannheim, *Ideology and Utopia* (New York: Harcourt, 1954), p. 236.

society is, as Paul Ricoeur also observes "a society without goals."[320] This is a point that the *Däqiqä Estifanos* have already made in the 15th century with their injunction to always aspire to "reach the summit."

The non-recognition of *säwrä tarik* is what prevents us from seeing the presence of *minab* within Ethiopian history/ society as the surplus meaning of the autochthonous associations, practices, and cultural expressions that the *people's people* have created in response to the challenges of living in conditions of powerlessness.[321] The pursuit of *minab* as an ideal is essential if Ethiopians are to win the intellectual, political, and economic battles that are indispensable for escaping the fate of becoming a disposable people, and for re-entering world history as agents that take part in shaping it. Ethiopians have to delve into the *minab* that *säwrä tarik* articulates and hammer out their own theories of democracy and social transformation to "reach the summit" and actualize their emancipatory interests and needs. Marx claimed that "philosophers have only *interpreted* the world in various ways; the point, however, is to *change* it."[322] This claim is false in the Ethiopian case. Ethiopians do not have critical interpretations of social transformation immanent to Ethiopian history/society, which could enable them to bring about emancipatory transformations. The task of interpreting Ethiopia in ways that disclose the emancipatory potentials and possibilities that gestate in her history is yet to be undertaken seriously.

3.3 *Säwrä tarik* and *yäwäl*: from property to use.

> Did God make the earth fruitful only for you?
> Did he not say: 'I am giving you [humans]
> the various plants so that you may *use* them'[323]
> Aba Estifanos (15th century)

Yäwäl (ያወል) means the commons. One must distinguish the commons as *yäwäl* from liberalism's nebulous ideas about the common good, equality, the "sharing

---

320 Paul Ricoeur, *Lectures on Ideology and Utopia*, ed. G. H. Taylor (New York: Columbia University Press, 1986), p. 283.
321 Mutual aid associations such as *iddir, kire, zakat, iqqub* and *ezen*; labour-sharing associations such as *däbo, wänfal, dafo, läfenty, jigge, mol'a, säddaka* and *bayto*; conflict resolution institutions such as *araaraa, jaarsummaa, biyyaas, afärsata, shimgelina, ayyanaa*; women's associations such as *ateetee, siiqqee, sänbäte, mahibär*
322 Howard Selsam and Harry Martel, eds., "Theses on Feuerbach, # 11," *Reader in Marxist Philosophy* (New York: International Publishers, 1971), p. 318.
323 Getatchew Haile, ደቂቀ እስጢፋኖስ በገነ አምላክ, trans. from Ge'ez (Collegeville, MN: 2004), p. 168.

economy," or solidarity. *Yäwäl* considers property, be it private or state-owned, of the conditions required for producing what is necessary for living detrimental to human welfare. *Yäwäl* replaces ownership with use. The idea of use as an alternative to ownership has roots in the Ethiopian monastic tradition of *gädam* / ገዳም wherein, unlike the hegemonic practice of ownership, the organizing principle of access to things necessary for life was the principle of "use." The concept of *yäwäl* (the commons) has also a presence among Ethiopians who practice communal ownership of land.[324] The concept of "use" could be considered as a *säwrä bahil* or a radical *andem* in the context of feudal Ethiopia wherein the Emperor and feudal lords owned the means of production of things necessary for life, i.e., land. In *yäwäl*, we could say, drawing on the *säwrä bahil* of the practice of *gädam*, that the use relationship to things and the conditions necessary for producing them is based on the collective deliberation and determination of needs, goals, and means through the co-responsibility of the members of the community to use resources in ways that enhance the individual, the community, and future generations of *gädam* members.

Since nothing is a "commons" in itself or naturally, the concept of *yäwäl* intimates the activity of "commoning" that transforms into a *yäwäl* (the commons) whatever is necessary for the individual and collective well-being. The concept of *tägbar* (ተግባር), which means mutual obligation, is internally related to *yäwäl* in that the activity that "commons" things also creates a co-obligation (*tägbar*) among the members of the community to ensure the proper use and reproduction or perpetuation of resources that are "commoned." As the *Däqiqä Estifanos* put it: each and all must "be a witness to those who will come after you."[325] The concept of *yäwäl* has no truck with collectivization, nationalization, or welfare economics, in so far as these assume the "state" as the "private" owner of property and encroach detrimentally on *arnät*. *Yäwäl* considers political, economic, social, and knowledge producing institutions, and all institutions that are necessary for the well-being of Ethiopians as commons and as subject to commoning.

We could grasp the meaning of the concept *yäwäl* (commons) from a response of Abba Estifanos, the 15th century monk, to the Emperor's claim that he owns all that exists in Ethiopia. The Emperor tells Abba Estifanos, "If you do not prostrate yourself before me as a recognition of my honor, on whose land do

---

324 Mohammud Abdulahi, "The Legal Status of the Communal Land Holding System in Ethiopia: The Case of Pastoral Communities," *International Journal on Minority and Group Rights* 14 (2007), 85-125.
325 [44] Getatchew Haile, ደቂቀ እስጢፋኖስ በገነ አምላክ, *supra*, p. 265.

you think you are living? Where do you believe you could go?"³²⁶ Abba Estifanos responds,

> I did not eat what you cultivated; I did not drink the water you stored. The book [the Bible] says 'the heavens are God's, but He gave the earth to humans [*läsäw*, ለሰው].' Did you help God create the heavens? Did God make the earth fruitful only for you? Did He not say, 'I am giving you [humans] the various plants so that you may *use* them'?³²⁷

Abba Estifanos articulates his response in a religious idiom. Nevertheless, there is a secular *säwrä bahil*, a secular *säwrä ras*, a secular *säwrä hiywät*, and a *lissan* trying to break through his religious discourse and articulate non-religious questions regarding property and power.

In rejecting the Emperor's claim that he owns the land and its produce and in telling him that "He [God] gave the earth to humans" and made her "fruitful" to all, Abba Estifanos's response gives voice to a *säwrä bahil*: the idea of "use" of things necessary for living and of the conditions necessary required for producing them as opposed to private or public "property" or "ownership" of these. Aba Estifanos, living in 15th century Ethiopia, refers to "land," which is the condition for the production of things necessary for living in an agricultural society. We could, however, extend through *zäräfa* the condition he refers to—"land"—to all things necessary for life and of their means of production in 21st century Ethiopia—capital, labour, land, and knowledge—and consider these from the perspective of *use* rather than from the perspective of ownership.

Yäwäl expresses the idea that human life is a commonly shared activity. It is the empirical expression and the symptom or *zäybé* of something more fundamental—the ontological primacy of becoming and relations over "being." It embraces the idea of trans-individual sharing of the sharing of society, an idea captured by the following *qiné*:

አገር ድንኳን ትሁን / Let my country be a tent
ጠቅልዬ የማዝላት / That I carry in her entirety
ስጎፉ እንድነቅላት / To save when thunder strikes
ሰረጋ እንድተክላት / To nourish when peace reigns ³²⁸

One finds here the idea of Ethiopia as a "tent" that Ethiopians pitch up collectively, protect collectively, but also take down collectively, if they do not take good care of it. The *qiné* refers to the contingency and fragility (ስጎፉ

---

326 Ibid., p.188.
327 Ibid., emphasis added.
328 Bäewqätu Siyum, ሰበሰብ ግጥሞች (Addis Ababa: Hitmat, 2001), p. 66.

እንድነቅላት / *To save when thunder strikes*) of social existence as well as of one's nation. *Yäwäl* is a dimension of *minab* (concrete utopia) and has no truck with *yählm injera* (abstract utopia). As a dimension of *minab*, *yäwäl* experiences "thunder": antagonisms, changes, and conflicts. *Yäwäl* considers Ethiopian society as a "shared tent" wherein not only all partake in whatever takes place in that tent and its organization and functioning, but also the partaking itself forms the participants and the "tent,' and in the process creates "thunder" or antagonisms that the inhabitants must cope with to bring "peace" through the use of commoning. "Thunder" stands for both internal and external antagonisms and commoning is the process that leads to the identification and resolution of these antagonisms. The "tent" is a "tent" because its inhabitants collectively "maintain" it and defend it through ideas and actions that enrich and deepen the commoning. They "make" the "tent" and the "tent" "makes" them. The *qiné* intimates that even if we deny it, society is a *yäwäl*, and denying this *yäwäl* nature of society could eventually lead to its collapsing from within, and to the suffering of the individuals in the "tent." Ethiopia is a "shared tent" that one cannot inhabit without experiencing the needs, interests, suffering, and the joy of the other as one's own. It is a "tent" within which freedom, rationality, equality, justice, responsibility, prosperity, and epistemic autonomy could exist intermeshed with each other and are equally available to all its inhabitants, if Ethiopians wish so and act accordingly. In other words, Ethiopia herself is, according to the *qiné*, a *yäwäl*.

Yäwäl creates the context and the means with which Ethiopians could maximize their freedom, equality, rationality, prosperity, responsibility, epistemic autonomy, and their capabilities. It is in *yäwäl* that Ethiopians discover the angelic experience of ፍስሃ (*fissiha* / joy, as opposed to the individualistic and utilitarian experience of happiness, ደስታ / *dästa*), to borrow an expression from the Ethiopian monastic tradition.[329] *Yäwäl* rejects utilitarian thinking, capitalist market relations, and state and private paternalism insofar as they undermine the full application of the rights and obligations that *säwrä tarik* uncovers, which we have seen in the discussion of *minab*.

In Ethiopia's secular tradition, one sees an aspect of *yäwäl* in the surplus meaning of *däbo* (ደቦ). In *däbo*, labour is "commoned"; it is a mutually shared use of labour, where labour is not comprehended as either private or public property, but as a commonly shared activity that enhances the *däbo* participants and the *däbo* association. The peasants participating in *däbo* deliberate as a collective on how to carry out the duties involved in farming—from ploughing

---

[329] Getatchew Haile, "Ethiopian Monasticism" in Aziz S Atiya, ed., *Coptic Encyclopedia*, vol. 3 (New York: Macmillan, 1991), pp. 993-94.

to harvesting. In *däbo*, the labour of each is the labour of all, and the labour of all is the labour of each.[330] The Awra Amba community also exemplifies the practice of *yäwäl*. Labour, land, goods and power are "commoned," and all the necessities of life are accessed in terms of "use" and not in terms of private or public ownership.[331]

From the perspective of *säwrä tarik*, the economy is a commons; it is not about *homo economicus*. *Yäwäl* is incompatible with the reduction of human labour to a commodity, of economic motivation to self-interest, and of human beings to market beings.[332] The concept and practice of *yäwäl* imply an alternative to market economy and state-owned economy: the economy as a commons; a new concept of interest as trans-subjectively shared interest; and a new concept of labour whose characteristics and meanings could be understood metaphorically as *däbo* labour or trans-individually shared labour as an alternative to wage labour.[333] As one could see in Awra Amba, the economy as *yäwäl* is an active social bond productive of resources and goods, and of freedom, equality, solidarity, and joy.[334] In *yäwäl*, the production, reproduction, circulation, and distribution of resources, goods, powers, and knowledge take place through commonly shared institutions, processes, and channels that in their functioning enhance the well-being of members, of the community as *wihdät*, and of future generations as well as of the process of "commoning."

Yäwäl also projects an alternative conception of knowledge: knowledge as a commons. With the increasing role of knowledge in the economy, an epochal shift is happening in the post-20th century that some describe as "cognitive capitalism": a form of capitalism based on the accumulation of "immaterial

---

330 On *däbo* Maimire Mennasemay, *Qiné Hermeneutics and Ethiopian Critical Theory* (Los Angeles: Tsehai Publishing, 2021), Chapter 10.
331 Ibid., Chapter 6, on Awra Amba. I conduct a *zäräfa* of what Pierre Dardot et Christian Laval in converting "commons" into a verb, "to common." Pierre Dardot et Christian Laval, *Commun. Essai sur la révolution au XXIe siècle* (Paris: La découverte, 2014), pp. 49, 51, 282-83, 440, 476-81.
332 On *säwrä tarik* (surplus history), see Chapter 2. Adam Smith, *The Wealth of Nations* (London: Penguin, 1982). On humans as market beings, Maurizio Lazzarato, *The Making of the Indebted Man*, trans., Joshua David Jordan (Los Angeles: by Semiotext(e), 2007).
333 For *yäwäl*, intersubjective interests are interests generated through *mädämamät* among participants in the economy or politics such that interests are more than individuals having similar understandings; rather interests generated through *mädämamät* express shared intentions, aims, goals, and courses of actions.
334 Maimire Mennasemay, *Qiné Hermeneutics and Ethiopian Critical Theory* (Los Angeles: Tsehai Publishing, 2021), Chapter 6.

capital," i.e. knowledge.[335] This means the goal of *arnät* cannot be reached with the kind of knowledge to which Ethiopia has access in terms of adaptive preferences. The knowledge that Ethiopia needs to carry out *arnät* enhancing economic transformations could be acquired only as a commodity, immaterial to be sure, for they are privately owned and are subject to patent rights. In other words, the transformation of knowledge into capital (immaterial) will accentuate the triple domination in which Ethiopia is currently trapped. Transforming knowledge into *yäwäl* is one of the crucial ways out of this deadly trap.

Unlike the capitalism-driven conception of knowledge that inheres in development theory and practice and considers knowledge as a commodity or as an intellectual object that is subject to ownership and exchange value, knowledge as *yäwäl* is knowledge as "use-value" accessible to all for living and flourishing.[336] In the present context, the pursuit of *arnät* requires that all knowledge produced in Ethiopia and on Ethiopia be part of the intellectual commons of Ethiopia. We cannot adopt the Gibbonist position and depend on knowledge others produce for us. Other-driven, state-driven and market-driven knowledge productions hollow out *arnät*: the first incubates a knowledge relationship that creates a hierarchical scheme between the "other" and Ethiopians and augments the power of the "other"; the second augments the power of the state over the *people's people*, and the third the power of the market over the *people's people*.[337] Only knowledge as a commons could enable Ethiopians to ensure the development and deepening of their epistemic autonomy and of *arnät*-enhancing knowledge, and the transformation of Ethiopian society into a learning society: a necessary condition for the flourishing of the Ethiopian "general intellect" or the collective intelligence of Ethiopian society.[338]

To be sure, the current global state of the commodification of knowledge is not something that Ethiopia could tackle alone. But she could be the catalyst to push for the commons of knowledge that are crucial for human well-being such as health, food production, communication, education, peace, prosperity,

---

335 Yann Mouler-Boutang, *Cognitive Capitalism* (Cambridge: Polity Press, 2012).
336 For a discussion of knowledge as a commons within the capitalist context, see Charlotte Hess, Elinor Ostrom, eds., *Understanding Knowledge as a Commons: From Theory to Practice* (Cambridge: MIT Press, 2007); Pierre Dardot et Christian Laval, *Commun....*, *supra*.
337 Patricia W. Elliot, *Free Knowledge: Confronting the Commodification of Human Discovery* (Regina_ University of Regina Press, 2015).
338 "General intellect" is Marx's expression to refer to the collective intelligence that a society gains in the process of its autonomous development at a given historical period. Karl Marx, *Grundrisse*, (Harmondsworth: Penguin, 1973) p.706.

a healthy environment, and so forth. *Yäwäl* expresses the freedom to have needs—material, social, political, cultural, cognitive, affective, and spiritual—and the power to have them satisfied by virtue of being human.

Yäwäl is not anti-state. To consider it anti-state is to misunderstand it. Rather, it is for a state that is a commons. And as a commons, its institutions are structured and function with the purpose of creating, managing and expanding the commons—political, economic, knowledge—so that they are freely and equally available to all Ethiopians and enhance the possibilities for leading a life of freedom, equality, justice, prosperity, and joy. Nor does *yäwäl* mean the end of social antagonisms and differences, for *yäwäl* is always *enkän* and its functioning will produce new and unforeseen problems and antagonisms. However, *yäwäl* is also a way of mobilizing antagonisms and differences for finding new ways and areas of "commoning," for continuing the expansion, improvement, and transformation of the commons and thus for further enriching the life of Ethiopians. To conclude, *yäwäl* (commons) is central to *minab* (utopianism without utopia). It is a dimension of *säwrä hiywät* and one of the core ideas of *säwrä tarik*.

4

Surplus History: The Emergence of *Hizb* and *Agär*

ከኢትዮጵያ ጋራ እየተፈራረድክ ነው
(I am litigating with Ethiopia)
ደቂቀ እስጢፋኖስ [339]

"The familiar, just because it is familiar
is not cognitively understood."
Hegel[340]

The history of Ethiopia is a long convoluted process—conflictual and cooperative, violent and peaceful, oppressive and liberative, contractive and expansive, integrative and disintegrative—that traverses centuries. The tortuous historical routes were the grounds from which emerged— characterized by political, economic, and social breaks, antagonisms, contradictions and reconstitutions—the gradual, intermittent and conflicted historical passage from "primary identification" (ethnic identity) to "secondary identification," or post-ethnic Ethiopian identity based on citizenship.[341] From the complex Ethiopian historical processes

---

339 Getatchew Haile, trans. from Ge'ez, ደቂቀ እስጢፋኖስ፣ በሕግ አምላክ (Collegeville, MN: 1996), p. 276.
340 G.W.F. Hegel, *Phenomenology of Spirit*, trans. A. V. Miller (Oxford: Oxford University Press), 1977, § 31, p. 18.
341 In primary identification one is "immersed in a particular life form in which he was born...his primordial 'organic community'." In secondary identification, one asserts oneself " as an 'autonomous individual'," by shifting one's "fundamental allegiance," by recognizing "the substance of his being in another, secondary

emerge gradually and intermittently the liberation from exclusive loyalties to closed or primary identities. I discuss below in five short sections, the transition from primary to secondary identification; becoming *hizb* and becoming *agär*; the primacy of *hizb* and *agär* over regimes; a critique of the borrowed concepts of people and nation; and the possibility of a democratic ethnic federalism by espousing an *Estifanosite* approach to the issue.

4.1 The transition from primary to secondary identification

A succinct review of some the vantage points of Ethiopian historical processes shows the emergence of surplus meanings or new political conceptions from within Ethiopian practices among which are *hizb*/ሕዝብ, and *agär*/አገር. Though the terms *hizb*/ሕዝብ, and *agär*/አገር are familiar to Ethiopians, they are not well understood. As Hegel notes in the exergue above, "the familiar, just because it is familiar is not cognitively understood." And this is certainly the case in Ethiopian politics and Ethiopian Studies regarding the terms of *hizb*/ሕዝብ, and *agär*/አገር.

Before discussing the emancipatory surplus meanings of these two terms, let me first zero in very briefly on five significant historical processes that could serve as vantage points for understanding the transition from primary to secondary identification and how this transition produced the historical meanings and specificity of *hizb*/ሕዝብ, and *agär*/አገር. These vantage points are: the adoption of Christianity, the adoption of Islam, the Grañ War, the *moggaasa* practice, and the *Zämänä Mäsafint*. One could add the war against Italy in 1896 that concluded with Ethiopia's victory at Adwa in which Ethiopians from the major regions participated, and the Patriotic resistance against Fascist Italy between 1936-1941 in which were active men and women from various Ethiopian regions. However, I will limit myself to the first five events and consider them as processes that made possible the transition from primary to secondary identification and the manifestation of pan-Ethiopian identity in the 1896 Adwa Victory and the trans-ethnic patriotic resistance against Fascist Italy.

I give below a limited but focussed description of the five watersheds of Ethiopian history to show their relevance for the present discussion on the

---

community [the nation, the state], which is universal and, simultaneously 'artificial'; no longer 'spontaneous' but 'mediated, ' sustained by the activity of independent free subjects." On "secondary identification," Slavoj Žižek, *The Ticklish Subject* (London: Verso, 2000), p. 90.

transition from primary to secondary identification and the historical emergence of *agär* as an alternative historical concept to "nation," and of *hizb* as an alternative historical concept to "people." I do not give a detailed historical description of the five processes and events for this is not my purpose. Nor do I suggest that there are no discontinuities, antagonisms and contradictions in Ethiopian history, nor that these watersheds are static, nor that they are the only vantage points Ethiopian history offers. However, considering these particular vantage points enables us to go beyond empiricist, Ethio-nationalist and ethno-nationalist or ethno-centric understandings of Ethiopia and disclose the emancipatory surplus meanings or the *säwrä tarik* of *agär* and *hizb*.

Let me briefly enucleate the *säwrä tarik* of the historical vantage points mentioned above. Christianity arrived in the region we now call Ethiopia circa 324 AD and the Pauline universalism that "There is neither Jew nor Greek, slave nor free, male nor female" (Galatians 3:28) percolated into the ambient culture with the spread of Christianity, loosening ethnic and regional identities.[342] The second vantage point is the introduction of Islam with the first migration of Muslims—the Hijra (circa 614 AD) to Ethiopia. Like Christianity, Islam also introduced the idea of universality into Ethiopia. It asserted that "Mankind was one single nation" (*The Holy Quran*, Surat I-baqarah, 2:213), and that God "made you into nations and tribes, that ye may know each other (not that ye may despise (each other)" (*The Holy Quran*, Sûrat I-hujur t, 49:13). It thus fostered practices that transcended regional and ethnic identities.[343] Both Christianity and Islam created trans-ethnic or pan-ethnic communities that transcended ethnic and regional identities. They thus contributed to the passage from primary to secondary identification in that both facilitated the emergence of the understanding and self-understanding of Ethiopians as "concrete universal" beings, that is, as beings that cannot be reduced to particular identities and who

---

342 Tewelde Beyene, "Inculturation and evangelisation in the history of Ethiopian Christianity," *Ethiopian Review of Cultures*, vol. 6-7 (1996-1997), pp.5-20. Very Rev. Mario Alexis Portella , "The Christianization and the Shaping of Ethiopian Society: From the Nine Saints to the 8-Monk Delegation at the Ecumenical Council of Florence" *Wissenschaftlichen Tagung der Gesellschaft Orbis Aethiopicus* 17. Salzburg/Österreich (Oktober 2015), pp. 1-26.

343 Hussein Ahmed, and Alessandro Gori. "Islam." In *Encyclopaedia Aethiopica*. Vol. 3. Edited by Siegbert Uhlig, Wiesbaden, Germany: Otto Harrassowitz Verlag, (2007), pp. 198–202; Jon Abbink, "An Historical-Anthropological Approach to Islam in Ethiopia: Issues of Identity and Politics." *Journal of African Cultural Studies* 11.2 (1998), pp. 109–124; Enrico Cerulli, "L'Islam en Éthiopie: Sa signification historique et ses méthodes." In *Colloque sur la sociologie musulmane: Actes, 11–14 septembre 1961*. Correspondance d'Orient 5. Brussels (1962), pp. 317–329.

have the capability to go beyond their particular determinations as Amhara, Oromo, Tigre, Sidama, Afar, Gurage, Wälayita, and so forth, and recognize in each other a commonly shared overarching identity that enables them to appropriate and practice the universal principles and values of freedom, equality, solidarity and justice, even if it is the case that these principles and values were articulated in religious terms. With Christianity and Islam, Ethiopians discover that one is more than one's own particular content, than one is more than what one is empirically, that one is more than the everything that one has, even if it is the case that this understanding is mediated by religion. That language borrowed from religious discourse often contributes to the development of a rational and universal understanding of the self is not peculiar to Ethiopia. It is part of humanity's history.[344]

The historical and living proof of the universalizing, particularity-transcending effects of these two universal religions on the actions, other-perception, and self-perception of Ethiopians are, to name the major ones, Wollo, Gondar, Gojjam, Tigray, Harar, and Shewa—the Ethiopian regions where Christians and Muslims Oromos, Amharas, Tigreans, and other ethnicities—have lived together, through peace and war, interacted with each other for centuries, exhibiting a high degree of religious and ethnic tolerance and "oscillation" such that it is quite common to see marriages that cross religious and ethnic boundaries and meet people with a Christian surname and a Muslim name, or vice versa, or with a name and forename from different ethnicities, among both the common people and the elites.[345]

This does not mean, however, there were no antagonisms and conflicts between Christians and Muslims, or between ethnicities. On the contrary, one of the most devastating wars in Ethiopian history took place between Christians and Muslims of the region: the Grañ war (1531-43). Grañ, whose name was Ahmad ibn Ibrahim al-Ghazi, came from the present day South-East Ethiopia.[346]

---

344 John Witte, "Christianity and Democracy: Past Contributions and Future Challenges," (1992). *Emory International Law Review*, Vol. 6, No. 1 (1992), pp. 55-69. Available at SSRN: https://ssrn.com/abstract=1851123. Sabri Ciftci, *Islam, Justice, and Democracy* (Philadelphia: Temple University Press, 2021).

345 Hussein Ahmed, *Islam in Nineteenth-Century Wallo, Ethiopia* (Leiden: Brill, 2001); Jon Abbink, "An Historical-Anthropological Approach to Islam in Ethiopia: Issues of Identity and Politics," *Journal of African Cultural Studies* 11, 2 (December 1998), p. 119; Prime Minister Abiy Ahmad personifies the crossing of ethnic and religious boundaries. His father is an Oromo Muslim, his mother an Amhara Orthodox, and he is a Pentecostal.

346 Sihab ad-Din Ahmadbin' Abd al-Qader bin Salem bin Utman, *The Conquest of Abyssinia (16th Century)*, trans. Paul Lester Stenhouse, annotations by Richard Pankhurst (Los Angeles: Tsehai Publishing, 2003).

The war he waged against the Christian region brought a great deal of destruction.³⁴⁷ However, the Grañ war has a *säwrä tarik* or surplus history that forces us to see beyond the destruction he brought to the Christian region. Indeed, that Grañ's war was destructive has nothing exceptional, for destructive wars have characterized the formation of states throughout human history. Ethiopian history is no exception; it overflows with wars between feudal lords whose destructiveness Marcus compares to "the infestation of locusts"—a biblical calamity for an agricultural society such as Ethiopia.³⁴⁸ Thus, the violence that accompanied Grañ's actions was not a historical aberration. What the official Ethiopian history fails to see is the *säwrä tarik* of Grañ's war.

A *qiné* hermeneutical reading of the Grañ war reveals it as, after Christianity and Islam, the third source of the transition from primary to secondary identification. Grañ's conquest of central and northern Ethiopia opened the door for wide-ranging and long-term demographic movements from the South to the North that led to the creation of new commercial relations, cultural interactions, and the establishment of powerful Oromo Muslim chiefdoms in Wallo, eventually leading to the Age of the Princes or the *Zämänä Mäsafint* (1769-1855), during which the Oromos became powerful members of the Ethiopian ruling elite in Gondar.³⁴⁹ Ultimately, these historical transformations paved the way for the move of Northerners (Tigreans and Amharas) to the South, intensifying other trans-regional demographic movements, cultural crossovers and cross-pollinations, and new economic interactions. The war thus weakened and, in many cases, rendered porous ethnic, cultural, commercial, and religious frontiers between the Northern and Southern parts of the region and transformed ethnic, cultural, and religious "diversities" from external to internal diversities, making them incubate circumstances that made possible the weaving of these internal diversities into a new, variegated, and unified (in the sense of *wihdät*) social, cultural, economic, and political tapestry. Grañ's war and its long-term reverberations triggered ethnic and cultural *métissage*, subverted ethnic and religious homogeneity in the various regions, and generated post-ethnicity, trans-ethnicity, multi-ethnicity, and multi-confessionalism. Grañ's war was a historical bathwater that infiltrated and eroded ethnic identity, cultural, and political boundaries and rendered them fluid and permeable. It triggered the historical processes that paved the way for the unification of the Ethiopian highlands and lowlands into a single political

---

347 Harold G. Marcus, *A History of Ethiopia* (Berkeley: University of California Press, 2002), p. 15.
348 Ibid.
349 Mordechai Abir, *The Era of the Princes: The Challenge of Islam and the Re-unification of the Christian empire, 1769-1855* (London: Longmans, 1968).

space, and contributed to the emergence of Ethiopians as a post-ethnic community or *hizb* and Ethiopia as a post-ethnic living space or *agär* (see below discussion on *hizb* and *agär*).

Grañ's understanding of unification was so original for the epoch that one could consider it as one of the great manifestations of *minab* or utopianism without utopia in Ethiopian history. It replaced the pre-Grañ Ethiopian emperors' practice of 'unity in diversity' (diversity as external relations between the Christian state and the surrounding Muslim sultanates) with the principle of "diversity-in-unity," with "diversity" understood as an internal articulation of diversities overdetermined by the principle of unity. One may object that Grañ's idea of unity and his desire to unify Ethiopians presupposed the Islamization of Christian Ethiopia and that his diversity-in-unity was intended to be an Islamic unity. This is probably true. However, *qiné* hermeneutics teaches us that we should produce the surplus meanings of social practices or *nägär* by treating them as *säm ena wärq* and subjecting the latter to *zäräfa*, dislocation and *détournement*, and not confine them to the given (a "two-eyed" vision) that limits them to their hegemonic meanings. This means that we cannot reduce Grañ's actions to his intention, or to his opponents' description of his intentions and actions, or to the immediate effects of the war—the destruction he brought to the Christian areas, which has been the main focus of mainstream Ethiopian history—for the outcomes of his actions escaped his intention and the immediate effects of the war. Intersecting with the long-term overt and subterranean material, political, military, cultural and belief processes taking place in Medieval Ethiopia, his actions generated a new political, economic, wider and deeper cultural aquifer and social interactions, and loosened and perforated ethnic and cultural boundaries, triggering social, cultural and political forces that created the internally complex political space and demography we now call Ethiopia.

Were we to ask counterfactually, "what if the Grañ war had not taken place?" the answer is that the current spatial, demographic, political, cultural, religious, and economic configuration of Ethiopia would have been radically different. Grañ is, *malgré lui*, one of the principal Ethiopian actors of the historical processes that created some of the necessary conditions for the transition from primary to secondary identification and for the formation of contemporary Ethiopia as *agär* and of Ethiopians as *hizb*. One could say that the Grañ war, a contingent event at the time, is, seen retroactively, one of the necessary conditions for the foundation of the indispensable elements of the spatial, demographic, cultural, economic, and confessional configuration we now call Ethiopia. He was one of the architects that laid the foundation of what has now become Ethiopia. Was that his intention? Probably not. But historical transformations and their effects are rarely limited by the intentions of historical actors, and the surplus meanings of historical actions reveal themselves only retroactively.[350]

The fourth historical process that gave rise to the transition from primary (ethnic) to secondary (post-ethnic or *hizb*) identification is the practice of *moggaasa* during the internal expansion of the Oromos in the various parts of what we now call Ethiopia leading to the process that Mohammed Hassen calls "Oromization."[351] The historical driver of Oromization is the practice of *butta*, which is the practice of war-making that each *luba* (generational class) engages in with the intent of conquering territory.[352] Let's not be distracted, however, by the fact that war-making (*butta*) is the immediate goal of each *luba*. From the perspective of our interest in the emergence of secondary identification, it is the relation of *butta* to the "process called *moggaasa* (adoption)," which is the venue of Oromization, that merits attention. *Moggaasa* is a process of "assimilation" that "claimed any non-Oromo, *defeated or otherwise*" to become a member of a larger community. *Butta* created the economic, social, and political conditions that triggered the process of *moggaasa*. Mohammed Hassen describes the practice of Oromization and *moggaasa* as follows:

> An important Oromo institution which seems to have facilitated the process [of Oromization] ... was [the practice of] ...*moggaasa* (adoption) [...], adoption into a clan or tribe. The adopted individual or group could be either Oromo or non-Oromo.... By this oath [taken during the process of adoption] of mutual responsibility and obligation, clans or tribes quickly enlarged their members, while the *weak Oromo or non-Oromo groups gained both protection and material benefit*.... After adoption, the concept of belonging was extended to include not only the clan that adopted, but also the tribe or confederacy to which the clan belonged. Through the new genealogy, the new members now became part of the Oromo people....[353]

Note that *moggaasa* applies not only to Oromos, but also to "*any non-Oromo, defeated or otherwise,*" and that it leads to the emergence of an identity that goes beyond primary identification thus triggering the process of secondary identification.[354] *Moggaasa* introduced a cultural, social, and political mutation

---

350 See for the Annales School understanding of history. André Burguière, *The Annales School: An Intellectual History*, Ithaca, Cornell University Press, 2009. On retroactivity and temporality, Slavoj Žižek, *Absolute Recoil*, (London: Verso, 2014), pp.23-38, 136-221.
351 Mohammed Hassen, *The Oromo of Ethiopia: A History 1570-1860* (Cambridge: Cambridge University Press, 1990), p. 21.
352 Asmarom Legesse, *Gada: Three Approaches to the Study of African Society* (New York: Free Press, 1973), p.8.
353 Mohammed Hassen, *The Oromo of Ethiopia: supra*, p.20. Emphasis added.
354 Ibid.

that triggered the advent of a new post-ethnic horizon or *admas* that articulates ethnic differences as internal to and reflective of a shared community and space articulated as *wihdät*.

In the practice of *moggaasa* towards non-Oromos, however violent it may have been, and it was insofar as it was associated with the practice of *butta* (each *luba*'s war campaign), one sees the emergence of a universal principle in Oromo culture, politics and history that rejects ethnic fixity and closure and intersects with the universality that Christianity and Islam introduced into Ethiopia. For *moggaasa*, it is our historical itineraries and not our origins that form our identities. It reveals ethnicity to be a fluid, plastic, and a permeable identity and demonstrates that ethnic identities could mutate historically into post-ethnic or non-ethnic differences by making the in-coming ethnic group part of the network of internal political, economic, and social relations of the expanded group. *Moggaasa* loosens pre-existing ethnic markers and differences, liberates facts and identities from ethnic closure, facilitates cultural creolization, and makes ethnic porosity rather than hermetic identity the main context of social relations. We could say that *moggaasa* introduces into Ethiopian history, together with Christianity and Islam, the transformative idea of tearing away oneself (*"defeated or otherwise"*) from one's primordial community (ethnic identity) and recognizing the substance of one's being in another, secondary community: the new over-arching post-ethnic community created through *moggaasa*. It thus subverts the ethno-centric impulse to ontologize ethnic identity that we see in *Oromummaa*. It transforms ethnic diversity from the fixed experience of rootedness that externalizes the "other" into the dynamic and transformative internal diversity expressive of transethnic and post-ethnic processes. Mohammed Hassen calls the new post-ethnic entity "a people" which he uses as a political concept that one must distinguish from the sociological concepts of ethnicity and population. The *moggaasa* practice of the universalizing "oath of mutual responsibility and obligation," whose goal is to ensure "protection and material benefit" to all, including "the *weak Oromo or non-Oromo*," is part of the process of de-ethnicization of newly inducted ethnic groups and of the host group, ushering a secondary community.[355] The practice of *moggaasa* thus announces a universalist politics and ethics, and introduces the idea and practice of diversity-in-unity that marks the transition from primary to secondary identification. *Moggaasa* harbours a critique of *Oromummaa avant la lettre*. One of the outcomes of this transition from primary to secondary identification is the full-fledged participation of the Oromo as active subjects in the development of the Ethiopian post-ethnic

---

355 Mohammed Hassen, *The Oromo of Ethiopia...*, *supra*, p.21.

identity and unity that modern Ethiopians have inherited. *Oromummaa* rejects this universalist dimension of Oromo culture and regresses to the pre-*moggaasa* notion of primordial identity.

The fifth event is the *Zämänä Mäsafint* (1769-1855), the highpoint of the transition from primary to secondary identification. The *Zämänä Mäsafint* is described in the hegemonic historical narratives as a period of political disintegration. A *qiné* hermeneutical reading of this period rejects this "two-eyed" (empiricist) reading and brings out its *säwrä tarik* as a historical period that intensified the brewing of additional integrative and universalizing forces and unifying tendencies unleashed by Grañ's war and the practice of *moggaasa*. The *Zämänä Mäsafint* overcame localism and parochialism by transforming the Oromo, the Amhara, the Tigre, the Christian and the Muslim ruling elites into Ethiopian competitors and allies for the control of national power at the center (Gondar) on the basis of the principle of diversity-in-unity (*wihdät*) that Christianity, Islam, Grañ, and the *moggaasa* practice introduced and developed. Unlike the leaders of the regimes based on the 1995 Constitution—the EPRDF and the PP regimes, and their member ethnic parties—these competitors for power identified themselves as Ethiopians, and not as ethnic leaders, attesting to the strength and depth of the secondary identification that Ethiopian historical processes have already sculpted. They did not pursue ethnic politics. Rather, the person who seized power, whatever his ethnicity or confession, tried to develop a national post-ethnic politics. The *Zämänä Mäsafint* thus deepened the transition from primary to secondary identification and furthered the forging of Ethiopians as *hizb*, a post-ethnic people, and Ethiopia as *agär*, a post-ethnic space. It thus contributed to the formation of Ethiopian political unity and identity. One could say that the *Zämänä Mäsafint* incubated the idea of a centripetal federalism that draws its strength from the integrating dimensions of diversity by mediating it through the principle of unity.

The above transitions from one historical period to the next constitute a civilizational progress in that they made possible the changeover from primary to secondary identification, from a worm-eye view of the self proper to primary identity to the concretely universalizing view of the self as a rational and universalizing mutual implication with the other. The surplus meanings of these historical processes and of their universalizing outcomes indicate the transition from primary to secondary identification as a process internal to Ethiopian history/society, and could be disclosed only through a theory that is immanent to Ethiopian history/society. However, it does not mean that the transition did not involve antagonisms and failures and that it was not punctuated by regressions. Nevertheless, despite the failures and the regressions, despite the antagonisms traversing Ethiopian society, a clear trend was visible in the rise and spread of secondary identification that led to the emergence of the concepts of *zegnät* (citizenship), and the consolidation of the concepts of *hizb* ("people") and *agär* ("nation"), indicating the emergence of a common space and time that all who live in what we now call Ethiopia shared, though the sharing was deeply marked by class and regional inequalities. The transition form primary to secondary identification that these five historical processes brought about is encapsulated in the *qiné* aphorisms discussed earlier, to wit, የኔ ቢጤ (*yäne bitie*), and ሰው ለሰው መድኃኒቱ / *säw läsäw mädhanitu*. As discussed earlier, the aphorisms express the ideas of universality, equality, autonomy, and solidarity that have historically emerged together with the emergence of *zegnät*, *hizb*, and *agär*. Though they have not been fully actualized, these ideas exist as part of *säwrä tarik*. One could see this also from the incubation of the universalizing principles considered earlier in the discussion of *minab* in Chapter 3.

The concepts of *hizb* and *agär* are occluded in Ethiopian Studies and politics when Ethiopia is subjected to the borrowed concepts of "people" and "nation," because the Western historical processes that gave rise to the concepts of "people" and "nation" and the realities these concepts describe are different from the historical processes constitutive of Ethiopia as a political space (*agär* / አገር) and a political community (*hizb* / ሕዝብ).

4.2. Becoming *hizb*, becoming *agär*

It is certain that there are other historical vantage points that indicate the emergence of universalizing principles, and of *hizb* and *agär*. However, the five historical vantage points—the Christianization and Islamization of Ethiopia, the Grañ war, the *moggaasa* practice, and the *Zämänä Mäsafint*— briefly discussed above carry within themselves the itinerary, traces, and outcomes of the internally-tensioned complex experience and self-experience of the historical emergence of Ethiopians as *hizb*, a post-ethnic political community that articulates diversity as internal relations (*wihdät*), and of Ethiopia as *agär*, a post-ethnic political space. These historical processes indicate that Ethiopian unity is not a given, but rather an active historical process, a contingent and open-ended political becoming of Ethiopians as a post-ethnic people, and Ethiopia as *agär* or as a post-ethnic space. These historical processes generated a new "cognitive mapping" that integrated the ideas of universality, shared history and shared destiny into the self-recognition of Ethiopians as a *hizb*, and Ethiopia as *agär*.[356] In this

---

356 On cognitive mapping, Fredric Jameson, "Cognitive Mapping," in C. Nelson and L. Grossberg, eds., *Marxism and the Interpretation of Culture* (Champaign: University of Illinois Press, 1990), pp. 347-60.

new cognitive mapping, *hizb* is not just a demographic entity that aggregates individuals and disparate groups, nor is *agär* an archipelago of ethnic regions. Both *hizb* and *agär* emerge as political subjects that transcend ethnic closures by transforming primary identities into new expressions of secondary identification in that the primary identities find their fulfillment in the universality that the secondary identification infuses into them such that becoming an Oromo, an Amhara, a Tigrean, a Sidama, a Somlai, an Afar, and so forth become new particular ways of becoming Ethiopian or of being a subject of *hizb* and *agär*. That is, ethnic identity is sublated into citizenship: a process that does not efface ethnic identity but keeps it as an open-to-the-other dimension of the self as a citizen. Hence, the unity Ethiopians manifested in Adwa (1896) and in the Patriotic resistance to Fascist Italy (1936-41). (see discussion below).

Becoming a *hizb* is a historical transformation that in the process of creating a new identity creates new divisions and new interactions that cut diagonally across ethnicities, confessions, and regions. It is important to emphasize that the transition from ethnicity to post-ethnicity does not mean the deletion of primary identifications and the creation of a homogeneous population. The new cognitive mapping that the historical becoming of *hizb* creates does not erase primary identifications; rather, it reinscribes them as different forms of appearance of the universal secondary identification: *hizb*. *Hizb* articulates heterogeneity and conflicts within unity (*wihdät*). Moreover, though it provides the political space of universality that makes possible to transcend immanently ethnic and other particularities, *hizb*, being always *enkän*, does not exist as an antagonism free zone.

Conflicts within *hizb* are qualitatively different from pre-*hizb* conflicts. The latter are external conflicts between communities. Moreover, they do not have *arnät* as their goal. Conflicts within *hizb*, on the other hand, are articulated through non-ethnic universal political categories, for the interests that generate the conflicts cut across *hizb* transversally and are expressed in universal terms as conflicts between oppressors and oppressed, exploiters and exploited, with members of different ethnies, regions and confessions present on both sides of these new transversal divisions and interactions. Consequently, unlike the inter-ethnic conflicts under the PP regime, which are driven by particular ethnic *official people's* interests, conflicts within *hizb* are vehicles for expressing the emancipatory demands of freedom, equality, justice solidarity, and knowledge, i.e., the emancipatory ideas and ideals articulated in *säwrä tarik*.

The Oromo aphorism, ሐርኪ ዑፉ መዳውሌ ሙረኒ እንዳርባን / (One does not amputate one's own hand because of a wound) speaks to this transversal nature of conflicts within *hizb*.[357] It tells us that since conflicts have evolved historically as post-ethnic phenomena with the becoming of *hizb*, their resolution requires *hizb*-oriented or post-ethnic solutions and not ethnic amputation or ethnic secession as expressed in article 39 of the 1995 Ethiopian Constitution. Secession is not "self-determination": it is crippling oneself politically and economically. Under the new historical conditions that have given birth to *hizb*, conflicts, even if they appear to be ethnic, are primarily triggered by issues that pertain to the post-ethnic relations of domination, which cut transversally the post-ethnic Ethiopian society. That is, conflicts require transversal solutions based on universal principles and not ethnic secession. To believe that ethnic separation dissolves conflicts is to fantasize that there are no internal antagonisms within an ethnicity, and that the interests of the ethnic *official people* and the *people's people* are identical. It is to create a more fertile ground for an *Oromummaa* type politics and ideology and thus fortify the presence of the triple domination.

The historical processes that gave birth to *hizb* are also the processes that led to the emergence of *agär*. *Agär* is more concrete, variegated, and universalist than the Western concept of "nation." *Agär* is a temporal and spatial political configuration that designates the space and time that is commonly shared by all those, whatever their particularities, who inhabit it and by virtue of which they constitute a *hizb*. Historically, the emergence of Ethiopia as *agär* through the historical processes of transition from primary to secondary identification marks the emergence of the real possibility of a political project that is inclusive and rational in that *agär* transcends primordial identities, enabling all who live in it to appropriate it as their political, social, economic, affective and cultural space.

The emergence of Ethiopia as *agär* is a historical process made up of peaceful and violent processes—the spread of Christianity and Islam, the incessant wars of pre-Medieval and Medieval Ethiopia, the *butta* wars, *moggaasa*, the Grañ War, the *Zämänä Mäsafint*, the contradictory actions and the failures and successes of Ethiopian Emperors up to 1974, the peasant uprisings of Wollo/ Gojjam / Tigre / Bale, to name a few. The war against the Derg in the 1980s, the war in Northern Ethiopia (2020-2022), the conflicts in the Amhara region since 2023, and the conflicts in Oromo and other regions since 2021 could be seen, like all the internal wars that have dotted the Ethiopian past, as part of the historical processes of the becoming of Ethiopia as *agär* and of Ethiopians as *hizb*. Recall the unintended consequences of the Grañ war discussed earlier.

---

357 Abdurahman Mohamed Korram, "Oromo Proverbs," *Journal of Ethiopian Studies* 7, No. 1 (January 1969), pp. 65-80, # 37.

The emergence of *agär* as the space and time of *hizb* makes *agär* more than the sum of its regions. *Agär* is both a "moral community" and a political project that is universalist, creating a space for freedom, equality, solidarity, and dignity though it is always *enkän*.[358] It is a becoming that is always incomplete, contradictory, under construction, and traversed by social antagonisms. It offers the best possible shared space for the struggle for and institutionalization of freedom, equality, solidarity, prosperity, justice, and emancipatory knowledge production precisely because its formation is rooted in a secondary identification that allows the emergence of the *people's people* as a political subject and the articulation of their emancipatory aspirations and projects. Because it emerges through the same historical processes and struggles that formed *hizb*, Ethiopians have been, are, and will always be in "litigation"— to use the *Däq Estifanos* vocabulary in the exergue—, peacefully or violently, with Ethiopia as *agär*. *Agär* is a dynamic, always-unfinished (*enkän*) spatial, temporal, and affective configuration within which "diversity" and antagonisms have been transformed from external into internal relations, from divisive to synergetic relations, creating the conditions for universalizing political, economic, and epistemic struggles and emancipation.

Unlike the Western concept of nation, which is based on exclusionary self-other binary that sees the different other as "an alien" (the American expression[359]) or in terms of a hierarchical scheme (mostly based on race or origin[360]), *agär* is an open-ended spatial, temporal, and political totality of a regionally, culturally, religiously, and ethnically diverse people, united as a unique historical political subject, *hizb*, which offers inclusive and universal relations of belonging. This universal relation of belonging historically emerges as ዜግነት (*zegnät*) understood as the legal, political, and cultural equality of all. However, as we could see with the primacy of ethnic identity in post-1995 Ethiopia, *zegnät*, like the other universal principles and values we saw in the discussion of *minab*, exists primarily as an emancipatory idea in *säwrä tarik* rather than as a reality in that its expression and practice are repressed in the functioning of the Ethiopian socio-political

---

358 On *agär* as a political community, Tesfaye Wolde-Medhin, "*Wänfäl* (Reciprocity) and the Constitution of *Agär* as Moral Community among Farmers in the Central Highlands of Ethiopia," *Journal of Ethiopian Studies,* vol.51, (December, 2018), pp. 1-38. He writes, "*agär* as a space of moral community, but also the very basis for the organization and persistence of the latter outside the intrusive and (dis) ordering structures of the "modernizing" state." p.2. See also pp.4, 32 ff.
359 "Alien," https://www.law.cornell.edu/wex/alien. Accessed, 8/9/2021.
360 Anthony W. Marx, *Making Race and Nation: A Comparison of South Africa, the United States, and Brazil* (New York: Cambridge University Press, 1997).

order in the past and in the present. From the perspective of *säwrä tarik*, the inhabitants of *agär* are Ethiopians: politically, socially, affectively, and legally, whatever their language, ethnicity, or religion. *Agär* transcends and makes Ethiopians transcend, the enclosures of primary identities by transforming these into so many new and different expressions of their historically emerging universal identity as *hizb* or Ethiopians. For *säwrä tarik*, *agär* is a *yäwäl*, *enkän* to be sure, but always being constructed through conflictual and peaceful relations.

It is the transition to post-ethnicity through the processes of secondary identification that explains the fact that Ethiopians generally understand themselves in terms of the historically constituted regions they come from—Gojjam, Wollega, Wollo, Sidamo, Arsi, Gondar, Harar, Shoa, Tigray, and so forth, all of which are trans-ethnic, post-ethnic, multi-ethnic, and multi-confessional to various degrees. These regions are known historically as *kiflä agär* (ክፍለ ሀገር). Unlike the ethnic *Blut und Boden* based *kilil* created by the 1995 Constitution, *kiflä agär*, meaning "a segment of *agär*," intimates that each region is expressive of the Ethiopian totality as *agär*: post-ethnic and multi-confessional. The historical constitution of each *kiflä agär* is part of the process of the transition from primary to secondary identification and of the formation of Ethiopians as internally diversified and interconnected *hizb*. At the same time, each *kiflä agär* has historical characteristics such that one could say that there is a Gojjame, a Wollega, a Wollo, a Sidama, an Arsi, a Gondar, a Harar, a Somali, a Shoa, a Tigray, a Gurage, a Wälayita, a Nuer, a Gumuz, an Anuak, and so forth, way of being Ethiopian, expressing unique characteristics. Thus, expressions such as *ye-Harar lij* (የሐረር ልጅ, the offspring of Harar), *ye-Wollo lij* (የወሎ ልጅ, the offspring of Wollo), *ye-Wollega lij* (የወለጋ ልጅ), and so forth, refer to the historical specificity of each *kiflä agär*, which at the same time transcends one's ethnicity or religion and point to the important role of secondary identification in the formation of *kiflä agär* as a post-ethnic region. It is the fluid, overlapping, oscillating, and interweaving identities formed through secondary identification that makes *agär* a diversity-in-unity or *wihdät*. Ethiopia is an *agär* whose *hizb* have multiple faces. *Agär* continues itself in the particularity and individuality of *kiflä agär* and therefore is in communion with itself through *kiflä agär*. Both *agär* and *hizb* are multifaceted because both embody diversity-in-unity. This is an outcome of Ethiopian history that the Gibbonist concepts of "nation" and "people" cannot grasp.

Agär exists insofar as its members actualize it by identifying themselves as the *hizb* of *agär* who share a common history and destiny and act accordingly. Simultaneously, *agär* generates its own actualization by motivating people to struggle for it. Ethiopian history gives ample evidence of this dialectical relation between Ethiopia as *agär* and Ethiopians as *hizb*. Consider the Ethiopian resistance to Italian colonialism in 1896 and the anti-Fascist Patriotic resistance (1936-41). Both attest to the active presence of secondary identification that sublate ethnic and confessional identities and affirm the self-identification of Ethiopians as *hizb* to whom *agär* is their historically and politically shared common space and time. It is interesting to note that the anti-Fascist Patriotic resistance was not organized by a central power but arose spontaneously. Its members, men and women, came from all corners of Ethiopia, creating a trans-regional and trans-ethnic resistance movement, which included "gada leaders," who "led a campaign of resistance against the Italian army," and Eritreans, among whom the most well-known are Abraha Deboch and Moges Asgedom, who made an attempt on the life of the Italian Viceroy on 19 February 1937, in Addis Ababa.[361] The participants saw themselves as members of *hizb*, of a commonly shared history and destiny—"We, the Ethiopian people"—and embraced Ethiopia as *agär*. We could then say that *hizb* and *agär* are not only historical political processes but they are also political subjects. In light of the above, the fact that *kilil* has replaced *kiflä agär* in post-1195 Ethiopia is a political and a historical regression. Its implicit premise that each *kilil* represents ethnic purity and homogeneity has led to ethnic-cleansing in *kilils*, thus undoing the historical civilizing achievement of Ethiopians: the secondary identification and the universalizing principles and processes that come with it.

4.3. The primacy of *hizb* and *agär* over regimes

Ethiopia as *agär* and Ethiopians as *hizb* stand above Ethiopian regimes. Historically, the loyalty of Ethiopians has been to *agär* and *hizb* and not to the regime in power. We could thus say that both *hizb* and *agär* are political categories that have universal normative valences: *hizb* and *agär* are subjects of politics and not mere objects of representation. One could see this from the history of Ethiopian resistance to external aggressions (1875, Gundet; 1887, Dogali; 1896, Adwa; 1935-41), and to internal domination—individual and group revolts ranging

---

361 Salome Gabre-Egziabher, "The Ethiopian Patriots 1936-1941," *Ethiopian Observer* 12, 2 (1969); Alberto Sbacchi, *Ethiopia Under Mussolini: Fascism and the Colonial Experience* (London: Zed Books, 1985); Bahru Zewde, *A History of Modern Ethiopia, 1855-1974* (London: James Currey, 1991), p.167; Asmarom Legesse, *Oromo Democracy: An Indigenous African Political System* (Trenton: The Red Sea Press, 2006), p. 218. Richard Pankhurst, "Events during the Fascist Occupation: in February 1937: Who Was the Third Man?", *Addis Ababa* Tribune, 27 February (2004) http://addistribune.com/Archives/2004/02/27-02-04/Events.htm. Accessed 2/9/2023.

from the *shifta* (ሽፍታ), to regional revolts (Gojjam, Tigray, Bale), to the resistance against the DERG, the TLF/EPRDF ethnic authoritarianism, and the budding resistance against the PP ethnic authoritarianism.[362] In the struggles against Ethiopian regimes, Ethiopians do not reject Ethiopia as *agär* and Ethiopians as *hizb*. Rather, in their uprisings against these regimes, they see themselves as a sovereign *hizb* who struggle to make their *agär* express its repressed *hizb* content by making it democratic, just, and prosperous. They consider the regimes in place obstacles for the realization of these aspirations. Historically, then, Ethiopians have given primacy to fidelity to *agär* and *hizb* over loyalty to the regimes in power. The primacy of *agär* and *hizb* over the regime in power is part of *säwrä tarik*.

The regime in power does not necessarily work to enhance *agär* and *hizb*. It is possible to have an anti-*agär* and anti-*hizb* regime. Although all Ethiopian regimes have been anti-*hizb* (oppressive), none of them, except for the regimes based on the 1995 Constitution (the EPRDF and the PP regimes), have been both anti-*agär* and anti-*hizb*. These regimes seem committed to undo the historically formed *agär* and *hizb* and return Ethiopians to the pre-Christianity, pre-Islam, pre-Grañ, pre-*moggaasa*, and pre-*Zämänä Mäsafint* historical condition of externally related ethnicities, euphemistically described as "unity in diversity" with unity instrumentalized to accentuate diversity in a way that leads to ethnic secession (1995 Constitution, article 39). It is certainly the case that the aspirations for political, economic and social emancipation that gestate in Ethiopia's *säwrä tarik* or surplus history have yet to be concretized. However, to deny that Ethiopians do not constitute a *hizb* that is rooted in *agär*, because they have not concretized their emancipatory aspirations, is as absurd as denying the

---

362 On *shifta* and regional revolts, Gebru Tareke, *Ethiopia: Power and Protest; Peasant Revolts in the Twentieth Century* (New York: Cambridge University Press, 1991); Donald Crummey, ed. , *Banditry, Rebellion and Social Protest in Africa* (James Curry, London 1986), pp.133-149. Resistance to external powers, Sven Rubenson, *The Survival of Ethiopian Independence*, (London: Heinemann, 1976); On patriotic resistance to fascist Italy, Charles Schaefer, "Serendipitous Resistance in Fascist-Occupied Ethiopia, 1936–1941," *Northeast African Studies New Series* 3.1 (1996), pp. 87–115; Salome Gabre-Egziabher, "The Ethiopian Patriots 1936-1941," *Ethiopian Observer*, Vol.12, No.2 (1969). Alberto Sbacchi, *Ethiopia Under Mussolini: Fascism and the Colonial Experience* (London: Zed Books, 1985); Bahru Zewde, *A History of Modern Ethiopia, 1855-1974* (London: James Currey, 1991), p. 167; Richard Pankhurst, "Events during the Fascist Occupation in February 1937: Who Was the Third Man?," *Addis Ababa Tribune*, 27 February (2004) http://addistribune.com/Archives/2004/02/27-02-04/Events.htm.

humanity of a man or a woman because they have failed to concretize their human capabilities.

In short, if one wants to use the Western concepts of "nation" and "people" in the Ethiopian case, then one must subject them to *zäräfa* in light of what a critical internal journey into Ethiopian historical processes (*säwrä tarik*) reveals and understand them as *agär* and *hizb*, respectively. Only then could one grasp the meanings and outcomes of the historical processes that created modern Ethiopia and free oneself from the misunderstandings of Ethiopia and the self-misinterpretations of Ethiopians that the Gibbonist concepts of "people" and "nation" generate.

4.4. Critique of the concepts of "people" and "nation"

With the above as our background, we could see the fatal theoretical error that the post-1960 revolutionaries, nationalists, and ethno-nationalists committed in their uncritical use of the concepts of "people" and "nation." The uncritical borrowing of the concepts of "people" and "nation" is rooted in the Gibbonist assumption that the Western historical processes of "people" and "nation" formation, and the understandings and the self-understandings they generate in the West, are the standards by which the outcome of Ethiopian historical processes are measured and judged. These borrowed concepts inevitably lead to a misunderstanding of Ethiopian history/society and to the self-misunderstanding of Ethiopians, generating political confusions, divisions, chaos, and violence, as we see since the 1960s—the decade the new westernized Ethiopian intellectuals, products of Gibbonist education, wielded the western concepts of "people" and "nation" as political tools. The use of these concepts occludes the historical specificities—material, political, intellectual, and cultural—of Ethiopia that are essential for an emancipatory self-understanding of Ethiopians and for an emancipatory transformation of Ethiopian society. From the perspective of *säwrä tarik*, the borrowed concepts of "people" and "nation" are zombie concepts that, though they are not connected to any Ethiopian historical reality, still remain alive within the thought systems of the *official people* and its organic intellectuals almost all of whom are the product of Gibbonist education.

The person who popularized the Gibbonist concepts of "nation" and "people" and made them the cornerstones of the post-1969 ideological and political discourses on Ethiopia, giving birth eventually to ethnic politics, is

Walleligne Mekonnen.[363] And Meles Zenawi is the politician who effectively put into practice and institutionalized the ethnic politics that Walleligne's uncritical appropriation of the Gibbonist concepts of nation and people generated.

Historically, the denial of Ethiopians as *hizb* and Ethiopia as *agär* was first attempted by Fascist Italy.[364] Based on this Gibbonist understanding of Ethiopia, the Italian fascist government established what it called *Governo of Eritrea*, *Governo of Amhara*, *Governo of Galla-Sidamo*, *Governo of Harrar*, and *Governo of Somalia*.[365] It was an "An attempt ... to draw the boundaries of the five *governi* in such a way that each will contain native peoples of essentially the same race and religion."[366] In a 1969 essay, Walleligne Mekonnen, the influential theoretician of the Ethiopian students' movement, espoused, unknowingly it seems, the claims of the Italian Ethiopianists who used the Western concepts of "nation" and "people" as special devices and the history of the West as a vantage point to describe Ethiopia as a backward ethnically fragmented society. He claimed, "There is no such thing as Ethiopian people" because there is no Ethiopian "nation."[367]

Walleligne adopted wholeheartedly the Gibbonist approach to Ethiopian history/society and used the Western concepts of "nation" and "people" as universal standards in his descriptions of Ethiopia. However, the West's conceptions of "nation" and "people" emerged from historical processes radically different from those that constituted *agär* and *hizb*, and it is far from

---

363 Walleligne Mekonnen, "On the Question of Nationalities in Ethiopia," *Arts IV* (Addis Ababa: November 17, 1969). Available at https://www.marxists.org/history/erol/ethiopia/nationalities.pdf.

364 H. Arthur Steiner, "The Government of Italian East Africa," *The American Political Science Review*, Vol. 30, No. 5 (Oct. 1936), pp. 884-902; Alberto Sbacchi. *Ethiopia under Mussolini: Fascism and the Colonial Experience* (London: Zed Books, 1985).

365 H. Arthur Steiner, "The Government of Italian East Africa," *supra*. Carlo Conti Rossini, *The History of Ethiopia: From Ancient Times to the Medieval Ages* (Trenton, NJ: Red Sea Press, 2001); Enrico Cerulli, *Peoples of Southwest Ethiopia and its Borderland*. Part III of Forde (London: International African Institute, 1956). Ernst Gellner claims that Ethiopia is a "prison house of nations." Ernst Gellner, *Nation and Nationalism* (London: Oxford University Press, 1983), p. 85.

366 H. Arthur Steiner, "The Government of Italian East Africa," *supra*, pp. 884-902, p. 892.

367 Walleligne Mekonnen, "On the Question of Nationalities in Ethiopia," *supra*; Bahru Zewde, *The Quest for Socialist Utopia: The Ethiopian Student Movement c.1960-1974* (London: James Curry, 2014), pp. 198-202; Messay Kebede, *Radicalism and Cultural Dislocation in Ethiopia, 1960-1974* (Rochester: University of Rochester Press, 2008), p. 152.

certain they could be considered as universal standards.[368] Walleligne identified Ethiopia in terms of what the West possesses but Ethiopia "lacks": being a "nation" and a "people" as the West understands these in terms of its own historical development. It is the non-acknowledgement of this historical difference, occluded by the anamorphic perception of Ethiopia and the epistemology of ignorance that Gibbonism imposes, that led to the application of an ahistorical and mechanical conception of "nation" and "people". The transcendental use of these borrowed concepts as universal devices and of their history as universal vantage points to understand Ethiopian society dehistoricizes both Ethiopian and Western processes of historical becoming and cancels the specificities of both Ethiopian and Western history/society. In terms of Ethiopian history/society, the Gibbonist concepts of "nation" and "people" are somnambulist concepts that, though seemingly awake, nevertheless do not see the historical and social realities that surround them.

Walleligne's Gibbonist use of the concepts of "nation' and "people" became the political dogma of the era and were influential among ethno-centric intellectuals and leaders. Out of this season of Gibbonism emerged militant ethno-politicians who condemned Ethiopia for not being a "nation" and a "people" in the Western sense, though she has never been a "nation" and a "people" in the Western sense. In typical Gibbonist fashion, Ethiopia is criticized for not being what she is not. To paraphrase an Ethiopian aphorism, it is like criticizing a lion for not being a dog. Her historically inherited identity as *agär* and of Ethiopians as *hizb* were discarded by peremptorily declaring Ethiopia to be a colonial empire.[369]

Walleligne and the ethno-nationalists who endorsed his use of the Gibbonist concepts of "people" and "nation" started with the correct observation that Ethiopian history is a history of political domination and economic exploitation. However, captives of Gibbonism, they caricatured Ethiopian history and jumped to the conclusion that Ethiopian history is a history of "colonization" of one group, identified by them as the "Amhara," of the territories that now form part of Ethiopia, and asserted that the ethnicities inhabiting these territories are "colonized" peoples that have the right of "self-determination." Their Gibbonism blinded them to the active historical agency of the Oromo, the Sidama, the

---

368 Jonathan Daly, *The Rise of Western Power: A Comparative History of Western Civilization* (New York:
(New York: Bloomsbury Academic, 2021).

369 For a contemporary restatement of this idea, see Bonnie K. Holcomb and Sisai Ibssa, *The Invention of Ethiopia* (Trenton, N.J.: Red Sea Press, 1990). The Amhara or the Habasha or the Abyssinians are usually identified as the "colonizers."

Wälayita, the Somali, the Harari, the Amhara, the Gurage, the Hadiya, the Tigreans, the Afars, Ethiopian Muslims and Christians, and so forth, in the passage from primary to secondary identification and in the construction of Ethiopia as *agär* and Ethiopians as *hizb*. Gibbonism led Walleligne and the ethno-nationalists to confuse domination, which characterizes all states, with "colonialism," and asserted that Ethiopia is, as Meles Zenawi wrote, a creation of Emperor Menelik's imperialism, a *deus ex machina* claim that cavalierly erases the long pre-Menelik history of Ethiopia.[370]

True, all domination creates internal antagonisms and historical wounds, but all domination is not colonialism. Colonialism establishes, as Fanon has argued and as the history of colonial racism attests, a radical gap between the colonizer and the colonized that ontologically inferiorizes the latter.[371] Since the beginning of the Axumite empire, Ethiopian history has been a continuous seesaw of victors and of the defeated. None of the historical relations between the victors and the defeated in Ethiopian history indicate the existence of practices that imply an ontological inferiorization of the defeated. As Gebru Tareke points out, in Ethiopian history, "*any person*, including a slave, could ascend the social ladder through acts of military valor or royal patronage."[372] The oppression and exploitation that the *official people* of Ethiopia inflict upon the *people's people* of Ethiopia cut across ethnicities and regions transversally, thus making antagonisms and historical wounds transethnic and systemic. Transversal conflicts demand transversal cures that heal systemic wounds and resolve systemic antagonisms with systemic solutions. To run away from transversal conflicts by degrading them into ethnic conflicts and opt for self-isolation dubbed ethnic self-determination not only keeps the existing antagonisms unresolved and the wounds festering in isolation, but it also fortifies the powers of oppression and exploitation that the *official people* wield over the *people's people*.[373]

The historical transformations highlighted above, including the emergence of a post-ethnic political community, *hizb*, and of a post-ethnic political space, *agär*, and their *säwrä tarik* intimate that Ethiopia is not trapped between the

---

370 Abraham Yayeh, የኤርትራ ህዝብ ትግል ከፍት ወደፍት (Washington D.C., 1992), pp. 36-40.
371 Frantz Fanon, *Black Skin, White Masks,* trans. R. Philcox (New York: Grove Press, 2008), p. 82; R.J. Ross, ed., *Racism and Colonialism: Essays on Ideology and Social Structure* (New York: Springer, 2011).
372 Gebru Tareke, *Ethiopia: Power and Protest; Peasant Revolts in the Twentieth Century* (New York: Cambridge University Press, 1991), p. 14. Emphasis added.
373 A case in point is the secession of Eritrea. Andebrhan Welde Giorgis, *Eritrea at a Crossroads: A Narrative of Triumph, Betrayal and Hope* (Strategic Book Publishing & Rights Agency, LLC, 2014)'

columbaria of ethnic *kilils* and the graveyard of centralism. From the perspective of *säwrä tarik*, democratic federalism, nourished with the emancipatory ideas of *säwrä tarik*, is the only emancipatory option. And the form and content of this federalism express diversity-in-unity, i.e., *wihdät*. To put it differently, democratic federalism is an idea that incubates in the *säwrä tarik* of the historical processes that transformed primary into secondary identification, constituted Ethiopians as *hizb* and formed Ethiopia as *agär* and its constituent parts as *kiflä-agär*. The dialectical historical relations between *agar* and *kiflä-agär* discussed earlier suggest that the idea of federalism as diversity in unity was already present in Ethiopia in an embryonic form, though it never developed beyond its blastula stage.[374] Many regions had their own *Negus* or rulers and enjoyed considerable autonomy, hence the expression of *Negusä Nägäst*: the leader of the ensemble of *Neguses* and rulers; and the *Zämänä Mäsafint* gestated surplus meanings that also intimated the idea of federalism as diversity in unity. Historically, centralization is a very new political phenomenon introduced into Ethiopia by Emperor Haile Selassie who enshrined it in the 1931 and 1955 Constitutions.[375]

For *säwrä tarik*, then, there is a conception of federalism that is immanent to Ethiopian history. The challenging task is to draw the meanings, ranges and implications of this conception by unpacking and expanding it in terns of the emancipatory *andemta* we develop through the articulation of our internal and external journeys. For *säwrä tarik*, federalism is not ethnic; it is territorial made up of historically constituted post-ethnic regions, *kiflä-agär*. The latter term mirrors the processes constitutive of *agär* and *hizb*. As we shall see below in the *Estifanosite* approach, *kiflä-agär* could be inhabited by a single ethnicity, but it owes its identity to the historical processes that formed it and not to primary identity. Examples are Gondar, Wollega, Tigray, Afar, and so forth. From the perspective of *säwrä tarik*, Ethiopian federalism must be rooted in the universality of the political principles that are inherent to the process of secondary identification—freedom, equality, solidarity, citizenship, and justice, i.e., *arnät*. Such a federalism ensures, in the words of *moggaasa* politics, "protection and material benefit" to all.[376] Moreover, the universality that backgrounds this

---

374 Blaten Geta Mahteme Selassie Welde Mesqel, ዝክረ ነገር (Addis Abeba, 1962 E.C.); Gebre-Sillasie, ታሪክ ዘመን ዳግማዊ ምኔልክ ንጉሰ ነገስት ሀኢትዮጵያ vol. 1 and vol II(Addis Abeba, 1967).
375 Zewde Reta, የቀዳማዊ ኃይለ ሥላሴ መንግስት (Boston: Laxmi Publications, 2012); Zewde Reta, ተፈሪ መኮንን (Addis Abeba: undated), Margary Perham, *The Government of Ethiopia* (London: Faber and Faber, 1969), pp. 423–432.
376 Mohammed Hassen, *The Oromo of Ethiopia: A History 1570-1860* (Cambridge: Cambridge University Press, 1990)., p. 21.

federation implies, *inter alia*, that all organizations, political parties, and public and state institutions—be they national, regional, or local—must be based on principles expressive of the universality inherent to *arnät*, i.e., freedom, equality, solidarity, citizenship, and justice.

4.5. Is a democratic ethnic federalism possible? The *Estifanosite* approach.

The inevitable question here is whether it is possible to have a democratic understanding of ethnic identity that allows the construction of an ethnic federalism that is also democratic. To answer this question, we have to examine what a democratic understanding of ethnic identity could be. Several possible answers could be contemplated.

The first possible approach is the French republican one that completely eschews ethnic, racial, religious, and other particular identity, and gives an absolute value to citizenship.[377] It offers a democratic federalism based on citizenship and eschews the political recognition of particular identities. These are relegated to the private sphere. Such a purist conception of politics and democratic federalism purports to be ethnicity-blind; however, it simply ignores the problem of the relationship between politics and ethnic identity. It is an approach that is not feasible in a historically multi-ethnic society such as Ethiopia.

A second possible approach may be derived from the political behaviour of the *official people* of the Ethiopian ethnic federation as well as of the ethnic *kilils*. The *official people* oscillate between citizenship and ethnic identity. Which mantle they don depends on which identity facilitates their pursuit of power and wealth at a given moment. Thus, we see politicians and public officials talk and act as ethnic nationalists on one occasion and talk and act as an Ethiopian nationalist-cum-citizen on another. Though this behaviour is cynical, the cynicism underlying their oscillation between ethnic identity and Ethiopian citizenship suggests the possibility of making citizenship a political identity that could replace ethnic identity under certain circumstances. The contentious point here is what counts as "certain circumstances." Could the *official people's* oscillation between these two identities be a political paradigm for all Ethiopians? Perhaps. But under what circumstances, when, and how? The fluid criteria that

---

[377] William Rogers Brubaker, "The French Revolution and the Invention of Citizenship," *French Politics and Society*, 1989, 7, No. 3, (1989), pp. 30-4.

underlie the determination of these circumstances may create more problems than they could solve. What appears to one an act of citizenship may appear to the other a pursuit of ethnic interest, or vice versa, thus creating a conflict of meanings and interests, for there is no guarantee that all will use or agree to use the same criteria of oscillation between citizenship and ethnic identity, and when, and how, and for what purpose. The quasi-impossibility of creating commonly shared universal criteria for oscillations between these two identities will certainly lead to unending political conflicts, violence and a full azimuth authoritarianism. Venturing to answer this question in practice will certainly open a political Pandora's Box that will release into Ethiopian society irreconcilable interests, unresolvable conflicts, unpredictable situations, and harmful political instabilities.

A third possible approach is what one could call the *Estifanosite* approach. I have discussed elsewhere the secular surplus meanings of the 15th century heretical movement of the *Däqiqä Estifanos*.[378] I will focus here on the parts that are relevant to our question. The membership of the *Däqiqä Estifanos* included Tigreans, Amharas, Wälayitas, Gamos, Agäws, Boshas, Hadiyas, and Oromos.[379] But as we shall see briefly, the *Däqiqä Estifanos* transformed their primary identification into a secondary identification through their membership in the organization such that they related to each other by giving primacy to that which is in their ethnic identity more than their ethnic identity: their humanity as the "children of God," to use their language. The organizing principle of their relation to authority was that of "standing up " to power, and the recognition of the equality between rulers and subjects; they were opposed to prostration to power, which they considered an insult to God and humanity, and believed that the voice of authority does not belong only to one person, thus affirming the autonomy, equality, and dignity (ማዕረግ, ma eräg) of each.[380] Note that, surprisingly for the 15th century, the *Däqiqä Estifanos* recognized both in theory and practice the equality of women: "is there any mystery that is given to men that women could not know?" asks Abuna Ezra, a member of the movement, and answers, no.[381] The *Däqiqä Estifanos* develop

---

378 Maimire Mennasemay, *Qiné Hermeneutics and Ethiopian Critical Theory* (Los Angeles: Tsehai Publishing, 2021), Chapter 8.
379 ደቂቀ እስቲፋኖስ: በሕግ አምላክ (translated from Ge'ez by Getatchew Haile (Collegeville, MN. 2004). p.46. I include the Oromos since we are in the 15th century, and according to Mohammed Hassen, Oromos were present in the Christian kingdoms of the north since at least the 13th century. Mohammed Hassen, *The Oromo and the Christian Kingdom of Ethiopia 1300– 1700* (Oxford: James Currey, 2015).
380 Ibid. pp. 102, 105-9, 112, 120, 122-7, 207. 30, 100, fn. 145.
381 Ibid, p. 298

a number of critical ideas. First, they point out that rulers would like to mould their subjects in their own image, and "People tend to resemble their rulers" because "this is what the ruler desires to see."[382] According to them, one has to stand up and resist the effort by the rulers to mould the people according to the interests of power; and the venue of this resistance is thinking autonomously. In addition, the *Däqiqä Estifanos* argue that one should not "remain at the foot of one's mountain" (of the given, such as one's primary identity, and the hegemonic ideas and beliefs), but rather one must "follow one's mind" and struggle until one "reaches the summit," that which is good and rational.[383] What is the "summit"? That which in oneself is more than oneself, i.e., one's universal dimension, or in the language of the Estifanosites, the Divine. This requires epistemic autonomy. Aba Estifanos asks his interlocutor: "Is your question a reflection of your judgment or a repetition of what others say? If you are making a judgment, you should first reflect upon what they say and what I say."[384] For the *Däqiqä Estifanos*, all issues that affect the community must be discussed with all the members of the community, hence their three statements—"I am engaged in litigation with Ethiopia," "Behold my evidence," and "Pray that I will not be an insult to the Ethiopian people."[385] One must treat these three fragments as brachylogia. When interpreted in ways that interrelate them, we discover that though the members of the *Däqiqä Estifanos* are of different ethnic origins— Tigreans, Amharas, Wälayitas, Gamos, Agäws, Boshas, Hadiyas, and Oromos—they believe that they should not remain at the "foot of the mountain" or their primary identities, but rather "scale" them until they could all say: "I am engaged in litigation with Ethiopia," and "Behold my evidence," and "Pray that I will not be an insult to the Ethiopian people."[386] It is precisely these universalist ideas that are articulated in their conviction that the rule of law is "just" only when it is the "rule of just law" (በሕግ አምላክ, BäHeg Amlak).[387] The *Däqiqä Estifanos* movement was rooted in the recognition of the autonomy of its members as embodiments, not of ethnicity, but of concrete universality— that which is in oneself more than oneself and puts one in reciprocal implications with the other.

---

382 Ibid. pp. 174, 211.
383 Ibid., p. 268
384 Ibid. p.70
385 Ibid. pp. 276, 302. Getatchew Haile, *A History of the First Stefanosite Monks*, translated from Ge'ez (Leuven: Uitgeverij Peeters, 2011), p.9.
386 Ibid.
387 ደቂቀ እስቲፋኖስ: በሕግ አምላክ, p. 156.

In our quest for an ethnic federalism that is also democratic, we could extrapolate from the surplus meanings of the ideas and practices of the *Estifanosites* and identify at least one possible answer. The core of the approach is democratizing ethnic identify—bringing to light "that which in oneself is more than oneself" or one's concrete universality politically and legally expressed as citizenship —such that its practice will be consistent, without annulling ethnic identity, with the practice and respect of autonomy, equality, justice, universality, and dignity. The solution I propose to derive from their approach will create out of each ethnicity with more than, say, three million people, multiple states (I am using an arbitrary figure for the sake of an example; it could be less or more as long as it does not prevent the democratization of ethnic identity) as a way of creating a space for the emergence of "that which is in oneself more than oneself," one's concrete universality that is the indispensable foundation of citizenship. I call these states *kiflä-agär* to underline their historical nature. The creation of multiple *kiflä-agär* avoids the identification of an entire ethnicity with a single ethnic space and boundaries that become walls that enclave, separate, and exclude. Avoiding the overlap of an entire ethnic group with a single space pre-empts the risk of the ethnicization of space, time, interests, and politics; it minimizes the emergence of monolithic group identity essentialism and ethnic extremism that an overlapping could bring in its wake. It nourishes secondary identification and fortifies the sense of citizenship. In the case of Ethiopia, whose population is around 120 million, the federation will be made up, based on the 3 million suggestion made above, of about 40 *kiflä-agär*. This *Estifanosite*-inspired approach has a number of advantages in that it provides the ground and creates the conditions for a federalism that is both democratic and ethnic and fosters the practices of autonomy, equality, justice, and dignity, without annulling ethnic identity. How?

First, it avoids the dangerous identification of ethnic identity with ethnic space, time, and boundaries. The absence of an overlapping of an entire ethnic group with a single space and time pre-empts the risk of ethnicization and sacralization of identity, space, time, and interests *à la Oromummaa*. It thus minimizes the emergence of monolithic group identity essentialism and atavistic ethno-nationalism. It creates a secular and open non-sectarian political, historical, social and psychological space within which ethnic identity is recognized, not as something fixed, but as a relation that is fluid and plastic. Second, it opens up the horizon of ethnic identity and gives it the opportunity to flourish by making ethnic identity an opening to others and a path of communication with others rather than a wall of separation that bottles up and stifles ethnicity in a bounded territory and a fixed essence. Third, at the same time, the absence of overlapping of an entire ethnicity with a single space and time reinforces secondary identification by historicizing ethnicity and transmuting primary identification into a transformed expression of the former. Fourth, the absence of a totalizing overlapping between space, time and ethnicity transmutes ethnic identity into language-identity and takes the venom out of monolithic group identity essentialism, for, given the dynamic, plastic and social nature of language, it is impossible to essentialize or mythologize a particular language *à la Oromummaa*.[388] The invention in the 1960s of a Latin alphabet-based Oromiffa script called *Qubee* attests to the historical and plastic nature of language. Fifth, it will push the various *kiflä-agär*, even if they speak the same language, to give primacy to their *kiflä-agär*'s and their inhabitants' interests thus avoiding the ethnicization of all issues, as is the case under the 1995 Constitution. There could be coalitions between the different federated *kiflä-agär*, but such coalitions are contingent since they are based on satisfying each *kiflä-agär*'s and its inhabitants' interests. Sixth, it creates a favorable ground for creating a federation that is both democratic and ethnic by making federalism an open system that allows ethnicity to be present through the representations of the various *kiflä-agär*, without such a representation congealing into walls of ethnic separation and monolithic identity essentialism, for each *kiflä-agär* will have its own particular interests. Shared common interests with other *kiflä-agär* will certainly exist, but they will be addressed as concrete rather than as ethnic issues, thus avoiding the prison of identity essentialism that prevents servicing the concrete issues of each *kiflä-agär* and its inhabitants. Seventh, it liberates federalism from the anti-democratic tasks of continuously trying to perpetuate monolithic group identity essentialism by continuously adjusting and changing its laws and regulations to accommodate the demands of monolithic group identity essentialism, as is the case under the 1995 Constitution. Eighth, it avoids the present practice of oppressive measures against those who are seen to flout the demand of monolithic group identity essentialism, as is the case under the 1995 Constitution.

The *Estifanosite* approach generates democratic ethnicity and a federalism that is both ethnic and democratic. For this to happen, the 1995 Constitution needs to be amended to make possible a transition from a system that makes an entire ethnicity overlap with a single ethnic space and time, creating boundaries that become walls of enclavement, separation, and exclusion, to a system of a non-spatially bounded ethnic identity that will surely evolve into a language-based, inclusive, open-ended and fluid ethnic identity, thus

---

388 Walter Benjamin, "On Language as such and on the Language of Man" in *Selected Writings*, vol. 1, 1913-1926, eds. Marcus Bullock and Michael W. Jennings (Cambridge: Harvard University Press, 1997), pp 62-74.

democratizing ethnic identity and federalism. A federalism based on this *Estifanosite* approach allows the development of public reason and of a public realm: "litigation with Ethiopia," the practice of "behold my evidence," and "Pray that I will not be an insult to the Ethiopian people," to use the *Däqiqä Estifanos* phrasings.

The problem with the 1995 Constitution is that, to use the language of the *Estifanosites*, it remains stuck at the "foot" of Ethiopia's history and primary identities. It is thus shackled to a worm's-eye view of Ethiopian society that sees only the immediately given: ethnic identities. It does not "scale" Ethiopian history and ethnic identity to their "summit" and discover the emancipatory horizon of freedom, equality, justice, and dignity they gestate without denying ethnic identity. It thus does not offer an emancipatory societal ideal to which Ethiopians could aspire.[389]

For *säwrä tarik*, a crucial component of the historical becoming of Ethiopians as *hizb* and Ethiopia as *agär* is the emergence of *adäbabay* (አደባባይ) and *lissan* or ልሳን (emancipatory discourse). *Adäbabay* means—as the *Däqiqä Estifanos* intimate in their ideas of "litigation with Ethiopia," "behold my evidence," and "Pray that I will not be an insult to the Ethiopian people," —public space and public time, or public realm, in short, wherein public debates flourish freely, creating the space necessary for the emergence of public reason, practically and institutionally. *Adäbabay* has deep roots in Ethiopian history. One finds it in the invitation of Lalibela (13th century) to the workers to discuss the worth of their labour, in the practices of the *Estifanosites*, the *Ewostatewos*, and the *Zamika'elites*, all of whom fearlessly expressed their views publicly, despite the persecutions they incurred.[390]

---

389 The Estifanosite approach could easily accommodate the cases of the small ethnicities (say, less than 3 million, as suggested above as an example).
390 Taddesse Tamrat, *Church and State in Ethiopia, 1270-1527* (Oxford: Clarendon Press, 1972)., pp. 209-219, 227; Gianfranco Ficcadori, "Ewosṭatewos" in Siegbert Uhlig, *Encyclopaedia Aethiopica* (Wiesbaden: Harrassowitz Verlag, 2005), pp. 464-472. Getachew Haile, "Ethiopian Heresies and Theological Controversies" in Coptic Encyclopedia, vol 2, ed. Aziz S. Atiya (New York: Macmillan, 1991), 984a-987b; Teweldeberhan Mezgebe Desta, *Gädlä Abäw wä-Aḥaw [Fourth Part]: Edition and Annotated Translation with Philological and Linguistic Commentary* (Addis Ababa: Addis Ababa University Dissertation, 2019). Getachew Haile, *A History of the First Stefanosite Monks*, translated from Ge'ez (Leuven: Uitgeverij Peeters, 2011), p.9. Maimire Mennasemay, *Qiné Hermeneutics and Ethiopian Critical Theory* (Los Angeles: Tsehai Publishers, 2021), Chapter 7.

Public reason is the political oxygen without which *arnät* and democratic federalism will suffocate and wither away.[391] Public reason functions through *mädämamät* or "dialogical dialogue" and *zäräfa* on social, economic, and political issues without resorting to authoritarianism, censorship, ethnic politics, violence, and corruption. It fosters the development of diverse and contrarian ideas, of *lissan* or emancipatory discourse. In erasing the ideas and practices of *hizb* and *agär*, the 1995 Constitution and ethnic federalism disintegrated Ethiopia's public space and time (*adäbabay*) into ethnic spaces and times. When ethnic space and time take over the public realm (*adäbabay*), the latter is fragmented, and public reason disintegrates. Its fragments are colonized by "private reason," whose form under the 1995 Constitution is "ethnic reason"—an oxymoron that grasps the impossibility of reconciling 'ethnic thinking' with thinking that is guided by the universal principles of freedom, equality, solidarity, citizenship, dignity, and justice. Ethnic thinking replaces pubic reason with verbal and physical violence, with printed and cyberspace violence, as we could see since 1995, the year 'ethnic thinking' was embedded in the Constitution and evicted public reason. Ethnic thinking is hostile to *hizb* and *agar*, to *adäbabay*, *lissan*, *zäräfa*, *mädämamät*, and *andemta*. It makes federalism that is both ethnic and democratic impossible. It subverts the quest for an Ethiopia liberated from political, economic, and epistemic unfreedoms and inequalities, and propels Ethiopians backwards into ethnic black holes where the only thing that matters is brute force. The constitutionalization of ethnic separation and the institutionalization of ethnic thinking have made Ethiopia an arena of deadly ethnic struggles for territory and scarce resources.[392] Unlike ethnic thinking, public reason

---

391 On public reason, Jurgen Habermas, *Between Facts and Norms: Contributions to a Discourse Theory of Law and Democracy*, tans. William Rehg (Cambridge: Polity, 1996); On private and public reason, Immanuel Kant, "What is Enlightenment?" in *Kant's Political Writings,* ed. Hans Reiss (Cambridge: Cambridge University Press, 1980), pp. 54-60.

392 Sarah Vaughan and Mesfin Gebremichael, *Rethinking Business and Politics in Ethiopia: The role of EFFORT, the Endowment Fund for the Rehabilitation of Tigray* (London: The Overseas Development Institute, 2011). Matthew J. McCracken, "Abusing Self-Determination and Democracy: How the TPLF is Looting Ethiopia." *Case Western Reserve Journal of International Law*, vol 36, 1 (2004) pp. 183-222. On page 185, he writes, "the TPLF-dominated EPRDF intentionally included Article 39 in Ethiopia's 1995 Constitution so that the Tigray region could loot Ethiopia of its resources, use the Ethiopian military to expand the borders of Tigray, and then secede from Ethiopia. Underlying this theory is the widely held opinion that the TPLF and EPRDF are not independent organizations, but symbiotic." This is an assessment shared by most scholars. Seid Hassan, "Aid, Predation and State Capture: The Role of Development Aid in Corruption and

embodies itself in public deliberations open to *hizb* and creates the space and time necessary to make democracy and federalism the expressions of *hizb* and *agär*, and through the mediations of these, of ethnicity.

4.6. Critique of *kilil* as a biopolitical space of necropower

With the above discussion as a background, we could now see how the *kilil* system that the 1995 Constitution created goes against the possibility of emancipation gestating in Ethiopian history and leads to a political system and practices that "subjugate life to the power of death."[393] That is, the 1995 Constitution has created *kilil* as a "biopolitical space" of "necropower."[394] *Kilil* institutes a biopolitical ordering of life based on ethnic identity. Its borders function as a Maginot Line that delineate a space of belonging that excludes other ethnicities as intruders to be prohibited from inhabiting it. Subjecting Mbembe to *zäräfa*, one could say that *kilil* borders function as lines of separation and exclusion and not as lines of communication and mutual understanding. By proclaiming that sovereignty resides in Ethiopian ethnicities (Article 8), and therefore in the ethnic *kilil*, and by making ethnic enclavement and separation the constitutive principles of political life, the 1995 Constitution created a "society of enmity."[395] The presence of members of other ethnicities in a *kilil* is perceived as an existential threat that must be thwarted by the *kilil*. The *official people* of *kilils* have set themselves to this task with a deadly enthusiasm. And this power to subject the other to a social or physical death is exercised as an expression of and legitimated by the "sovereignty" the 1995 Constitution bestows on each ethnicity. The upshot is the imposition of "the

---

Undermining Governance: The Case of Ethiopia," *Ethiopian e-Journal for Research and Innovation Foresight (Ee-JRIF)*, vol 5, 1 (2013), pp. 51-93. Note the arrest of many prominent members of the Meles Zenawi regime for corruption in November 2018. በሰብዓዊ መብት ጥሰቶችና በክፍተኛ የሙስና ወንጀል የተጠረጠሩ ግለሰቦች ፍርድ ቤት ቀረቡ, *The Reporter* (in Amharic) 14 November 2018. The destructive war that the TPLF instigated in 2020 is one of the outcome of the ethnic elites' predatory behaviour and struggle for scarce resources.

393 Achille Mbembe, *Necropolitics* (Durham: Duke University Press, 2019), p. 92. This section draws on a *zäräfa* of Achlle Mbembe's reflections on necropolitics

394 Biopolitics is the power the state has to administer and discipline life through social interventions and policies. On biopolitics, Michel Foucault, *Society Must Be Defended* (London: Penguin, 2004), pp. 239-265; Timothy Campbell and Adam Sitze, eds., *Biopolitics: A Reader* (Durham: Duke University Press, 2013).On necropower, Achille Mbembe, *Necropolitics*, supra.

395 Achille Mbembe, *Necropolitics*, pp. 42-65.

status of rightlessness as a biopolitical necessity" on those who do not belong to a *kilil* by virtue of blood and soil.[396] The creation of *kilils* naturalized ethnicity, introduced ethnic separation based on the principle of blood and soil, rendered the other ethnic group a foreigner, entertained the fantasy of ethnic purity, and laid the ground for the spatial, political, psychological, cultural separation between Ethiopian ethnicities, transforming Ethiopia into a society of archfoes. Those who are of other ethnies in a given *kilil* are identified as not being of the blood and soil of the *kilil* and are perceived as enemies to be subjected to exclusion, abjection, and selective elimination. The *kilil* thus became for the non-indigenous a space of terror and death.

Ethnic sovereignty, whose institutional embodiment is the *kilil*, has bestowed on each *kilil* the power "to define who matters and who does not, who is *disposable* and who is not", making the social or physical killing of the "other" a "regulative practice" of governing and a tool and a condition of necropower.[397] Thus, *kilils* in Ethiopia are the constitutionally created "sovereign" agents of necropolitics: a politics that subjects populations identified as not belonging to the *kilil* to "living conditions that confer upon them the status of the living dead."[398]

Consequently, the principles of freedom, equality, solidarity, and justice are amputated of their universality and reduced to ethnic rights that are governed by the laws of autochthony. For those who do not "belong" to the *kilil*, these rights are wielded against them as weapons of necropower. Thus, the ethnic cleansing of Amharas, other non-Oromos, and pro-Ethiopian Oromos from the Oromo *kilil* in the name of the "right of ethnic self-determination." It is to be noted that Prime Minister Abiy Ahmed, a Nobel Peace Prize winner, has not uttered a word of condemnation on the openly conducted massive ethnic cleansing in the Oromo *kilil*. Similar necropolitical practices directed at those considered "intruders" or as being not of the "the land and blood" of the *kilils* take place in other *kilils*. The *kilils* have become "death worlds," which are "new and unique forms of social existence in which" members of ethnicities that do not "belong" to a *kilil*'s biopolitcal space are regulated through social or physical death. In these death worlds called *kilils*, those who do not "belong" to the *kilil* lose their humanity and become bodies without values to be socially or physically eliminated, even if they have lived in the area for generations. Those identified of being not of the *kilil* are subjected to a life of perpetual humiliation, exclusion, abjection, and total insecurity. They survive on the precipice of

---

396 Achille Mbembe, *Necropolitics*, p. 98.
397 Achille Mbembe, *Necropolitics*, p. 80.
398 Achille Mbembe, *Necropolitics*, p. 92.

annihilation, abandoned to their fate of being the "living dead," without either the federal or the *kilil* governments raising a finger to protect them. Theirs is a "life in death."

As Walter Benjamin has written, "There is no document of civilization which is not at the same time a document of barbarism."[399] That is, every civilization is a *säm ena wärq*. The likelihood that the "barbarism," which is present in Ethiopian history, could return and demolish the civilizational achievements or *wärq* of Ethiopians— secondary identification, *hizb, agar, adäbabay*, public reason, diversity-in-unity (*wihdät*), universality—if primary identities continue to be the foundation of politics cannot be underestimated. The unfettering of our barbarisms is what has resulted from the monolithic identity essentialism enshrined in the 1995 Constitution and the ethnic federalism it created. Wars, local (*kilil*) tyrannies, ethnic-cleansings, institutional ethnicism and nano-ethnicism, and authoritarianism are more prevalent now than in any other time of Ethiopian history. The anti-*hizb*, anti-*agär*, anti-democratic 1995 Constitution and ethnic federation have created a historical deadlock that not only engulfs the lives of Ethiopians in an unrelenting political violence but also surely condemns the present ethnic federalism to death, sooner or later. The question is: how? Would ethnic federalism collapse through a *coup d'état*, or would it disintegrate through violent ethnic conflicts *à la* Yugoslavia? Or, would it be the wrong choice that through its destructive after-effects will persuade Ethiopians to make the right choice—*arnät* infused democratic federalism? Only time will tell.

---

399 Walter Benjamin, "Theses on the Philosophy of History," in *Illuminations*, edited and with an introduction by Hannah Arendt, trans. Harry Zohn (New York: Schocken Books, 1968), p. 256.

5

Conclusion: Ethioperspectivism and Becoming Ethiopian

ዕውቀትን ስጠኝ የሃብቶች ራስ የሆነችውን
ከነጻ ጌታ ጋር እኩል የምታደርግ ባሪያውን

(Give me knowledge, for it is superior to wealth,
And makes the slave the equal of the free lord.)
        Aba Bahrey (Late 16th Century monk and historian)[400]

Turina keessatt killen millaan adeemti
(By persevering the egg walks on legs)
        An Oromiffa aphorism

"A life without thinking is quite possible; it then fails to develop
its own essence – it is not merely meaningless; it is not fully alive.
Unthinking men are like sleepwalkers."
        Hannah Arendt[401]

As the discussions in the previous chapters indicate, Ethioperspectivism is an emancipatory *andemta* that emerges from our critical internal and external journeys from the perspective of the *säwrä tarik* disclosed by our critical internal journey. Ethioperspectivism and the reflection on Becoming Ethiopian are triggered by the historically informed consciousness that *säwrä tarik* generates:

---

400 Getatchew Haile, የአባ ባጎራይ ድርሰቶች [16th Century] (Collegeville, Minnesota, 2002), p. 49.
401 Hannah Arendt, *The Life of the Mind* (New York: A Harvest Book, 1971), p.191.

that there is "something wrong" in contemporary Ethiopia, an obscure temptation to commit a national suicide. Ethioperspectivism aims to expose the roots of the "something that is wrong" and throw light on how to overcome it through a process of critical reflection that lead to transformative actions—political, economic, social, cultural, and epistemic. Since we cannot resist effectively and transform what we do not understand, Ethioperspectivism requires thinking that develops critical ideas immanent to Ethiopian history/society in order to expose and overcome the "something wrong" that is consuming Ethiopia from within. Ethioperspectivism, being rooted in *qiné* hermeneutics, understands thinking in the critical *qiné* hermeneutical sense of asking fundamental questions.[402] It scrutinizes and seeks (*qisäla* and *mirmära*) new and emancipatory ways of seeing and conceptualizing our conditions, our selves and the world we live in, and our relations to our past, present and future, and the emancipatory potentials that gestate in these. To engage in this emancipation oriented knowledge production, Ethioperspectivism must be based on and guided by epistemic autonomy on pain of failing like the Gibbonist social sciences.

For the sake of facilitating the grasp of the threads of the discussion of the issue of Ethioperspectivism and Becoming Ethiopian, I will briefly define Becoming Ethiopian as a process that creates an Ethiopian society whose political, economic, social, intellectual, and cultural institutions and practices prevent the breeding of political, economic, social and epistemic powerlessness, and generate an Ethiopian life-context in which each and all Ethiopians flourish politically, economically, and epistemically. I argue that Ethioperspectivism is the approach necessary for achieving this goal and discus it in five steps: critique of knowledge welfare; de-Gibbonizing or de-Westernizing knowledge; de-Gobbinizing or de-Westernizing Ethiopian poverty; de-Gibbonizing or de-Westernizing democracy; and against falling out of history.

---

402 Writing about *qiné* schools, Sumner quotes a qiné scholar, "In such a school [*qiné* school] discussion and *asking questions* [ጥያቄ / *tiyaqé*, plural ጥያቄዎች, *tiyaqéwoch*] is (*sic*) encouraged. Since the students in such an atmosphere throughout the Ethiopian tradition have been trained to think rather than believe, they have been dissenters more often than not. Since they tend to rely on reason rather than on mere faith, they tend to be more philosophical than their counterparts the priests are. Indeed, it can be said that Ethiopian philosophy in its true sense, i.e., philosophy based on primacy of reason, originated in the kine [*qiné*] school." Solomon Gebre Chiogis, quoted in Claude Sumner, *Classical Ethiopian Philosophy* (Los Angeles: Adey Publishing Company, 1994), p. 224. Italics added. On *wistä wäyra reading*, see Chapter 1 above.

5.1. Critique of Knowledge welfare

When Addis Alemayehu, Ethiopia's literary giant, wrote, "Education is the second creator of the human being," (ትምርት ለሰው ሁለተኛ ፈጣሪው) he was expressing the *qiné* hermeneutical tradition's idea that human beings are born twice: first from their mothers, and second, from their education.[403] According to Addis, it is the second birth that shapes and molds the Ethiopian and eventually Ethiopia. For Addis, education should create Ethiopians who see themselves as citizens who are committed to freedom, equality and justice, acknowledge their interdependence, practice civility, and trust each other, and pursue their individual and collective flourishing. For Addis, the issue of Becoming Ethiopian in the context of modernization is intimately associated with the "cultural production" of the modern educated Ethiopian.[404]

Since the signing of the Point Four Program in 1951 between the government of Emperor Haile Selassie and the government of the United States, Gibbonism has been the foundation of the cultural production of the modern educated Ethiopian. The form, content, methodology, concepts, and theories in post-secondary education and knowledge production on Ethiopia give absolute primacy to the epistemology, methodology, and theories of Western social sciences.[405] Absent from the cultural formation of the modern educated Ethiopians are important areas of Ethiopia's intellectual traditions: her manuscript culture, *qiné* hermeneutics, the philosophical, legal and political surplus meanings of *Fitha Nägäst*, the ideas and surplus meanings of the 19th century Wollo Muslim scholars and *mänzuma* compositions, the surplus meanings of aphorisms, *andemta* commentaries, *gädl* texts, historical chronicles, Ethiopian literature and arts, the surplus meanings of autopoietic organizations (*däbo, iddir, iqqub, araaraa, jaarsummaa, biyyaas, ayyanaa*, etc.), of social / political practices such as *moggaasa, luba, butta*, social practices such as *ateetee, afersata, gudifecha*, the eight-generation rule, and other Ethiopian institutions and practices.

Certainly, one could find in Ethiopian Studies research papers and studies on Ethiopia's manuscript culture and the above Ethiopian practices and institutions. However, these studies are framed by Gibbonism. They are bounded by and

---

403 Addis Alemayehu, የልም ገት (Addis Ababa: Kuraz Printing Press, 1980), p.373.
404 On the cultural production of the educated person, see Levinson, B. A., Foley, D. E. and Holland, D. eds., *The Cultural Production of the Educated Person: Critical Ethnographies of Schooling and Local Practice* (New York: SUNY, 1996), pp. 1-54; Aklilu Habte, Menguesha Gebre Hewit and Monika Kehoe, "Higher Education in Ethiopia," *Journal of Ethiopian Studies*, 1963, vol 1, No. 1 (January 1963), pp. 3- 7.
405 The discussion bears only on the social sciences and philosophy.

rooted in the ontological, epistemological, teleological, and methodological assumptions of Western social sciences. Ethiopian practices and institutions are temporally frozen in their context and rarely considered as *nägär* that should be problematized and subjected to *zäräfa* in order to enucleate and develop the emancipatory questions, ideas, norms, methods, possibilities and aspirations that could be germinating in them and that could speak to the questions, needs, and interests of present-day Ethiopians. It is as if present day Ethiopia exists without an intellectual tradition that raises questions and intimates responses, indirect as these may be, bearing on the Ethiopian present and future context of life and the various issues they raise; it is as if contemporary Ethiopians exist in a cognitive night— *"slept near a thousand years,"* as Gibbon wrote—waiting for the "light" of Western knowledge that enables Ethiopians to see, recognize and understand themselves. Inevitably, the cultural formation of modern educated Ethiopians submits them to the unrestrained authority of the West's epistemic paternalism and makes them internalize the practice of uncritical borrowing of knowledge as the only form of knowledge acquisition. Since it is difficult to cultivate epistemic autonomy from an educational system that does not include it in some form, it is not surprising that modern educated Ethiopians rarely attain epistemic autonomy and depend without much questioning on the ideas, paradigms and procedures they acquire through Gibbonist education.

As we have already seen, Gibbonist education blocks and excludes epistemic autonomy. The lack of epistemic autonomy puts out of our intellectual reach a critical approach to Ethiopia's conditions and her relations to others . The absence of a critical internal journey into the intellectual history and *nägär* of Ethiopia, both vertically and laterally, inevitably renders *säwrä tarik* invisible and unavailable. Ethiopian students pursue their acquisition of knowledge on Ethiopia, as if Ethiopia were a cognitive *tabula rasa*, an intellectually silent and blind society that needs the epistemology, the concepts, theories, and methodologies of the West to see, hear, understand and express herself. The transformation of Ethiopia into an intellectually mute society in the process of the cultural formation of modern educated Ethiopians propels them into self-forgetfulness, plunging them into a whirlpool of ignorance of themselves (historically) and of each other (laterally). This self-forgetfulness *cum* self-ignorance forces them into a number of deadlocks.

First, they resort to mythologizing their past and their identity—national or ethnic. Thus, the proliferation of "invented traditions" such as *Oromummaa* or mythologized national and ethnic narratives. Mythologized national and ethnic narratives often mutate into prohibitions of autonomous thinking and impose group thinking. Second, they see Ethiopia's present conditions and future development through the lens of the West. Self-forgetfulness *cum* self-ignorance have disabled modern Ethiopians from engaging in a critical internal journey and conduct *zäräfa* on the knowledge, traditions and practices of Ethiopia—both vertical and lateral—and enucleate their *säwrä tarik*. Thus, they cannot produce the emancipatory questions, interests, ideas, aspirations and practices immanent in these two historical dimensions and forge an *andemta* of commonly shared emancipatory visons, ideas and projects. Third, modern Ethiopians are unable to engage in a critical external journey and conduct *zäräfa* on the knowledge and practices of the West (or the "other"), because, being deprived of a critical internal journey, they do not have the knowledge of the *säwrä tarik* that provides the necessary ground, framework, and questions for a critical external journey into the intellectual and practical achievements of the West (or other) from an Ethiopian emancipatory perspective. Consequently, producing an *andemta* of Ethiopian and Western horizons of understanding from the perspective of Ethiopia's emancipatory questions, interests, needs, ideas, practices, and aspirations becomes unfeasible. The acquisition of what Gibbon calls "the arts and ingenuity of Europe" becomes a process of unquestioned unidirectional *mäsmat*-based learning of what the West produces, a process that the *andemta* commentary would describe as "breathing from the air [the] master breathes, ... resting where he [the master] rests, and ... preserving the teaching as he has received it, without the slightest change, or difference of opinion."[406]

It is crucial to recognize that what prevents modern educated Ethiopians to achieve epistemic autonomy is not their lack of "reason." Rather, we could say, citing Kant, that it is the absence of the *"the courage to use"* their own understanding that prevents them from achieving epistemic autonomy.[407] However, we should submit Kant's concept of "courage" to *zäräfa* and understand "courage" as *wäne* (ወኔ), which in Amharic has a more potent meaning than Kant's term for courage, *der Mut*.[408] *Wäne* (ወኔ) is the decision to confront the impossible when one is in a situations of hopelessness, for it is only when one knows that defeat

---

406 Roger W. Cowley, "Old Testament Introduction in the Andemta Commentary Tradition," *Journal of Ethiopian Studies* 12, 1 (1974), p. 170.
407 Kant writes, *"Enlightenment is man's leaving his self-caused immaturity. Immaturity is the inability to use one's own understanding without the guidance of another. This immaturity is self-incurred if its cause is not lack of understanding, but by lack of resolution and courage to use it without the guidance of another. The motto of the enlightenment is therefore: Sapere Aude.! Have the courage to use your own understanding!" Kant's Political Writings,* ed. Hans Reiss (Cambridge: Cambridge University Press, 1980), p. 54. Italics in the original.
408 The Amharic word *wäne* (ወኔ) is more complex and more multi-dimensional that the English word "courage" or the German word that Kant uses, *der Mut* ("Sapere aude! Habe Mut, dich deines eigenen Verstandes zu bedienen! ist also der Wahlspruch der Aufklärung"). Immanuel Kant, "Was ist Aufklärung?" https://

is inevitable that one develops the cognitive and affective resoluteness, the unyielding drive, the steadfast will, the militant hope, fidelity to one's emancipatory aspirations, and the knowledge necessary to snatch victory from the jaws of hopelessness and make the impossible possible. It is not the lack of "reason" but the lack of intellectual *wäne* that has led modern educated Ethiopians down the path of epistemic vassalage and cultural cringe.

One could say then that under the reign of Gibbonism, the "will to ignorance" has replaced intellectual *wäne* in Ethiopian Studies. "The will to ignorance…is not simply the tendency or desire not to know some things. It…also turn[s] upon itself and become[s] *the will not to know that one is failing to know many things in the process of coming to know one.*"[409] That is, Gibbonist education cultivates the will to ignorance and makes the acquisition of knowledge an ensemble of cognitive mechanisms of self-deception, self-ignorance, self-forgetfulness, and epistemic submission to the West. It implies not only the epistemological disqualification but also the ontological disqualification of Ethiopians in that it treats them as beings who are essentially incapacitated to "think" that which in Ethiopian history/society is "more" than Ethiopian history/society—emancipated life and emancipatory knowledge; it condemns them to the condition of eternal "knowledge welfare" recipients. It is thus not surprising that Ethiopian Studies have failed to produce a coherent theory that can successfully guide Ethiopians out of the triple domination—political, economic, and epistemic—under which they live.

Modern educated Ethiopians who get their education abroad are as equally trapped in Gibbonism as those who get their higher education in Ethiopia. When Ethiopians go to Western universities for higher studies, they rarely do research and write their thesis from an Ethiopian perspective on the sociological, psychological, political, economic, historical, gnoseological, and anthropological issues of the countries—America, France, Britain, Russia, China, and so forth—where they are studying. That is, they do not engage in a critical external journey into Western (other) society and knowledge based on the questions Ethiopia's *säwrä tarik* raises, because they do not know what these questions are, not having conducted a critical internal journey into Ethiopian knowledge traditions, intellectual history, and their place in Ethiopian history/society. Westerners, on the other hand, come to Ethiopia to study Ethiopians using Western paradigms of knowledge that emerge from their own critical internal journey into their

---

www.rosalux.de/fileadmin/rls_uploads/pdfs/159_kant.pdf, p.5. Accessed 1/30/2016.
409 On the "will to ignorance," Alexander Nehamas, *Nietzsche: Life as Literature* (Cambridge, MA: Harvard University Press, 1985), p. 69. Emphasis added.

own history, society, and knowledge traditions. They engage in a critical external journey into Ethiopian society based on the paradigms, questions, theories and methods their own society's critical internal journey into itself has created. Unlike Westerners who come to study Ethiopia armed with their theories and methodologies, Ethiopian students who go to the West go epistemically naked and do not and cannot study the West from an Ethiopian perspective. Rather, during their stay in the West, they study Ethiopia using Western theories and methodologies. Often, they go back to Ethiopia and bring along their borrowed paradigms to do field work, return to the Western university where they study, and write their thesis and articles on Ethiopia, expanding thus the domination of the Western episteme on and in Ethiopia, and increasing the Western fund of knowledge, while impoverishing Ethiopia as a space for producing new paradigms, new theories, and new methodologies, and new knowledge. Thus, the higher education of Ethiopians, both within and outside Ethiopia, dispossesses modern educated Ethiopians of their epistemic autonomy and of the possibility of engaging in both critical internal and external journeys. Thus Ethiopia suffers a double "accumulation by dispossession": material and intellectual.[410] Material and intellectual production in/on Ethiopia augment the material and intellectual capital of the West and, in the process, create the material and intellectual impoverishment of Ethiopia.

The formation of the modern Ethiopian intellectual instills in the educated a "cultural cringe."[411] Thus the post-secondary educational institutions in Ethiopia produce "as-if form of knowledge," knowledge that assumes "as if" the West's social sciences and philosophy were the only ways of understanding Ethiopian reality, and indeed the world.[412] Inevitably, Ethiopian reality becomes impenetrable to this "as-if" knowledge. Hence, the repeated political and economic failures and the untold sufferings wrought on Ethiopia by the modern educated Ethiopians in their pursuit to uncritically impose on Ethiopians the Western understanding of nation, people, ethnicity, democracy, revolution, and development, "as if" these were simply transferable from the West to the Ethiopian historical, political, economic, psychological, and social contexts without being subjected to *zäräfa* from the perspective of the emancipatory questions, needs, and interests that *säwrä tarik* articulates. It is precisely the

---

410 On "accumulation by dispossession", see David Harvey, *A Brief History of Neoliberalism* (Oxford: Oxford University Press, 2007), p. 159. I extend through *zäräfa* the idea of "accumulation by dispossession" to the field of knowledge production by modern educated Ethiopians.
411 On cultural cringe, see Introduction.
412 http://www.raewynconnell.net/2013/02/the-cultural-cringe-and-social-science.html. Accessed 10/29/2021. The expression "as if form of knowledge" is Raewyn Connel's.

failures of political and economic development based on "as-if" knowledge that generated the failed Revolution of 1974 that begat the authoritarian regimes of the DERG, the EPRDF, and the PP. In the oft quoted words of Walter Benjamin, "behind every fascism, there is a failed revolution."[413]

Knowledge welfare, the offspring of Gibbonism, has created zombie ideas that have made modern educated Ethiopians intellectual noctambulists in their relations to each other, to Ethiopian issues, and to the West, preventing them from effectively understanding themselves, the West, and their relation to and their place in the world. The completely gratuitous wars in the Tigrai, Amhara, and Oromo *kilils* since 2020 and the fantasies the participants in these wars spin on official and social media are proofs of the intellectual noctambulism that has struck educated Ethiopians. In Gibbonist education lies thus the answer to two crucial questions: How is it that almost a century of Western higher education in Ethiopia has failed to give rise to educated Ethiopians who are capable of creating and developing emancipatory theories and practices that enthuse and grasp Ethiopians? How is it that this education has created modern educated Ethiopians who pursue "adaptive preferences" that reduce "democracy" to ethnic othering, and "development" to an extraverted economy and a process of large-scale corruption, and knowledge production to "as if" knowledge?[414]

Gibbon wrote that Ethiopians were "forgetful of the world, by whom they were forgotten." But the situation has radically changed now. We could now say that modern educated Ethiopians are no longer "forgetful of the world," nor are they "forgotten" by it. They are now aware of the world as the world is of them. However, they have become "forgetful" of themselves and have forgotten that they have become "forgetful" of themselves.[415] Not surprisingly, given the "will to ignorance" and the "self-forgetfulness" that drive the cultural formation of the modern educated Ethiopian, the hotbeds of ethnic unrest in Ethiopia are

---

413 Quoted in Slavoj Žižek, *In Defense of Lost Causes* (New York: Verso, 2008), p. 386..
414 On corruption and development in Ethiopia, *Transparency International Corruption Index*, https://www.transparency.org/en/cpi/2022. Accessed 7/2/2023. Ethiopia is among the most corrupt countries.
415 The propensity of modern educated Ethiopians for uncritical borrowing of knowledge, led an observer of modern Ethiopian students to note "the speed with which they gave up their traditional habits and manners" and to compare them to "their Japanese counterparts," who followed Western education but "continued to adhere to their traditions. Bahru Zewde, *Pioneers of Change in Ethiopia: The Reformist Intellectuals of the early Twentieth Century* (Oxford: James Curry, 2002), p. 80.

institutions of higher education. Ethiopia's Ministry of Science and Higher Education announced on January 17, 2020, that ethnic unrest in 22 universities have caused 35,000 students to quit class.[416] The ethnic animosity among the internally and externally educated Ethiopians continues unabated.[417] Addis Alemayehu's idea that education should create Ethiopians who see themselves as citizens that are free and equal, that practice civility, solidarity, have a critical spirit, and trust each other has been thoroughly undermined by Gibbonist education. Knowledge welfare has saddled modern Ethiopia with Potemkin knowledge: an elaborate intellectual façade, made up of political, economic, social and cultural studies, and over 30 public universities, which has little relation to Ethiopian reality and emancipatory needs, but is making this reality increasingly chaotic and pathological due to the pursuit of politics and the formulation of policies based on this ersatz knowledge. In modern Ethiopia, knowledge welfare has led to a contraction of the conceivable, an implosion of the intelligence, a stunting of the imagination, and a cancelation of possible alternatives.

Aba Bahrey, the 16th century monk and historian wrote in መልክዐ ገብርኤል (*Mälka Gäbriel*) addressing himself to God— "ጸግወኒ ረአስ ሀብታት እንተ ይኣቲ ኣአምሮ / ምስለ አግዓዚ. እግዚአ ዘታዔሪ ገብር." "Give me knowledge, for it is superior to wealth / And makes the slave the equal of the free lord."[418] Only with the rejection of Gibbonism and the appropriation of epistemic autonomy could Ethiopians be free, produce emancipatory knowledge, prosper, and be "the equal of the free lord." *Zäräfa* shows that for the modern educated Ethiopians the "free lord" is the West. Ethiopia is still the recipient of "knowledge welfare" from this "free lord." Aba Bahrey's prayer is yet to be answered.

5.2. De-Gibbonizing or de-Westernizing knowledge

Mesfin Welde Mariam, the well-known geographer and human rights militant, raises a poignant question with a whiff of pessimism: "የጭካኔ አገዛዝ ውስጥ ሌላ ምርጫ አለ ወይ? / Is there really an alternative to an oppressive state?"[419] Despite

---

416 https://africa.cgtn.com/2020/01/17/unrest-in-ethiopian-universities-forces-35000-students-to-quit-class/. Accessed on 1/18/2020.
417 Ethiopian cyberspace media accounts of Twitter, YouTube, FaceBook, mainly run by young modern educated Ethiopians, have become venues for disseminating ethnic hatred. Among these, OMN, the Oromo Media Network, is without contest the Ethiopian equivalent of the infamous Radio Collines (Radio-Television Libre des Mille Collines) of Rwanda in its unrelenting preaching of hatred of the Amhara.
418 In Getatchew Haile, የአባ ባሕራይ ድርስቶች (Collegeville, Minnesota, 2002), p. 49.
419 Mesfin Welde Mariam, አዳፍኔ፡ ፍርሃትና መከሸፍ (Addis Ababa, 2007), p. 263.

Ethiopia's long history of oppressive governments, Ethiopians should not hesitate to answer in the affirmative. However, such an affirmative answer is effective only if we formulate emancipatory questions and concepts, blend theoretical thought and emancipatory imagination in terms of the *andemta* of the outcomes of our critical internal and external journeys. I will call Ethioperspectivism the outcome of such a knowledge activity and the ideas and approaches we develop based on it.

Ethioperspectivism is for unconditional universalism, and institutes epistemic autonomy as the necessary ground for knowledge production by Ethiopians. It is based on the belief that we Ethiopians "have in us what we could become": free, equal, prosperous, just, and knowledge producing people, if we were to liberate ourselves from the clutches of Gibbonism and appropriate our *säwrä tarik*.[420] Ethioperspectivism de-Gibbonizes the Western social sciences, hegemonic in Ethiopia's higher education and research institutions. It discards the West's sanitization of its oppressive and exploitive history, ideas and practices, and considers the role its knowledge production has played in the imposition of the triple domination on Ethiopia and others in order to purge it of its anti-emancipatory forms and contents. It rejects its assumptions that its understanding of the world is the limit to our understanding of the world, and that its social sciences provide universal and objective knowledge. Ethioperspectivism decenters and dislocates the borrowed social sciences and practices and subjects them to *antsar* and *wistä wäyra* readings from the perspective of *säwrä tarik*. In the process, it unveils and rejects the zombie concepts, the methodological Westernism, and the somnambulistic practices that have dissociated knowledge production on Ethiopia from Ethiopian reality and the emancipatory needs of Ethiopians. Ethioperspectivism requires that we actively unlearn the Gibbonist problematization of development, democracy, people, nation, ethnicity, and knowledge. Only then could we abandon the present practice of choosing political, economic and cognitive adaptive preferences, and reject the Ptolemization of ethnic politics as democracy, of the *official people*'s enrichment as development, and of studies on Ethiopian politics, economy and society that sweat epistemic servility from every pore as knowledge. The de-Westernization of knowledge does not usher relativism. Rather, it makes the emancipation of Ethiopians the measure by which the universality of an

---

420 A *zäräfa* of Ernst Bloch's idea on what human beings could become. Ernst Bloch, *The Principle of Hope* I, trans. Neville Plaice, Stephen Plaice and Paul Knight (Cambridge, MA: MIT Press, 1986), p. 927.

idea, an act, a practice, or a belief, whatever its source may be, is judged. As such, it rejects the present practice of "knowledge welfare" that cultivates cognitive dependency through epistemic servility.

What has characterized Ethiopia since the institutionalization of Gibbonism is massive poverty, making Ethiopia the world-wide symbol of hunger and suffering.[421] Despite the massive international aid and internationally funded poverty alleviation programs, despite the Ethiopian governments' projects and policies to reduce poverty, and despite the efforts of local and international NGOs, hunger still stalks more than 20 million Ethiopians (the 2023 figure), and the number of Ethiopians who will suffer from hunger is expected to rise in the coming years.[422] One must then ask: why have poverty alleviation programs and policies failed so starkly? These failures are not the outcome of the lack of efforts, sincerity, and diligence on the part of those who are implementing these programs. They are the outcome of the Gibbonist problematization of poverty based on knowledge welfare through whose concepts we identify the "problem" of poverty and develop "solutions" for it.

5.3. De-Gibbonizing or de-Westernizing Ethiopian poverty

The Gibbonist approach to Ethiopian poverty does not problematize it as a systemic political outcome of the normal functioning of the processes of development and democratization in Ethiopia. Nor does it problematize it in terms of the emancipatory needs of Ethiopians. The Gibbonist approach treats poverty and solutions to it as non-political matters amenable to piecemeal technical and bureaucratic procedures. As one could see in the UN Millenium Development Goals and the projects inspired by them, poverty is fragmented into discrete items and considered through a micro-level

---

421 Famine has struck in 1958, 1966, 1973-75, 1984-85, 2003, 2022-23. These famines were not limited to Northern Ethiopia, They also affected the Borena and Ogaden regions. Patrick Webb, J.von Braun, Y. Yohannes, , *Famine in Ethiopia: Policy Implications of Coping Failure at National and Household Levels* (International Food Policy Research Institute Research Report, 1992); B.G. Kumar, "Ethiopian Famines 1973–1985: A CasevStudy, https://doi.org/10.1093/acprof:oso/9780198286363.003. 0004 (accessed, 7/1/2020; Peter Gill, Peter. 2010. *Famine and Foreigners: Ethiopia since Live Aid* . (Oxford: Oxford University Press (2010).

422 According to the World Food Program, more than 21 million Ethiopians are threatened by extreme food insecurity https://www.wfp.org/countries/ethiopia. Accessed: 6/23/2023

approach.⁴²³ What we have in this micro-level approach is a neo-liberal updated Gibbonism. It dehistoricizes poverty, individualizes it, conceives the micro-level as the relevant representation of reality, ignores poverty as a systemic political question, considers it as a technical problem resolved through the administration of things by experts, and gears poverty alleviation towards the employment needs of the market. Poverty alleviation programs create, at best, precarious labour at the mercy of employers.⁴²⁴ The neo-liberal updating of Gibbonism is a manifestation of "capitalist realism" that has globalized a neo-liberal ontology in which the market is the arbiter of all interests, needs, and values.⁴²⁵ The Gibbonist conception of poverty in the context of capitalist realism is unconnected to the lived political reality and emancipatory needs of the *people's people.* Poverty's unquantifiable dimensions—political, social, economic, affective, and epistemic powerlessness—essential for problematizing it and its solutions are excluded outright.

The Gibbonist poverty alleviation discourses, programs and projects make possible a confluence of the interests of the Ethiopian state, global capital, and NGOs. This approach meets the Ethiopian state's interest, which is to depoliticize poverty and occlude the latter's structural and political origins; it meets the interest of global capital to whom the passage from extreme to acceptable poverty makes available cheap labour, as one could see with the recent growth of Asian and Western corporations' investment in sweatshop manufacturing in Ethiopia.⁴²⁶ It also meets the interests of NGOs, in that considering poverty as a

---

423 UN, *Millennium Development Goals*. Available at http://www.un.org/en/mdg/summit2010/. Accessed 10/9/ 2012.
424 https://addisstandard.com/analysis-ethiopias-industrialization-comes-at-a-cost-as-workers-left-struggling-with-alarmingly-low-wages/ . Accessed 12/7/2023.
425 Mark Fisher, *Capitalist Realism: Is There No Alternative?* (Winchester: Zero Books, 2009), pp. 16-7.
426 Ethiopia plans to have 15 industrial parks by 2018. See the reports by the Ethiopian Investment Commission, http://www.investethiopia.gov.et/about-us/how-we-can-help?id=485; Laura Dean, "Ethiopia Touts Good Conditions in Factories for Brands Like H&M and Calvin Klein, but Workers Scrape By on $1 a Day," *The Intercept* (July 8, 2018), https://theintercept.com/2018/07/08/ethiopia-garment-industry/. Laura Dean notes, "In the Hawassa Industrial Park, factory operators make 750 Ethiopian *birr*, or about $27 a month. Out of this sum, workers must pay for rent and food." Accessed 20/7/2018. James Ferguson, *Global shadows: Africa in the neoliberal world order* (Durham: Duke University Press, 2006). Paul M. Barrett and Dorothee Baumann-Pauly, "Made in Ethiopia: Challenges in the Garment's Industry New Frontiers." They write that Ethiopian garment industry workers are the lowest paid in the world. https://issuu.com/nyusterncenterforbusinessandhumanri/docs/nyu_ethiopia_final_online?e=31640827/69644612. Accessed 2019/05/07.

micro-level problem resolved through micro-level approaches allows them to don and maintain the mask of political atheism, propose development projects based on adaptive preferences, Ptolemize these projects as development, and ensure the perpetuation of the conditions necessary for their indefinite self-reproduction as NGOs. Since, the poor, even if they are working, cannot meet their housing, heath, educational, and nutrition needs, NGOs kick in to provide certain essential services that neither the state nor capital is willing to provide.[427] The confluence of the interests of the Ethiopian state, global capital, and NGOs in Ethiopia severs the *people's people* from the political, economic, and epistemic means necessary for overcoming the conditions of powerlessness that are at the root of their poverty.

From the perspective of *säwrä tarik*, the Gibbonist social science concept of poverty that informs poverty studies and policies in Ethiopia is a zombie concept. It occludes that the life of poverty is primarily a political condition that deprives the *people's people* the ability to be the masters of the political, economic, and epistemic structures and relations that frame and determine their daily existence. From the perspective of *säwrä tarik*, Ethiopians do not suffer from poverty. They suffer from what Amartya Sen calls "poor living."[428] Amartya Sen discusses the idea of "poor living," which he drives from the Aristotelian concept of the "good life."[429] *Säwrä tarik* offers a more potent concept: *säwrä hiywät*. As we have seen in Chapter 1, *säwrä hiywät* refers to a life of *fissiha* (joy) that comes from living a life of *arnät*. Sen's understanding of the good life is limited in that he frames it within the capitalist horizon, which he thinks is unsurpassable. Thus, it must be subjected to *zäräfa*. From the perspective of *säwrä tarik*, "poor living" is the necessary outcome of capitalism in a subaltern capitalist country

---

427 Paul M. Barrett and Dorothée Baumann-Pauly, *Made in Ethiopia...*, *supra*. Huihui Wang et al., *A World Bank Study, Ethiopia Health Extension Program. An Institutionalized Community Approach for Universal Health Coverage* (Washington: The World Bank, 2016).

428 Amartya Sen, "Social Exclusion: Concept, Application, and Scrutiny," *Social Development Papers No. 1* (Manila: Asian Development Bank, 2000), p. 3. Amartya Sen, *The Idea of Justice* (Cambridge: Harvard University Press, 2009), pp. 225-252; . Amartya Sen, *Resources, Values and Development*, (London: Basil Blackwell, 1984), p. 309; Amartya Sen, *Development as Freedom* (Oxford: Oxford University Press, 1999). https://www.oxfam.org/sites/www.oxfam.org/files/file_attachments/bp-reward-work-not-wealth-220118. Accessed 1/25/2018. Even the most developed capitalist democracy, the USA, is unable to eradicate extreme poverty. United Nations General Assembly, Human Rights Council, *Report of the Special Rapporteur on extreme poverty and human rights on his mission to the United States of America*, A/HRC/38/33/Add.1. Accessed 4 May, 2019.

429 For the "good life" or good living, Aristotle, *Nicomachean Ethics*, ed/trans., Roger Crisp (Cambridge: Cambridge University Press. 2000).

such as Ethiopia and the authoritarianism and the depoliticization of the economy it fosters. Poverty alleviation programs may enable some Ethiopians to transit from "extreme poverty" to "poverty" but they cannot overcome the causes of poverty in the context of a capitalist economy, a point that Sen does not consider. Indeed, that good living is possible for the great majority of the world's population under the regime of capitalism seems to be belied by the increasing inequalities of wealth and power worldwide, including the rich capitalist liberal democracies.[430]

From the perspective of *säwrä hiywät*, poor living is a form of life that is characterized by political, economic, social, and educational structures and relations that in their very functioning necessarily produce political, economic, social, and epistemic powerlessness. "Poor living" is opposed to *säwrä hiywät* or "good living," *Säwrä hiywät* is a life wherein citizens participate fully in their political, economic, and epistemic governance: they do not face the state, the economy, and knowledge as radically separate power structures that produce the powerlessness of citizens.

Poor living in Ethiopia is not an individual condition. It is a dynamic ensemble of political, economic, social, and epistemic structures and relations that generate a generalized framework of living wherein the great majority of Ethiopians—the *people's people*—have no access to the political, economic, social, and epistemic powers that could enable them to create a context of life free from the inherited and development and democratization induced unfreedoms, injustices, inequalities, and non-emancipatory knowledge. Poverty is just one of the inevitable consequences of poor living. Poverty is a political wrong that the *official people* inflict on the *people's people* insofar as the former incapacitate the latter politically, economically, and epistemically, a condition the poet Abe Gubegna called "ሞት" (*mot*, meaning death) and led him to ask, as we have already seen, "Is there something better than the death they call life?"[431] The *official people* create the conditions of poor living that block the emancipatory demands and efforts of the *people's people* but augment the power and wealth of the *official people*. Poverty will be eliminated only when poor living is eliminated, which means when the political, economic, social, and epistemic structures and

---

430 https://www.oxfam.org/sites/www.oxfam.org/files/file_attachments/bp-reward-work-not-wealth-220118-. Accessed 1/25/2018. Even the most developed capitalist democracy, the USA, is unable to eradicate extreme poverty. United Nations General Assembly, Human Rights Council, *Report of the Special Rapporteur on extreme poverty and human rights on his mission to the United States of America*, A/HRC/38/33/Add.1. Accessed 4 May, 2019.
431 Abe Gubegna, ስብስብ ሥራዎች, (Addis Ababa Ezop Publishing, 2010), p.255.

relations that produce and reproduce the powerlessness of the *people's people* are eradicated through the agency of the *people's people*.

One may object that the current struggle against poverty in Ethiopia involves the participation of the poor in poverty alleviation programs and development schemes, and that this participation gives them some power over their daily lives. It does, without however putting in question the political, economic, and epistemic parameters of the regime that produce poverty as a normal outcome of their functioning. Participation is the key term in poverty alleviation programs in Ethiopia. However, as one could see from the subtexts of MDG projects and the Charities and Societies Proclamation, and the activities of NGOs, "participation" subordinates the agency of the participants to the agency of development experts, NGO organizers, and state bureaucrats, for these are the conceptualizers of poverty and of the means to alleviate it. Note that the purpose they pursue is not the eradication of poverty. As the Millennium Development Goals (MDG) states, the goal is not to eradicate "Hunger and Poverty"; it is to "Eradicate *Extreme* Hunger and Poverty."[432] Jeffrey Sachs, United Nations Secretary-General's Special Adviser on the MDG, makes the same point. He writes, the goal of poverty reduction "is to end *extreme* poverty, *not to end all poverty*, and *still less … to close the gap* between the rich and the poor."[433]

Participation, as understood in development theory and practice, takes place within an individualistic and market-oriented framework. The political economy that subtends the theory and practice of development in Ethiopia converts structural inequalities into individual problems: it assumes that individuals could overcome poverty if they work hard enough (participate in the market), that their failure to extricate themselves from poverty is an indicator of their moral weakness (their non-participation in the market), and that the market is the arbiter of success and failure in exiting from poverty.[434] Poverty alleviation programs and projects are supposed to provide skills useful for individuals to enhance their income generating capacities and their abilities to

---

432 UN, *Millennium Development Goals*. Available at http://www.un.org/en/mdg/summit2010/. Accessed 10/9/2012.
433 Jeffery D. Sachs, *The End of Poverty* (New York: Penguin, 2005), p. 289. Emphasis added.
434 Nana Poku and Jim Whitman, *Africa under Neoliberalism*, (New York: Routledge, 2018); Melkamu Dires Asabu, "Successes and Failures of International Financial Institutions (IFIs) in Exporting Neoliberalism in Africa: The Case of Ethiopia,". *International. Journal of Political Science Development*, 5, 6 (2017), pp. 203-209; Tebeje Molla "Neoliberal Shock Therapy in Ethiopia," *Review of African Political Economy* (June 2019); Wendy Brown, "Neo-Liberalism and the End of Liberal Democracy." *Theory & Event* 7,1 (2003), pp.1-19.

participate in the market competitively. It is based on a scheme that individualizes poverty and is geared towards creating capitalism-friendly market conditions such as the supply of cheap labour, and promoting the free play of market forces, even when these are mediated by the state, as is the case in Ethiopia's purported "developmental state."[435] Individual and local participation in development projects is designed as an activity that sees the acquisition of skills and knowledge as social capital and human capital, which are considered necessary for facilitating one's access to the market. Participation in the context of capitalism is grounded in the assumption that transforming oneself into an "entrepreneur of the self" and investing in oneself to enhance one's participation and competitivity in the market counts as "development."[436] From the perspective of *säwrä tarik*, to consider skills and knowhows as "capital" is to frame them within the capitalist problematic of the market and scarcity. It means considering them as private assets. This is incompatible with *säwrä tarik* and its ideal of *säwrä hiywät* or good living.

Participation, as practiced within the context of development and democratization, is a zombie concept. It is not based on institutions and practices that make the *people's people* the identifiers and problematizers of their needs, and the thinkers and authors of policies and projects to meet their needs. Rather, it makes the participants experience their participation through the ideas,

---

[435] Meles Zenawi, the late Prime Minister (1919-2012) considered "social capital" necessary for the "developmental state." That "social capital" is necessary for development is a view that the World bank and neo-liberal theorists promote. Meles Zenawi, "States and Markets: Neoliberal Limitations and the Case for a developmental state," in Akbar Noman *et al.*, *Good Growth and Governance in Africa* (New York: Oxford University Press, 2012), p. 147, 140-174. Christiaan Grootaert and Thierry van Bastelaer, *Understanding and Measuring Social Capital: A Synthesis of Findings and Recommendations from the Social Capital Initiative* (Washington: The World Bank, 2001).

[436] Christiaan Grootaert and Thierry van Bastelaer, *Understanding and Measuring Social Capital...*, *supra*; Maryann K Cusimano, ed. *Beyond Sovereignty: Issues for a Global Agenda* (Boston: Bedford, 2000); G. Cheema, and Rondinelli. *Decentralisation and Development: Policy Implementation in Developing Countries* (London, Sage, 1983); J. Wolfensohn, *The Challenges of Inclusion*, (Washington, D.C.: World Bank, 1997); K.M. Seethi, "Postmodernism, Neoliberalism and Civil Society: A Critique of the Development Strategies in the Era of Globalisation," *The Indian Journal of Political Science*, 62, 3 (2001), pp. 307-320; David Harvey, *A Brief History of Neoliberalism* (Oxford, Oxford University Press, 2005); Francis Fukuyama, "Social capital, civil society and development". *Third World Quarterly*, 22, 1 (2001), pp.7-20.

activities, and programs others design for them.[437] This is what one could call "interpassive participation."[438] An interpassive participation depoliticizes the participants by making them spectators of their poverty and of the solutions to it. It makes them the moral patients of NGOs, poverty experts and bureaucrats. The development experts and bureaucrat are present in the participation process as the "subjects supposed to know" through whom the poor believe that the poverty alleviation program is what is fit for them, because the "subject supposed to know" believes so. The participants are reduced to being "subjects supposed to believe." One sees here the workings of "Leviathan logic" that makes the poor believe that what the experts believe is good for the poor, because the experts believe so. Interpassive participation makes the poor participate in a process that reinforces the existing order, which is an order that produces and reproduces adaptive preferences—authoritarianism, economic subalternization, epistemic servility—that reproduce poverty. Interpassive participation allows the *official people* to Ptolemize poverty alleviation programs as solutions to poverty through they do not make a dent in poor living. The overcoming of poor living and the promotion of emancipatory interests and needs of Ethiopians are not within the purview of development and democratization and the interpassive participation they promote.

---

437 Federal Democratic Republic of Ethiopia, "Charities and Societies Proclamation [CSP] No. 621/2009." *Federal Negarit Gazzeta*, No. 25. (Addis Ababa: Berhanena Selam Printing Press 2009). CSP mandates civil society organization to "actively participate in the process of strengthening democratization and election, particularly in the process of conducting educational seminars on current affairs, understanding the platforms of candidates, observing the electoral process and cooperating with electoral organs." In practice participation is based on the "Leviathan logic." It makes clear that the participation is organized from above; it does not allow for questions that challenge the parameters of the regime. It is a participation that is apolitical, and its purpose is to reinforce the regime's policies and legitimacy. On Leviathan logic, Jeremy Gilbert, *Common Ground: Democracy and Collectivity in an Age of Individualism* (London: Pluto Press, 2014), pp. 69-70.

438 I am conducting here a *zäräfa* of the concept of "interpassivity" as "delegated enjoyment." Robert Pfaller, *Interpassivity: The Aesthetics of Delegated Enjoyment* (Edinbourgh: Edinburgh University Press. 2017); Slavoj Žižek, *The Plague of Fantasies* (London: Verso, 1997), pp. 109-112, 144-7. An interpassive participant is one who believes or enjoys through the other. Participants see those who lead the participation as "subjects supposed to know," and the participants believe what these "subjects" say is true because the participants believe that what these "subjects" say is true. Interpassivity functions through such a tautological operation. Also, Ethiopians who outsource or delegate their enjoyment of knowledge production on development and democracy to the Western social scientists' active production of knowledge on development and democratization in Ethiopia are engaged in "interpassive" activity.

"Participation," a keyword in the discourse of Ethiopian regimes, is, as Lefort notes, "a smoke screen": the authorities give the order and the people obey.[439] One should not be misled by the busyness that accompanies the participation Ethiopian regimes and NGOs promote. "Active" participation is indeed the standard "interpassive" mode of participation in Ethiopia: in politics, it takes the form of campaign meetings and voting, though the *official people* predetermine the outcome of the elections; in economics, it takes the form of busyness—participation in all kinds of development projects, and "social capital" and "human capital" creating activities.[440] In knowledge production, interpassive participation is encapsulated in epistemic servility that is Ptolemized as activities of knowledge acquisition and research. The main characteristic of this Ptolemized knowledge is its disconnect from the emancipatory needs of the *people's people* and from *säwrä tarik*. Interpassive participation, however active it may look, eschews the issues of political, economic, and epistemic powerlessness and considers the existing regime as a non-questioned background of its activities. Emancipatory participation wherein the *people's people* problematize the sources of their powerlessness and how they could appropriate the political, economic, and epistemic powers they need to get rid of poor living is outside the horizon of interpassive participation however active it may appear. One should see interpassive participation as a form of "objective violence" that, though it is not as visible as "subjective violence," it is nevertheless more harmful politically, for it makes the participants accomplices in the reproduction of poor living and thus collaborators in their own dispossession and oppression.[441]

From the perspective of *säwrä tarik*, unless the understanding of poverty is not de-Gibbonized or de-Westernized, all the efforts that are expended now and

---

439 René Lefort, "The Theory and Practice of Meles Zenawi: A Response to Alex de Waal," *African Affairs*, Vol. 112, No. 448 (2013), p. 462. On the "centralism" of the TPLF/EPRDF, Gebru Tareke, *The Ethiopian Revolution - War in the Horn of Africa* (New Haven, CT.: Yale University Press, 2009).
440 The CSP leaves no doubt that interpassive participation is the only kind of participation available to Ethiopians in "development" and "democratization" processes. Federal Democratic Republic of Ethiopia, "Charities and Societies Proclamation [CSP] No. 621/2009." *Federal Negarit Gazzeta*, No. 25. (Addis Ababa: Berhanena Selam Printing Press 2009).
441 On the difference between objective and subjective violence, see Slavoj Žižek, *Violence* (New York: Picador: 2008), pp. 9-15. Objective violence is the economic, social, and psychological harms produced systemically by the apparently peaceful and objective operation of the political, economic, and epistemic regime, whereas subjective violence is the visible violence that identifiable subjects—individuals, rioters, etc.—commit.

in the future on poverty alleviation will reproduce the poverty of the *people's people*. Emancipatory participation is an activity that requires the *people's people* to be the primary agents who identify and problematize the political, economic, and epistemic structures and relations of poor living, who work out the ways of neutralizing these structures and relations, and who propose alternatives to political, economic, and epistemic powerlessness. It is the only type of participation that could bring *arnät* to the *people's people*.

5.4. De-Gibbonizing or de-Westernizing democracy.

Given capitalism's generation of increasing inequalities in the global production, reproduction, and consumption of wealth and knowledge, and given the contradictions and fractures it creates in the very process of its self-reproduction as globalization without universalization, one could use the failures, contradictions and fissures of the democratization and development processes in Ethiopia as a trampoline for subjecting to *zäräfa* the Western theories and practices of development and democracy from the perspective of the emancipatory needs and possibilities disclosed through the *andemta* of our critical internal and external journeys. The goal is to develop an emancipatory theory, strike a new path and create new institutions and new political practices that have no filiation with the hegemonic theories and practices of the West. Such is the route Ethioperspectivism proposes. It makes possible to carry out novel types of emancipatory social transformations while still being engaged with the capitalist global order. This is not an easy task. Ethiopia's emancipatory social transformation is a project that demands perseverance in discarding the anti-emancipatory political, economic, social and epistemic practices, processes and the pathological effects of democratization and development, while at the same time dislocating them from their theoretical and practical contexts and appropriating them from an emancipatory perspective what they have accomplished in Ethiopia up to the present. Note that the *qiné* hermeneutical approach intimates that every historical situation is *nägär*, internally complex, contradictory and incomplete (*enkän*), and thus pregnant with qualitatively different possibilities that could be elicited through *zäräfa*. That is, every situation is potentially dis-locatable and transformable through *zäräfa* to advance *arnät*.

Two questions arise here. First, given that Ethiopia is stuck at the lowest end of the capitalist international order, radically dependent on external sources for capital, knowledge, and technology, how does Ethioperspectivism deal with this situation? Second, how could Ethiopia jointly pursue its *aim* (work within the present global economic and political context) and its *goal: arnät* or emancipatory democracy and emancipatory development? In the current historical context, the *goal* and the *aim* pull in opposite directions and pursuing the two jointly seems to be in the realm of the impossible.

Under neo-liberalism, capitalist market values have effectively penetrated Western societies politically, economically, culturally, cognitively, and psychologically to an extent that Westerners see themselves as "human capital" and engage in self-regarding investment to enhance their competitivity and marketability.[442] The pervasive "colonization" of Western life by capitalism has created a "unidimensional system" where all "that is solid melts into air," defanging and coopting all critical possibilities from inside, and making society an arena of quantitative variations of the same, devoid of negativity and otherness.[443] The hold of capitalism on Western life is so deep that, as Fredric Jameson notes, it is easier for Westerners to imagine the end of the world than to imagine the end of capitalism.[444] However, such is not the outcome of capitalist-driven development in Ethiopia. Development in Ethiopia is the embodiment of "necropolitics" and "necrocapitalism": a political-economical system that subjugates the lives of Ethiopians to political and economic horrors whose forms are famine, poverty, authoritarianism, political violence, adaptive preferences, social and physical death, and the deadly ethnic struggles for the crumbs of the subaltern capitalism that globalization without universalization promotes in Ethiopia as development.[445]

---

442 Peter Kelly, *The Self as Enterprise: Foucault and the Spirit of 21st Century Capitalism* (New York: Routledge, 2013); Robin Blackburn, "Finance and the Fourth Dimension," *New Left Review* 39 (May–June 2006), pp. 39–70.

443 Marshall Berman, *All That Is Solid Melts Into Air* (New York: Verso, 2010); Herbert Marcuse, *One Dimensional Man* (Boston: Beacon Press 1991). "The vocabulary of customer, consumer choice, of markets moulds both our conception of ourselves and our understanding of and relationship to the world." Doreen Massey, quoted in Marnie Holborow, ed., *Language and Neoliberalism* (New York: Routledge, 2015), p. 1.

444 Fredric Jameson, "Future City," *New Left Review* 21 (May-June 2003), p. 76. In considering that there is no alternative to capitalism, Anthony Giddens concurs with Jameson. Anthony Giddens, *The Third Way: The Renewal of Social Democracy* (Cambridge, Polity Press, 1999).

445 Ethiopia's economy is a necro-economy. See the yearly minimum wage rate. https://www.minimum-wage.org/international/ethiopia. Accessed 6/2/ 2023. Helen Tesfaye, "Study to weigh pros and cons of minimum wage as Ethiopia hesitates," *The Reporter,* July 1, 2023. https://www.thereporterethiopia.com/35257/ Accessed 8/2/2023. When one considers the new international poverty line for acceptable poverty set by the World Bank ($1.90 US), we see how problematic the distinction between acceptable and non-acceptable poverty is. In Ethiopia, living just above the international poverty line means living in destitution. Jason Hickel, "The true extent of global poverty and hunger: Questioning the good news narrative of the

The radical difference in the outcomes of the operation of capitalism in Ethiopia and in the West creates a critical space of otherness and negativity—a space for *minab* thinking and visions—in Ethiopia that could be disclosed through *antsar* and *wistä wäyra* readings of Ethiopian and global conditions, Such readings could indicate ways of figuring out methods, policies, and actions for dealing with Ethiopia's internal and external antagonisms so that the contradictions they generate could be mined for advancing *arnät*. Such readings could disclose conditions that could show that the possibility of the impossible becoming possible exists as a latency in these conditions and thus offers Ethiopians the opportunity to practice "politics as the art of the impossible" in the pursuit of *arnät*. This possibility exists because the political, economic, and epistemic miseries that capitalist-driven development inflicts on Ethiopians have created vast swaths of political, economic, cultural, and psychological spaces that are uncolonized by capitalism.[446] True, currently, these uncolonized spaces are filled with ethnic politics. But this regression to ethnic politics is itself a *zäybé* of the quest for an alternative Ethiopia and of the latent presence of the possibility of the impossible becoming possible that Ethiopians have failed to seize since the 1960 coup d'état.

Democratization and development have created in Ethiopia a space of otherness and forces of negativity that offer the opportunity to generate a critical understanding of Ethiopia's conditions and of the global situation in which Ethiopia is inserted. Ethiopians could thus explore the hidden emancipatory possibilities that Ethiopia's specific internal and external triple dominations gestate in the very antagonisms they create. Such an understanding, emerging from the *andemta* of our critical internal and external journeys, enables Ethiopians to say "no" to "poor living," and lay down the foundations for an *arnät*-centered political, economic, and epistemic transformation as an alternative to the capitalist-centered democratization, development, and knowledge production that the West proposes to Ethiopians in the form of adaptive preferences. One could say that for Ethiopians, unlike Westerners, "it is easier to imagine the end of subaltern capitalism than to imagine the end of the world."

Millennium Development Goals," *Third World Quarterly* 37, 5 (2016), pp. 749-767. UNDP, https://report.hdr.undp.org/intro (2021-2022). Ethiopia is 175th (out of 191) on the Human Development index, below poor countries such as Sudan, Equatorial Guinea, Benin, Togo. On necropolitics, see Achille Mbembe, *Necropolitics* (Durham: Duke University Press, 2019); on necrocapitalism, see Bobby Banerjee, "Necrocapitalism", *Organization Studies* 29 (2008), pp. 1541-1563.

446 On "politics as the art of the impossible," see Chapter 2.5 above.

Democratization is a term touted by the borrowed social sciences, NGOs, the apostles of civil society, Ethiopia's *official people*, be they in power or waiting on the sidelines, Western "experts" on Ethiopia, Western governments, and international institutions. Without exception, the exemplar of democracy from which the ideas and practice of democratization are drawn is Western liberal democracy. However, given that Western liberal democracy has become the political and ideological supplement of capitalism, and given its role in the oppression and exploitation of the non-West, could the triple domination that weighs on Ethiopia be eliminated and *arnät* established for good if democracy is not subjected to *zäräfa*, and thus de-Gibbonized or de-Westernized, dislocated and subjected to *détournement*? From the perspective of *säwrä tarik*, the answer is no. Under globalization without universalization, liberal democracy has betrayed the emancipatory core of democracy. Democracy has become a floating signifier that capitalism has captured to mold institutions, practices, behaviours, and knowledge to serve its interests.[447] What the practice of Western democracy under globalization without universalization has disclosed in Asia, Africa, and Latin America is that regular competitive multi-party elections do not reduce, let alone eliminate, the triple powerlessness—political, economic, and epistemic—and sufferings that weigh on the *people's people* of these countries. This is even more true for Ethiopia.

From the perspective of *säwrä tarik*, the de-Westernization and dislocation of democracy is necessary to liberate Ethiopia from Potemkin democracy. For Ethioperspectivism, democracy cannot be reduced to competitive multi-party elections, parliamentary representation and debates, and the free press. To be sure, all these are necessary. However, given the triple domination that weighs on Ethiopia, they are not sufficient to block the transformation of the borrowed practice of Western democracy into Potemkin democracy. Moreover, the rise of anti-democratic populism in the West is precisely a *zäybé* of the disconnection of Western democracy from the needs of the people.[448] Democracy understood as *arnät* requires that the Ethiopian people be the active constitutive agents of all sources of power—political, economic, epistemic, organizational and

---

[447] Yann Moulier-Boutang, *Cognitive Capitalism* (Cambridge: Polity Press, 2012); M. Olssen and M. A. Peters, "Neoliberalism, higher education and the knowledge economy: from the free market to knowledge capitalism," *Journal of Education Policy*, vol. 20, 3 (2005), pp. 313–345; Wolfgang Streeck, *Buying Time: The Delayed Crisis of Democratic Capitalism* (London: Verso, 2014). Hakan Ergül and Simten Cosar, *Universities in the Neoliberal Era* (London: Palgrave Macmillan, 2017).

[448] Takis S. Pappas, *Populism and Liberal Democracy: A Comparative and Theoretical Analysis* (New York: Oxford University Press, 2019).

institutional, and cultural sources—in order to eliminate the political, economic and epistemic domination of the *people's people* by the *official people*. The de-westernization of democracy requires then subjecting it to *zäräfa* and repurposing it to make it serve the continuous and active minimization of political, economic, epistemic, organizational and institutional, and cultural powerlessness and the continuous enhancement of the capabilities necessary for *säwrä hiywät* or "good living."

Ethioperspectivism treats liberal democracy as *nägär*. It transforms into questions its positive self-interpretations and narcissistic self-presentations. The goal of this questioning is to liberate ourselves from the intellectual and affective captivity in which the self-absorbed self-representation of liberal democracy has trapped us, rendering us blind and deaf to the injustices, inequalities, unfreedoms, and epistemic servility it generates in the name of democracy. A liberation from the spell of the narcistic and religious-like investment of liberal democracy in itself could enable us to de-Westernize / de-Gibbonize and re-invent both democratization and development as *arnät*.[449] Note that were Ethiopia to achieve liberal democracy *à la West*, she would still not be able to eradicate the triple powerlessness she suffers, which will continue to thrive behind the mask of liberal democracy.[450] Liberal democracy in the context of globalization without universalization creates structural inequalities and insecurities, and justifies these as the expressions of the free functioning of democracy. It makes the "unequal" and the "poor" themselves responsible for the inequalities and suffering that the political-economic system generates; liberal democracy thinks and acts only in terms of alleviating inequalities and poverty and not in terms of abolishing the structures and relations that produce inequalities and poverty in their very functioning. To believe that liberal democracy will liberate Ethiopia from the triple domination that weighs down on her is as credible as the belief

---

449 *Iqqub*'s surplus meanings suggest the kind of emancipatory democracy that is immanent to Ethiopian history and social practices, and that could de-westernize / de-Gibbonize democracy and liberate us from the spell of liberal democracy's self-adulation. Maimire Mennasemay, *Qiné Hermeneutics and Ethiopian Critical Theory* (Los Angeles: Tsehai Publishing, 2021), pp. 398-407.

450 One could ask if it is not in the very nature and operation of liberal capitalist democracy to generate the exclusion and oppression of some of the people who live under it. Consider the issue of mass incarceration in liberal democratic societies. Michelle Alexander, *The New Jim Crow: Mass incarceration in the age of colorblindness* (New York: The New Press, 2010); Peter Mair, *Ruling the Void: The Hollowing out of Western Democracy* (New York: Verso, 2013); 3 (Aug. 2003), pp. 425-446. United Nations General Assembly, Human Rights Council, *Report of the Special Rapporteur on extreme poverty and human rights on his mission to the United States of America*, A/HRC/38/33/Add.1. Accessed 4 May, 2019.

of Mamo Qilo, the popular naive character in an Ethiopian children's story, that he could cut down a full-grown tree with his teeth. The de-westernization of democracy forestalls the emergence of new forms of Ethiopian authoritarianism—the *Zära Yacob syndrome*— cloaked as "liberal democracy," as is the case currently.[451]

As a theory immanent to Ethiopian society and history, Ethioperspectivism critically reflects not only on Ethiopian conditions, possibilities of emancipatory transformations, and the actions and ways that lead to *arnät* or emancipatory democracy and emancipatory social transformation, but also on itself for it is aware of its own *enkän* or incompleteness. It has an epistemological concern with the ground of its own activity. It critically reflects on the concepts, principles, and methods of the theories it articulates: it examines their social implications and evaluates their political consequences. The aim of these critiques (*hiss*) internal to Ethioperspectivism is double: (a) to prevent the congealing of Ethioperspectivism into a dogma that prevents *zäräfa* to operate continuously, and (b) to prevent the ossification of *arnät* into a system of domination that produces new unfreedoms, inequalities, and injustices.[452]

5.5. Against falling out of world history

The idea that all *nägär* is *säm ena wärq* assumes that to think critically is not only necessary, but it is also an act of resistance to the given. According to *säwrä tarik*, to think demands from us that we formulate questions pertinent to the emancipatory needs of the *people's people*, and that we enucleate from Ethiopia's conditions the *wärq* or the emancipatory possibilities that are excluded by the hegemonic political, economic, and epistemic parameters, and conceptualize these possibilities in ways that make *arnät* feasible.[453] As we could see in the rise of ethnic politics since 1991, the fidelity of modern educated Ethiopians to Gib-

---

451 The *Zära Yacob syndrome* refers to the homegrown historically Ethiopian authoritarianism. Maimire Mennasemay, *Qiné Hermeneutics and Ethiopian Critical Theory*, pp.463-7.
452 This double critique is crucial to avoid the fate of liberal democracy and Marxism befalling *arnät*: the transformation of liberal democracy into a cover for inequalities and the degeneration of Marxism into dictatorship. Peter Mair, *Ruling the Void: The Hollowing out of Western Democracy* (New York: Verso, 2013); Leon Trotsky, *The Revolution Betrayed* (New York: Dover Publications, 2004).
453 The *qiné* hermeneutical idea of thinking as resistance, whose discursive form is *säm ena wärq*, is one that other civilizations also recognize. "Whoever thinks, offers resistance." Theodor W. Adorno, 1998. *Critical Models*: *Interventions and Catchwords*, trans. Henry W. Pickford (New York: Columbia University Press, 1998), p. 263.

bonism has led to less and less thinking (in the *qiné* hermeneutical sense), and, inevitably, to more and more political, economic, and cognitive regression. One cannot deny that the quest for "ethnic self-determination" as defined by the 1995 Constitution will not and cannot allow Ethiopians to confront and overcome the triple domination—political, economic, epistemic—that crushes Ethiopians. On the contrary, it will intensify it.

One cannot overestimate the importance of reviving critical thinking in Ethiopia, because Gibbonism has replaced the Ethiopian *qiné* hermeneutical culture of critical thinking with the culture of borrowing the finished product of the thinking of the West. As Arendt points out (see exergue above), "A life without thinking is quite possible," but it makes us "sleepwalkers" who use zombie concepts, pushing Ethiopia into falling out of world history.[454] "A life without thinking" is what regression to our ethnic wombs has spawned. Since the DERG dictatorship, Ethiopians have been subjected to increasing political and economic barbarisms such that Ethiopian society is currently strained to the breaking point. There is a real risk that Ethiopians now are on the verge of falling out of world history and becoming a permanently oppressed, exploited, ethnicized, fragmented, and disposable people. One may object that Ethiopians are not falling out of world history, that Addis Ababa is the seat of international organizations, and that Ethiopia plays an important role in Africa. But we have to separate the wheat from the chaff and ask serious questions. Isn't Addis Ababa, often touted by the *official people* as a modern city, a "Potemkin village" with a fake modern face that hides the painful and ugly reality of the unrelenting "development" of suffering that has befallen the rest of the country: 6 million internally displaced persons, 20 million living on the cusp of hunger, thousands subjected to ethnic cleansing, and endless political violence? Could not one say that Ethiopia is falling out of world history insofar as all the decisions that affect humanity are taken without her substantive participation and without considering her interests? Are not Ethiopians falling out of world history by drowning themselves in ethnic narcissism and conflicts when others are actively engaged in mastering internal and external nature, relegating us to impotent spectators of their achievements?[455] Are not Ethiopians falling out of world history by becoming dependent on foreign aid

---

454 Hannah Arendt, *The Life of the Mind* (New York: A Harvest Book, 1971), p.191.
455 Since one cannot claim epistemic autonomy, capabilities, and flourishing in the present era without significant scientific and technological research and development, one could speak of the "epistemic deprivation" of Ethiopians, a consequence of epistemic servility, in that they are dependent on foreign sources for the sciences and technologies. Jamil Salmi, Andrée Sursock, and Anna Olefir, *Improving the Performance of Ethiopian Universities in Science and Technology*

for everything, from knowledge to food, and objectively becoming a disposable population from the perspective of the dynamics of global capitalism? If the doors were open to immigration to the West, how many of the youth of Ethiopia would stay in Ethiopia?[456]

To escape the fate of falling out of world history and to become a full-fledged autonomous people participating as an equal among equals in the making of world history, *säwrä tarik* proposes Becoming Ethiopian as the goal and Ethioperspectivism as the approach to achieve it. Becoming Ethiopian—making Ethiopia "Ethiopian" and Ethiopians "Ethiopians"— is a process whose goal is to create an Ethiopian society whose political, economic, social, intellectual, and cultural institutions and practices actively prevent the generation of political, economic, social, and epistemic powerlessness, while actively creating the conditions necessary for the political, economic, and epistemic flourishing of Ethiopians. It aims to make Ethiopians the thinkers, architects, and builders of their society in conformity with their emancipatory needs and interests.

However, Becoming Ethiopian confronts Westernization: a dynamic hegemonic system of ideas, norms institutions, and practices that currently operates as globalization without universalization and is embedded in the hegemonic theories and practices of development and democratization. This situation forces us to ask: Is "Becoming Ethiopian" possible in the present political and economic context of capitalist hegemony, whose most potent form is Westernization?

Westernization denotes a specific historical process that is unique to the West.[457] It refers to a historical process of social transformation rooted in the birth and growth of capitalism in the West.[458] It sees itself explicitly or implicitly as the teleological model towards which other countries evolve via "modernization."[459] In its current hegemonic form, Westernization champions

---

(World Bank, 2017). They write, "There is a serious lack of research capacity in Ethiopian universities." p. 10.

456 The Washington Post, "Many Ethiopians see illegal migration as the only escape from violence" washingtonpost.com, https://www.washingtonpost.com › politics › 2022/07/19. Accessed 2023.02, 24.

457 Alex Anievas and Kerem Nisancioglu, *How the West Came to Rule: The Geopolitical Origins of Capitalism* (London: Pluto, 2014).

458 Immanuel Wallerstein, *The Capitalist World Economy* (Cambridge: Cambridge University Press, 1979); Immanuel Wallerstein, *Historical Capitalism with Capitalist Civilization* (London: Verso, 2011); David Harvey, *A Brief History of Neoliberalism* (Oxford: Oxford University Press, 2007).

459 Nils Gilman, *Mandarins of the Future: Modernization Theory in Cold War America* (Baltimore. MD. Johns Hopkins University, 2003). Francis Fukuyama, *The End of*

ontological individualism, a conception of society as an aggregate of freestanding and unattached individuals.[460] Epistemologically, it denies the implication of the knowing agent in the assertion of truth about the world, and it is committed to methodological individualism; it affirms the separation of facts and values and claims that knowledge is value-free. Economically, Westernization conceptualizes the economy as a free market economy and gives priority to market rights over social rights.[461] It conceives labour as a commodity, champions privatization, competition and deregulation, and regards the individual as an "entrepreneur of the self" and society as a "market society."[462] Politically, it considers liberal democracy as the most preferable system of political life and thought. Historically, Westernization sanitizes the history of capitalism and represents capitalism as an economic system to which there is no better alternative. The capitalist perspective has become all-pervasive and Ethiopia is exposed to its relentless logic of accumulation by dispossession.[463]

Among the major obstacles that Ethiopians have to overcome in their quest for *arnät* are the internal and external economic, political, social, cultural and epistemic anti-*arnät* effects of globalization without universalization. Though the West—the author and actor of globalization without universalization—acknowledges the political, economic and social needs of Ethiopians, it does so from the perspective of the interests of liberal capitalist democracy. It does not treat Ethiopians as autonomous authors and actors of their lives who could meet their needs through their own agency. At best, its sees them as a source of cheap labour for export oriented manufacturing and cash crop production, and considers them as discardable labour whenever they do not meet the needs of the export market or its strategic economic and political interests, as one could see from the suspension of Ethiopia from the AGOA agreement by the US

History and the Last Man (Washington: Free Press, 2006).
460 Charles Taylor, "Interpretation and the Sciences of Man," in *Philosophy and the Human Sciences,* vol. 2 (Cambridge University Press, 1988), pp. 15-57, 187-210.
461 Maurizio Lazzarato, *The Making of the Indebted Man: An Essay on the Neoliberal Condition*, trans. Joshua David Jordan (Amsterdam: Semiotext (e), 2012); Pierre Dardot and Christian Laval, *The New Way of the World: On Neo-liberal Society*, trans. Gregory Elliot (London: Verso: 2013); Peter Kelly, *The Self as Enterprise* (New York: Routledge, 2013).
462 Ibid.
463 Pierre Dardot and Christian Laval, *The New Way of the World…, supra*; Henry Veltmeyer, ed. *Development in an Era of Neoliberal Globalization* (New York: Routledge, 2013); On "accumulation by dispossession", see David Harvey, *A Brief History of Neoliberalism* (Oxford: Oxford University Press, 2007)

government in 2022.⁴⁶⁴ Public and private international aid agencies and Western NGOs claim to combat human suffering in Ethiopia while working with the Ethiopian political, economic, and knowledge institutions that in their very functioning generate the suffering of the *people's people*. This peculiar situation of helping the victims while providing support to the *official people*'s political and economic institutions that create the miseries of the *people's people* calls for reflection. It is a process that amounts to "carceral humanitarianism," to adapt Kelly Oliver's expression for a humanitarianism that imprisons its recipients in a permanent state of dependence on foreign aid, interests and needs.⁴⁶⁵ In brief, one could observe a parallel between international humanitarian aid providers and the godly person who, out "of the love he has for himself" yearns for the reproduction of the suffering of others so that he could through his "self-sacrifice" alleviate their sufferings and thus gain self-righteous moral satisfaction and happiness.⁴⁶⁶ Since they accept the conditions that generate the miseries of the *people's people*, aid institutions and international NGOs could reproduce themselves endlessly, thus guaranteeing the extension of their moral satisfaction and happiness into the indefinite future. However, the recipients of this aid see in this hopeless future their existence as disposable objects and desire to escape it. The yearning to escape this hopeless condition is foremost in the minds of the young Ethiopian generation, making immigration to the West their dream for escaping this predicament.

To recognize that globalization is a barrier to Becoming Ethiopian in the sense already defined does not mean that Ethiopia should isolate herself from the capitalist world, because the conditions of oppression and exploitation in Ethiopia are created through the political, economic, and epistemic interactions of internal and external forces and agents.⁴⁶⁷ Rather, Ethiopia could use globalization as a trampoline for achieving *arnät*. For this strategy, a *zäräfa* of Laclau's idea that a coordinated and strategic "acceptance of the transformations

---

464 "Ethiopia lost its AGOA beneficiary status effective 1 January 2022,". https://agoa.info/profiles/ethiopia.html, Accessed 8/2/2022.
465 Kelly Oliver uses the terms to refer to the intolerable conditions of refugees.. Kelly Oliver, *Carceral Humanitarianism: Logics of Refugee Detention* (Minneapolis: University of Minnesota Press, 2017).
466 On this Malebranchian way of looking at NGOs, see Donald Rutherford, "Malebranche's Theodicy" in *The Cambridge Companion to Malebranche*, ed. S. Nadler (Cambridge: Cambridge University Press, 2000), 165-89; Henri Gouhier, *La philosophie de Malebranche et son expérience religieuse* (Paris: Vrin, 1948).
467 I do not mean "de-linking" in the sense popularized by Samir Amin. China shows that one could work with capitalism and still have an auto-centric people-centered form of development. Samir Amin, *Delinking: Towards a Polycentric World* (London: Zed Books Press, 1989).

entailed by capitalism and the construction of an alternative project that is *based on the ground created by those transformations and not on opposition to them*" could be productive.[468] In the Ethiopian context, this means two things: first, transforming the borrowed social science theories of democracy and development through *zäräfa* that subjects them to the criteria and standards of *säwrä tarik* rather than their outright dismissal; second, subjecting the transformations entailed by democratization and development to *zäräfa* to elicit their emancipatory but repressed elements from the perspective of *säwrä tarik* rather than their elimination. This implies that appropriating what democratization and development have produced in Ethiopia must be articulated with the purging of the deleterious conditions and outcomes that the inchoate capitalism of the Haile Selassie regime, the muddled "state capitalism" of the DERG, the "ethnic developmental state" capitalism of the TPLF, and the "ethnic" neoliberalism of the PP regime have created. That is, the anti-emancipatory theories, institutions, practices, policies, projects, forms, aims, standards, measures, characteristics and contents that informed these regimes must be purged in the process of appropriating the positive but repressed changes democratization and development have wrought. In this process, Ethiopians are the imaginers, thinkers, planners, and builders of their own emancipation, which necessitates a *gädl* / struggle to transform the capitalist globalization processes that entered Ethiopia into tools for minimizing continuously unfreedoms, inequalities, injustices and epistemic servility, and for generating the capabilities necessary for continuously developing *arnät*. This means that Becoming Ethiopian or the achievement of *arnät* requires, among other things, figuring out ways of transforming globalization without universalization into globalization *with* universalization for Ethiopia, that is, participating in globalization and using it as a trampoline for the universalization of freedom, equality, justice, prosperity, and epistemic autonomy. But is this possible?

Indeed, the Ethiopian experience of "development" shows that capitalist globalization limits Ethiopia to choosing development policies, institutions, projects, and knowledge that promote primarily capitalism's interests.[469]

---

468 Ernesto Laclau, *New Reflections on the Revolution of Our Time* (London: Verso, 1990), p. 55.
469 Habtamu Legese, "Determinants of foreign direct investment in Ethiopia: Systematic review ,"*International Journal of Business and Economic Development*, 6,3 (2018), pp. 38-47; Amanuel Mekonnen Workneh, "Factors Affecting FDI Flow in Ethiopia: An Empirical Investigation," *European Journal of Business and Management*, vol6, 20 (2014), pp, 118-125. On sweatshops in Ethiopia, http://www.investethiopia.gov.et/about-us/how-we-can-help?id=485; Ayelech Tiruwha Melese and A. H. J. (Bert)

Through its claimed neutral and objective market logic, it imposes on Ethiopia adaptive preferences as "development," "democratization," and "appropriate" knowledge.[470] The challenge Ethioperspectivism confronts is how to develop and implement the ideas and practices necessary for Becoming Ethiopian in the face of a liberal capitalist democracy that celebrates capitalism and liberal democracy as the best possible frameworks of our economic and political lives, considers alternative political and economic systems inferior to it, and pushes Ethiopia into adaptive preferences and practices humanitarian aid, whose subtext is the defence of the liberal capitalist hegemony.[471]

Still, Ethioperspectivism refuses to isolate Ethiopia from the world, for the conditions that created and still create poor living—politically, economically, and epistemically—are outcomes of internal and external circumstances that relate to each other dynamically through the triple relations of domination, to wit, political, economic, and epistemic. Understanding Ethiopian conditions and resolving the deadlocks that inhabit them thus require tackling internal and external circumstances and the interconnections between them. Hence, the importance of engaging in critical internal and external journeys. Being rooted in *säwrä tarik*, Ethioperspectivism rejects dualism such as Euro-centrism/Ethio-centrism, tradition/modernity, individual/collective, and so forth. Inspired by *qiné* hermeneutics, Ethioperspectivism sees both Ethiopian and Western thinking and societies as *nägär*, therefore as *säm ena wärq*. As such, it considers them *enkän* and subjects them to *zäräfa* to generate their emancipatory surplus meanings.

Having acquired higher education through knowledge welfare, modern educated Ethiopians are imprisoned in a cultural cringe that has normalized the strange belief that borrowed knowledge is an application-ready knowledge already cleansed from errors by the processes that produced it in the West and which they apply transcendently to Ethiopian issues. What we fail to recognize is the crucial importance of we ourselves producing knowledge by settling

---

Helmsing, "Endogenisation or Enclave Formation? The Development of the Ethiopian Cut Flower Industry," *The Journal of Modern African Studies*, vol. 48, 1 (2010), pp. 35-66.

470 The so-called "appropriate technology," Aaron Segal, "Appropriate Technology: The African Experience," *Journal of Asian and African Studies* (1992) Volume 27 (1992): Issue 1-2 (Jan 1992), pp. 124-133; Harvey Brooks, "A Critique of the Concept of Appropriate Technology," *Bulletin of the American Academy of Arts and Sciences*, Vol. 34, No. 6 (1981), pp. 16-37.

471 Fidèle Ingiyimbere, *Domesticating Human Rights: A Reappraisal of their Cultural-Political Critiques and their Imperialistic Use* (New York: Springer, 2017). Fukuyama is the silent partner of the current hegemonic development and democratization theories. Francis Fukuyama, *The End of History and the Last Man* (Washington: Free Press, 2006).

accounts with the errors we make. As the practice of *zäräfa* shows, it is impossible to disconnect the errors committed in the process of knowing from the process that constructs the correct answers that are finally produced.[472] That is, errors are the path that lead to true knowledge (*wärq*), and true knowledge (*wärq*) is attained by working through the errors we commit, which means that it is essential that we ourselves make the errors and learn from them by being engaged in the active process of knowing. Such a process changes not only the object of knowledge but also, crucially, Ethiopians engaged in the production of knowledge. The *qiné* lines—ይስጠኝ ብትል የት ይሆናል /ያልተዘራ መች ይበቅላል (Borrowing is a dead-end / What you do not sow, does not sprout.)—intimate that there is a crucial sense in which one could say that there is an emancipatory dimension, both subjectively and objectively, in "re-inventing the wheel." Simply "borrowing the wheel" confines us to epistemic servility, while "re-inventing the wheel"—subjecting it to *zäräfa*, i.e., "over-reading" and "re-constructing" it to meet our emancipatory purposes—gives us mastery over our conditions, the knowledge we acquire, and ourselves. Even if we fail, the failure itself is a source of new knowledge of the subjective and objective conditions that led to the failure, and prepares us for a cognitive leap forward. It is a process that develops our epistemic autonomy. It is in this sense that we should embrace all our failures to bring about political economic emancipation in Ethiopia in 1960, 1974, 1991, and 2020, and subject these failures to *zäräfa* and use them as trampolines for reflecting on why we failed to actualize the emancipatory possibilities gestating in these watershed years, and how we could mobilize these failures as negative and positive sources for achieving the goals of Ethioperspectivism. In engaging in the *zäräfa* of our failures, we affirm our epistemic and political autonomy. The epistemic autonomy that informs Ethioperspectivism opens the political, economic, social, cognitive, and affective spaces for an alternative and autonomous way of thinking, imagining, feeling, acting and becoming, and for formulating new questions and creating new concepts (*tsinsä hassab*). It gives us self-esteem and self-respect, and generates the conditions for epistemological egalitarianism between us and the West (or other). It makes us the authors and actors of our *arnät*.

Some may object that Ethioperspectivism envisages a social transformation of Ethiopia that exceeds the material conditions of Ethiopia. *Qiné* hermeneutical readings of Ethiopian history/society challenge the teleology, determinism, and dualism lodged in this thinking. If only material conditions of Ethiopian

---

472 The importance of error-making in the production of knowledge is what the universal history of knowledge production shows. Stuart Firestein, *Failure: Why Science Is So Successful* (New York: Oxford University Press, 2015).

society were to determine what is possible politically, the 1896 war between materially advanced Italy and materially weak Ethiopia would have ended with the victory of Italy. Also, the radical changes Christianity and Islam brought to Ethiopia, including the transition from primary to secondary identification, as indicated earlier, show that ideas and visions convert themselves into material forces that make possible that which may appear to be impossible from the deterministic or dualistic perspective.[473]

An Oromiffa aphorism tells us, *"Turina keessatt killen millaan adeemti"* ("By persevering the egg walks on legs"). It intimates that it is not by rejecting but by traversing our errors and failures that we find our balance and walk confidently on our own legs. The errors and the failures themselves create the space for the emergence of the possibility of *arnät*, hence the need for perseverance when one practices politics as the art of the impossible.[474] Only through such a process could Ethiopians develop the collective intelligence of Ethiopian society for whom emancipatory democracy and emancipatory economic transformation—*arnät*—become the normal practice and context of life. Faced with the dangers of Gibbonism, the early 20th century Ethiopian thinker, Hiywet Baykedagn, wrote, "ዕውቀት የሌለው ሕዝብ ሁሉ ለብቻው መንግሥት ቢኖረውም ዕውቀት ያላቸው ሕዝቦች ይገዙታል።"[475] That is, "A people deprived of knowledge, even if it has an independent state, will be dominated by those who master knowledge." If as Marx says, "it is not enough that thought should seek to realize itself, reality must also strive towards thought" for achieving emancipation (*arnät*), then Gibbonism and the epistemic servility it has engendered must be overthrown, for they have frozen thinking in Ethiopia into living without "thought" and prevented Ethiopian reality from "striving towards thought," making contemporary Ethiopia an intellectual wasteland.[476] Without epistemic

---

473 Even Marx recognizes the primacy of ideas. He wrote, "theory also becomes a material force as soon as it has gripped the masses." Karl Marx, "Introduction," *Critique of Hegel's Philosophy of Right* (London: Oxford University Press, 1970), p. 5.

474 This idea, which arises from the practice of *zäräfa*, is similar to the Hegelian idea that Žižek renders as follows: "Yes, 'truth emerges out of error,' but that in no way implies that this error, this fall into illusion, could be reduced to Machiavellian cunning on the part of truth, which would have used this stratagem in order to achieve its ends and its ultimate victory. It is quite literally the error itself that creates, that opens, the (still) empty space of truth." Slavoj Žižek, *The Most Sublime Hysteric: Hegel with Lacan* (Cambridge: Polity Press: 2014), p. 84.

475 Negadras Gebre Hiywet Baykedagn, ሥራዎች (Addis Ababa: Addis Ababa University Press, 2007), p.75.

476 Karl Marx, "Contribution to the Critique of Hegel's Philosophy of Right. Introduction," in Karl Marx, *Early Writings*, ed. T. B. Bottomore (New York: McGraw-Hill, 1964), p. 54.

autonomy, Ethiopian reality cannot "strive towards thought": a necessary condition for enabling Ethiopians to raise the questions, invent the concepts, and develop the theories they need to become the imaginers, thinkers, planners, and builders of a democratic (in the sense of *arnät*) and prosperous Ethiopia. Ethioperspectivism tells us that "Becoming Ethiopian" demands that Ethiopians be the father, the mother, the midwife, the offspring, the teacher, the student, and the labourer of the process of *arnät*: emancipatory democracy and emancipatory development. For this to happen, Ethiopia needs, as the following lines from a post-1995 song puts it,

>አዲስ ሰማይ ኢትዮጵያ ላይ / A new sky in Ethiopia
>አዲስ ፀሃይ ኢትዮጵያ ላይ / A new sun in Ethiopia
>አዲስ ዝናብ ኢትዮጵያ ላይ / A new rain in Ethiopia
>አዲስ ሃሳብ ኢትዮጵያ ላይ / A new idea in Ethiopia
>ይንገስ ኢትዮጵያ ላይ   / Let these reign in Ethiopia[477]

A "new sky," a "new sun," a "new rain," and a "new idea" must reign in Ethiopia if Ethiopians are to flourish in the modern world in all areas of human endeavour and if Ethiopia is to become a full-fledged actor in the making of the world to come. This "new" that Ethiopians have to comprehend and grasp gestates in Ethiopia's *säwrä tarik* (surplus history), which they have to use as the trampoline for constructing Ethioperspectivism. Although Ethioperspectivism does not, cannot, and should not offer a blueprint for an emancipated Ethiopia, it clearly identifies what Ethiopians and Ethiopia *should not do* and could and must do to achieve *arnät*. Its approach to Becoming Ethiopian is a *säm ena wärq* process that traverses contradictions and antagonisms in its pursuit of an unrelenting *minimization* of unfreedoms, injustices, material and cultural poverty, and epistemic servility and of an equally unrelenting *maximization* of the conditions that enhance *säwrä hiywät*: the political, economic, cultural and epistemic capabilities and flourishing of Ethiopians.

Another Ethiopia is possible.

---

477 Betty G. አዲስ ሰማይ, 2021.

Glossary of qiné hermeneutical terms

A

abiy agäbab, ዓቢይ አገባብ (refers to contradictory or subversive or reflexive understanding)

absho, አብሾ (refers to a person who has a productive and restless imagination)

adäbabay, አደባባይ public realm (public space and public time)

admas, አድማስ (horizon)

aëmrowawi, አአምሮዋዊ (rational)

afla zäybé, አፍላ ዘይቤ (comparable to metonymy)

afrash zäybé, አፍራሽ ዘይቤ (negation, contradiction, antagonism)

agär, አገር (combines the notion of country, homeland, and nation without exclusionary self-other binary)

alama, ዓላማ (aim, goal)

andem, አንድም (and one, said repeatedly for each new interpretation)

andemta, አንድምታ (fusion of horizons of understandings)

antsar nibab, አንጻር ንባብ (reading or interpretation that uses distanciation)

antsar t'mir zäybé, አንጻር ጥምር ዘይቤ (determinate negation)

antsar zäybé, አንጻር ዘይቤ (distanciation)

arat ayn, አራት ዓይን (four-eyed, reality cannot be reduced to the empirical knowledge we have of it). It also means parallax views.

arnät, አርነት (democracy that embraces political, economic, and epistemic emancipation)

atsäfa, አጻፋ (reciprocity)

aynä hileena, ዓይነ ሕሊና (eye of the mind and of the imagination)

azmari, አዝማሪ (minstrel)

B

bähig amlak, በሕግ አምላክ (The god of Law/ the Law of God, the rule of just law)

bahil, ባህል (tradition)

bahtawi, ባህታዊ (hermit)

biltsigina, ብልጽግና (just prosperity)

butta (a war-like activity that serves as a passage of rite towards societal responsibilities)

däbo, ደቦ (voluntarily organized communal labour among peasants)

Dagmawi Tinsa'e, ዳግማዊ ትንሣኤ (the Second Resurrection, resurrection in a secular sense)
däqiq agäbab, ደቂቅ አገባብ (refers to analytical or inferential understanding)
dästa, ደስታ (happiness)
dingay, ድንጋይ (stone, metaphor for oppression)

E

eger, እግር (leg, metaphor for being servile)
ena, እና (and that articulates tensions and contradictions in säm ena wärq)
enkän, እንክን (incompleteness, open-endedness, internal contradiction)
entsarawi gälätsa zäybé, እንጻራዊ ገላጻ ዘይቤ (metaphor, catachresis, double entendre)
equlinät, እኩልነት (equality)
ewen, እውን (reality)
ewnät, እውነት (truth)
ewqät, እውቀት (knowledge)

F

fich, ፍች (explanation)
filatsa zäybé, ፍላጻ ዘይቤ (allegory_
fissiha, ፍስሃ (joy).
fithe, ፍትህ (justice)

G

gada (traditional Oromo system of governance)
gädl, ገድል (struggle, deeds)
gädlo madän zäybé, ገድሎ ማደን ዘይቤ (expresses an affirmative by negating its opposite)
gourangur, ጉራንጉር (heterogeneous with contradictions between the constitutive elements)

H

hassabä ewen, ሃሳብ እውን (metaphysics)
hatäta, ሐተታ (dialectical reasoning)
hazan, ሓዘን (sorrow)
hibrä qal, ሕብረ ቃል (harmonizer)
hibrä qiné, ሕብረ ቅኔ (an old qiné that is often the source of aphorisms)
hibrät, ኅብረት (solidarity)
hilawi, ህላዊ (essence)
hiss, ሂስ, (critique). Zäräfa is an important tool of hiss.
huläntänawi, ሁለንተናዊ (universal)
huläntänawinät, ሁለንተናዊነት (universality)

I

iddir, ዕድር (voluntary self-help association)
iqqub, ዕቁብ (voluntary saving association)

K

kiflä agär, ክፍለ አገር (province or region)

L

lib wäläd, ልብ ወለድ (that which originates in the heart)
libsä wärq zäybé, ልብስ ወርቅ ዘይቤ (indicates a false self-evidence)
lissan, ልሳን (language of critical or emancipatory discourse)
luba (age group among the Oromo, basis of societal organization)

M

mäbit, ሙብት (right)
mädämamät, መደማምጥ (critical dialogical dialogue)
mahibär, ማህበር (association of like-minded people to pursue collectively a commonly shared goal)
mälk, መልክ (appearance)
mängäd, መንገድ (way that leads from symptom to cause, another term for zäybé)
mäsiya zäybé, መሲያ ዘይቤ (refers to a hidden, the unsaid, unheard, unseen, or a virtual dimension)
mäsmat, መስማት (to hear)
mastawäl, ማስታወል (observation)
ma'eräg, ማዕረግ (dignity)
miknyat, ምክንያት (reason)
minab, ምናብ (concrete utopia or utopianism without utopia)
mirmära, ምርመራ (research)
misät zäybé, ምጻት ዘይቤ (refers to contraries)
mist'ir, ምስጢር (a secret)
moggaasa, ሞጋሳ (the Oromo political process of creating a post-ethnic people)

N

n'oos agäbab, ንዑስ አገባብ (refers to reductive or subtractive understanding)
näftäña, ነፍጠኛ (old meaning: settler; post-1991 meaning: a person who believes that democracy should be based on citizenship and not on ethnic identity)
nägär, ነገር (all that is human made, be it material or mental, individual or collective, and so forth)
nätäla tirgum, ነጠላ ትርጉም (simple or direct translation)

nätsanät, ነጻነት (liberty as freedom from domination)

Q

qälb, ቀልብ (reason, rational)
qiné, ቅኔ (classical poetry)
qisäla, ቅጸላ (preliminary or preparatory steps before embarking on full-fledged research)
quanqua, ቋንቋ (language of hegemonic discourse)
qulqul zäybé, ቁልቁል ዘይቤ (similar to synecdoche)

S

säbäb, ሰበብ (cause)
säm ena wärq, ሰም እና ወርቅ (wax and gold)
säm läbäs zäybé, ሰም ለበስ ዘይቤ (disguised as something familiar or non-important)
säw, ሰው (humanity; also refers to man and to woman)
säwigna zäybé, ሰውኛ ዘይቤ (refers to anthropomorphism)
säwrä bahil, ሰውረ ባሕል (non-tradition)
säwrä hiywät, ሰውረ ሕይወት (surplus life)
säwrä ras, ሰውረ ራስ (surplus self)
säwrä tarik, ሰውረ ታሪh (surplus history)
silitané, ስልጣኔ (civilisation, culture)
silt, ስልት (method as an approach to a subject matter that considers its singularity)
sinä ewen, ሥነ እውን (ontology)
sinä ewqät arnät, ሥነ እውቀት አርነት (epistemic autonomy)
sinä ewqät, ሥነ እውቀት (epistemology)
sinä mädräsha, ሥነ መድረሻ (teleology)
sinä migbar, ሥነ ምግባር (ethics)
sinä silt, ሥነ ስልት (methodology)
sineñ, ስንኝ (a line from a qiné)

T

t'mir, ጥምር (tensions and contradiction)
tägbar, ተግባር (duty, obligation)
täläwach zäybé, ተለዋጭ ዘይቤ (alludes to indirect meanings)
tämssalit zäybé, ተምሳሊት ዘይቤ (refers to false similarities and dissimilarities)
tänätsatsari zäybé, ተነጻጻሪ ዘይቤ (refers to opposition between things, ideas, persons, values)
täqlala agäbab, ጠቅላላ አገባብ (refers to comprehensive or synthetic understanding)

täsfa, ተስፋ (hope)
tähägagari hiss, ተሸጋጋሪ ሂስ (transcritique)
tässalqo zäybé, ተሳልቆ ዘይቤ (refers to brachylogy, conjoining opposed terms or fragments)
tichit, ትችት (commentaire de texte)
Tinsa'e, ትንሳኤ (The Resurrection)
tintena, ትንተና (analytical reasoning)
tiqtiq, ጥቅጥቅ (heterogeneous with tension between the constitutive elements)
tirgum, ትርጉም (a critical translation that reveals that which is not visible in the original text)
tiyaqé, ጥያቄ (question)
tiyaqé, ጥያቄ (question)
tiyaqewotch, ጥያቄዎች (questions)
tizita, ትዝታ (the remembered past as a promise of a better future)
tkazie, ትካዜ (sadness)
tsärä qälb, ፀረ ቀልብ (irrational)
tsinsä hassab, ፅንስ ሓሳብ (concept)
tzärä-bahil, ፀረ ባሕል (anti-tradition)
tzärä, ፀረ (anti)

W

wäné, ወኔ (courage that drives one to change things at the roots and for the better)
wärqa wärq zäybé, ወርቃ ወርቅ ዘይቤ (refers to something disguised as true, authentic)
wäyim, ወይም (or in the sense of mutually exclusive)
wihdät, ውህደት (unity in the sense of unity "without mixture or separation")
wistä wäyra nibab, ውስጠ ወይራ ንባብ (symptomatic reading)
wistä wäyra zäybé, ውስጠ ወይራ ዘይቤ (refers to signs that lead to a hidden or repressed meaning)

Y

yählm injära, የሕልም እንጀራ (bread made from dreams or abstract utopia)
yämist'ir tirgum, የምስጢር ትርጉም (a translation that makes the hidden, a "secret," visible)
yäne bitie, የኔ ቢጤ (a phrase that acknowledged the commonly shared humanity of all)
yäwäl, የወል (commons)

Z

zälängä hassab, ዘለንገ ሐሳብ (induction)

zäläsäña, ዘለሰኛ (melancholy, expression of a repressed surplus life)

zängä hassab, ዘንገ ሐሳብ (deduction)

zar, ዛር (spiritual possession)

Zäräfa englobes hiss, andem, tirgum, täshägagari hiss cum mädämamät, and arat ayn. And each of these uses *zäräfa*.

zäräfa, ዘረፉ (decentering, diverting, subjecting ideas, norms, and practices to détournement).

zäybé, ዘይቤ (rhetorical figure, symptom, way). The main zäybé are

zega, ዜጋ (citizen)

zeginät, ዜግነት (citizenship)

zimd zäybé, ዝምድ ዘይቤ (refers to analogy)

Bibliography

Ethiopian names are indicated according to the Ethiopian convention: first name followed by last name.

Abba Paulos Tzadua, "Foreword," *The Fetha Nägäst: The Law of the Kings*, trans. Abba Paulos Tzadua, ed. Peter L. Strauss (Addis Ababa: Haile Selassie I University, 1968).
Abe Gubegna, አልወለድም (Addis Ababa: Berana Printing Press, 1986 E. C.).
_____, ስብስብ ሥራዎች, (Addis Ababa Ezop Publishing, 2010).
Abiy Ahmed, መደመር (*Mädämer*) (in Amharic) (Los Angeles: Tsehai Publishers, 2019).
Abraham Yayeh, የኤርትራ ህዝብ ትግል ከዬት ወደዬት (Washington D.C., 1992).
Addis Alemayhu, *Fiqer eskä Mäqaber* (Addis Ababa: Mega, 1992, first published in 1965).
_____, የልም ዝት (Addis Ababa: Kuraz Printing Press, 1980).
Admasu Jembere, መጽሐፈ ቅኔ (Addis Ababa, Berhan ena Selam Printing Press, 1963).
Alaka Imbakom Kalewold, *Traditional Ethiopian Church Education*, trans. Menghestu Lemma (New York: Teachers College Press, 1970).
Aläka Imbakom Kalewold, ቅኔ ትምህርት ና ስለ ጥቅሙ, Proceedings of the Third International Conference of Ethiopian Studies (Addis Ababa, 1966).
Alemayhu Mogess, መልከዐ ኢትዮጵያ, *Mälkea Ethiopia* (Asmara: Graphic Printing Press, 1952 E.C.).
_____, ሰም ና ወርቅ, 2 vols. (Asmara, Graphic Printing Press, 1953 E. C.).
_____, ኢትዮጵያዊ ቅኔ (Asmara: Graphic Printing Press, 1959, E. C.).
Allen, Amy, *The End of Progress* (New York: Columbia University Press, 2015).
አማርኛ መዝገበ ቃላት (Addis Ababa: Addis Ababa University, 1993).
Archbishop Gabriel, ትምህርት ሃይማኖት ኦርቶዶክሳዊ (Addis Ababa: Addis Printers, 2001).
Archbishop Mekarios *et al.*, eds., *The Ethiopian Orthodox Täwahedo Church Faith, Order of Worship and Ecumenical Relations* (Addis Ababa: Tinsae ZeGubae Printing Press, 1996).

Bäalu Girma, ሀዲስ (Addis Ababa: Ethiopia Book center, 1982).
Bäewqätu Siyum, ስብስብ ግጥሞች (Addis Ababa: Hitmat, 2001).
Bahru Zewde, *Pioneers of Change in Ethiopia: The Reformist Intellectuals of the early Twentieth Century* (Addis Ababa: Addis Ababa University Press, 2002).
_____, *The Quest of Socialist Utopia: the Ethiopian Student Movement c. 1960-1974* (Rochester, NY: James Curry, 2014).
Balambaras Mahtem Selasse Welde Mesqel, አማሪኛ ቅኔ (Addis Ababa: Artistic Printing Press, 1955, E. C.).

Bibliography

Ethiopian names are indicated according to the Ethiopian convention: first name followed by last name.

Abba Paulos Tzadua, "Foreword," *The Fetha Nägäst: The Law of the Kings*, trans. Abba Paulos Tzadua, ed. Peter L. Strauss (Addis Ababa: Haile Selassie I University, 1968).
Abe Gubegna, አልወለድም (Addis Ababa: Berana Printing Press, 1986 E. C.).
_____, ስብስብ ሥራዎች, (Addis Ababa Ezop Publishing, 2010).
Abiy Ahmed, መደመር (*Mädämer*) (in Amharic) (Los Angeles: Tsehai Publishers, 2019).
Abraham Yayeh, የኤርትራ ህዝብ ትግል ከየት ወደየት (Washington D.C., 1992).
Addis Alemayhu, *Fiqer eskä Mäqaber* (Addis Ababa: Mega, 1992, first published in 1965).
_____, የልም ዝት (Addis Ababa: Kuraz Printing Press, 1980).
Admasu Jembere, መጽሐፈ ቅኔ (Addis Ababa, Berhan ena Selam Printing Press, 1963).
Alaka Imbakom Kalewold, *Traditional Ethiopian Church Education*, trans. Menghestu Lemma (New York: Teachers College Press, 1970).
Aläka Imbakom Kalewold, ቅኔ ትምህርት ና ስለ ጥቅሙ, Proceedings of the Third International Conference of Ethiopian Studies (Addis Ababa, 1966).
Alemayhu Mogess, መልከዐ ኢትዮጵያ, *Mälkea Ethiopia* (Asmara: Graphic Printing Press, 1952 E.C.).
_____, ሰም ና ወርቅ, 2 vols. (Asmara, Graphic Printing Press, 1953 E. C.).
_____, ኢትዮጵያዊ ቅኔ (Asmara: Graphic Printing Press, 1959, E. C.).
Allen, Amy, *The End of Progress* (New York: Columbia University Press, 2015).
አማርኛ መዝገበ ቃላት (Addis Ababa: Addis Ababa University, 1993).
Archbishop Gabriel, ትምህርተ ሃይማኖት ኦርቶዶክሳዊ (Addis Ababa: Addis Printers, 2001).
Archbishop Mekarios et al., eds., *The Ethiopian Orthodox Täwahedo Church Faith, Order of Worship and Ecumenical Relations* (Addis Ababa: Tinsae ZeGubae Printing Press, 1996).

Bäalu Girma, ሀዲስ (Addis Ababa: Ethiopia Book center, 1982).
Bäewqätu Siyum, ስብስብ ግጥሞች (Addis Ababa: Hitmat, 2001).
Bahru Zewde, *Pioneers of Change in Ethiopia: The Reformist Intellectuals of the early Twentieth Century* (Addis Ababa: Addis Ababa University Press, 2002).
_____, *The Quest of Socialist Utopia: the Ethiopian Student Movement c. 1960-1974* (Rochester, NY: James Curry, 2014).
Balambaras Mahtem Selasse Welde Mesqel, አማሪኛ ቅኔ (Addis Ababa: Artistic Printing Press, 1955, E. C.).

Baltrusaitis, Jurgis, *Anamorphic Art*, trans. W. J. Strachan (New York: Harry N. Abrams, 1977).
Birhanu Gebeyhu, የአማርኛ ስነ ግጥም (Addis Ababa: Alfa Printing, 2003).
Binyam Hailemeskel Kidane, ኢትዮጵያዊ የትምህርት ፍልስፍና (2021), https://mail.google.com/mail/u/0/#inbox/FMfcgzGtxKKflLZmlCCtxncKKSwjbcxK. Accessed 9/2/2023
Blaten Geta Mahteme Selassie Welde Mesqel, ዝክረ ነገር (Addis Abeba, 1962 E.C.)
Bloch, Ernst, *The Principle of Hope*, trans. Neville Plaice, Stephen Plaice and Paul Knight (Cambridge, MA: MIT Press, 1986).
_____, *The Spirit of Utopia*, trans. Anthony A. Nassar (Redwood City, CA: Stanford University Press, 2000).
Bookstaber, Richard, *The End of Theory: Financial Crises, the Failure of Economics and the Sweep of Human Interaction* (Princeton, NJ: Princeton University Press, 2017).

Campbell, Timothy and Sitze, Adam, eds., *Biopolitics: A Reader* (Durham: Duke University Press, 2013).
Cherenet Abebe. መሰርአዊ የመጽሐፍ ቅዱስ አጠናን ዘዴ (Addis Ababa: Foundational Bible Study, 2011).
Cicovacki, Predrag, *Anamorphosis: Kant on Knowledge and Ignorance* (New York: University of America Press, 1997).
Clark, Jeffery, *Civil Society, NGOs, and Development in Ethiopia* (Washington: The World Bank, 2000),
Claude Sumner, *Classical Ethiopian Philosophy* (Los Angeles: Adey Publishing Company, 1994).
Cohen Jean L. and Andrew Arato, *Civil Society and Political Theory* (Cambridge: MIT Press, 1992).
Cuoq, Joseph, *L'Islam en Ethiopie: des origines au XVI siècle* (Paris: Nouvelles Editions Latines, 1981).
Cowley, Roger W., "Old Testament Introduction in the Andemta Commentary Tradition," *Journal of Ethiopian Studies* 12, 1 (1974).
_____, *Ethiopian Biblical Interpretation: A Study in Exegetical Tradition and Hermeneutics* (Cambridge: Cambridge University Press, 1988).
_____, *The Traditional Interpretation of the Apocalypse of St John in the Ethiopian Orthodox Church* (Cambridge: Cambridge University Press, 1983).

Dardot, Pierre et Laval, Christian, *Commun. Essai sur la révolution au XXIe siècle* (Paris: La découverte, 2014).
Davis, Colin, *Critical excess: overreading in Derrida, Deleuze, Levinas, Žižek and Cavell* (Stanford: Stanford University Press, 2010).
de la Boétie, Etienne, *Discours on voluntary servitude,* trans. James B. Atkinson and David Sices (Indianapolis: Hackett, 2012).
Debebe Seyfu, የብርሃን ፍቅር (Addis Ababa: Hassab Publishers, 2013).
Dessalegn Rahmato, "Civil Society Organizations in Ethiopia," in *Ethiopia: The Challenge of Democracy from Below*, eds. Bahru Zewde and Siegfried Pausewang (Addis Ababa: Forum for Social Studies, 2002), pp. 103-119.

Elleni Centime Zeleke, *Ethiopia in Theory: Revolution and Knowledge Production, 1964-2016* (Leiden and Boston: Brill 2019).

Foucault, Michel, *Society Must Be Defended* (London: Penguin, 2004).

Gadamer, Hans-Georg, *Truth and Method*, Second Revised Edition; translation revised by Joel Weinsheimer and Donald G. Marshall (New York: Continuum, 2004/2006).

Gebre-Sillasie, ታሪክ ዘመን ዳግማዊ ምኔልክ ንጉስ ነገስት ዘኢትዮጵያ (Addis Abeba, 1967).

Gebru Tareke, *Ethiopia: Power and Protest* (New York: Cambridge University Press, 1991).

Getahun Benti, *Addis Ababa: Migration and the Making of a Multiethnic Metropolis: 1941-1974* (Trenton: The Red Sea Press, 2007).

Getatchew Haile, *A History of the First Stefanosite Monks*, trans. from Ge'ez (Leuven: Uitgeverij Peeters, 2011).

_____, የአባ ባጎራይ ድርሰቶች (Collegeville, Minnesota, 2002).

_____, ደቂቀ እስጢፋኖስ በገግ አምላክ, trans. from Ge'ez (Collegeville, MN, 2004).

_____, ግዕዝ በቀላሉ (New York: Kilsna Yetsfafa Etim, 2015).

_____, "Ethiopian Monasticism" in Aziz S Atiya, ed., *Coptic Encyclopedia*, vol. 3 (New York: Macmillan, 1991), pp. 993-9

_____, "Ethiopian Heresies and Theological Controversies" in *Coptic Encyclopedia*, vol 2, ed. Aziz S. Atiya (New York: Macmillan, 1991), 984a-987b.

Groys, Boris, *On the New*, trans. G. M. Goshgarian (London: Verso, 2014).

Harvey, David, *A Brief History of Neoliberalism* (Oxford: Oxford University Press, 2007)

Hiruie Ermias, *The Issues of 'Aggabāb (Classic Gəʿəz Grammar) According to the Tradition of Qəne Schools*, PhD Dissertation in Ethiopian Studies, Faculty of Humanities at the University of Hamburg, (2019).

Hiwot Teffera, ጉዞዋ, (Addis Ababa, Eclipse Printing Press, 2009).

Hussein Ahmed, *Islam in Nineteenth-Century Wallo, Ethiopia* (Leiden: Brill, 2001).

Jalata, Asafa, *Oromia and Ethiopia: State Formation and Ethnonational Conflict, 1868-2004* (Trenton, NJ: Red Sea Press, 2005).

_____, *The Oromo Movement and Imperial Politics: Culture and Ideology in Oromia and Ethiopia* (Lexington Books, 2005).

_____, *Oromo Nationalism and the Ethiopian Discourse: The Search for Freedom and Democracy* (Trenton, NJ. ʃRed Sea Press, 1998).

_____, *Oromia and Ethiopia: State Formation and Ethnonational Conflict, 1868-2004* (Trenton, NJ. ʃRed Sea Press, 2005).

_____, The Concept of Oromummaa and Identity Formation in Contemporary Oromo Society" (2007); https://trace.tennessee.edu/cgi/viewcontent.cgi?article=1009&context= utk_socopubs.

_____, "Promoting and Developing Oromummaa" (2012). https://trace.tennessee.edu/utk_socopubs/83.

Kant. I., *Kant's Political Writings*, ed. Hans Reiss (Cambridge: Cambridge University Press, 1970).
Karatani, Kojin, *Transcritique: On Kant and Marx*, trans. Sabu Koshu (Cambridge: MIT Press, 2003).
Kearney, Richard and Brian Treanor, eds., *Carnal Hermeneutics* (New York: Fordham University Press, 2015).
Kebede, G/Medhin, ሳይንሳዊ የቅኔ አፈታት ስልት (Addis Ababa: Birana Matëmia Bet, 1992).
Kebede, Michael, የቅኔ ውበት (Addis Ababa: Mega Printing, 1994).
Kidane Weld Kifle, መጽሐፈ ሰዋስው ወግስ ወመዝገበ ቃላት ሐዲስ (Addis Ababa: Artistic Printing Press, 1978. E. C.).

Laclau, Ernesto, *New Reflections on the Revolution of Our Time* (London: Verso, 1990)
Leiris, Michel, *La Possession et ses aspects théâtraux chez les Éthiopiens de Gondar* (Paris: Plon, 1958).
Leslau, Wolf, *Comparative Dictionary of Ge'ez (Classical Ethiopic)* (Wiesbaden: Otto Harrassowitz, 1991).
_____, *Ethiopians Speak* (Berkeley: University of California Press, 1966).
Levine, Donald D., *Wax and Gold* (Chicago: University of Chicago Press, 1972).
Levinson, B. A., Foley, D. E. and Holland, D. eds., *The Cultural Production of the Educated Person: Critical Ethnographies of Schooling and Local Practice* (New York: SUNY, 1996).
Levitas, Ruth, *Utopia as Method: The Imaginary Reconstitution of Society* (New York: Palgrave Macmillan, 2013) .
Liqä Siltanat Habtä Mariam Werqneh, ጥንታዊ የኢትዮጲያ ትምህርት (Addis Ababa, Berhan ena Selam Printing Press, 1962 /63/ 70).

Maimire Mennasemay, *Qiné Hermeneutics and Ethiopian Critical Theory* (Los Angeles: Tsehai Publishers, 2021).
Mannheim, Karl. *Ideology and Utopia* (New York: Harcourt, 1954).
Mannoni, Octave, *Clefs pour l'imaginaire ou l'autre scène* (Paris : Seuil, 1969).
Martín Alcoff, Linda, "Epistemologies of Ignorance: Three Types," in Shannon Sullivan and Nancy Tuana, eds. *Race and Epistemologies of Ignorance* (New York: State University of New York Press, 2007).
Mbembe, Achille, *Necropolitics* (Durham: Duke University Press, 2019).
McGowan, Todd, *Emancipation After Hegel* (New York: Cambridge University Press, 2019).
Mebratu Kiros Gebru, *Miaphysite Christology: An Ethiopian Perspective* (Piscataway, NJ: Gorgias Press, 2010).
Melake Berhan Admassu Jembere, ዝክረ ሊቃዊት (Addis Ababa: Tinsae Zegubae Printing Press, 1970).

Memhir Gebrekidan Desta, የትግራይ ህዝብና የትምክህተኞች ሴራ ከትናንት እስከ ዛሬ (Addis Ababa, 1998).

Merse Hazen Weld Qirqos, የሀያኛው ክፍለ ዘመን መባቻ 1896-1922 (Addis Abeba: Addis Abeba University Press, 1999).

Menghestu Lemma, "Appendix: Ethiopian classical poetry" in Alaka Imbakom Kalewold, *Traditional Ethiopian Church Education*, trans. Menghestu Lemma (New York: Teachers College Press, 1970).

_____, የአማርኛ ግጥም ዓይነቱ ሥረቱ ሥርዓቱ (offprint, undated).

_____, መጽሐፈ ትዝታ (Addis Ababa: Berhan ena Selam Printing Press, 1959).

Messay Kebede, *Radicalism and Cultural Dislocation in Ethiopia, 1960-1974* (Rochester: University of Rochester Press, 2008).

_____, *Survival and Modernization, Ethiopia's Enigmatic Present: A Philosophical Discourse* (Lawrenceville, NJ: The Red Sea Press, 1999).

Michel Foucault, *Power/Knowledge: Selected Interviews and Other Writings, 1972-1977*, Colin Gordon, ed. (New York: Pantheon Books, 1980).

Mohamed Hassen, *The Oromo and the Christian Kingdom of Ethiopia: 1300-1700* (London: James Curry, 2017).

_____, *The Oromo of Ethiopia: A History 1570-1860* (Cambridge: Cambridge University Press, 1990).

Mohammed Girma, "Whose Meaning? The Wax and Gold Tradition as a Philosophical Foundation for an Ethiopian Hermeneutic," *Sophia* 50 (2011).

_____, *Understanding Religion and Social Change in Ethiopia: Toward a Hermeneutic of Covenant* (New York: Palgrave Macmillan, 2012).

Negadras Gebre Hiywet Baykedagn, ሥራዎች (Addis Ababa: Addis Ababa University Press, 2007).

Negussie Andre Dominic, *The Fetha Nägäst and its Ecclesiology* (New York: Peter Lang, 2010).

Ngusse Nagaw Dagaga, የቅኔ አፈታት ዜዳዎች ና የምርጥ ቅኔዎች ስብስብ, Second edition (Addis Ababa: Mega, 1993).

Panikkar, Raimon, *Myth, Faith and Hermeneutics* (New York: Paulist Press, 1979).

Ricoeur, Paul, *Lectures on Ideology and Utopia*, ed. G. H. Taylor (New York: Columbia University Press, 1986).

_____, *From Text to Action: Essays in Hermeneutics*, II (Chicago: Northwestern University Press, 1991).

_____, *Hermeneutics and the Human Sciences: Essays on Language, Action and Interpretation*, ed. and trans. J. B. Thompson (Cambridge: Cambridge University Press, 1981).

Rist, Gilbert, *The history of development: from Western origins to global faith*, trans. Patrick Camiller (London: Zed Books, 2014).

Salmi, Jamil, Andrée Sursock, and Anna Olefir, *Improving the Performance of Ethiopian Universities in Science and Technology* (World Bank, 2017).

Salome Gabre-Egziabher, "The Ethiopian Patriots 1936-1941," *Ethiopian Observer* 12, 2 (1969).
Sen, Amartya, *Development as Freedom* (Oxford, Oxford University Press, 1999).
Sergew Hable Sellassie, *Ancient and Medieval Ethiopian History* (Addis Ababa: United Printers, 1972).
_____, *The Church of Ethiopia - A panorama of History and Spiritual Life* (Addis Ababa: Berhanena Selam, 1997).
_____, የአማርኛ የቤተ ክርስቲያን መዝገበ ቃላት ፥ ረቂቅ, 13 volumes (Addis Ababa: Hand-written manuscript, 1977-1990).
_____, and Taddesse Tamrat, *The Church of Ethiopia, a Panorama of History and Spiritual Life* (Addis Ababa: EOTC, 1970).
Sohn-Rethel, Alfred, *Intellectual and Manual Labour: A Critique of Epistemology* (London: MacMillan, 1978).
Sumner, Claude, *Classical Ethiopian Philosophy* (Los Angeles: Adey Publishing Company, 1994).

Tessema Eshete, ሰምና ወርቅ, presented by Yidneqachew Tessema (Addis Ababa: 1985).
Tadesse Tamrat, *Church and State in Ethiopia 1270-1527* (Oxford: Clarendon Press, 1972).
Taylor, Charles, *Philosophy and the Human Sciences,* vol. 2 (Cambridge: Cambridge University Press, 1988).
Tesfaye Wolde-Medhin, "Wänfäl (Reciprocity) and the Constitution of Agär as Moral Community among Farmers in the Central Highlands of Ethiopia," *Journal of Ethiopian Studies*, vol.51, (December, 2018), pp. 1-38.
Teweldeberhan Mezgebe Desta, *Gädlä Abäw wä-A aw [Fourth Part]: Edition and Annotated Translation with Philological and Linguistic Commentary* (Addis Ababa: Addis Ababa University Dissertation, 2019).
Tsegaye Gebre Medhin (Poet Laureate), እሳት ወይ አበባ (Addis Ababa: Graphics Printing Press, 1999).

Wolff, Kurt H., ed., *From Karl Mannheim* (New Brunswick: Transition Publishers, 1993).

Yitbarek Gidäy, የቅኔ ቤት ባህል ና የሕይወቴ ገጠመኝ (Addis Ababa: Artistic Printing Press, undated).

Zewde Reta, የቀዳማዊ ኃይለ ሥላሴ መንግስት (Boston: Laxmi Publications, 2012).
_____, ተፈሪ መኮንን (Addis Abeba: Central Printing Press, undated).
Žižek, Slavoj, *The Plague of Fantasies* (London: Verso, 1997).
_____, *The Ticklish Subject* (London: Verso, 2000)
_____, *The Universal Exception* (New York: Continuum, 2006).
_____, *The Sublime Object of Ideology* (London: Verso, 1989).

Index

adäbabay, አደባባይ, 187-3, 188-3, 191, 227

adaptive preferences, 149-153, 159, 200-202, 205, 209, 212-3, 222

addis semay, አዲስ ሰማይ, 40, 225

admas, አድማስ, 20, 54-5, 63-4, 69-70, 83-4, 103, 118, 145-6, 168, 227

agär, አገር, 162-3, 166, 169-81, 187-9, 191, 227

anamorphic, 6, 8-9, 179

andem, አንድም, 33, 37, 82-3, 99, 123, 146, 155, 227

andemta, አንድምታ, ix, 2, 16-7, 20, 30, 46, 51, 53-4, 57-9, 61, 64, 67-70, 73-4, 81-4, 86, 92, 129, 141, 181, 188, 193, 195, 197, 202, 211, 213, 227

antsar, አንጻር, 20, 48, 53, 57, 61, 69, 72, 82-4, 93, 98, 144, 202, 213, 227

arat ayn, አራት ዓይን, 20, 27, 33, 35, 46, 51-4, 57, 82-3, 87, 129, 143, 146, 227

arnät, አርነት, 20-1, 25, 30, 44, 65, 90, 92, 93-4, 122-4, 126, 129-30, 132-7, 139-41, 144, 146-8, 153, 155, 170, 181-2, 188, 191, 205, 211-6, 219-21, 223-5, 227

aynä hileena, ዓይነ ሕሊና, 143, 227

bähig amlak, በሕግ አምላክ, 20, 78-81, 227

bahil, ባህል, 37-8, 227

biopolitics, 189

butta, 57, 167-8, 172, 195, 227

capitalism, 8, 41, 58, 79, 123, 134-5, 137, 145, 150, 158-9, 205-6, 208, 211-4, 218-9, 221-2

Christianity, 41, 106-7, 110, 113, 162-5, 168-9, 172, 176, 224

citizenship, 38, 103-4, 113, 118, 151, 161, 170-1, 181-3, 185, 188

civil society, 8, 12-3, 60, 127, 214

commons, 20, 76, 93, 132, 140, 147, 154-5, 158-60

däbo, ደቦ, 12, 39, 41, 97, 157-8, 195, 227

Dagmawi Tinsa'e, ዳግማዊ ትንሳኤ, 20, 77, 123, 228

Däqiqä Estifanos, 40, 43, 77, 80, 128, 148, 153-5, 183-4, 187

democracy, 2-3, 8-9, 12, 14, 37-8, 49, 58, 60, 62-3, 79, 103-4, 117-9, 122, 126-8, 133-6, 138, 141, 151, 153-4, 189, 194, 199-200, 202, 211-2, 214-6, 219, 221-2, 224-5

dingay, ድንጋይ, 140-1

dispossession, 199, 210, 219

domination, 12, 16, 18, 20, 22, 29, 31, 41, 43, 43, 57-60, 63, 90, 94, 98-100, 118, 122, 126, 130, 133-5, 137, 141, 144, 146-7, 149, 153, 159, 172, 175, 179-80, 198-9, 202, 213-7, 222

education, 3, 5, 11, 48, 101-3, 118, 125, 127, 139, 159, 177, 195-6, 198-202, 205-6, 222

emancipation, 2, 19-20, 25, 28-31, 42, 44, 57-9, 63, 65, 67, 69, 84, 87, 90-4, 97-100, 118, 123-4, 126-7, 129-30, 132-3, 135-40, 144, 147, 152, 173, 176, 189, 194, 202, 221, 223-4

ena, እና, 17, 20, 22-30, 32-3, 47, 52-3, 56, 61, 65, 71-3, 82-3, 87, 90, 93, 109, 129,

131, 139, 141, 145, 166, 191, 216, 222, 225, 228

enkän, እንከን, 20, 24-5, 29, 31-4, 36-7, 51-4, 56, 59-61, 65, 69, 84, 87, 90, 93, 113, 134-5, 146, 160, 171, 173-4, 211, 216, 222, 228

epistemic, 2, 4-5, 9, 11-3, 15-8, 28, 30, 35-6, 39, 41, 43-5, 52-3, 58, 62-3, 70, 77, 80, 82, 84, 90-2, 94-8, 111, 118, 121-4, 126-7, 129-30, 132-5, 140, 142, 145-7, 149-53, 157, 159, 173, 184, 188, 194, 196-9, 201-7, 209-11, 213-25

epistemology, 6-8, 13, 26, 33, 61, 96, 179, 195-6

Estifanosite, 128, 162, 181-7

Ethioperspectivism, 193-4, 202, 211, 214-6, 218, 222-3, 225

ethnic, 1, 5, 10-1, 13-5, 17, 38, 43-4, 49, 56, 58, 60, 63, 65-7, 70, 90-1, 100-7, 110-21, 127, 130-1, 133, 136, 139, 142, 144, 151-2, 161-202, 212-3, 216-7, 221

Ewostatewos, 128, 148, 187

ewen, እውን, 26, 32, 38, 143, 228

ewnät, እውነት, 20, 29-32, 36-7, 55, 59, 63, 72, 96-7, 140, 147, 228

ewqät, እውቀት, 20, 26, 29-32, 36-7, 55, 59, 63, 72, 96-7, 140, 147, 228

fantasy, 107, 109, 114-5, 145, 190

federalism 15, 65, 101, 151, 162, 169, 181-2, 185-9, 191

fitch, ፍች, 19-20, 22, 29, 36, 69, 87, 93, 228

fithe, ፍትህ, 20, 78, 147, 228

gada, 63, 108-9, 175

gädl, ገድል, 4, 20, 23, 27-9, 31, 60, 67, 75, 83, 126, 129, 134, 149, 195, 221, 228

Gibbonism, 5-7, 9-10, 14, 92, 111, 126, 129, 141, 179-80, 195, 198, 200-4, 217, 224

globalization, 150, 211-2, 214-5, 218-21

gourangur, ጉራንጉር, 21, 228

hassabä ewen, ሃሳበ እውን, 26, 228

hatäta, ሐተታ 45, 228

hermeneutics/ hermeneutical, 11-2, 14, 16-7, 19, 21-7, 29-38, 41-2, 45-8, 50-3, 55-6, 58-64, 68-9, 71-6, 78, 81-4, 87, 90-4, 96, 98, 109, 124, 131, 143, 145-6, 165-6, 169, 194-5, 211, 217, 222-3

hibrä qal, ሕብረ ቃል, 20, 48-9, 82-3, 126-7, 228

hiss, ሂስ, 20, 23, 27, 33, 35, 44-6, 50, 53-4, 56-7, 60, 68-9, 74-5, 82, 84, 129, 216, 228

hizb, ህዝብ, 100, 102-3, 120, 161-3, 166-7, 169-81, 187-9, 191, 228

huläntänawi, ሁለንተናዊ, 29, 33, 228

ignorance, 2, 6-8, 84, 179, 196, 198, 200

iddir, ዕድር, 12, 39, 41, 97, 102, 195, 229

imagination, 4, 32, 34-6, 83-4, 118, 130, 143, 201-2

iqqub, ዕቁብ, 12, 39, 41, 97, 102, 195, 229

Islam, 41, 106-7, 110, 113, 162-6, 168-70, 172, 176, 224

kiflä agär, ክፍለ አገር, 174-5, 181, 185-6, 229

knowledge, 1, 3-4, 7-13, 15-7, 19-21, 23, 29-1, 35-6, 38-9, 43-4, 51-6, 58, 68-9, 71-2, 82-3, 89, 91-2, 94-9, 104, 106, 121-2, 126-8, 132, 135, 137-8, 139-42, 146-7, 149, 152-3, 155-6, 158-60, 171, 173, 193-208, 210-1, 213-4, 218-4

Lalibela, 40, 69, 77, 148, 187
lib wäläd, ልብ ወለድ, 143, 229
liberal democracy, 58, 79, 135-6, 151, 214-6, 219, 222
lissan, ልሳን, 19-20, 57-60, 70, 76, 83-4, 156, 187-8, 229
luba 57, 167-8, 195, 229

mäbit, መብት 147, 229
mädämamät, መደማመጥ, 20, 33, 46, 53-4, 56-7, 69, 74-6, 82, 84, 18, 229
maeräg, ማዕረግ, 147, 183, 229
mängäd, መንገድ, 46, 83-5, 229
mäsmat, መስማት, 75, 197, 229
methodological Westernism, 12, 61, 71, 73, 202
minab, ምናብ, 20-1, 25, 76, 93, 132, 141-9, 151-4, 157, 160, 166, 170, 173, 213, 229
mirmära, ምርመራ, 17, 20, 34-7, 53, 61, 71, 76, 83, 194, 229
moggaasa, 57, 118, 162, 167-70, 172, 176, 181, 195

nägär, ነገር, 14, 20-4, 27-37, 39, 42, 44-8, 50-6, 60-5, 70-5, 82-3, 85-7, 93, 97, 109, 111, 113, 129, 139, 146, 166, 196, 211, 215-6, 222, 229
nätäla tirgum, ነጠላ ትርጉም, 81, 230
nation, 3, 6, 13, 66, 98, 103-6, 142, 153, 157, 163-3, 170, 172-4, 177-9, 199, 202, 207
nätsanät, ነጻነት, 135, 147, 230
necropolitics, 14, 190, 212
necropower, 101, 122, 189-90
nibab, ንባብ, 20, 48, 53, 61, 70, 82, 84, 86, 93, 230

official people, 89, 99-109, 111-2, 114-6, 118-20, 122, 126-130, 136, 144-5, 151-2, 171-2, 177, 180, 182, 189, 202, 206, 209-10, 214-5, 217, 220
oppression, 27-8, 30-1, 40-3, 49, 57-8, 66, 69, 72, 77, 79-80, 90, 94-5, 98-9, 102, 113, 122, 127, 132, 137, 139-40, 146-8, 150, 180, 210, 214, 220
Oromumma, 89, 101, 105-9, 111-20, 126, 168-9, 172, 185-6, 196

people's people, 99-100, 102, 104-5, 107, 109, 112-4, 118, 120, 122-4, 127-30, 132-4, 138-40, 144-6, 149, 151-4, 159, 172-3, 180, 204-8, 210-1, 214-6, 220
poor living, 39, 205-6, 209-1, 213, 222
poverty, 13, 48, 97, 194, 203-12, 215, 225
primary identification, 167, 171, 183, 186
private reason, 188
public reason, 187-8, 191

qälb, ቀልብ, 29, 33, 230
qiné, ቅኔ, 11, 14, 16-9, 21-38, 40-3, 45-6, 48, 50-3, 55-6, 58-64, 68-73, 75-6, 78, 81-4, 86-7, 90-6, 98, 123-4, 129-31, 139-43, 145-6, 153, 156-7, 165-6, 169-70, 194-5, 211, 217, 222-3, 230
qisäla, ቅጸላ, 20, 34-6, 53, 61, 71, 76, 83, 194, 230
quanqua, ቋንቋ, 20, 46, 57-60, 63, 66, 75, 83-5, 87, 230

säm ena wärq, ሰም እና ወርቅ, 17, 20, 22-30, 32-3, 47, 52-3, 56, 61, 65, 71-3, 82-3, 87, 90, 93, 109, 129, 131, 139, 141, 145, 166, 191, 216, 222, 225, 230
säw läsäw, ሰው ለሰው, 40-1, 131, 135, 170, 230
säwrä bahil, ሰውረ ባሕል, 20, 29-31, 37-9, 43, 61, 69, 78, 93, 95-6, 146, 155-6, 230

säwrä hiywät, ሰውረ ሕይወት, 20, 29-32, 39-42, 61, 69, 77, 93, 134, 146, 156, 160, 205-6, 208, 215, 225, 230

säwrä ras, ሰውረ ራስ, 20, 29-31, 39, 42-4, 61, 69, 77, 93, 97, 125-6, 129-30, 144, 146, 156, 230

säwrä tarik, ሰውረ ታሪክ, 18-21, 29-30, 34, 44, 63, 69, 81, 89-91, 93-100, 106, 108-9, 111, 113, 118, 120-4, 126, 128-30, 132-5, 139-44, 147-9, 152, 154, 156, 158, 160, 163, 165, 169-71, 173-4, 176-7, 180-1, 187, 193, 196-9, 202, 205, 208, 210, 214, 216, 218, 221-2, 225, 230

secondary identification, 57, 161-3, 165-75, 180-1, 183, 185-6, 191, 224

self-determination, 49, 58, 60, 65, 103, 107, 111, 119, 130, 139, 172, 179-80, 190, 217

silt, ስልት, 20, 70-3, 86, 230

somnambulist, 13, 72, 179, 202

subjectivization, 42, 44

tägbar, ተግባር, 147, 155

täshägagari hiss, ተሸጋጋሪ ሂስ, 33, 46, 50, 53-4, 56-7, 60, 68-9, 74-5, 84, 231

tichit, ትችት, 44-5, 231

tintena, ትንተና, 44-5, 231

tirgum, ትርጉም, 20, 27, 33, 35, 46, 53-7, 81-3, 129, 231

tiyaqé, ጥያቄ, 35, 75-6, 231

tzärä-bahil, ፀረ ባሕል, 37-8, 231

tsinsä hassab, ፅንስ ሓሳብ, 20, 54, 57, 61-3, 69-70, 86, 223, 231

universal, 9, 13-4, 29-30, 33, 43, 71-3, 104, 114, 116, 132, 150, 163-4, 168, 171-5, 178-9, 183-4, 188, 202

universalization, 150, 211-2, 214-5, 218-9, 221

wäné, ወኔ, 28, 231

wäyim, ወይም, 26, 28, 231

wihdät, ውህደት , 20, 31, 64-7, 83-4, 92, 95, 98, 122, 125, 132, 135, 158, 165, 168-71, 174, 181, 191, 231

wistä wäyra, ውስት ወይራ, 20, 48, 53, 57, 61, 69, 72, 82, 84-6, 93, 144, 202, 213, 231

yählm injära, የሕልም እንጀራ . 143, 231

yämist'ir tirgum, የምስጢር ትርጉም, 81-2, 231

yäne bitie, የኔ ቢጤ , 43, 131, 135, 170, 231

yäwäl, የወል, 20-1, 76, 93, 132, 140, 147, 154-60, 174, 231

zäläsäña, ዘለሰኛ . 25, 40, 95-6, 232

zäräfa, ዘረፋ, 16, 20, 27, 33, 46, 52-61, 64, 68-72, 74-6, 78, 82-3, 85-6, 93-4, 96, 100, 118, 122-3, 129, 134, 141, 144, 146-7, 156, 166, 177, 188-9, 196-7, 199, 201, 205, 211, 214-6, 220-3, 232

zäybé, ዘይቤ, 20, 24, 43, 46-50, 52, 63, 77, 82-5, 87, 95, 98, 124-5, 140-1, 145, 148, 156, 213-4, 232

zega, ዜጋ , 102-3, 151, 232

Zamika'elites, 128, 148, 187

zombie concept, 13-4, 119, 177, 202, 205, 208, 217

zega, ዜጋ , 93, 137, 209, 232

Zamika'elites, 116, 134, 172

zombie concept, 11-3, 108, 163,182, 184, 187, 190, 198

ABOUT THE AUTHOR:

Maimire Mennasemay, PhD, is a distinguished academic with a rich background in critical theory, world views, and ethics, primarily through his role in the Humanities/Philosophy Department at Dawson College. He holds the position of scholar in residence at the same institution and is notable for his authorship of *Qine Hermeneutics and Ethiopian Critical Theory*.

Dr. Mennasemay is a founding and active member of S.P.A.C.E (Science, Philosophy, Arts, and Community Education), a project that integrates diverse disciplines like the sciences, philosophy, humanities, and the arts. His editorial experience is extensive, having served as the book review editor for *Labour, Capital and Society / Travail, Capital et Société* and being a part of its current editorial team. He also contributed to the editorial staff of the now-defunct *Horn of Africa* and is a senior editor at the *International Journal of Ethiopian Studies*.

His academic contributions are primarily in Ethiopian Studies, hermeneutics, and critical theory. Among his notable works is *Language, Theory, and African Emancipation*, published by the University of Liverpool. His scholarly articles have been featured in several esteemed journals, including the *Canadian Journal of Modern African Studies*, *North East African Studies*, *Horn of Africa*, *International Journal of Ethiopian Studies*, and *Africa Today*. Additionally, Dr. Mennasemay has enriched various edited books with his insightful chapters.

ALSO BY THE SAME AUTHOR:

Qine Hermeneutics and Ethiopian Critical Theory

Author: Maimire Mennasemay, Ph.D.

ISBNs:
 978-1-59-907234-0 (paperback)
 978-1-59-907235-7 (hardcover)
Language : English
Book Format: 6" x 9"
Page numbers: 532
Publication Date: Fall 2021

Available at www.tsehaipublishers.com
and everywhere where books are sold.

Qine Hermeneutics and Ethiopian Critical Theory is a profound work that delves deep into the critical concepts and interpretative methods of qiné hermeneutics, aiming to uncover and articulate a uniquely Ethiopian critical tradition. This tradition is envisioned as being capable of addressing the diverse intellectual, social, and political challenges present in the modern world.

The book undertakes a rigorous internal exploration of Ethiopia's intellectual traditions, shedding light on the emancipatory ideas inherent within them. It then embarks on an external journey, critically engaging with the Western social sciences that predominantly influence Ethiopian studies. In this process, the book not only critiques and redirects the borrowed knowledge but also reinterprets it through the lens of emancipatory concepts uncovered in the internal journey.

Central to the text is the proposition of "Ethioperspectivism," a unique approach that advocates for the epistemic independence of Ethiopian studies. This approach harmonizes the insights gained from both the internal and external journeys, aiming to create knowledge about Ethiopia that is deeply rooted in its own history and intellectual traditions while simultaneously aligning with the emancipatory interests of the Ethiopian people. This synthesis of internal and external perspectives forms the crux of the book, presenting a compelling case for a more autonomous and culturally resonant approach to Ethiopian studies.

> Written by one of the most intriguing philosophers of our time, *Qiné Hermeneutics* is a crucial input in any discussion on the role and meaning of education for the self and for the society at large.
> —Tekeste Negash, Ph.D.

International Journal of Ethiopian Studies

ISSN: 1543-4133

Language : English/Amharic
Journal Format: 6" x 9"
Publication time: Twice a year

EDITORIAL DIRECTOR: Elias Wondimu
SENIOR EDITOR: Maimire Mennasemay, Ph.D.

*Available at www.tsehaipublishers.com,
www.jstor.com and everywhere where journals
and books are sold.*

The *International Journal of Ethiopian Studies* (IJES) is a unique interdisciplinary and refereed journal, established in 2002, dedicated to academic research that is relevant to or informed by the Ethiopian experience. IJES is distinctive in its commitment to publishing original works in both English and Amharic, catering to a global readership.

The journal focuses on Ethiopia and the Horn of Africa, offering a blend of original articles, reviews, and insightful features that delve into significant issues impacting the region. Its publication of two issues per year makes it a critical platform for sharing and nurturing research by scholars who are invested in matters pertinent to the region. IJES also facilitates the cross-fertilization of ideas among experts in the field.

Significantly, IJES represents a crucial and long-awaited initiative in the Ethiopian academic landscape. It provides Ethiopian scholars with a dedicated platform to engage deeply and critically with issues specific to Ethiopia, from a scholarly perspective. This is particularly important considering the historical context where African nations, including Ethiopia, have often been relegated to mere subjects in global knowledge discourse. The journal is seen as a step towards reversing this trend, offering a space for Ethiopian scholars to assert their subjectivity and contribute to defining, understanding, and solving their own societal issues. This initiative is a move towards empowering Ethiopian voices in academic discourse, breaking free from external (European and American) dominance in defining and interpreting Ethiopian identity and challenges.

WWW.TSEHAIPUBLISHERS.COM

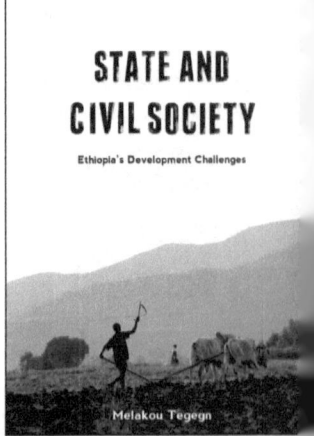

www.ingramcontent.com/pod-product-compliance
Lightning Source LLC
Chambersburg PA
CBHW030537230426
43665CB00010B/931